The Maritime
Political Boundaries
of the World

THE MARITIME
POLITICAL BOUNDARIES
OF THE WORLD

J. R. V. PRESCOTT

METHUEN

London & New York

First published in 1985 by
Methuen & Co. Ltd
11 New Fetter Lane,
London EC4P 4EE

First published in the USA in 1986 by
Methuen & Co.
in association with Methuen, Inc.
29 West 35th Street,
New York NY 10001

Typeset by Scarborough Typesetting Services
and printed in Great Britain at
the University Press, Cambridge

British Library Cataloguing in Publication Data

Prescott, J. R. V.
The maritime political boundaries of the world.
1. Territorial waters   2. Boundaries
I. Title
341.4'48   JX4131

ISBN 0–416–41750–7

*Library of Congress Cataloging in Publication
Data*

Prescott, J. R. V. (John Robert Victor)
The maritime political boundaries of the world.
Bibliography: p.
Includes index.
1. Economic zones (Maritime law)
2. Territorial waters.
I. Title.
JX4144.5.P733   1985   341.4'48   85–11465
ISBN 0–416–41750–7

This book is dedicated to
DOROTHY, MARGARET
AND PHILIP

Contents

Figures

Tables

Preface

My thanks are due and willingly given to Harm de Blij, who suggested that I should write this book; to the staff of the Environment and Policy Institute of the East–West Center, Honolulu, for giving me such a pleasant environment to study the maritime boundaries of the South China Sea; to the staff of the Departments of Foreign Affairs and National Assessments in Canberra for providing complete copies of many international agreements on maritime boundaries and many unilateral claims to maritime zones; and to Rob Bartlett for drawing the maps.

This is essentially a practical book written by a political geographer. There is no attempt to develop a theory of ocean boundary-making because in my experience of observing and sometimes working with governments, theoretical considerations have no place in developing policies or strategies. In every case policies and strategies have been selected because they are perceived to be the best way of serving national self-interest.

The book is organized in two sections. The first five chapters treat maritime claims and their boundaries in a systematic way. The remaining nine chapters provide a regional treatment of the world's oceans and seas.

In order to leave as much space as possible for the detailed regional treatment two subjects have not been considered in the systematic chapters and one has been treated in a general manner. There is no discussion of the evolution of maritime claims since earliest times because that information is already available in some excellent studies by Baty (1928), Bouchez (1964), Fenn (1926), Gidel (1932), Jessup (1927), Kent (1954) and Walker (1945).

Intra-national maritime boundaries have not been considered because even if it had proved possible to acquire the mass of information dealing with the internal boundaries of national maritime zones there would have been no opportunity to describe and analyse this information in the regional sections. It is safe to predict that the questions associated with intra-national maritime boundaries will attract more attention from scholars in the future.

While landlocked states have not been ignored in this study they have not been given a separate focus. There are two reasons for this approach. First it is my view that the apparent gains which landlocked states have made through various articles in the 1982 Convention may prove to be illusory. It seems more likely that the transit and other rights which landlocked states presently enjoy and will continue to enjoy will owe most to earlier conventions. Second there is a large and detailed literature about landlocked states which is recorded in the bibliography prepared by Glassner (1980).

Wherever possible I have tried to use technical terms connected with boundaries in a precise manner. Unfortunately there are no precise terms dealing with the fixing of maritime boundaries in the same manner that the terms such as *allocation*, *delimitation* and *demarcation* apply to the fixing of boundaries on land. The 1982 Convention was carefully inspected to discover whether particular terms such as *delimit* or *determine* had been used in special and consistent ways. This investigation revealed no consistency in the use of these terms and so in this book the words *delimit*, *determine*, *delineate*, *draw*, *establish* and *construct* are used as synonyms for the process of fixing maritime boundaries.

J. R. V. PRESCOTT

References

Baty, T. (1928) 'The three mile limit', *American Journal of International Law*, 22, 503–37.

Bouchez, L. J. (1964) *The Regime of Bays in International Law*, Leyden.

Fenn, P. T. (1926) 'Origins of the theory of territorial waters', *American Journal of International Law*, 20, 465–82.

Gidel, G. (1932) *Le Droit international public de la mer* [Public international law of the sea], Châteauroux.

Glassner, M. I. (1980) *Bibliography on Landlocked States*, Alphen aan den Rijn, the Netherlands.

Jessup, P. C. (1927) *The Law of Territorial Waters and Maritime Jurisdiction*, New York.

Kent, H. S. K. (1954) 'The historical origins of the three-mile limit', *American Journal of International Law*, 48, 537–53.

Walker, W. L. (1945) 'Territorial waters: the cannon shot rule', *The British Yearbook of International Law*, 22, 210–31.

Note on place names and references to maritime claims and boundaries

Wherever possible the place names used in this book have been taken from *The Times Atlas of the World*, Comprehensive Edition, published in Edinburgh in 1980. Where the atlas did not record a name for some small feature the name used by the country concerned was adopted.

With very few exceptions, the analysis of unilateral maritime claims and bilateral maritime agreements was based on documents supplied either by one of the countries concerned or by the Departments of Foreign Affairs or National Assessments in Canberra. I prefer to work from such documents for three reasons. First, there is no risk of misprints. Second, the entire document is provided rather than an edited version. Third, maps attached to such documents are also available, whereas in many collections of treaties maps are not reproduced.

Thus, apart from a few exceptions, where an original version could not be obtained, treaties and unilateral proclamations are identified by the date of signing and date of ratification. These dates will enable readers to identify the documents in collections of treaties, of which the following are the best.

United Nations (1970–) *National Legislation and Treaties Relating to the Law of the Sea*, Legislative Series, New York.

Churchill, R., Lay, S. H., Nordquist, M., and Simmonds, K. R. (1975–) *New Directions in the Law of the Sea*, London.

Nordquist, M. and Park, C.-H. (1981) *North America and Asia-Pacific and the Development of the Law of the Sea*, 2 vols, New York.

Sebek, V. (1979) *The East European States and the Development of the Law of the Sea*, 2 vols, New York.

Szekely, A. (1980) *Latin America and the Development of the Law of the Sea*, 2 vols, New York.

The Geographer (1969–) 'Limits in the Seas' series, Washington, DC.

1

Political geographers
and the oceans

It is a hotly debated question whether connexion with the sea is to the advantage or the detriment of a well ordered state.

(Aristotle, *Politics*, Book VII, chapter VI, translated by Barker 1968, 294)

The potential future strength of world powers will be in proportion to the length of their fronts on the Pacific Ocean and the kind of resources possessed by their respective hinterlands. Small wonder, therefore, that the Pacific Ocean exerts so great a drawing power on expansionist, imperialistically minded young nations.

(Ratzel 1900, 73, translated by Gyorgy 1944, 158)

Whether the origins of political geography are traced back thousands of years to the writings of Aristotle, or only a century to Ratzel's diligent scholarship, there is evidence of a consistent interest in the political importance of the world's seas. That interest has encompassed the influence of the oceans on the fortunes of a single state, on the direction and rate of exploration, on the acquisition of colonies, on the development of international commerce, and on conflict between great powers. The attention given to these subjects focused almost exclusively on the waters near to inhabited areas, because it is there that the great harvest of marine creatures was gathered, there that the commercial sea lanes converged, and there that nearly all the great naval battles were fought.

Before 1914 the work of political geographers centred on three main themes: the role of the sea in influencing national characteristics, the priorities of national naval strategies, and the political significance of coastal features. While the analysis of some of these themes continued into the inter-war period, the 1920s and 1930s marked an intellectual frontier in the subject. In that period new interests developed alongside of the three traditional themes, and after 1945 these new interests had supplanted them. The new interests concerned the law of the sea. At the very end of this transition period Whittlesey (1944, 589) had written that the interplay of law and regions was incessant, each affecting the other and in the process being itself modified. He could not have known, as he wrote those views and criticized the lack of specific studies of the interplay of the law and geography, that there was to be a flood of literature, which shows no signs of receding, on the law and the new regions of the seas which were claimed by countries.

The flavour of the traditional themes can be sampled by reference to a few of the renowned studies. Semple was one of the geographers who followed Ratzel's lead in exploring the impact of proximity to the sea and the nature of the coastline upon the characteristics of coastal inhabitants. She had no doubts about the importance of this relationship.

> Inaccessibility from the land, a high degree of accessibility from the sea, and a paucity of local resources unite to thrust the inhabitants of such [fjord] coasts out upon the deep to make of them fishermen, seamen and ocean carriers.
>
> Here where a mild climate enables the boatman race to make a companion of the deep, where every landscape is a seascape, where every diplomatic visit or war campaign, every trading journey or search for a new coco-palm plantation means a voyage beyond the narrow confines of the home island, there dwells a race whose splendid chest and arm muscles were developed in the gymnasium of the sea.
>
> (Semple 1911, 282)

These generalizations and similar ones by Fairgrieve (1941, 51) always applied to early periods of history when technical developments in navigation, gunnery and fishing were at a comparatively low level. Studies of this kind do not seem to be made by geographers today.

Investigation of the relationships between the oceans and the exercise of national power was the most vigorous of the traditional themes, and occasional papers on the subject appeared after 1945. Mahan, Ratzel, Mackinder, Whittlesey and Spykman were all concerned with the significance of factors of location and space in the continual struggle for pre-eminence amongst the major powers. Mahan attached more importance to sea power than any of the other authors mentioned. This characteristic might be attributed to his naval background and the fact that he was writing at a time when naval power was patently effective about a period in the seventeenth and eighteenth centuries when naval strength had sometimes been decisive in settling international issues. Mahan (1890) identified six conditions which influenced the sea power of states. These were: the location of the state, the nature and length of its coastline, the number of citizens, the national character and the quality of government. Certainly the first four conditions are appropriate for consideration by political geographers, and were examined by both Ritter and Ratzel. Thus the location of the state will determine the number of seas to which it has access, and influence the extent to which it can control strategic routes and important fishing and mineral resources. The nature and length of the coastline will have important implications for policies connected with the defence of the state and the operation of an active merchant marine and navy. The numbers of people and the relation of that population to resources on land will affect the extent to which attempts are made to discover resources within the sea or across the sea. While not openly advocating the acquisition of colonies, Mahan disclosed his attitude by reflecting with enthusiasm on the benefits which Britain had enjoyed by owning a string of bases around the world. It seems probable that Mahan deserves some credit for the policies which led the United

States to secure bases in Hawaii, Guam, Puerto Rico, the Philippines, the Virgin Islands and Panama. New developments in the construction of ships, missiles and the means of propelling them, and fresh processes of international negotiation, have reduced Mahan's concepts and proposals to subjects of historic interest.

Mackinder (1904 and 1919) was concerned with the strength of land and sea powers and the possible conflict between them. Mackinder's perceived dichotomy between land and sea powers was false and remains so; great powers then and now have large armies and powerful navies, to which of course have been added, since the twilight of Mackinder's life, destructive air forces. This basic weakness, together with Mackinder's obsession with inner Asia as a pivotal heartland in world affairs, led him to make some simplistic judgements about the strength and limitations of sea power. He regarded the navigability of rivers from accessible oceans as being critical in determining the theatres in which maritime and land powers held sway. Yet by the time he wrote his best-known paper in 1904 the maritime powers Britain and France dominated Africa, a continent singularly deficient in navigable rivers, and the location of a second heartland which he developed in his later study. In common with the ideas of Mahan, Mackinder's concepts have been rendered obsolete by subsequent technical and political developments.

Spykman (1942 and 1944) inverted Mackinder's thesis by placing the United States at the centre of a map on a Mercator projection instead of central Asia. The map made it appear that the United States was surrounded and that the obvious strategy for that country was to avoid the unification of the opposite shores of the Atlantic and Pacific Ocean under a single enemy or alliance of hostile powers. German and Japanese advances along these coasts during the 1940s gave Spykman's writings a vogue which critical analysis of his work suggests was unjustified (Prescott 1968, ch. 2).

Cohen (1964) is one of the few geographers to have tackled this subject in the modern period. He presented a geographical view of contemporary international politics by suggesting a division of the world into geo-strategic and geo-political regions and then describing the power cores of the world and the zones of contact between the major powers. The regional boundaries drawn by Cohen were extended across the oceans, although it was not clear on what basis the waters had been divided. The prime division between the trade-dependent maritime world and the Eurasian continental world owed something to the heartland concept of Mackinder, and throughout his book Cohen made references to naval strategy, of which the following quotations are typical.

What we cannot afford to do, however, is to take the American Mediterranean for granted.

As long as its most important allies are so heavily dependent upon overseas trade the United States has to help them maintain their sea contacts.

(Cohen 1964, 66 and 138)

Cohen also refines Spykman's ideas by urging a selective American commitment in the rimland states which surround the Soviet Union.

The third traditional theme dealt with the political significance of particular coastal situations. Early writers such as Fairgrieve and later contributors, including Whittlesey (1944) and Fischer (1957), examined the political significance of peninsulas, isthmuses, islands, fjords, deltas, lagoons and narrow straits. Fairgrieve gave considerable weight to the importance of some of these features in trying to explain the sequential development of empires; however, this deterministic approach was discarded by geographers during the strong reaction to the German school of *Geopolitik*. It is now recognized that the significance of any particular coastal landform will be conditioned by many variables. The most obvious of these will include its location, the nature of political relations between the state which owns the coastal feature and its near neighbours, and the technical skills available to the government in control of the area. It is impossible to make valid generalizations about the political significance of islands or deltas in different parts of the world. Each feature would have to be examined in the context of the region's political geography to reach any proper conclusion. This realization should not prevent comparative studies by political geographers. It would, for example, be interesting to investigate the political importance of the deltas of the Niger, Mekong, Ganges and Nile, but predictably the scholar would learn more about the variable interaction of geography and politics than make progress in the construction of generalizations about the political relevance of deltas.

It is regrettable that while political geographers have abandoned the global strategic analyses so beloved of Mackinder and Mahan, scholars in other disciplines, especially political science, continue to equate political geography with such studies. There can be no excuse for this distortion in view of the large volume of detailed studies published by political geographers since 1945. To make sure that this intellectual skeleton in the cupboard is laid to rest the following section reviews the more important modern studies by political geographers interested in the oceans.

A survey of modern studies of the oceans by political geographers

It must be stressed at the beginning of this section that this survey is not an attempt to define a particular area of study which should be reserved for political geographers interested in oceans. Its sole aim is to display the geographer's range of interests in that zone of scholarship related to the oceans which lies between the fields of geography, law, economics and politics. It is a field which is shared with lawyers, economists and political scientists, and examples of their work will be cited to indicate this joint concern. In the remainder of the book references have been selected solely on the basis of their quality, without any reference to the particular discipline of the author.

Regional studies

The most important contribution of political geographers to this literature in terms of volume and originality is to specific regional studies. They have usually been of two kinds. First there are studies of the complex of conflicting claims and management problems in semi-enclosed seas. Second there are the studies which deal with a single segment of boundary, or a single dispute.

The South China Sea and the waters of southeast Asia have proved to be an attractive subject. Senftleben (1976), Lee Yong Leng (1980) and Prescott (1981) have all written on this region. Senftleben's paper begins by surveying the historical importance of the South China Sea, then reviews specific national claims and their bases. He concludes that China is judged to be the strongest regional power and that all indications show that China will not retreat from its claim to all the islands and banks in the South China Sea. Finally he expresses the faint hope that if specific boundaries cannot be agreed arrangements for joint development of the region should be made.

Lee Yong Leng has published a short monograph which examines, from a geographical standpoint, the main contentious issues debated at the United Nations Law of the Sea Conference as they apply to the waters of southeast Asia. There are separate chapters on the territorial seas, the seabed and its resources, fishing zones, landlocked states and international straits. This is a useful introduction to the subject and the region, and it leads to the gloomy conclusion that Laos, Singapore, Thailand and Kampuchea are not well placed in relation to the sea and will be the losers in the scramble for ocean resources. Professor Leng also notes that the proposals in the United Nations Law of the Sea Conference do not provide any effective redress for such disadvantaged states.

Melamid (1947 and 1959) and Fielden (1978) have focused on the Red Sea. Melamid's two studies deal with the political geography of the Gulf of Aqaba and its legal status. Prior to Israel's occupation of Sharm el Sheikh in 1967 the question of that country's right to send ships through the Strait of Tiran was fiercely debated. Fielden's monograph on the political geography of the Red Sea region deals more with the origins of the conflicts involving the countries which border that sea than with the Red Sea itself; however, he does provide an excellent background to anyone wishing to study the specific problems of conflicting maritime claims in the region.

Blacksell (1979) and Bierman (1978) have examined claims to the waters of the European Economic Community and Soviet Arctic regions. Blacksell shows how the Community's problems over continental shelf claims and exclusive fishing zones developed, and in the case of fish stocks have persisted. Bierman's interesting paper records the technical progress which has made it possible for navigation through the Arctic Ocean to increase, and then chronicles Russian claims to internal and historic waters. It is then explained how different interpretations of points of international law have created ambiguities about the right of innocent passage through such waters.

Regional papers by scholars in other fields include very useful studies by Symmons (1979a) on disputed claims to waters surrounding the United Kingdom, and by Chiu and Park (1976) on the legal status of the Spratly and Paracel Islands.

While many geographers have published examinations of specific boundary disputes it is proposed to refer to only the 'Limits in the Seas' series, which was started by Hodgson in 1970. This series has involved the publication of about eight boundary studies each year and is an indispensable research tool for any scholar interested in the oceans. The studies are generally short, but their chief merits are that they are totally objective, reproduce the declaration or agreement which creates the boundary, and show the agreed boundary or disputed lines on clear maps. This series is a fitting monument to Hodgson, who was The Geographer in the American Department of State, and who, before his untimely death in 1979, found time to write many other useful articles on maritime boundaries.

Specific boundary studies by other scholars include the investigation of the importance of Rockall as a basis for claims to large areas of the seabed of the north Atlantic Ocean by Symmons (1975) and by Brown (1978), and the examination of the fishing dispute in the Yellow and East China Seas involving China and Japan by Park (1974).

Technical aspects of boundaries

The second group of papers and monographs contributed by geographers deals with technical questions of boundary construction and the interpretation of geographical terms used in the law of the sea. Boggs (1930 and 1937) set a very high original standard for this group. These papers on the delimitation of the territorial sea and the definition of water boundaries marked Boggs's major contribution to the field of political geography and helped in the solution of problems associated with the construction of maritime boundaries. Other writers, such as Jones (1945) and Moodie (1956), tended to follow Boggs, and then Hodgson (1977) and Hodgson and Cooper (1976) built on that secure foundation and carried boundary construction into the age of computers, so that the laborious graphical method of constructing lines of equidistance can be avoided.

Other useful studies of particular technical questions include the review by Hodgson (1973) of the use of islands in normal and special circumstances to claim maritime zones, and the analysis of the strategic attributes of international straits by Smith (1974). Other scholars have been prominent in this field. Early studies by Bruel (1947) on international straits, and Strohl (1963) on bays, have been matched more recently by the excellent volume on the maritime zones of islands in international law by Symmons (1979b), and the masterly papers by Hedberg (1972 and 1976), who is a geologist, on the outer limits of the continental margin.

Landlocked states

The third aspect of the oceans considered by political geographers deals with landlocked states. While Glassner has not made this field his own, he is certainly the most prolific writer on it. After fleeting references to the topic by Bowman (1923) and Whittlesey (1944), Pounds (1959) and East (1960), apparently working separately, laid the foundation for this subject. Pounds concentrated on the methods by which landlocked states seek access for their goods and citizens to the high seas. The three methods identified were by the use of international rivers, by securing transit rights, and by acquiring a corridor of land to the sea, thus effectively ending the landlocked condition. Pound's paper was illustrated by historic and contemporary cases. East began his analysis of the geography of landlocked states by comparing the characteristics of fourteen such countries. This activity revealed that they had nothing in common save their aloofness from the sea, so he turned to their formation. Now he found that eleven could be considered buffer states; the exceptions were Lichtenstein, San Marino and the Vatican. The first major work by Glassner (1970) received a mixed reception from his fellow geographers. He presented detailed studies of Uganda, Bolivia and Afghanistan and included some general chapters. While General Marshall-Cornwall thought that the book dealt fully and cogently with the whole subject, Minghi, a specialist political geographer, regretted the lack of an innovative classification of landlocked states. Fortunately Glassner has persisted with this topic and his studies in 1974 and 1977 have now been crowned with a most useful bibliography published in 1980. Other economic geographers such as Whittington (1966) and Hilling (1968) have provided useful case studies of landlocked states and their efforts to solve their transport problems in southern and west Africa respectively. Childs (1972) and Caflisch (1978) are lawyers who have produced good general studies on the problems of landlocked states and their consideration at the United Nations Law of the Sea Conference.

Marine resources

It is disappointing that geographers have not made the contribution to the study of marine resources which might have been expected, although this criticism applies more to the issue of minerals than the fishing industry. Geographers do not appear to have entered into the debate over regulations governing mining at the United Nations Law of the Sea Conference in any significant role. Davies (1977) explored the extent to which discoveries of oil fields off the coast of Scotland have been a blessing or bane to that region. He examines the benefits of employment opportunities against the strain on existing roads and services and the risk of increased pollution. French (1979) has provided a very interesting account of exploration for hydrocarbon deposits in Canada's High Arctic Islands. He reveals how the original discovery of some deposits on land in the western Sverdrup Basin, between latitudes 76° north and 79° north, encouraged the development of offshore ice-platform drilling techniques, to allow similar offshore structures to be tested. His paper also gives a good account of the problems which may be faced in seeking to ensure that drilling and exploitation does no lasting damage to the environment. There is a much higher volume of articles on offshore mining for hydrocarbons and manganese nodules by economists and others. For example, Siddayao (1978) has produced an account of the offshore petroleum resources of southeast Asia, while Frazer (1977) has published information on revised estimates of the reserves of manganese nodules available for harvesting. There is scope for economic geographers to contribute to the debate on the quotas suggested for nodule mining, and on proposals to levy an impost on revenue derived from resources mined on the seabed more than 200 nautical miles from the coast.

Investigation of issues concerned with fishing fleets and new claims to extended maritime zones has attracted more attention from geographers than mining the seabed. The excellent early works by Black (1960) on the Labrador cod fishing industry, by Alexander (1960) on the fishing grounds of northwest Europe, and by Minghi (1961) on conflicting salmon policies in the north Pacific Ocean have been continued by recent studies. Coull and Jonnson (1979) survey the situation of Iceland's cod fishing industry after it had successfully claimed an extended fishing zone. The most critical problems are identified to stem from inflation rather than from any decline in fish stocks. The desire of the European Economic Community to protect its fishing grounds is the subject of an illuminating paper by Bloch and Fournet (1977), which focuses clearly on the problems raised by universal claims to exclusive economic zones 200 nautical miles wide. The theme of a paper by Lotz (1978) is that fisheries in the western Atlantic Ocean will be revived by extended claims, because it will be possible to exert closer control over this renewable source in deep waters.

The declaration of wide fishing zones by countries has prompted many economists, lawyers and political scientists to write on the arrangements which developing countries are now concluding with those developed countries possessing distant fishing fleets. For example, Franklin and Duncan (1982) have provided a useful account of the different kinds of provisions contained in the sixty agreements which countries in the southwest Pacific Ocean have concluded with fishing fleets from other countries. Loring (1971) has provided a helpful review of the dispute which developed between the United States and Peru over the latter country's exercise of jurisdiction over fishing fleets within 200 nautical miles of its coast.

The Law of the Sea Conference

Geographers have not published many studies dealing with the progress of the United Nations Law of the Sea Conference; it has been left to lawyers to flood journals with articles and notes which record every important and unimportant development at that conference. Alexander and Hodgson (1976) made a rare foray into this field when they recounted the role played by geographically disadvantaged states in the deliberations of the conference; however, Alexander has also written an article which could be the herald for more on the same topic. In this article Alexander (1977) draws attention to the frequent use of the word 'region' in the documents springing from the Law of the Sea Conference, and the growing number of regional arrangements which are being concluded by groups or interested states to solve common maritime problems. He then reviews the characteristics of regions and the types of maritime regions which have been defined. It will be surprising if geographers do not play a more prominent role in refining the concept of maritime regions and contributing to the practical construction of regional arrangements.

Conclusions

In academic terms one of the chief results of the rash of extended maritime claims since 1945, and of the long United Nations Law of the Sea Conference, has been to open a new field for scholars. In the past two decades we have witnessed a research rush which has had an important effect on the ·fortunes of some academics, just as the gold rushes of past times made the fortunes of some prospectors. Workers from different disciplines bring different skills to the new field, and it is essential that these different skills should not be used to stake claims to particular areas and to erect notices telling others to keep out. Instead the skills should be employed to produce a complete and full development of the whole field.

Geographers bring a number of skills and attitudes which are useful in conducting research into maritime issues. Their familiarity with maps and charts is helpful in a number of ways. It enables sensible interpretation of historic maps which might be used in disputes over coastal waters. Such maps played a decisive role in the disputes between Argentina and Chile over the Beagle Channel, and between Australia and Papua New Guinea over Torres Strait. Geographers are also able to detect the incorrect use of maps and charts by countries to score particular points. They are aware of the error of drawing equidistant baselines trending east–west in mid to high latitudes on charts based on the Mercator projection. Finally geographers are capable of constructing maps to illustrate the important features connected with agreements or disagreements over maritime claims.

The special contribution which geographers have made to coastal geomorphology has produced an understanding of processes leading to coastal change. This understanding allied with skills in fieldwork in general and surveying in particular allows some geographers to play a very important role in planning for coastal regions and offshore activities to avoid damage to the coastal environment. These same abilities help the geographers to interpret the rules which have been agreed by politicians and framed by lawyers, in respect of specific sections of coast and offshore waters. Analysis of this kind enables geographers to comment on the extent to which national claims contravene the letter of such regulations. This facility also permits geographers to comment on the problems associated with the practical application of existing and proposed rules, and this is a skill appreciated by surveyors who are often presented with the difficult task of fixing maritime limits by their political masters.

The regional approach, which is the hallmark of geography, is appropriate for the analysis of different zones claimed by a single country, of closed and semi-enclosed seas, and of overlapping claims by two or more countries. The need for geographers to synthesize and correlate information for a particular region, proves to be a benefit when it is necessary, for example, to relate strategic, economic and environmental issues or uses to particular regions of the sea. The tradition of conducting regional analysis will also be helpful when attempts are being made to solve boundary problems on an equitable basis, when predictably opposite sides will be trying to introduce matters which best suit their case.

Political geographers have made a major contribution to the study of land boundaries for many decades, and the accumulated experience and knowledge have been translated for use in respect of maritime boundaries. The study of their evolution and definition, as well as disputes over their location and the impact which they have upon state relations and economic activities, are subjects which geographers are well qualified to explore.

Finally, some geographers, in common with many other academics in economics and political science, are capable of making good guesses about how the implementation of a particular policy will influence the development of coastal regions. Such guesses will be based on earlier studies of the evolution of the settlement and economic patterns along coasts in past periods.

While the willingness of scholars in different fields to share the fruits of their research is a desirable step, it does not go far enough. There must also be a will-ingness to share those results with governments. This is necessary so that the policies which governments produce are based on the best possible information; however, there can be no guarantee that making research results available to governments will produce good policies. It remains a fact that all the important decisions and many of the minor decisions about the marine environment are made by politicians for political reasons. Only occasionally will an objective analysis and a political analysis yield identical policies.

References

Alexander, L. M. (1960) 'Offshore claims and fisheries in northwest Europe', *Yearbook of World Affairs*, 14, 236–60.

Alexander, L. M. (1977) 'Regional arrangements in the ocean', *American Journal of International Law*, 71, 84–109.

Alexander, L. M. and Hodgson, R. D. (1976) 'The role of geographically disadvantaged states in the law of the sea', *San Diego Law Review*, 13, 558–82.

Barker, E. (1968) *The Politics of Aristotle*, Oxford.

Bierman, D. E. (1978) 'Soviet territorial claims in the Arctic and their economic and political implications', *Soviet Geography: Review and Translation*, 19 (7), 490–6.

Black, W. A. (1960) 'The Labrador codfishery', *Annals of the Association of American Geographers*, 50, 267–96.

Blacksell, M. (1979) 'Frontiers at sea', *Geographical Magazine*, 51 (8), 521–4.

Bloch, P. and Fournet, P. (1977) 'Le Nouveau Droit de la mer et ses incidences sur les pêches maritimes françaises' [The new law of the sea and its effect on French sea fishing], *Cahiers d'outre mer*, 30 (120), 326–47.

Boggs, S. W. (1930) 'Delimitation of the territorial sea', *American Journal of International Law*, 24, 541–55.

Boggs, S. W. (1937) 'Problems of water boundary definitions', *Geographical Review*, 27, 451–6.

Bowman, I. (1923) *The New World*, New York.

Brown, E. D. (1978) 'Rockall and the limits of national jurisdiction', *Marine Policy*, 2 (3), 181–211 and 2 (4), 275–302.

Bruel, E. (1947) *International Straits*, London.

Caflisch, L. C. (1978) 'Landlocked states and their access to and from the sea', *British Yearbook of International Law*, 49, 71–100.

Childs, P. (1972) 'The interests of land-locked states in law of the sea', *San Diego Law Review*, 9 (3), 701–34.

Chiu, H. and Park, C.-H. (1976) 'Legal status of the Paracel and Spratly Islands', *Ocean Development and International Law*, 3, 1–28.

Cohen, S. B. (1964) *Geography and Politics in a Divided World*, New York.

Coull, J. R. and Jonnson, S. (1979) 'Iceland after the cod war', *Geography*, 64 (2), 129–33.

Davies, J. F. (1977) 'Bane or boom? North Sea oil and gas development off northeast Scotland', *Great Plains Mountain Geographical Journal*, 6 (2), 204–11.

East, W. G. (1960) 'The geography of landlocked states', *Transactions of the Institute of British Geographers*, 28, 1–22.

Fairgrieve, J. (1941) *Geography and World Power*, 8th edn, London.

Fielden, D. G. (1978) *The Political Geography of the Red Sea Region*, Department of Geography, University of Durham, Occasional Publications (new series), 13.

Fischer, E. (1957) 'Location', a chapter in Weigert, H. W. (ed.) *Principles of Political Geography*, New York, 124–8.

Franklin, P. G. and Duncan, A. (1982) 'Economic profile and evaluation of activities of distant water fishing fleets in south and western Pacific skipjack/tuna fisheries', paper presented to a workshop on the harmonization and co-ordination of fisheries regimes and access agreements, Suva.

Frazer, J. Z. (1977) 'Manganese nodule reserves: an updated estimate', *Marine Mining*, 1 (1–2), 103–23.

French, H. M. (1979) 'Oil and gas exploration in the High Arctic Island: problems and prospects', *Marburger Geographische Schriften*, 79, 13–26.

Glassner, M. I. (1970) *Access to the Sea for Developing Landlocked States*, The Hague.

Glassner, M. I. (1974) 'Developing landlocked states and the resources of the seabed', *San Diego Law Review*, 11, 633–55.

Glassner, M. I. (1977) 'Landlocked nations and development', *International Development Review*, 19, 19–23.

Glassner, M. I. (1980) *Bibliography on landlocked states*, Alphen aan den Rijn, the Netherlands.

Gyorgy, A. (1944) 'Geopolitics: the new German science', *University of California Publications in International Relations*, 3 (3), 141–304.

Hedberg, H. D. (1972) *National-international Jurisdictional Boundary on the Ocean Floor*, Law of the Sea Institute Rhode Island, Occasional Paper No. 16.

Hedberg, H. D. (1976) 'Relation of political boundaries on the ocean floor to the continental margin', *Virginia Journal of International Law*, 17, 57–75.

Hilling, D. (1968) 'The problem of West African landlocked states', in Fisher, C. A. (ed.) *Essays in Political Geography*, London, ch. 14.

Hodgson, R. D. (1973) *Islands: Normal and Special Circumstances*, Research Study, Bureau of Intelligence and Research, Washington, DC.

Hodgson, R. D. (1977) 'Maritime limits and boundaries', *Marine Geodesy*, 1 (2), 155–64.

Hodgson, R. D. and Cooper, E. J. (1976) 'The technical delimitation of a modern equidistant boundary', *Ocean Development and International Law*, 3, 361–88.

Jones, S. B. (1945) *Boundary Making: A Handbook for Statesmen, Treaty Editors and Boundary Commissioners*, Washington, DC.

Lee Yong Leng (1980) *Southeast Asia and the Law of the Sea*, Singapore.

'Limits in the Seas' series, issued at irregular intervals by The Geographer, Department of State, Washington, DC.

Loring, D. C. (1971) 'The United States–Peruvian "fisheries" dispute', *Stanford Law Review*, 23 (3), 391–453.

Lotz, J. (1978) '200 mile limit revives Atlantic fisheries', *Canadian Geographical Journal*, 97 (2), 40–5.

Mackinder, H. J. (1904) 'The geographical pivot of history', *Geographical Journal*, 23, 421–37.

Mackinder, H. J. (1919) *Democratic Ideals and Reality*, London.

Mahan, A. T. (1890) *The Influence of Sea Power upon History 1660–1783*, Boston.

Melamid, A. (1947) 'The political geography of the Gulf of Aqaba', *Annals of the Association of American Geographers*, 37, 231–40.

Melamid, A. (1959) 'Legal status of the Gulf of Aqaba', *American Journal of International Law*, 53, 412–14.

Minghi, J. (1961) 'The conflict of salmon fishing policies in the north Pacific', *Pacific Viewpoint*, 2, 59–86.

Moodie, A. E. (1956) 'Maritime boundaries', in East, W. G. and Moodie, A. E. (eds) *The Changing World*, London, 942–59.

Park, C.-H. (1974) 'Fishing under troubled waters: the Northeast Asia fisheries controversy', *Ocean Development and International Law*, 2, 93–136.

Pounds, N. J. G. (1959) 'Access to the sea', *Annals of the Association of American Geographers*, 49, 256–68.

Prescott, J. R. V. (1968) *The Geography of State Policies*, London.

Prescott, J. R. V. (1981) *Maritime Jurisdiction in Southeast Asia: A Commentary and Map*, EAPI Research Report no. 2, East–West Center, Honolulu.

Ratzel, F. (1900) *Das Meer als Quelle der Volkergrösse* [The sea as a source of world power], Munich.

Ritter, K. (1865) *Comparative Geography*, Edinburgh.

Semple, E. C. (1911) *Influence of Geography and Environment*, New York.

Senftleben, W. (1976) 'Political geography of the South China Sea', *Philippine Geographical Journal*, 20 (4), 163–75.

Siddayao, C. (1978) *The Offshore Petroleum Resources of Southeast Asia*, Kuala Lumpur.

Smith, R. W. (1974) 'An analysis of the strategic attributes of international straits: a geographical perspective', *Maritime Studies and Management*, 2 (2) 88–101.

Spykman, N. J. (1942) *American Strategy in World Politics*, New York.

Spykman, N. J. (1944) *The Geography of the Peace*, ed. H. R. Nicholl, New York.

Strohl, M. P. (1963) *The International Law of Bays*, The Hague.

Symmons, C. R. (1975) 'The Rockall dispute', *Irish Geography*, 8, 122–6.

Symmons, C. R. (1979a) 'British offshore continental shelf and fishery limit boundaries: an analysis of overlapping zones', *International and Comparative Law Quarterly*, 28 (4), 703–33.

Symmons, C. R. (1979b) *The Maritime Zones of Islands in International Law*, The Hague.

Whittington, G. (1966) 'The Swaziland railway', *Tidjschrift voor economische en sociale geographie*, 57, 68–73.

Whittlesey, D. (1944) *The Earth and the State*, New York.

2
The physical nature of oceans and coasts

> The nearshore and estuarine waters are the part of the sea that overwhelmingly dominates the everyday affairs of mankind.   (Inman 1974, 351)

> Three broad groups of factors may be recognised as important in influencing geographical variation in coastal development. They are physical factors operating from landward, physical factors in the sea, and, thirdly, biological factors operating along the shoreline itself.   (Davies 1972, 2)

When Shepard (1973) published the third edition of *Submarine Geology*, he noted that the increase in knowledge about the continental margin in the decade since the second edition appeared had been truly staggering. The same assessment would have been true of the increase in knowledge about the physics of the oceans, processes in the atmosphere above the oceans, and processes of change in coastal landforms. Further, that rate of increase has persisted through the 1970s and into the 1980s.

It is not the intention of this chapter to attempt any review of the mass of detailed data about the physical nature of the oceans and surrounding coasts. Instead it examines in general terms the significance of these characteristics to claims which countries can make to the oceans and the seabed, and to the use of the claimed areas. It will be impossible to develop predictive laws about the significance of the physical nature of the oceans and coasts to the extent of political claims or the type and intensity of economic activity. The operation and significance of these physical factors will depend in part on the interpretations by governments of rules dealing with national claims, and in part on the willingness of governments to subsidize economic activities and promote technical innovation. For example, it is only by a perverse interpretation of Article 13 of the 1958 *Convention on the Territorial Sea and Contiguous Zone* that Argentina and Uruguay have closed the mouth of the Rio de la Plata by a straight line about 120 nautical miles in length. This article applies to rivers which flow directly into the sea; it does not apply to vast estuaries such as that of the Rio de la Plata. Thus there is no value in a detailed objective description of coasts as a guide to the kinds of claims which can be made from them; accordingly this chapter presents a large-scale regional review of important coastal features. Later regional chapters will present more detailed information.

An example of straight necessity overcoming the economic constraints of an adverse environment and remoteness from market is provided by the development of oil fields off the north shore of Alaska and the construction of a pipeline to deliver it southwards. Knowledge about the tundra environment of the shores of the Beaufort Sea, their ice-bound condition in winter, and the environmental risks associated with developing the oil field and building the pipeline across a region of permafrost might have suggested that the field would not be developed. But these difficulties were faced and overcome because of the determination of the government in Washington to reduce, as far as possible, American dependence on imported petroleum.

While the extent of national claims will be influenced only by the nature of the coast, the use of offshore areas will be influenced by the nature of the coast and the characteristics of the offshore waters.

The influence of the nature of the coast on national claims

Coastal topography

The coastal topography might be important in determining whether a country can claim internal waters. Coastlines which are deeply indented, such as the fjord coasts of Norway, western Canada and southern Chile, or which have a chain of islands in the vicinity of the coast, are entitled to draw straight baselines and convert the landward waters to internal waters. An inspection of the coastlines of the continents on maps in *The Times Atlas of the World* (1980) reveals the following main points.

There is less scope for drawing straight baselines along iented coasts or coasts fringed with islands in Africa than in any other continent. The short coasts of Ethiopia and Guinea-Bissau seem to offer the best justification for straight baselines. The other southern continents offer marginally more opportunities. The fretted coast of the Antarctic Peninsula with its fringing islands provides a classic case for a straight baseline if the ownership of that region is ever settled. In South America ideal conditions for proclaiming straight baselines occur in southern Chile, that part of Tierra del Fuego which belongs to Argentina, and the Brazilian coast between Belém and São Luis, east of the mouth of the Amazon. In Australia and New Zealand straight baselines appear to be appropriate along the Archipelago of the Recherche, the Bonaparte Archipelago, the Great Barrier Reef, and the fretted coasts of western Southland and Otago, of northeastern Northland, and of northern Marlborough.

In the northern hemisphere Europe abounds with examples of indented coasts, sometimes also fringed with islands, in Scandinavia, and on the west coasts of Scotland and Eire, Devon and Cornwall, Bretagne, the west coast of Galicia in Spain, many of the south-facing coasts of Greece, and the west coast of Turkey. Coasts fringed with islands where straight baselines would be appropriate are found along the coasts of West Germany, Denmark, the Netherlands and Yugoslavia. In North America the longest sections of indented coasts, sometimes with fringing islands, are found along the coasts of British Columbia and southern Alaska, Newfoundland and Greenland, and the eastern shores of Baffin Island and Ellesmere Island. Shorter sections are located in Maine, Nova Scotia, Massachusetts, South Carolina and Georgia. In Asia the main sections of indented coasts are found along the southern and west coasts of South Korea, the Chinese coast south of Shanghai, and the coasts of Novaya Zemlya and Poluostrov Taymyr in the Soviet Union. The best example of coasts fringed with islands in Asia occurs in south Burma and west Thailand.

Baselines may also be proclaimed around coasts which are unstable. This rule is generally considered to have been devised to deal with the coasts of deltas which are retreating because fluvial sediments are no longer nourishing their growth. Deltas of some major rivers, such as the Nile and the Volga, are retreating, probably because of the dams built along their courses. Some other deltas, including those of the Mississippi, Niger and Ganges, are showing growth in one section and retreat in another. Bird and Ongkosongo (1980) have described simultaneous advance and retreat on the deltas of the Bangkaderes, Pemali, Bosok and Cimanuk Rivers of Indonesia. The main deltas which appear to be growing steadily without any retreat are at the mouths of the Irrawaddy River of Burma, the Mekong River of Vietnam and the Mahakam River of Indonesia. There is too little information to assess changes in Russia's deltas on the Arctic Coast, although the delta of the Mackenzie River in Canada is stable.

This description of major regions where straight baselines could be proclaimed represents the minimum number of situations, but not all the countries concerned have determined their baselines yet, and there are cases where other countries have declared baselines on smooth coasts.

It is predictable that unless straight baselines are drawn with a total disregard for the agreed rules, the changes in the areas of maritime zones claimed will be greatest near the coast. This point is supported by measurements made along part of the coast of northwest Australia. Along the 270 nautical miles of coast separating Cape Leveque and Cape Talbot, there are seven major deep indentations, including King Sound and Admiralty Gulf, and countless small indentations. There are also at least 132 islands and unnumbered rocks and low-tide elevations in the offshore waters. When the areas which fall within the categories of internal waters, territorial seas, contiguous zone and fishing zone are measured first from the low-water mark of the coast, and second from a straight baseline connecting those islands close to the coast, the following changes occur. The use of the straight baseline increases the area of internal waters by 7666 square nautical miles most of which were territorial waters when measurements were made from the low-water mark. The new outer limit of territorial waters eroded 876 square nautical miles from the former contiguous zone, while the displacement of the contiguous zone incorporated 228 square nautical miles of waters which had previously been part of the fishing zone. The outer boundary of the fishing zone, which is 200 nautical miles from the baselines, was the same whether measured from the low-water mark or the straight baseline.

While it is not proposed to consider the distribution of bays at the world scale of this chapter, it is important to note the distribution of major gulfs and semi-enclosed seas. Although there are no agreed rules about which gulfs can be claimed as historic bays, such bays have been claimed for a long time by various countries. For example, Canada has claimed Hudson Bay as an historic bay since 1906, and in 1959 Thailand claimed the Bight of Thailand north of parallel 12° 35' 45" north (The Geographer 1971, 8).

A survey of major gulfs which fall entirely within the coast of a single country shows that Russia has the main chance of claiming such features as historic bays. The Sea of Okhotsk with the smaller Zaliv Shelikhova at its head, the Kara Sea, Beloye More (White Sea), Obskaya Guba and Sea of Azov are all gulfs for which Soviet authorities might attempt to make a case to justify their incorporation as historic bays or historic waters. Butler (1971, 104–15) records that there is uncertainty about the status claimed for these areas by Russia.

There are three large gulfs or bays on the west coast of Alaska: Bristol Bay, Norton Sound and Kotzebue Sound. However, it seems unlikely that the United States would claim these features as historic bays, since that action would encourage other states to make similar claims along their coasts. There are four large gulfs around the Australian coast; they are Spencer Gulf and Gulf St Vincent in South Australia, Bonaparte Gulf straddling the coasts of Western Australia and the Northern Territory, and the Gulf of Carpentaria, which is shared by the Northern Territory and Queensland. Discussion about the possibility of proclaiming the Gulf of Carpentaria an historic bay in 1968, when Mexico claimed that status for the head of the Golfo de California, led to the conclusion that such a claim would be inappropriate.

Argentina claimed the waters of Golfo San Matias and Golfo de San Jorge on 29 December 1966, even though their respective mouths are 65 and 123 nautical miles wide. No other country possesses more than one major gulf along its coastline. The other gulfs in South America are Golfo de Panama on the west coast of Panama, Golfo de Darien on the north shore of Colombia, and Golfo de Venezuela on Venezuela's coast. There are only two major gulfs on the African littoral; they are Khalij Surt and Golfe de Gabes on the Libyan and Tunisian coasts respectively. Finally, separated from the Yellow Sea by the Shantung Peninsula is Bo Hai which is the only major gulf on the Chinese coast. Because there are no agreed rules governing proclamations of sovereignty over major gulfs, it is impossible to predict which gulfs might be claimed; however, such claims will have a better chance of success when no other state has a traditional economic or strategic interest in the gulf in question. It appears that the lack of any compelling strategic or economic interests on the part of other countries was the major factor which allowed Burma to proclaim a closing line 222 nautical miles wide across the Gulf of Martaban on 15 November 1968, without any challenge.

The closure of major gulfs by straight baselines will cause more erosion of the high seas than the definition of straight baselines along indented coasts or coasts fringed with islands. However, the extension of national claims along coasts possessing any of these characteristics will be much less than the extensions which result from the existence of offshore islands beyond the immediate vicinity of the shore, which cannot be considered as fringing islands. This fact can be illustrated by calculating the area of sea which lies within 200 nautical miles of a tiny island; the answer is 125,600 square nautical miles.

Offshore islands

Figure 2.1 records the areas of ocean more than 200 nautical miles from land. The width of the zone which separates these waters from the coasts of the continents is determined by the number of offshore islands. The map shows that the main concentrations of islands are found in Southeast Asia, the southwest Pacific Ocean and the Caribbean Sea. Although not shown on this map the Arctic Ocean also contains many islands, especially north of Canada. It follows that islands are only useful for extending claims when they belong to the country possessing the mainland. This can be seen on figure 2.1 by the manner in which Chile's claims are extended by ownership of Islas Juan Fernandez, Sala y Gomez and Easter Island. Alien islands offshore limit the claims which can be made from the mainland; this is a disadvantage which has been faced by Turkey, Papua New Guinea, Cameroon, Mozambique, Somalia, Cambodia, North Korea and Madagascar.

The nature of the continental margin

Figure 2.1 also shows those parts of the continental margin which lie more than 200 nautical miles from the nearest land. The map does not distinguish which parts of the distant margin consist of continental shelf, continental slope and continental rise. Since states may claim authority over the seabed to the outer edge of the continental margin, it follows that those countries with wide offshore margins have an advantage and that the extent of the claim is determined by the nature of these submarine prolongations of the continents. A striking difference is revealed between the Pacific Ocean and the Indian and Atlantic Oceans. Wide margins are more common in the Indian and Atlantic Oceans than in the Pacific Ocean, where the two main occurrences are found near Alaska and between Australia and New Zealand. The explanation for this difference is found in an understanding of plate tectonics. This subject deals with the movement of enormous crustal plates from zones of spreading to zones of convergence (Davies 1972, 8). The relationship of the continental coasts to the direction of these movements provides a fundamental twofold classification. Where two plates converge a collision coast results; the oceanic plate moves under the continental plate producing, amongst other features, a deep trench and narrow continental margins. Where a continental plate is moving in a similar direction to the spreading oceanic plate a trailing edge coast is formed. Such coasts are often bounded by comparatively wide margins, although there are variants where

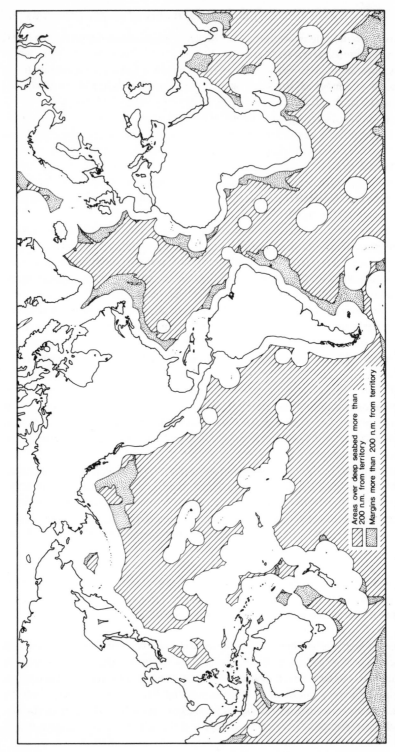

Areas over deep seabed more than 200 n.m. from territory

Margins more than 200 n.m. from territory

Figure 2.1 Seas and continental margins more than 200 nautical miles from land

narrow margins might be found. Such variants are associated with continents pulling apart in narrow seas, as in the Red Sea.

The Pacific Ocean is bounded by collision coasts, a fact which is demonstrated by the deep trenches off the Kuril Islands, the Philippines and Fiji, by the folding of coastal sediments, most clearly in the Rocky Mountains and Andes, and by the narrow continental margins. The wider margin near southern Alaska might be explained by the deposition of turbidites. These are sediments moved by ocean currents after massive landslides and landslips associated with vulcanism. Heezen and MacGregor (1973, 105) show a section through the northern Pacific Ocean which depicts thick deposits of turbidites in the vicinity of the Alaskan shelf. The wide margin between Australia and New Zealand is associated with complex plate movements in this region.

Although the map does not show them, there are some wide shelves off the Asian coast of the Pacific Ocean. They are formed behind the tectonic dams identified by Emery (1969, 111), which have sealed the Sea of Okhotsk and the Yellow Sea. Because these seas are bounded by islands they do not appear on the map as being more than 200 nautical miles from land.

The widespread occurrence of wide margins along the coasts of the Atlantic Ocean is explained by the fact that they are trailing edge coasts. The greater extent of wide shelves along the east coast of the Americas compared with the margins off the African coast is explained by the higher relief of the western Americas compared with the African interior. This fact ensures that the major American rivers carry a larger load of sediment than the African rivers, and the discharge of sediment contributes to the extent of the continental margin. This characteristic helps to explain the wide margins in the Bay of Bengal, which are nourished by the discharge of sediments from the Ganges and Irrawaddy Rivers draining the Himalaya Mountains.

The projection of the map does not permit the Arctic Ocean to be shown, but Dietz and Holden (1970, 38–9) have shown that in terms of plate tectonics this region is a continuation of the Atlantic Ocean. The zone of spreading in the north Atlantic Ocean has extended into the Arctic Ocean, between Iceland and Greenland, to a point 250 nautical miles north of Ostrov Vrangelya (Wrangel Island). This means that the wide margin off Russia is associated with a trailing edge coast. While the Canadian margin beyond the northernmost islands is not remarkably wide, the margin beyond the mainland is very wide. The widening of the Atlantic Ocean and the narrowing of the Pacific Ocean means that Bering Strait and the Chukchi Sea is the current hinge around which this movement is occurring.

Around much of Antarctica the continental margin is more than 200 nautical miles wide. The Antarctic plate is essentially fixed, although it appears to be rotating slowly eastwards (Dietz and Holden 1970, 39). The wide margin consists mainly of continental rise derived from material scoured from the continent by ice. Lovering and Prescott (1979, 27) have noted that the sediments in the rise generally exceed 1000 metres.

The influence of the physical nature of coasts and oceans on the use of offshore regions

The main economic activities in offshore regions are fishing, mining and recreation. It is not proposed to consider recreation, although it must be accepted that in some areas with a heavy recreational use, it is necessary to harmonize this and other economic activities. Such concern is at the heart of plans to organize sections of the Great Barrier Reef Marine Park Region off the coast of Queensland. The offshore areas of the continents vary in the opportunities they provide for commercial fishing and mining, and it is not a safe assumption that countries with longer coasts will have access to more of the wealth of the oceans than states with shorter coasts. Fishing grounds and mineralized regions can be very localized. For example, Iceland derives more wealth from its offshore fisheries than Brazil which has a much longer coastline, and while rich oil and gas fields have been found off the short coast of Cabinda, lying north of the mouth of the Zaire River, the search continues without much encouragement in terms of discoveries off the long coast of South Africa.

The living resources of the sea

A large number of factors, interrelated in a complex way, influence the location of any particular fish stock at any time. It is only necessary in this world survey to consider the most important. The basic food source for fish is phytoplankton, which consists of microscopic plants. The location of phytoplankton varies significantly across the surface layers of the oceans. The Geographer (1972) has produced an excellent map on Mercator's projection showing the daily average production of phytoplankton in the world's seas between parallels 60° south and 84° north, excluding areas off northern Canada and Greenland. Figure 2.2 is based on that map and shows those areas where phytoplankton production is higher than 250 milligrams of carbon per square metre per day. The most striking feature of the map is the concentration of high-yielding areas around the world's coasts. The richest phytoplankton pastures lie within 200 nautical miles of the continents; by contrast the central areas of the oceans are comparative phytoplankton deserts, relieved only by a few small oases associated with parts of the mid-ocean ridges and some island groups. There are also high-yielding areas in the waters around Antarctica, which are not shown on figure 2.2. These lush phytoplankton pastures support the dense krill stocks which Everson (1976) has identified in the Ross and Weddell Seas, and off Enderby Land, Queen Mary Land and Alexander Island.

Phytoplankton need a supply of mineral salts and sunlight for growth. Sunlight and salts such as sodium chloride and calcium carbonate are commonly available in the upper layers of the oceans. Therefore it is the availability of phosphates and nitrates, which are unevenly distributed throughout the seas, which are critical in influencing the production of phytoplankton. These salts are most readily available in deep waters, where they accumulate as a result of the decay of unused

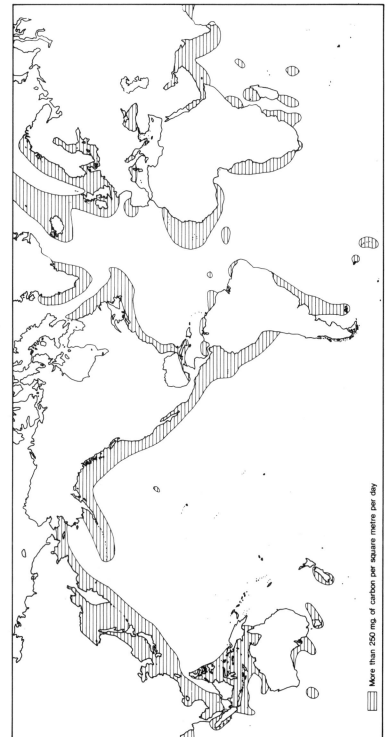

Figure 2.2 The distribution of rich phytoplankton pastures

More than 250 mg. of carbon per square metre per day

phytoplankton, and they become available in the upper layers when there are strong vertical and horizontal movements of water. Several situations will encourage or discourage such movements. They are obviously encouraged over continental shelves, where the shallow depths allow a more rapid recycling of the critical nutrients. The effects of tides and deep waves are not available in areas of very deep water. Stormy weather will also encourage the formation of waves and facilitate vertical movements, whereas the areas of light winds in the central parts of tropical oceans will lack this advantage. The absence of marked temperature differences between deep and surface waters will encourage vertical water movements. The lowest temperature gradients in the oceans will be found in the temperate and sub-arctic areas. In tropical regions the surface waters can be as much as 10°C warmer than the deeper waters, and the resulting thermocline discourages the vertical movement of water. Strong currents and streams in the oceans will improve the chance of vertical mixing; such movements are strongest near the continents. Finally, strong persistent offshore winds will promote the upwelling of cold water from deep basins near the coast.

It is therefore possible to describe the characteristics of the most favourable areas, in terms of the vertical and horizontal exchange of waters, which will create concentrations of phosphates and nitrates. Such areas would be located over continental shelves or mid-ocean banks, in temperate regions where the thermocline between surface and deep waters was either very shallow or absent, where the tidal range was considerable and storms prevalent for part of the year, and across the path of major streams and currents. These characteristics are found over extensive parts of the northern littorals of the Atlantic and Pacific Oceans. Deep upwelling, associated in some cases with the major circulatory movements of the oceans and persistent offshore winds, provides favourable conditions for the growth of phytoplankton off the west coasts of continents in lower latitudes. This is particularly true of the west coast of Africa from the Canary Islands to the Ivory Coast, and from Gabon to South Africa, and of the west coast of the Americas between California and the Tropic of Capricorn. It is also true of the east coast of the Arabian peninsula.

The significance of temperature does not end with consideration of the thermocline between surface and deeper waters; absolute temperatures also impose physiological limits on some species of fish. For example, the main concentrations of north Atlantic cod are found in waters where the temperature range is from 2°C to 5°C (Coull 1972, 39–40). The main concentrations of hake occur in waters with a temperature range of 4°C to 7°C, and the bluefin tuna shows much more tolerance by ranging in waters varying from 5°C to 29°C (Coull 1972, 42–3). Coull also notes that variations in salinity are mainly important in enclosed or semi-enclosed seas, where comparative high or low levels of salinity may alter the types of fish available.

Fluctuations in the location of fish stocks occur over short and long periods. The short-term changes may be due to migrations associated with different stages of the life cycle; for example, the northern North Sea herring stock generally spends winter near the western edge of the Norwegian Trench. In spring, melting snow and ice causes a marked increase in the flow of fresh water into the Baltic Sea, and this causes an outflow of cold water, rich in nutrients, into the northern North Sea. The herrings move westwards feeding on the new plankton pastures and spawn off Shetland. From September, the herring shoals move slowly back to their winter quarters near the Norwegian Trench. Coull has collected many similar accounts of fish migrations in European fishing grounds, and fishermen of most countries with long coastlines would be able to give evidence about similar movements. There are also long-term fluctuations in the location and size of fish stocks, but these have not been satisfactorily explained and there is a risk that the easy answer of over-fishing will be accepted, even though such changes have occurred in historic times without any evidence of over-fishing.

The resources of the continental margin are conveniently divided into living and inanimate categories. The living resources include molluscs, bêche de mer, seaweed and coral. Each of these commodities may be locally of some importance, but the total value of such products is only a tiny fraction of the value of non-sedentary species caught in the waters above the continental margin. It is also true that some of these commodities had more commercial importance in the past than they have today. For example, trade in natural pearls and pearl-shell was more important in the past than today. Reputedly the best natural pearls are found in the Persian Gulf, along the coast between Oman and Qatar, where the Mohar variety of *Meleagrina vulgaris* occurs. Large fleets of dhows search for these pearls in the period from May to September each year. Pearl fisheries off the coast of Sri Lanka, in the Gulf of Mannar, are now less important than they were, but the collection of chank shells is still locally significant. The chank is a gastropod producing a thick, heavy shell. This shell is used as a religious symbol associated with the worship of Vishnu, and some of the shells are fashioned into bangles and other ornaments and sold throughout Sri Lanka and southern India. Some of the best waters for collecting pearl-shell occur off the northern coasts of Western Australia and Queensland, and around Papua New Guinea. In these waters the shell of the *Pinctada magaritifera* grows to a considerable size, but since 1920 the industry based in Australia has recorded a major decline. In 1920 there were 3738 men employed on 515 boats and they harvested 2126 tonnes of shell, of which 1570 tonnes were exported. In 1973, there were 233 men employed on 17 boats, and they collected 233.8 tonnes of shell. It is not known what proportion of the catch was exported, but Australian exports and re-exports amounted to 547 tonnes. The value of the pearl-shell harvested in Australian waters was $A 203,000 while the value of products associated with pearl culture operations was $A 4,114,000 (Miller 1974, 918, 923–4 and 927). Seaweed is harvested in Japan for the preparation of some foods, while in Ireland and Iceland seaweed is used as a fertilizer.

The mineral resources of the seabed
The inanimate resources of the continental margin may be usefully divided into

three types. First, there are the accumulations of the remains of living organisms; second, there are mineral deposits which lie on, or just below, the surface of the margin in unconsolidated deposits; and third, there are mineral and hydrocarbon deposits lying deep beneath the surface of the continental margin in consolidated and unconsolidated material. The best recent accounts of these resources have been provided by Kent (1980) and Earney (1980). They both provide much useful technical information, and while the former has a useful glossary, the latter has an extensive bibliography. Consideration of manganese nodules is delayed until chapter 5.

The most useful remains of living organisms are coral reefs and shell beds. Mero (1964, 16–18 and 55–7) has described the commercial use of shell beds in Iceland and Texas. A deposit of crushed shells was discovered 10 nautical miles offshore in Faxafloi Bay on the west coast of Iceland in 1949. The shells are washed off rocky areas to the southwest during winter storms and are pulverized as they are washed eastwards. The beds vary from 1–4 metres (3–13 feet) in thickness and are found in water which does not exceed 22 fathoms. Since more shell is washed into the area each year than is mined, the deposit would seem to have an excellent future. Layered shell deposits are found in the Gulf of Mexico off the south coast of the United States of America, and Texan companies extracted 45 million tonnes of shell in the period 1945–65. Crushed coral can be used in the manufacture of cement and lime in those volcanic areas where limestone is scarce. It is also sometimes used in road building.

Mineral deposits on or close to the surface of the continental margin are found in concretions or sedimentary layers. The best-known concretions are of phosphorite nodules which vary in size and occur either as flat slabs or irregular masses; they have been described by a number of authors including Emery (1960), Chesterman (1952), Hanna (1952) and Dietz, Emery and Shepard (1942). Although the exact method of formation is not understood, the environment where nodules generally occur has been identified. They are found in areas where large numbers of small marine organisms are killed either by fluctuations in temperature, caused by the mixing of cool and warm water, or by fluctuations in salinity caused by the discharge of large rivers in flood. Off California the nodules are found on the walls of submarine canyons, on fault scarps, and on the outer edge of the continental shelf close to the top of the continental slope. These are all areas where there is normally very little deposition because of the concentration of ocean currents. Since there is no evidence to the contrary, it is assumed by Mero (1964, 69) that the nodules form deposits only one layer thick. Mero (1964, 75–6) also describes barium sulphate concretions which have been located off Colombo in the Indian Ocean, near the Kai Islands of Indonesia in the eastern Banda Sea, and off the southern end of San Clemente Island of California. He judges, however, that extensive deposits of these nodules are unlikely to be found.

The sedimentary layers on the continental shelf are composed of material derived from the land catchment or the outer edge of the continental shelf. There is no known mechanism for raising sediments from the abyssal plain to the continental shelf via the steep continental slope or submarine canyons. Plainly the material moved shorewards from the outer edge of the continental shelf may be former terrestrial deposits laid down in an earlier geological phase or material eroded from the bedrock of the sea floor (Bird, 1966). It follows from this that the geological composition of the land and submarine catchments will be one of the most important variables determining the location of continental shelf deposits. It is usually considered that the most valuable surface sedimentary deposits have been mainly derived from terrestrial sources. They include diamonds, gold, platinum, tin and heavy mineral sands, such as ilmenite, monazite, rutile and zircon. These valuable minerals will be released from the solid rock on land by the normal processes of denudation and weathering, and they will then be transported by rivers to the sea. The valuable proportion of the river's load will be deposited fairly close to the mouth, and from there it may be moved and sorted by wave action. Bird (1966, 4) has described two distinct situations in which sorting occurs. Where the sandy deposits overlie a shallow rock platform backed by a cliff, wave action will accumulate in the lower levels of the deposit, in contact with the platform. In some cases, as with the diamonds mined at Oranjemund on the coast of southwest Africa, the gems or minerals will be trapped in crevices and runnels of the rock platform. Where the sand deposits are much thicker they will be subject to alternations of erosion by high-energy waves during stormy weather, and of renewal by the action of gentle swells during calm weather. This alternation of cutting and filling in what is called the sweep zone creates variable laminae of the heavier minerals, and these laminae will be resorted and reformed on many occasions. Extreme storm waves will throw deposits of heavy minerals above the mean high-tide level. On beaches that are prograding, these heavy mineral deposits may form discontinuous seams for considerable distances. Now it is evident that these processes will be creating useful mineral deposits near certain coasts, and well within the outer limit of the narrowest territorial seas. But the relevance of these processes to the present subject stems from the sea-level changes during the Quaternary period. During the glacial periods sea-levels fell as increasing volumes of water drawn from the oceans were retained as ice on the land; during the inter-glacial and post-glacial phases sea-levels rose as water was returned to the oceans faster than it was evaporated. This means that during the glacial periods considerable areas of the present continental shelves stood above the seas, and coasts were located seawards of their present position. There is still debate about the maximum extent of the seas' retreat and the issue is complicated by subsequent tectonic movements, but there is some consensus on a level 90–140 metres (300–450 feet) below present sea-level (Guilcher 1970 and Shepard 1963). This means that former beaches are now under varying depths of water on the continental shelf. Whether these former beach sites are occupied by surface sedimentary deposits depends upon a number of interrelated and variable factors. First, the climate over the land would play a major role in influencing the volume of sediment delivered to the coast. Humid climates would encourage the formation and flow of rivers, which would be largely absent in coasts off tropical deserts and polar and temperate ice-caps. The amount of sediment generated would be influenced by the major gradients found throughout the catchment. The rate of marine transgression during the inter-glacial and post-glacial periods would also be an important factor. Where the rise in sea-level was rapid there would be less opportunity for the critical zone of wave action to destroy the drowned, thick beach deposits. This would be particularly true where the beach deposits were protected by overlying dunes. A slower rate of marine transgression would allow the wave zone to move the drowned beach deposits landwards. It should be noted however, that a rapid rise in sea-level across a rock platform backed by a cliff would result in a notch on the seabed where subsequent accumulation of sediment could take place. The location of mineral deposits on the continental shelf would also be affected by tectonic movements, by the growth of coral reefs which would reduce wave energy along the coast, and by the headward and lateral extension of submarine canyons.

The rivers which delivered sediment to glacial shorelines, excavated valleys in the continental shelves which they crossed. During the drowning process these lower river courses have been filled with sediment carried by the river, and by unconsolidated material on the shelf which has been transported by waves and currents along the coast. Some of these drowned valleys extend 480 kilometres (300 miles) from the coast.

The main minerals which are obtained from deposits formed in the manners described are tin, especially off the coasts of Thailand and the Indonesian islands of Belitung, Bangka and Singkep, diamonds near Oranjemund, and beach sands in Queensland and Natal. However it is probable that if the value of sand and gravel dredged from the surface of the continental shelf could be calculated, it would be found to exceed the value of minerals derived from the same area.

Mero (1964) has referred to deposits of glauconite on the continental shelf. This authigenic material is a hydrated potassium, iron, aluminium silicate which could be used as a source of potash or potassium. It is mentioned here because the deposits are found in muds and oozes along coasts where there are no major rivers and where sedimentation from terrestrial sources is very slow.

Probably every type of mineral resource is represented somewhere under the surface of the continental shelf. However, the additional expense of finding and mining such occurrences on the continental shelf, compared with similar deposits on land, probably means that only a small proportion of these prospects will be developed. Because there is a lower incidence of igneous intrusions on the continental shelf than on land the occurrence of metallic minerals is limited. Such deposits occur at the contact between igneous and other rocks, in fissured zones and in igneous intrusions. It is also a disadvantage that metallic bodies are often harder to mine than mineral deposits in sedimentary rocks. Both sedimentary and vein deposits are mined by galleries driven from land, and reference has been made to such operations listed by Wenk (1969) and Gidel (1932). Mero (1964, 96–7) has described the mining of tabular veins of magnetite under the Gulf of Finland from tunnels driven from Jussaro and Stenlandet.

There is no doubt that the great prize associated with ownership of continental margins consists of hydrocarbon fields. Since 1945, and especially since 1973 when the sharp rise in petroleum prices started, companies and countries have increasingly turned their attention to the exploration of offshore areas for oil and natural gas fields. Many countries, including Australia, Angola, Mexico and Nigeria have made important discoveries on their continental margins, which have either permitted lucrative exports or shielded domestic consumers from the worst effects of rapid increases in the cost of imported fuels. The petroleum and gas deposits may be trapped in anticlines formed during the tectonic warping of parts of the shelf, or by traps created by salt domes. These salt structures occur in large numbers off the northern coast of the Gulf of Mexico. As the salt dome thrusts upwards through overlying strata it drags the sedimentary layers upwards, forming traps along its edges and on the top of the plug.

Deep-drilling techniques have also revealed that fields can be located on the continental slope and the rise, although it is normal for such fields to be smaller than those associated with the major submarine alluvial fans found on the shelf off some coasts. In 1980 it seemed that conventional platforms were exploiting fields under seas not more than 220 fathoms deep; however, experimental techniques are already available which allow productive wells under much deeper water. The deepest water under which an exploration hole was drilled is 800 fathoms off Gander in Newfoundland.

Coasts and offshore economic development

Before examining the significance of the nature of the coast and of the sea and seabed to offshore economic activities, it is necessary to distinguish those economic activities which will require near-by shore installations. The existence of distant fishing fleets demonstrates the fact that some fishing can occur without relying on shore installations in the vicinity of the fishing grounds. The operation of factory ships and the provision of refrigerated holds ensures that fish can be caught and stored for periods which will enable the vessels to travel long distances to home ports. Nevertheless distant fishing fleets will sometimes make use of convenient foreign ports to purchase stores, or to discharge some of their catch if that requirement is written into agreements with the coastal state which controls the offshore waters.

Fishermen engaged in harvesting shellfish for the domestic market will usually operate comparatively close to the home port, because such fishing is usually done from small boats lacking large cold stores and because the price paid for the product is related to its freshness.

It is usual for mining on the seabed to be directly related to nearby shore installations. In the mining of placer deposits it is usually cheaper to refine the product close to the mine rather than transport all the dredged material to distant factories. It is also usual for petroleum products to be brought ashore by pipelines, although it is possible for tankers to be loaded near the offshore wellhead.

Oil can be fed to giant buoys to which tankers can be attached and the oil transferred to the tankers. This arrangement avoids problems associated with tides because the buoys and tankers will rise and fall together. However, the arrangement does not avoid problems associated with bad weather. For this reason buoys are often used as a temporary device to promote a cash flow while the pipeline to shore is being completed. Pipelines to shore have also become essential in cases where gas and oil are produced together. It is no longer acceptable for companies to waste the gas component by flaring. It is not possible to predict how big the area needed for shore installations servicing offshore oilfields will be. The area will depend on decisions taken by the company on how to market the product or combination of products. If the output from the field is in the form of crude petroleum without any significant gas or condensate component, the company may settle for a small pumping station driving the oil to distant refineries through pipelines. If there is a major gas or condensate component, then it might be necessary to establish some processing capacity. For example, because much of the output of natural gas fields on the northwest shelf of Australia will be exported, it is necessary to construct a liquefaction plant. This process will cool the raw gas to minus 160 degrees Celsius, and the resulting liquid will occupy one six-hundredth of the original gas volume. The liquid will be transported in special tankers of about 200,000 deadweight tonnes. So there will have to be space for storage tanks, and for berths for the tankers. Because of the risks of fire and explosion associated with the petroleum industry it is also necessary to construct a secure area, sufficiently remote from residential suburbs.

It thus appears that the nature of the coast might be significant to offshore activities concerned with harvesting shellfish and mining; these activities might also be influenced by the nature of offshore waters and seabed, and those characteristics will also influence other forms of fishing.

McGill (1958) has produced the most detailed world map of coastal landforms. However, a careful examination of this excellent map does not reveal any correlation between coastal landform and economic development. It is not surprising that the explanation of variations in the economic development of coasts will be found in such factors as onshore resources, climate, landforms, population pressure and government policies. Rather than reviewing each of these factors in turn it is proposed to consider the advantages and disadvantages of new offshore activities off densely settled and lightly populated coasts.

It would be rare for new shellfish grounds to be discovered and developed, but the reliance of this form of fishing on rapid delivery to market makes the densely settled coast more attractive. The development of new shellfish grounds off sparsely populated coasts would require additional costs for refrigeration or canning.

When offshore mining is considered no consistent balance of advantage and disadvantage exists between settled and underpopulated areas. Dredging for sand and gravel on the continental shelf generally occurs close to developed areas where the building industry is most active. It seems likely that placer mining of tin and other minerals which do not command a high price will be most conveniently conducted close to settled areas where infrastructures of ports and power supplies already exist. The placer mining of valuable commodities such as gold and diamonds does not face such large transport costs and so can be profitably pursued in remote locations on sparsely populated shores. Indeed, because of the strict security which must be enforced the remote location of the placer mining for diamonds at Oranjemund, in the extreme south of South West Africa/Namibia, is most convenient. Because of the need to erect a huge sand dam to hold back the Atlantic Ocean while the diamonds are extracted from the exhumed, ancient wave-cut platform, it is also an advantage that this coast has no tourist or recreational activities. Miners of beach sands on Fraser Island, 100 miles north of Brisbane, were forced to cease production after the Australian government revoked their export contracts in response to groups defending the recreational value of Fraser Island and alleging that sand mining would damage the environment.

Because petroleum products are valuable most countries have to develop all fields which are discovered to contain commercial quantities, and therefore oil companies have to make the best of their location off densely settled and lightly populated coasts. There are advantages and disadvantages in each case. Settled coasts possess the infrastructure of transport and power; they may contain a reservoir of skilled labour to work on the development projects and oil rigs; they may provide a ready market for the refined products either to domestic or industrial customers. This means that transport costs will be comparatively low and there will not be the difficulties associated with securing rights to build long pipelines. Of course if the particular field requires a large onshore installation, land will be expensive to buy on settled coasts, and there might be strong opposition from conservation groups actively defending the restricted recreational areas near major settlements. If the final product is destined for export then the proximity to the domestic market is no longer an advantage. There will probably be plenty of available land on lightly populated coasts if it is necessary to construct extensive onshore plants. While there might be less opposition from conservation groups to preserve restricted recreational areas, it is possible that opposition will be mounted against possible interference with wilderness regions. If the product is aimed at the domestic market it will be necessary to use tankers or long pipelines to transport the oil or natural gas, and there will be the difficulty of obtaining permission to build pipelines across private and public land, apart from any technical problems which the nature of the terrain might present to the pipe layers. The lightly populated areas will probably lack the infrastructure of railways, power supplies and ports; thus a larger cost will fall on the company, which will also have to allow a longer period of preparation before the field will start earning revenue. The workforce required for the construction of tanker berths, storage tanks, pipelines and processing plants will mainly have to be imported. The influx of many men, often single and well paid, into local communities can cause social and industrial stresses, and companies must plan to avoid or reduce such problems. Certainly Shell and other companies engaged in developing the gas fields on the shelf off northwest Australia are aware of the potential problems when 4500 workers are brought into the local community of 11,000 around Dampier, to build the onshore installations over a period of four years.

If the coast is lightly populated because of extremely adverse environments, such as those associated with the tropical and polar deserts, the disadvantages listed above will be increased. It will be necessary to develop special houses which are either centrally heated or air-conditioned, and in the tropical deserts the supply of water might be costly. In addition it is likely that wages will have to be very high and that leave conditions will need to be generous to attract and retain employees. As the engineers developing the fields off north Alaska in the Beaufort Sea found, Arctic conditions present special technical problems which extended to the construction of the pipeline. Figure 2.3 shows the location of coasts which form part of tropical and polar deserts.

A major disadvantage which inhibits the use of offshore waters in some areas is the absence of sites for ports. Such coasts are very often straight and assailed by fierce surfs, through which, prior to the construction of deep-water piers, lighters conveyed cargo between the shore and ships moored in roadsteads. Taylor (1977) has described the artificial port of Acajutla, the major port of El Salvador, which was built after 1961, 2 miles south of the old port of the same name. While the protective breakwaters reduce the height of the waves from about 6 feet to 1 foot, a slightly higher wave every two or three minutes causes the movement of moored vessels in an inconvenient and sometimes dangerous manner.

Namibia is unfortunate because the only deep-water port along its entire coast belongs to South Africa. The port of Walvis Bay is the only remaining bay on the coast; similar bays which once existed to the south of Sandwich Harbour and Conception Bay were closed by the northward drift of sediment extending the sheltering spit until it rejoined the coast and enclosed a lagoon. Luderitz is only a small fishing port, because the bed of the port is rocky and cannot be deepened. In any case Luderitz is located away from the main mining and cattle areas of the central and northern part of the country.

The influence of the sea and seabed on economic development
Finally it is necessary to consider the significance of the nature of the seas and seabed to offshore economic activities. The chief characteristic of the seas which concern people engaged in offshore activities relates to the propensity for hazardous sailing conditions to develop. Such conditions may increase the risk of vessels foundering, or colliding with each other or with some fixed structure such as an oil well platform. Figure 2.3 records some of the occurrences which create hazardous sailing conditions. It shows that tropical storm tracks are concentrated in the western Pacific Ocean and Indian Ocean and in the seas off Central America. While such storms can be detected earlier by using satellite photographs, they still create dangerous conditions for small vessels engaged in fishing, trading and tourism, and ferries heavily laden with people and vehicles plying

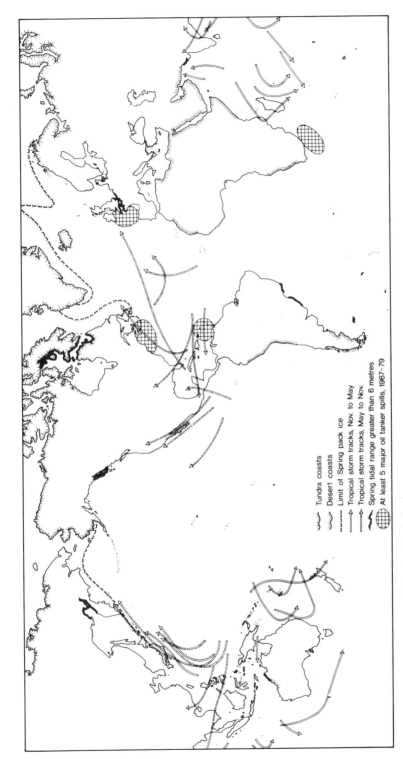

Figure 2.3 Coasts which possess geographical disadvantages

between islands. Gales in temperate areas carry the same dangers for vessels, and such disturbances are common in the winter months off the shores of Western Europe, eastern Canada, Greenland, Iceland, Kamchatka and the Aleutian Islands. When these gales are accompanied by icing conditions, as sometimes occurs off Iceland and Greenland, very dangerous conditions can develop for trawlers, as heavy ice on the superstructure raises the ship's centre of gravity and makes it more liable to capsize in high seas. High-latitude gales are less trouble-some to countries in the southern hemisphere, except in southern Chile and Argentina. However, they would be a factor to be considered in any exploitation of the offshore areas of Antarctica.

Icebergs no longer seem to threaten disaster as they did at the time of the sinking of the *Titanic*. The use of radar and satellite photography has helped to reduce the danger. However, icebergs do present problems to drilling vessels operating at a fixed location. Davis Strait, between Canada and Greenland, is known as 'Iceberg Alley', and the vessels which have drilled the seabed of that strait must maintain a constant vigilance for this danger. Similar dangers would attend any programme of drilling on the continental margin around Antarctica. The development of pack ice in the polar regions prohibits certain kinds of activity in winter; the map shows the mean limits of pack ice which covers half the sea at the time of its greatest extent. Unfortunately this mean limit is useful only as a very general indication because of the wide variations in the extent of ice from year to year.

Fog is another circumstance which can endanger shipping and it is prevalent on the west coasts of continents when warmer moist air passes over a colder sea. The South African port of Walvis Bay suffers from a surfeit of fogs.

Sea fogs are frequent off this coast at all seasons, but are more so near the shore, in autumn and winter (April to September). They may appear at any time of the day with a SW wind, even of force 5, and in winter with a NW wind. The low sandy nature of the coastline renders it very dangerous to approach during fog so great caution is needed.   (Hydrographer of the Navy 1977, 155)

The Benguela Current of cold water which creates this problem for Walvis Bay is matched by the Peru Current along the Chilean coast, and by the Kamchatka, Labrador and Californian Currents in the northern hemisphere. Some other persistent fog areas are shown on the map in the vicinity of the Antarctic Conver-gence, where the colder polar waters sink under the warmer, lighter seas to the north.

While exceptionally high tides themselves do not create hazardous sailing conditions if their existence is known, they can restrict the times when vessels can enter some ports, or they can require particularly deep channels to be dredged to overcome this handicap. Those coasts where the spring tidal range is more than 6 metres (20 feet) are shown in figure 2.3.

The final point relating to the development of hazardous sailing conditions relates to tsunamis which are large waves generated by tectonic activity on the sea floor or along coasts. Such destructive waves are usually associated with the Pacific Ocean, where the collision coasts promote volcanic and tectonic activity. Japan and the east coast of Hawaii Island have earned the worst record of suffering damage from tsunamis.

There are three ways in which the nature of the seabed can create problems for offshore economic activities. First there are those shores where the configuration of the seabed is constantly altering, as waves and currents create and remove shoals. Such uncertain conditions create difficulties for small vessels and if big ships must negotiate the hazard it is necessary to spend large sums on surveying, marking and dredging navigable channels.

Two of the other problems concern the extraction of hydrocarbons from the seabed. Conventional platforms require firm foundations which are also level. If the surface is covered with thick, unconsolidated sediments it can sometimes be difficult to find secure foundations, or it might be necessary to engage in major excavations. If the production platform is located at some distance from the shore, it might be difficult to find a satisfactory pipeline route if there are deep and wide chasms between the well and the shore installation.

Finally, the nature of the seabed can influence the extent to which trawling is a worthwhile activity. If the seabed includes irregular obstructions which can tear nets and snag expensive equipment, trawlers are likely to give it a wide berth.

Conclusions

The physical nature of the coasts and offshore seas do not determine either the extent of national claims or the use which is made of the offshore areas, but they do affect the options which are available for governments. For example, if a coastal state possesses a coast which lacks indentations and a fringe of near-by islands, its government can only proclaim straight baselines if it is prepared to act in contravention of customary international law. It must also be prepared to run the risk that its claims will be challenged by other countries with commercial fleets which transit the area, or by countries with traditional fishing rights in the additional exclusive fishing areas claimed by the use of those straight baselines. While the physical nature of coasts and offshore waters will influence the profitability of particular fishing and mining ventures, that issue will not always be decisive. It might happen that for political or strategic reasons a government will be prepared to subsidize offshore activities.

While national claims will only be influenced by the nature of the coasts and continental margin, the use of offshore areas will be influenced by those characteristics and by the nature of the offshore waters and atmosphere.

It is certain that the construction of straight baselines along coasts will cause little erosion of the high seas by fishing zones 200 nautical miles wide, unless those baselines are drawn with total disregard for customary rules. However, the construction of straight baselines will significantly influence the composition of waters close to the coast, and their main effect will be to increase sharply the area of internal waters claimed by any state. The first part of this generalization does not apply to closing lines drawn across wide bays and gulfs; such closing lines will cause significant erosion of the high seas by exclusive fishing zones 200 nautical miles wide.

The general occurrence of continental margins wider than 200 nautical miles along coasts of the Atlantic, Arctic and Indian Oceans, compared with the general lack of such coasts in the Pacific Ocean, is due to the process known as plate tectonics. The most productive activity in the oceans occurs in the vicinity of the continental margins. It is there that the largest fish stocks exist and there that mining can proceed most easily. However, the occurrence of fish stocks, placer deposits and oil and natural gas fields is highly irregular, and the ownership of wide areas of continental margin is not a guarantee that the state will possess good fishing grounds or hydrocarbon deposits.

Offshore activities will be influenced by the nature of available resources and by the characteristics of the waters and the coast and seabed. Events which create problems of navigation, such as an exceptional tidal range, a high incidence of fogs and storms, and the risk of encountering icebergs, or icing conditions, either restrict the time when offshore activities can be prosecuted or increase the costs of maintaining activity and production. The nature of the coast might also influence the offshore activities which need near-by, onshore installations, and the nature of the seabed can create problems for oil and gas producers establishing platforms and constructing pipelines from the wells to the coast.

References

Bird, E. C. F. (1966) *Preliminary Report on the Possible Existence of Heavy Mineral Deposits on the Sea Floor around the Australian Coast* (Presented to the Planet Mining Company Pty Ltd), mimeo., Melbourne.

Bird, E. C. F. and Ongkosongo, A. S. R. (1980) *Environment Changes on the Coasts of Indonesia*, Tokyo.

Butler, W. E. (1971) *The Soviet Union and the Law of the Sea*, Baltimore.

Chesterman, C. W. (1952) 'Descriptive petrography of rocks dredged off the coast of central California', *Proceedings of the Californian Academy of Sciences*, 27, 359–74.

Coull, J. R. (1972) *The Fisheries of Europe: An Economic Geography*, London.

Davies, J. L. (1972) *Geographical Variation in Coastal Development*, Edinburgh.

Dietz, R. S., Emery, K. O. and Shepard, F. P. (1942) 'Phosphorite deposits on the sea floor off southern California', *Bulletin of the Geological Society of America*, 53, 815–48.

Dietz, R. S. and Holden, J. C. (1970) 'The breakup of Pangaea', *Scientific American*, 222 (4), 30–41.

Earney, F. C. F. (1980) *Petroleum and Hard Minerals from the Sea*, Suffolk.

Emery, K. O. (1960) *The Sea off Southern California*, New York.

Emery, K. O. (1969) 'The continental shelves', *Scientific American*, 221 (3), 107–22.

Everson, I. (1976) 'Antarctic krill: A reappraisal of its distribution', *Polar Record*, 18, 15–23.

Gidel, G. (1932) *Le Droit international public de la mer* [Public international law of the sea], Châteauroux.

Guilcher, A. (1970) 'Quaternary events on the continental shelves of the world', in Delany, F. M. (ed.) *The Geology of the East Atlantic Continental Margin*, New York, 31–46.

Hanna, G. D. (1952) 'Geology of the continental slope off central California', *Proceedings of the Californian Academy of Sciences*, 27, 325–58.

Heezen, B. C. and MacGregor, I. D. (1973) 'The evolution of the Pacific', *Scientific American*, 225 (5), 102–12.

Hydrographer of the Navy (1977) *Africa Pilot*, 2, London.

Inman, D. L. (1974) 'Shore processes', in Vetter, R. C. (ed.) *Oceanography: The Last Frontier*, Washington, DC, 351–74.

Kent, Sir P. (1980) *Minerals from the Marine Environment*, London.

Lovering, J. F. and Prescott, J. R. V. (1979) *Last of Lands: Antarctica*, Melbourne.

McGill, J. T. (1958) 'Map of coastal landforms of the world', *Geographical Review*, 48, 402–5.

Mero, J. L. (1964) *The Mineral Resources of the Sea*, New York.

Miller, J. G. (1974) *Official Yearbook of Australia*, 60, Canberra.

Shepard, F. P. (1963) 'Thirty-five thousand years of sea-level', in Clements, T. (ed.) *Essays in Marine Geology in Honor of K. O. Emery*, Los Angeles, 1–10.

Shepard, F. P. (1973) *Submarine Geology*, 3rd edn, New York.

Taylor, S. (1977) 'Changed role for a conquistador port', *Geographical Magazine*, 49, 383–8.

The Geographer (1971) *Thailand*, 'Limits in the Seas' series, no. 31, Washington, DC.

The Geographer (1972) *Phytoplankton Production*, 512518 1–72, Washington, DC.

The Times Atlas of the World (1980) Edinburgh.

Wenk, E. (1969) 'The physical resources of the ocean', *Scientific American*, 221 (1), 167–76.

3

National maritime claims

Natural conditions differ in various parts of the world. The length and curvature of the coastlines of coastal countries, the depth and inclination of the seabed along their coasts, the specific conditions of their coastal resources and the joining of neighbouring countries in the same area are diversified. Moreover, the needs of economic development and national security differ for the people of each country. It is, therefore, entirely proper, legitimate and irreproachable for coastal countries to delimit in a reasonable way their own territorial sea. (*New China News* 1973, 15)

It should be observed that, however justified the rule in question may be, it is devoid of any mathematical precision. (International Court of Justice 1951, 141–2)

The long quotation from a Chinese representative at the United Nations Law of the Sea Conference, and the pithy comment by the judges who tried the fisheries case between Britain and Norway, point in the same direction. Because of the peculiar circumstances which occur along the coasts of individual states those countries must have some latitude in defining their maritime claims, and in any case no precise, mathematical rules can be devised to govern the formulation of such claims.

This chapter is divided into three parts. The first describes the maritime zones which states have or may claim. The second section reviews the rights of the claimant states and other states in the claimed zones in respect of navigation, overflight, fishing, marine scientific research, the laying of submarine cables and legislation to protect the environment. The third part surveys the means by which the boundaries of the claimed maritime zones are delimited.

Maritime zones

States which have the necessary strength to defend their claims can claim rights over the adjacent seas, for a variety of purposes, out to differing distances. Fortunately, apart from rare exceptions, such as North Korea's claim to a military warning zone, coastal countries have restricted themselves to conventional maritime claims. For coastal states there are five conventional zones. Proceeding seawards from the coast the zones are designated internal waters, territorial waters or seas, contiguous zone, exclusive economic zone or fishing zone, and continental shelf or continental margin. In the case of archipelagic states there will be an additional zone which is called archipelagic waters. Figure 3.1 shows the sequence of these zones in plan and profile for a mainland coastal country. This diagram makes it clear that the zones overlap. For example, rights to the continental shelf are confirmed by claims to territorial waters, exclusive economic zone

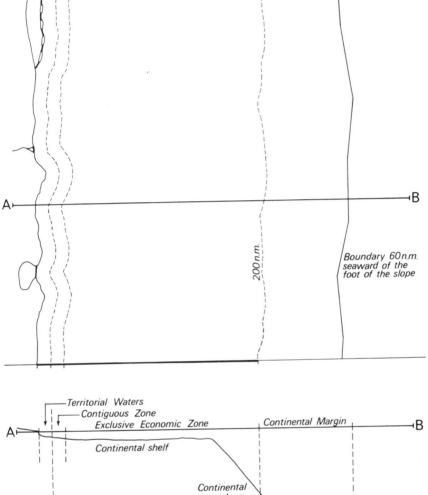

Figure 3.1 The plan and profile of national maritime claims

and the continental shelf. This means that even if a state did not claim rights over the continental shelf specifically, it would possess such rights to the shelf which lay below claimed territorial waters and exclusive economic zone. This means that the continental shelf under territorial seas is claimed three times by states which claim the whole suite of maritime zones, while the fishing rights in the territorial seas are claimed twice.

Internal waters are created when baselines other than a low-water mark are selected. Thus straight lines closing bays or river mouths, and straight baselines drawn along coasts which are deeply indented or fringed with islands, will create areas of internal waters between the shore and the baseline. When archipelagic states draw baselines around the outermost points of their outermost islands the waters encompassed by the baselines are considered to be archipelagic waters. However, archipelagic states may define internal waters within their archipelagic waters. Thus the Indonesian authorities could close the mouth of Teluk Saleh on the island of Sumbawa with a straight line, and the waters of this bay would become internal waters (Convention, Articles 8, 47 and 50).

Territorial waters consist of a belt of offshore waters measured seawards from the baseline (Convention, Articles 2 and 3). This maritime zone will form a continuous belt, unlike internal waters, which may be divided into unequal areas as straight baselines alternate with baselines along the low-water mark.

While the contiguous zone is measured from the same baseline as the territorial sea, it provides a fringe along the outer edge of that maritime zone, and its function is to provide protection for the territorial waters (Convention, Article 33). It overlaps that part of the exclusive economic zone closest to the shore.

The exclusive economic zone or fishing zone is an area beyond and adjacent to the territorial waters, and within this region the coastal state has sovereign rights over the economic use of fish and mineral resources (Convention, Articles 55 and 56). Finally, the continental shelf or continental margin consists of that part of the seabed adjacent to the coast as far as the outer edge of the continental margin, which marks the line at which the deep abyssal plain begins and international control over mining replaces national control (Convention, Article 76). This means that rights to the continental shelf alone are only made beyond the exclusive economic zone.

Some rights of nationals and aliens in claimed maritime zones

In order to achieve the compromise necessary to produce the Convention, some of the language of its sections is vague and capable of more than one interpretation. It is certain that there will be legal and political wrangles between governments in the future. For this reason it is necessary to note that in this review of the rights of nationals and aliens in the various maritime zones, the language of the Convention has been taken at face value. Possible complications have not been sought, and the survey has been restricted to the activities of navigation, overflight, fishing, the conduct of scientific research, laying submarine cables, mining and promulgating environmental legislation.

Table 3.1 records the information about alien rights in the various maritime zones for all activities except the promulgation of environmental legislation, where the information is provided about the rights of the coastal state. The commentary on the table is most conveniently arranged by considering how alien rights change as the individual travels seawards. Archipelagic waters have been placed at the end of table 3.1 because only a minority of states are able to claim them.

Navigation rights

Only in the case of internal waters which have existed for a very long time does an alien lack any navigation rights. Such waters would include the Gippsland Lakes in Victoria, Australia and Great South Bay on Long Island in the United States of America. Where internal waters have been created recently by drawing straight baselines around waters not considered previously to enjoy that status, the right of innocent passage remains (Convention, Article 8 [2]). Thus internal waters created in this fashion are indistinguishable from territorial waters in terms of alien navigation.

According to the Convention (Articles 18 and 19) innocent passage means continuous and expeditious transit, through the territorial waters or internal waters, *en route* to or from the high seas, in a manner which does not prejudice the peace, good order and security of the coastal state. The Convention spells out some of the acts which would be considered prejudicial to the coastal state. They include the launching, landing and taking on board of any aircraft, collecting information about the defences of the coastal state, practice with weapons of any kind, and the carrying out of any survey activities. It is also stipulated that submarines must navigate on the surface and display their flag (Convention, Article 20). Of course all alien vessels must also comply with accepted international regulations to avoid collisions at sea.

There were long debates at the Law of the Sea Conference about the rights of aliens to traverse those international straits which have recently been totally claimed as territorial waters by flanking states. Some of these features, such as the Strait of Bab al Mandab and the Strait of Hormuz, which are respectively 9.4 and 20.6 nautical miles wide, previously had a central strip of high seas when coastal states only claimed territorial seas 3 nautical miles wide. The Convention (Article 38) permits aliens to enjoy the right of transit passage, which in practical terms seems almost indistinguishable from innocent passage. There are, however, three differences between these forms of passage which should be mentioned. First, transit passage also includes overflight. Second, the right of transit passage may not be suspended. Third, the provisions of transit passage make no reference to warships including submarines. This transit right does not apply to those straits which are formed by offshore islands where an equally convenient route in terms of navigational and hydrographic characteristics exists in an exclusive economic zone or high seas seaward of the island. Coastal states have the right to designate sea lanes and traffic separation schemes to promote the safety of ships, and aliens

Table 3.1 The rights of aliens in national maritime zones

	INTERNAL WATERS	TERRITORIAL WATERS	CONTIGUOUS ZONE
NAVIGATION	Aliens have no rights except where a straight baseline has converted waters to the internal status. In such cases the right of innocent passage remains (8.2).	Aliens have the right of innocent passage providing they comply with legitimate laws and regulations adopted by the coastal state and with accepted international regulations to prevent collisions at sea (21). Aliens have the right of transit passage through straits used for international navigation (38). Aliens must follow designated sea lanes and traffic separation schemes (22 and 41).	Aliens have full navigation rights providing they have not infringed regulations relating to the territorial sea (33).
OVERFLIGHT	Aliens have no rights.	Aliens may overfly straits used for international navigation (38).	Aliens have full overflight rights.
FISHING	Aliens have no rights.	Aliens have no rights.	Aliens would possess rights to fish if no fishing zone or exclusive economic zone had been proclaimed extending beyond the seaward limit of the territorial sea. Sedentary species could not be caught (77.4).
SCIENTIFIC RESEARCH	Aliens have no rights.	Research can only be conducted with the express consent of the coastal state (245).	Aliens would possess rights to conduct research in the water column if no fishing zone or exclusive economic zone had been proclaimed extending beyond the seaward limit of the territorial sea. However, no research could be conducted on any continental shelf underlying the contiguous zone in this situation (246).
LAYING SUBMARINE CABLES	Aliens have no rights.	Aliens have no rights.	Aliens possess rights.
MINING	Aliens have no rights.	Aliens have no rights.	Aliens have no rights
IMPOSITION OF ENVIRONMENTAL LEGISLATION	The coastal state has complete authority (8).	The coastal state has complete authority (21 d and f), providing it does not hamper innocent passage (211.4). Warships are exempted because they possess sovereign immunity (236).	The coastal state would have authority only if the contiguous zone was overlapped by an exclusive economic zone or underlain by the continental shelf. In the first case the state would have authority over the seabed and the water column; in the second case the state could only legislate for the seabed. Such regulations would have to be consistent with rights of aliens in this zone. Warships are exempt because they possess sovereign immunity (236).

Note:
Numbers and letters in brackets refer to sections of the Draft Convention on the Law of the Sea (Informal Text).
Source: Author's research.

EXCLUSIVE ECONOMIC ZONE	CONTINENTAL SHELF	ARCHIPELAGIC WATERS	HIGH SEAS
Aliens have full navigation rights providing they observe safety zones designated by the coastal state around artificial islands, installations and structures (58 and 60.6).	Aliens have full navigation rights providing that they observe safety zones designated by the coastal state around artificial islands, installations and structures (80).	Aliens have the right of innocent passage though the archipelagic state may designate sea lanes for continuous and expeditious passage, and may close certain areas temporarily for the protection of its security (52 and 53). Where archipelagic waters intrude between two parts of a neighbouring state existing traditional rights and interests will be preserved (47.7).	All operators have equal rights (87.a).
Aliens have full overflight rights.	Aliens have full overflight rights.	Aliens have overflight rights, although they might be restricted to designated corridors (53).	All operators have equal rights (87.b).
Aliens may have access to the surplus allowable catch, determined by the coastal state, through agreements or other arrangements with the coastal state, which shall take into account the need to minimize economic dislocation to aliens who have habitually fished these waters (62). Under certain circumstances, aliens of landlocked states and of states with special geographical characteristics have the right to participate on an equitable basis, in the exploitation of an appropriate part of the surplus living resources in the EEZ of near-by coastal states (69 and 70).	Aliens have rights to fish in the water column; they are prohibited from catching sedentary species (77.4 and 78).	Aliens have traditional or agreed rights in waters prior to them being declared archi-pelagic waters and shall have those rights respected through the concluding of bilateral treaties (51).	All operators have equal rights and obligations (87.e and 116–120).
Research can only be conducted with the consent of the coastal state (246).	Research can be conducted in the water column, but consent of the coastal state would be required for research on the seabed (246 and 257).	Research can only be conducted with the consent of the archipelagic state (54 and 40).	All operators have equal rights, although these do not include the continental shelf which underlies high seas (87.f and 257).
Aliens possess rights (58).	Aliens possess rights (79).	Existing cables shall be respected and may be maintained (51).	All operators have equal rights (87.c).
Aliens have no rights.	Aliens have no rights.	Aliens have no rights.	All operators have equal rights (141).
The coastal state has complete authority (56.b.iii), providing the rights of aliens are not adversely affected (52.2). Regulations dealing with pollution from vessels should give effect to generally accepted international rules and standards (211.5). Provision exists for imposing special regulations dealing with pollution from vessels after consultation with the competent international authority (211.6). Warships are exempt because they possess sovereign immunity (236).	The coastal state has complete authority to legislate for the protection of the seabed environment (194.2 and 200) providing such regulations do not unjustifiably interfere with the rights and duties of aliens (194.4). Aliens have rights to conduct scientific research in those areas of the shelf, more than 200 nm from the baseline, which have not been designated by the coastal state as areas within which exploration or exploitation will occur in a reasonable time (246.6). Warships are exempt because they possess sovereign immunity (236).	Archipelagic states have complete authority to legislate for protection of the environment in these waters (50 and 42), and are bound not to use regulations to hamper innocent passage (50, 42.2 and 44). Warships are exempt because they possess sovereign immunity (236).	All operators have equal responsibilities (116–120).

must conform with such regulations. Such a scheme is now in operation in the Strait of Malacca.

In the contiguous zone aliens have full navigation rights providing they have not infringed regulations relating to the territorial sea. If there have been infringements the vessel can still be intercepted and the owners punished. Finally, in the exclusive economic zone and waters over the distant continental shelf, alien vessels must simply observe safety zones designated by the coastal state around any artificial islands, installations and structures which might exist (Convention, Articles 58 and 60 [6], and 80).

In the case of archipelagic waters aliens have the right of innocent passage, although the coastal state may suspend that right in specified areas for the protection of its security, and it may designate sea lanes for the continuous and expeditious transit passage of alien vessels (Convention, Articles 52 and 53). At the insistence of Malaysia the Convention (Article 47 [8]) contained a clause ensuring that where archipelagic waters lie between two parts of an immediately adjacent state, the traditional rights and interests exercised in those waters shall continue. The Malaysian authorities were anxious to ensure that the location of Indonesia's Anambas, Natuna and Bunguran Selatan Islands between peninsula Malaysia and Sarawak did not hinder communication or cancel traditional fishing interests. Those Malaysian fears were finally allayed by an agreement with Indonesia in 1981.

The position regarding overflight of maritime zones can be quickly described. Aliens have no rights of overflight over internal or territorial waters except where those territorial waters are located in an international strait (Convention, Article 38). Planes have the right of overflight across archipelagic waters, although the coastal state may designate air routes for the continuous and expeditious passage of alien aircraft (Convention, Article 53). Over all other zones aircraft have the right of overflight.

Fishing rights

Aliens have no fishing rights in internal waters or territorial seas. Aliens would be able to fish in the contiguous zone if the coastal state had not proclaimed any exclusive economic zone or fishing zone. However, it would not be permissible to harvest sedentary species, which are defined as living organisms which at the harvestable stage either are immobile on or under the seabed or unable to move except in contact with it (Convention, Article 77 [4]). Such species belong to the state which has rights over the continental shelf, and those rights exist whether or not the state has made a formal claim to the continental shelf (Convention, Article 77 [3]). In the exclusive economic zone or fishing zone aliens have no express fishing rights. Those coastal states which are incapable of harvesting the entire available catch, should, through bilateral agreements, give nationals of other states access to the surplus catch (Convention, Article 62). The Convention sets out some of the regulations which the coastal state is entitled to enforce and which alien fishermen must observe. They include the need to land all or part of the catch in ports of the coastal state; the conduct of fisheries research under the control of the coastal state; the placing of trainees or observers on alien vessels by the coastal state; and fixing quotas for vessels. It is plain that there is enough scope in these and other requirements to enable coastal states wishing to avoid this sharing of resources to do so.

The Convention (Articles 69 and 70) also tries to ensure that landlocked states and states with special geographical circumstances will be allowed to share in the surplus available catch of coastal states in the same sub-region or region. The terms under which such participation will be arranged include the need to avoid effects detrimental to the fishing communities or fishing industries of the coastal state; the nutritional needs of the populations of the various countries; and the extent to which the landlocked states and states with special geographical characteristics are participating or entitled to participate in fishing the waters of other coastal states. Once again there are enough qualifications to be met to enable any coastal states wishing to avoid sharing its fish stocks to do so. States with special geographical circumstances are deemed to be those whose geographical situation makes them depend on exploiting the living resources in the exclusive economic zones of neighbouring states to feed their citizens adequately or coastal states which cannot claim any exclusive economic zone of their own.

As explained earlier in discussing the rights of aliens in the contiguous zone, aliens are entitled to fish in the water column above the continental shelf which lies outside other maritime zones, such as the territorial sea and the exclusive economic zone or fishing zone. However, the sedentary species may not be harvested and remain available for fishermen of the coastal state. The Convention (Article 51) deals with the rights of aliens to fish in archipelagic waters. The only rights which exist belong to those countries whose nationals have enjoyed traditional fishing rights in the waters which have been enclosed within the archipelagic baselines, or who have fished the waters under an existing agreement. Such traditional rights and existing agreements shall be respected and codified by bilateral treaties which specify the conditions under which the rights are continued. Once again there will be plenty of scope for archipelagic states wishing to eliminate these rights of aliens to delay the conclusion of bilateral treaties indefinitely.

Rights to conduct research
When the rights of aliens to conduct marine scientific research are considered it is clear that no rights exist in internal waters, and the consent of the coastal state must be obtained for research programmes in the territorial seas, the exclusive economic zone or fishing zone, and the continental shelf. If the coastal state does not claim any exclusive economic zone or fishing zone beyond its territorial sea then aliens could conduct research in the contiguous zone without obtaining consent, providing the programme did not involve the seabed. While the Convention (Article 246 [3]) notes that permission will not be withheld in normal circumstances, there is no definition of normal circumstances, except to note that they

can exist in the absence of diplomatic relations. States are entitled to withhold consent if the programme is of direct significance for the exploration and exploitation of resources, and of course the decision on the relevance of any programme to resource use is made by the coastal state. There is one glimmer of hope for aliens wishing to conduct marine scientific research on the seabed more than 200 nautical miles from the baselines from which the coastal state measures its maritime claims. The Convention (Article 246 [6]) stipulates that coastal states may not withhold permission for research in such areas unless they have been designated as areas within which exploitation or detailed exploratory processes are being conducted, or will be conducted within a reasonable period of time. This is far from being a cast-iron guarantee for research workers, and coastal states will be able to stall programmes without contravening the letter of this provision.

Rights to lay and repair submarine cables

Submarine cables are no longer vitally important for international communication, but alien states do have the right to lay such cables in the exclusive economic zone or fishing zone and the continental shelf (Convention, Articles 58 and 79). Such right would also be available in the contiguous zone providing no exclusive economic zone or fishing zone had been proclaimed. Any cable-laying must be undertaken with due regard for the rights of the coastal state, and in the case of the continental shelf, the route taken by the cable must be approved by the coastal state. In respect of archipelagic waters the Convention (Article 51) provides that states owning cables traversing such waters are entitled to maintain them, and if necessary replace them.

Mining rights

Aliens have no mining rights in any of the maritime zones claimed by coastal states. Any opportunities which arise for mining ventures by aliens will follow negotiations with the authorities of the coastal state.

Environmental legislation

Turning now to the rights of the coastal states to impose environmental legislation in its maritime zones, it seems certain that this activity will be a lawyer's delight. The coastal state has complete authority over the imposition of such legislation in its internal waters. In the other zones the rights of coastal states are tempered by the need to avoid any adverse effect upon the rights of aliens. Thus, the Convention (Article 24, 211 [4]) prohibits coastal states from hampering the innocent passage of aliens by the imposition of environmental legislation relating to pollution standards, or the design, construction, manning or equipment of foreign vessels. There is scope within the various articles dealing with this matter for different interpretations on the part of coastal states and states which register commercial vessels. Warships are exempt from environmental legislation because they possess sovereign immunity (Convention, Article 236); however, it seems very unlikely that naval commanders would want to incur the bad publicity which would result for their country if they flouted environmental requirements.

This survey indicates that it is in activities connected with communication that aliens have the most rights in the maritime zones of coastal states. There is more opportunity for navigation, overflight and the laying of submarine cables than for fishing and research, while there is no alien right concerned with mining.

A special comment should be made about the rights of landlocked states under the terms of the Convention. Although landlocked states form only about 20 per cent of all countries, they possess diverse characteristics of location, size, numbers of neighbours and wealth. This diversity makes generalizations about landlocked states unwise, except perhaps to observe that such states normally try to secure more than one outlet for transit trade.

The bloc of landlocked and geographically disadvantaged states managed to secure serious treatment of their major concerns at the Conference on the Law of the Sea, and to have articles included in the Convention which dealt with them. It appears, however, that the language of these articles is sufficiently imprecise to guarantee that the landlocked states will certainly be able to insist on the rights conferred.

The section dealing with transit rights confirms existing conventions rather than breaking new ground. That part dealing with revenue contributions from states with broad continental shelves seems unlikely to generate large amounts of money, unless those states are uncharacteristically generous. The articles dealing with the access of landlocked states to the living resources of exclusive economic zones is sufficiently ambiguous to allow any obdurate coastal state to stall applications from landlocked states indefinitely.

Landlocked states also had the minor success of being noted for favourable treatment in the operations of the Enterprise, which is the international body created to control mining of the deep seabed beyond national jurisdiction. Various articles note that the participation of landlocked states in activities in The Area will be promoted; that the Authority may discriminate in its functions in favour of landlocked states; and that representatives of landlocked states will be appointed to the Council which is the executive organ of the Authority. None of these references confer any benefit for landlocked states which is likely to produce tangible gains in the foreseeable future.

However, it is a matter for satisfaction that landlocked states have survived, with varying degrees of success, without the new special rights contained in the Convention. There can be no question that the secure future in a strategic and economic sense for landlocked countries will owe more to good relations with coastal neighbours than to the letter of articles in the Convention.

The delimitation of maritime boundaries

There are three basic problems in delimiting maritime boundaries. First, it is necessary to establish the baseline to be used by the coastal state. The selection of this line will immediately fix the outer edge of the state's internal waters, and then permit the mechanical determination of the outer edges of the territorial waters, the contiguous zone, and the exclusive economic zone or fishing zone, since each of them consists of a uniform distance measured seawards from the baseline. In the case of archipelagic states the establishment of the baselines will instantly determine the extent of archipelagic waters.

The second problem concerns the determination of the outer edge of the continental margin. This boundary is not related to the baseline, except that in the case of submarine ridges, other than oceanic submarine ridges which cannot be claimed, the boundary may not be drawn more than 350 nautical miles beyond the baseline.

The third problem centres on the need for countries to draw common international limits. This need arises when countries are so close together that if each claimed the full suite of maritime zones, some of them would overlap.

All countries with coasts must face these three problems, because there is no country which is so far from its neighbours that the construction of international boundaries is unnecessary. There are some detached parts of countries, such as Hawaii and the Azores, which are so remote that they involve the construction of no international boundaries, but the United States and Portugal have other international boundaries to settle around their mainlands.

At first sight it appears that shelf-locked countries, which are hemmed in by close neighbours, would not need to concern themselves with the outer edge of their continental margin, but that impression is false. Because states may claim the seabed which is the natural prolongation of their land territories, such states can argue that equidistant boundaries are inappropriate.

Because the construction of international maritime boundaries is a major topic it is treated separately in the next chapter. The remainder of this chapter examines first the problems of drawing baselines and then the difficulty of identifying the outer edge of the continental margin.

The delimitation of baselines

Normal baselines

The Convention (Article 5) states that the normal baseline for the measurement of maritime zones is the low-water mark along the coast which is marked on large-scale charts officially recognized by the coastal country. The advantage of selecting a low-water mark is that the coastal state secures the widest possible area of sea. Different countries use different datums, for it is possible to make a selection from a range of low-water marks. For example, the Mean Low-Water Neaps is the average height of low neap tides taken over a long period. Because neap tides occur at times when the forces exerted by the moon and sun are operating at right angles to each other, the Low-Water Neaps do not fall as far as the Low-Water Springs, when the forces exerted by the sun and moon operate in the same direction. Nor will the High-Water Neaps rise as high as the High-Water Springs.

Therefore countries would usually select the Mean Low-Water Springs. This low-water level was advocated by the international conference at The Hague in 1930, and it is obtained by measuring successive low waters during those periods of 24 hours during the year, when the maximum declination of the moon is 23° 30'.

In some countries, including Australia, there have been moves to use a lower datum called Indian Spring Low-Water, and even the Lowest Astronomic Tide, which refers to the lowest water level normally reached. The search for ever-lower water lines has two possible advantages. First, the baseline is pushed seawards and therefore the area of sea claimed is increased. Second, the lower datums might expose more low-tide elevations from which claims to territorial seas could be made, providing they lie within the normal territorial waters claimed from land which stands permanently above high tide. However, these advantages must be qualified. First, except on gently shelving coasts, such as the Bay of Fundy between Nova Scotia and New Brunswick, and the Baie du Mont St Michel near St Malo in France, the horizontal distance between various low-water marks will not be very long. Second, the low-tide elevations will only be significant in extending the zone of territorial seas and contiguous zone, which are normally 12 and 24 nautical miles wide. Low-tide elevations, which must be within 12 nautical miles of the coast to act as part of the baseline, will have little or no effect on the location of the outer boundary of an exclusive economic zone 200 nautical miles wide. Third, the surveying of low-water marks or the collection and processing of tidal data can be expensive for countries with long coastlines, seeking the Lowest Astronomic Tide, and the expense is increased if new charts have to be published corrected to the new datum.

In most cases countries will accept their existing charts and use that low-water mark, or will be guided by the data available from existing stations for a long period. For example, on hydrographic charts of Australia the tidal datum used in 51 of the 59 standard ports is either Indian Spring Low-Water or some value close to that level. Therefore it makes good sense for Australia to use Indian Spring Low-Water as its baseline. This conclusion is reinforced by the fact that at six locations the Lowest Astronomic Tide as presently computed is above the Indian Spring Low-Water at the same location; that the highest tides in Australia occur in the vicinity of King Sound, a sector of coast which could be surrounded by a straight baseline; and that the level of Indian Spring Low-Water can be un-ambiguously defined by a formula, whereas the level of the Lowest Astronomic Tide cannot be defined, only the conditions which will produce it can be described.

Only when countries have strategic needs to extend their territorial seas and contiguous zones to the maximum extent is it likely to be worth the expense and time to determine the lowest possible datums. Presumably, since the Convention does not stipulate that the low-water mark must be uniform on all official charts, countries which regard the matter as critical could determine the lowest water line for strategic sections of coast, and use readily available datums in other areas.

There is also a technical problem of fixing a low-water mark on high energy coasts, with persistent heavy surf. One solution to the problem would be to take aerial photographs of the coastline at the time of low tide, and to use the photographs as evidence of the location of the baseline.

Atolls

The sixth article specifies that islands situated on atolls or islands which possess fringing reefs may draw their baselines along the seaward low-water line of the reef. An atoll consists of a reef which encloses a lagoon, and which is surmounted by one or more islands. The reefs normally have a circular or ovoid shape, and the islands are generally elongated. Bird (1976, 226) has noted that it is also a characteristic of atolls that the reefs are punctuated by channels, often on the leeward side, and that the depth of water in the lagoon exceeds 35 fathoms.

Atolls are formed by coral and associated organisms which create a skeletal structure within which sediment and other material can accumulate, creating a reef. The high growth of coral at the seaward edge of the underlying platform is explained by the higher oxygen content of the sea as the waves break, and by the better supply of nutrients compared with the floor of the lagoon. The oxygen content of the lagoon is lower than at the fringes of the reef, and there is frequently an accumulation of sediment which adversely affects coral growth. The islands formed on the reef are derived from rubble thrown by waves from the coral edge on to the reef, and by the accumulation of sand produced by the destruction of coral. If the islands are colonized by vegetation then further growth is made easier.

Fairbridge (1950) has recognized three kinds of atolls. First there are oceanic atolls which have localized foundations, usually of volcanic origin, at depths of at least 550 metres. These features are most common in the western Pacific Ocean. Ailuk Atoll in the Marshall Islands and Fakaofo in Tokelau are representatives of oceanic atolls. Peros Banhos provides an example from the Chagos Archipelago in the Indian Ocean. The second class of atolls are called shelf atolls; they are located on continental shelves and usually have foundations shallower than 550 metres. Good examples are provided by Seringapatam and Scott Reef located off the northwest coast of Australia. The third type of atolls are called compound atolls and, as the name suggests, they consist of recent atolls enclosing remnants of former atolls. The Houtman Abrolhos Islands off the coast of Western Australia provide a clear example of this type.

The Convention makes no distinction between these kinds of atolls and all would qualify under the terms of the sixth article. To this stage the discussion has centred on atolls recognized by geomorphologists. However, there is no evidence that those who drafted the Convention took such a restricted view, and it is therefore necessary to consider features which have the appearance of atolls.

There are features known as 'almost-atolls' (Bird 1976, 229). They consist of circular reefs formed about an island which is subsiding. Thus the appearance develops of a central island standing in a lagoon enclosed by a circular reef. There are sometimes distortions of this pattern if structural tilting occurs. For example, Aitutaki in the Cook Islands consists of a reef built in this way about the remnants of a volcano. Because of tilting the island is tied to the northern part of the reef system.

Horseshoe reefs can also form an atoll. They are formed as the growth of reefs responds to a fairly constant wave pattern. Bird (1976, 226) has identified Pickersgill Reef off the coast of northern Queensland as a horseshoe reef. Its alignment results from the dominance of southeast trade winds in this region; the oldest part of the structure is found in the southeast of the reef, and from this origin twin arms have developed towards the northwest.

Finally there are systems called faros. These structures appear to be atolls in every respect except that they have shallow lagoons. Their formation is uncertain. They could result from the continued subsidence of an island which forms an 'almost-atoll'. Manihiki in Tokelau and Karavaratti in the Lkashadweep Group provide good examples of faros.

It seems probable that all features which have reefs enclosing lagoons will be deemed to be subject to the provisions of this article if that is to the benefit of the country concerned.

It is also true that while geomorphologists understand fringing reefs to have a biological source, there are also structural fringing reefs created by erosion and variations in sea-level. Biological fringing reefs can be created around islands in three ways. First, as is the case with Mangaia in the Cook Islands, coral reefs grow around the edge of an island. Second, it is possible for the reef to be created first. If a coral platform is built and reaches the surface of the sea, it is possible that cays, which are sand islands, will be built on top of the reef. Of course such features will have a ready-made coral fringe. Iles Glorieuses, situated north of Madagascar and belonging to France, provide a good example of cays formed in this way. Finally, Bird (1976, 223) has noted that nearshore coral reefs can become fringing reefs if the intervening lagoon is filled with sediment.

It is also possible that some countries will decide that coral barrier reefs, which are located at some distance from the coasts of major islands, will be regarded as fringing reefs in the sense of Article 6. The best barrier reefs are found off the coast of Queensland, New Caledonia, Fiji, Papua and Sulawesi. It will not generally matter very much if structural reefs are considered under the terms of this article, because providing they lie within the normal territorial sea they could be considered as low-tide elevations.

There is one small remaining problem about drawing baselines around fringing reefs of atolls. Is it permissible to draw straight lines across the channels in the reef? If this is not permissible, and there is no specific authorization in the Convention, then large atolls with wide mouths, such as Bikini Atoll, could be considered to include waters within the lagoon which lay outside the zone of territorial waters. The authorities in Tokelau, in the marine areas act dated 23 December 1977, have specified that straight lines will be drawn across the channels in fringing reefs. That seems to be a sensible attitude.

Local straight baselines

There are two situations where straight lines can be used to replace the low-water mark as the baseline for maritime zones. First, there are local circumstances where short straight lines are appropriate; they include the mouths of rivers and small bays. Since the maximum closing line for a bay is 24 nautical miles these local straight baselines will generally be shorter than that distance, and they will be connected by sections of coast where the low-water mark is used. Second, there are regional circumstances where the nature of the coast and offshore areas makes the use of longer straight baselines appropriate. Norway's fjord coast provides a classical example of such a situation. These longer, regional baselines also include archipelagic baselines drawn around the constituent islands of countries such as the Philippines.

There are probably three main reasons why countries substitute straight lines for low-water marks. First, and probably most important, is the desire to simplify the administration of regulations governing offshore areas. If the low-water mark was used throughout the coastline of a country such as Canada or Yugoslavia, it is certain that the outer edge of the territorial sea in some sections would be highly convoluted. Such an irregular line makes it very difficult for navigators on vessels to know whether they are inside or outside territorial waters, and equally difficult for navigators on patrol vessels and aircraft to know whether regulations are being broken by alien vessels. In some cases, such as the Australian Great Barrier Reef, the use of low-water marks throughout would ensure that enclaves of non-territorial waters were surrounded by territorial seas.

The second reason for drawing straight baselines is to increase the area of seas claimed. As was shown in the last chapter the effect of straight baselines will be greatly to increase the area of internal waters, rather than to extend the outer limit of the exclusive economic zone. The outer limit of the economic zone would only be significantly displaced seawards if the baseline was drawn with complete disregard for the rules governing baseline selection in the Convention (Article 7). The third reason which some countries might entertain for drawing straight baselines would be to secure an advantage over a neighbouring state in the negotiation of a common international maritime boundary. This would seem to be a vain hope, because predictably any country which was placed at this disadvantage would be likely to proclaim its own straight baselines to regain equality. It is generally considered that while Malaysia has never proclaimed baselines, during negotiations with Indonesia over their common boundary in Malacca Strait it was assumed that Malaysian baselines existed. The apparent existence of these baselines was confirmed in maps issued by Malaysia in 1979, showing the country's territorial waters at a scale of 1:1.5 millions. The straight outer boundaries of these waters could only have been produced by measurements from straight baselines.

Rivers

There are three local situations where short straight lines may be substituted for the low-water mark. First, the mouths of rivers which flow directly into the sea may be closed by a line linking the low-water mark on its opposite banks. The spirit of this section of the Convention (Article 9) is clear; it refers to rivers with comparatively small mouths which do not possess estuaries (figure 3.2). But the letter of the article is imprecise. There is no mention of any maximum width, and the reference to rivers flowing directly into the sea is capable of interpretation to include estuaries. The obvious manner to tighten this definition to avoid the extreme claims of Argentina and Uruguay to close the mouth of the Rio de la Plata by a straight line 120 nautical miles long, would have been to specify a maximum width for river mouths. It would have seemed reasonable to use the same width employed to determine bays.

Bays

Bays provide the second local circumstance which permits the use of a closing line. It is doubtful whether any other subject dealing with maritime boundaries has inspired more written commentary by lawyers and others than bays. The long studies by Strohl (1963) and Bouchez (1964) cite a multitude of references published during the last century.

The Convention restricts its concern to bays which are bounded by coasts owned by a single country; there is no provision for bays which are shared by two or more countries. This restriction follows the line taken by the International Law Commission in its report (United Nations 1956, 16), but that Commission admitted that its decision to avoid examination of shared bays was due to lack of time and data. It is surprising that in the years that have elapsed since that report was published, no satisfactory treatment of this question has been possible.

Bays subject to this part of the Convention are described in two ways: first there are four descriptive phrases, then there is a mathematical test.

For the purposes of the Convention, a bay is a well-marked indentation whose penetration is in such proportion to the width of its mouth as to contain land-locked waters and constitute more than a mere curvature of the coast.

(Convention Article 10)

The references to a bay being a well-marked indentation and more than a mere curvature of the coast convey the same message. It is expected that the bay will be marked by a large change in the azimuth of the coast. Part of the coast of North Borneo provides examples of curved and embayed coasts. Brunei Bay is a well-marked indentation, and the general direction of the coast changes sharply at Brunei Bluff and Tanjong Sakat, which mark the mouth of this bay. In contrast with this situation, east of Tanjong Baram there is a gently curved section of coast measuring 58 nautical miles which cannot be considered as a bay for the purposes of the Convention.

The other pair of phrases also belong together. There has to be a degree of penetration by the sea into the land so that waters may be considered to be land-locked. Beazley (1978, 13) expresses the opinion that a seaman would understand

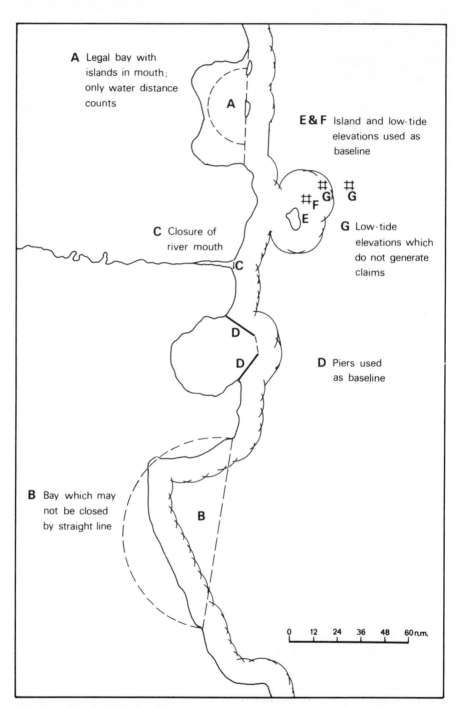

Figure 3.2 Local straight baselines

the description 'landlocked' to mean that there is land on all sides but one, and that there is shelter from all except that one direction. He might also have added that seamen would also regard landlocked waters as difficult to enter or leave when the weather conditions are adverse.

But these useful phrases would not permit agreement on the point along a continuum of coastal features, when legal bays which can be closed are distinguished from mere curvatures of the coast which cannot be closed as bays. That exact distinction is provided by a mathematical rule.

> An indentation shall not, however, be regarded as a bay unless its area is as large as, or larger than, that of a semi-circle whose diameter is a line drawn across the mouth of that indentation.   (Convention, Article 10)

The paragraph is clear in intent, but there are some difficulties in application which are partially addressed in the remainder of Article 10. Before examining these difficulties it should be noted that in a strict legal sense this semi-circle test should only be applied after it has been decided that the bay is a well-marked indentation. In practice it is inconceivable that any country would refuse to close a bay which satisfied the semi-circle test on the ground that it was not a well-marked indentation. The only exception to this generalization might be provided by a federal government which has granted its constituent states exclusive mining rights to the continental margin overlain by internal waters and territorial seas. The continental margin reserved for the federal authorities would be augmented by avoiding the closure of bays.

Since there is reference to 'the mouth of that indentation' it follows that a bay can have only one mouth, even though islands in that mouth may create a number of entrances. Plainly this is an essential condition, because if a bay had more than one mouth a country would always be able to describe the semi-circle on the diameter of the smallest mouth.

In order accurately to compare the area of the bay and the area of the semi-circle, it is necessary to establish the closing line, and to discover the line which delimits the bay around the coast.

There are three points which complicate determining the proper closing line. First, it is necessary to select the natural entrance points to the bay, which are specifically mentioned in Article 10. Second, it is necessary to choose a particular point on those entrance points which will act as termini for the baseline. Third, decisions must be taken about how to deal with islands in the mouth of the bay.

Sometimes bays have well-marked points guarding the entrance to the sheltered waters. Mabo Harbour on Malaita in the Solomon Islands and Gwadar West Bay on the coast of Pakistan serve as excellent examples of such bays. But in the case of other bays there could be disagreement amongst observers on the correct natural entrance points. Such a case is shown in figure 3.3 which depicts Wanderer Bay on Guadalcanal in the Solomon Islands. There are six possible closing lines to this bay. It must be admitted that there is no irrefutable argument in favour of one rather than another line, and it can be assumed that a state would be entitled to

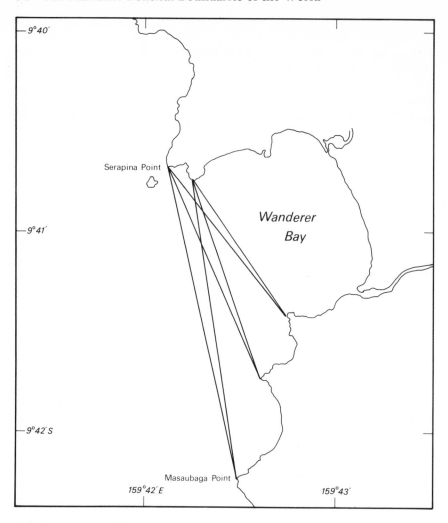

Figure 3.3 Wanderer Bay, Guadalcanal

select any set of entrance points which still satisfied the other conditions of this test.

A special problem arises when a bay is formed by a projecting headland at one end of a smooth coast. The problem is demonstrated in figure 3.4 which represents Port Waitangi, on Chatham Island in the south Pacific Ocean. Point Hanson marks the westerly natural entrance point, but there is no obvious entrance point on the smooth Waitangi beach. Encounter Bay in South Australia, Saint Helena Bay in Cape Province of South Africa and Walvis Bay in southwest Africa all have this type of configuration. One reasonable approach to this

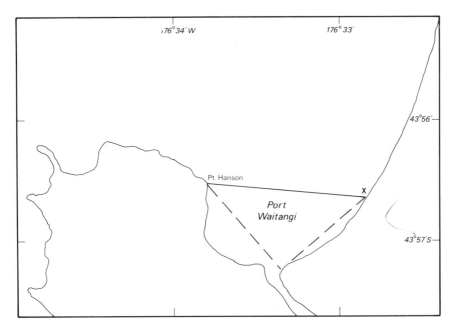

Figure 3.4 Port Waitangi, Chatham Island

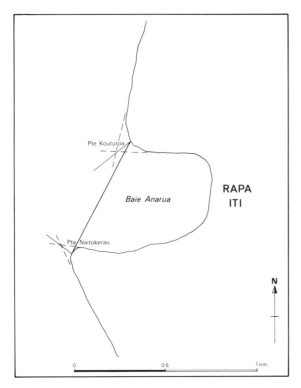

Figure 3.5 Baie Anarua, French Polynesia

problem would be to measure the distance between the natural entrance point and the position on the coast where the headland merges with the smooth coast. Then the arbitrary terminus could be fixed an equal distance along the smooth coast; such a position is shown at the point marked X in figure 3.4.

When a bay is marked by a natural entrance point which is rounded there is the problem of deciding the exact point at which the baseline should terminate. Figure 3.5 shows Baie Anarua on the coast of Rapa Iti in French Polynesia. It would be possible to select a number of different termini on the rounded entrance points of this bay. The method recommended by Shalowitz (1962, 64–5) involves constructing intersecting lines along the general direction of the open coast and the bay. The angle formed by these lines is then bisected and the entrance point fixed where the bisector first crosses the coast. His method could also be used for fixing the termini of lines closing river mouths where there was no obvious natural point.

The question of islands in the mouth of the bay is addressed in Article 10. Where multiple entrances occur in the mouth of a bay, the semi-circle is constructed on a diameter equal to the total widths of those various entrances. However, there is no guidance on how much latitude states have in interpreting this provision. In short it is not clear whether islands to which this provision applies must be on a direct line between the natural entrance points of the bay. If it is decided that they do not have to be astride that line, then it is uncertain how far inside or outside the bay they can be located before this provision does not apply. Perhaps this point was not considered to be important, because geometry tells us that due to a restriction that closing lines may not measure more than 24 nautical miles, a single island could not lie more than just under 12 nautical miles from the baseline. That distance could be extended if there were a number of islands, but in that case a regional baseline might be appropriate on the grounds that they are fringing islands.

Before leaving the subject of islands in the mouth of a bay, it is necessary to examine the question which was raised in a case between the United States and Louisiana (1969, 60–6). It was whether the headland of a bay could be located on an island. The question could be rephrased to ask whether an island, because of its juxtaposition with the coast, can create a bay.

The counsel for the United States argued that islands could not create bays, and if a baseline was drawn to some point on an island then it must be continued from some other point on the island to reach the mainland. This means that a bay closing line must go from mainland to mainland. In such a case the island would be indistinguishable from one in the entrance to a bay.

The judges appeared to agree with this view.

Of course, the general understanding has been – and under the Convention certainly remains – that bays are indentations in the mainland, and that islands off the shore are not headlands, but at the most create multiple mouths to the Bay.   (*United States* v. *Louisiana*, 1969, 62)

Any hopes for a favourable verdict which these words might have raised in the minds of the United States representatives were soon dashed. The judgement continued in the following terms:

> In most instances and on most coasts it is no doubt true that islands would play only that restricted role in the delimitation of bays. But much of the Louisiana coast does not fit the usual mold.   (*United States* v. *Louisiana*, 1969, 62–3)

The Court held that there were cases where islands could be considered to be the natural headlands of bays:

> The Convention does not prohibit the drawing of bay-closing lines to islands where (as is true of much of the Louisiana coast) insular configurations really are 'part of the mainland'; and it is left to the Special Master initially to determine whether islands which Louisiana has designated as headlands of bays are so integrally related to the mainland as realistically to be parts of the 'coast' within the meaning of the Convention.   (*United States* v. *Louisiana*, 1969, 13)

This view that islands can form the natural entrance points of bays was quoted with approval by a number of judges in the Australian High Court in a case concerning the limits of South Australia (*Raptis* v. *South Australia*, 1976). On the strength of these two endorsements it would seem very hard to argue that an island cannot form a bay with the mainland.

In 1961 the Director of the United States Coast and Geodetic Service set out general principles for drawing baselines in response to a request from the Solicitor General of the United States. The Director set out his views in the following terms:

> The coast line should not depart from the mainland to embrace offshore islands, except where such islands form a portico to the mainland and are so situated that the waters between them and the mainland are sufficiently enclosed to constitute inland waters, or they form an integral part of a land form.   (Shalowitz 1962, 161)

In analysing this statement Shalowitz came to the reasonable conclusion that there is no precise standard to determine which islands can be considered to be an integral part of the mainland. Fortunately the judges in the American case did offer some guidance to the Special Master:

> While there is little objective evidence on this question to be found in international law, the question whether a particular island is to be treated as part of the mainland would depend on such factors as its size, its distance from the mainland, the depth and utility of the intervening waters, the shape of the island, and its relationship to the configuration of the coast.
> (*United States* v. *Louisiana*, 1969, 67)

Because the combination of these factors at various scales offers a wide range of situations, there is no point in trying to assess which factor will be critical in any case.

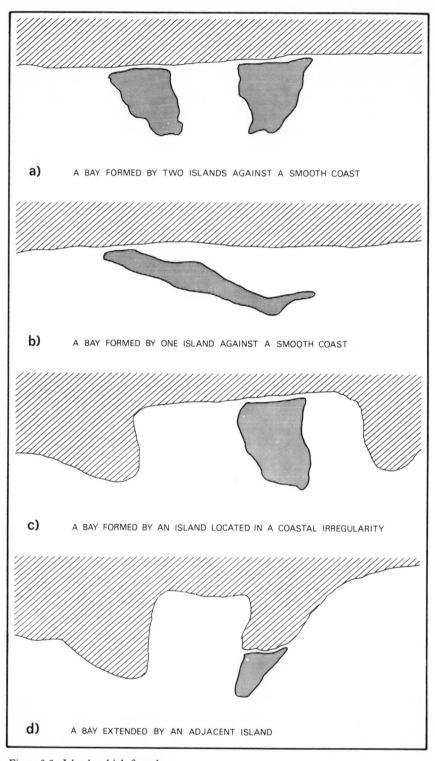

Figure 3.6 Islands which form bays

Instead it is worth reflecting on the four basic situations in which islands might be considered to produce bays. The cases are shown in figure 3.6. First, there is the case of two islands forming a bay along a smooth coast. It has proved impossible to find a perfect example of this situation, although off the coast of Finnmark Kyaloyo and Seiland enclose waters against the mainland. This is almost an inverted bay, since the expanse of waters broadens towards the coast.

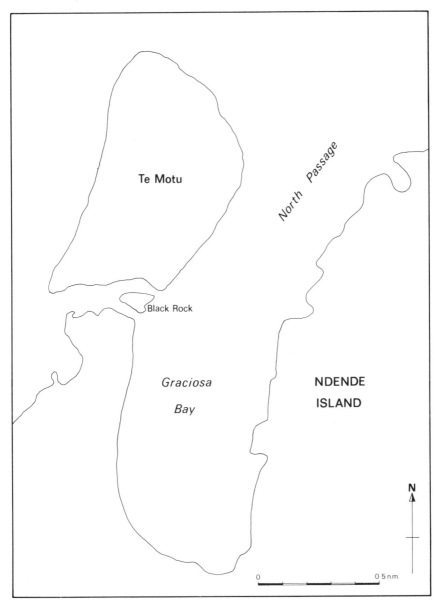

Figure 3.7 Graciosa Bay, Santa Cruz Islands

The second situation (figure 3.6b) shows a single linear island forming a bay against a smooth coast. Fraser Island on the coast of Queensland encloses Hervey Bay in this fashion. A very large rectangular island could also serve the same purpose. Caernarfon Bay is formed by the west coast of Anglesey and the smooth north coast of Lleyn peninsula in northwest Wales.

The third general case occurs when an island is located against an indented coast to form a bay. Manevai Bay in the Santa Cruz Islands is formed by Tevaii Island being lodged in a well-marked irregularity in the coast.

In the fourth situation an island may simply extend a bay which already exists. Figure 3.7 shows Graciosa Bay in the Santa Cruz Islands, and it is plainly extended by Black Rock and Te Motu.

If the view becomes general that islands may sometimes constitute the natural entrance points of bays, then the application of this set of provisions in the Convention will be complicated. At least the United States counsel was correct when he insisted that the island which forms the natural entrance point must still be tied to the mainland on the other side. If that is not done then there will not be a complete enclosure of the internal waters in the bay.

Once the problem about fixing the closing line has been settled there still remains the task of fixing the line around the shore of the bay, so that its area can be compared to a semi-circle. That line will normally be the same low-water mark that the state uses as its normal baseline. However, if there are tributary waters it is important to consider whether these waters can be included in calculating the area of the lake. For example, if there is a tidal river, then presumably the area of the river to the limit of tidal influences can be claimed as part of the bay. If there was a large tidal range, and the gradient of the shoreline was gentle, then it would be in the interest of the state wishing to establish a legal bay to use a high-water line in the bay. That would give the largest possible area for the bay. The tidal influences would also reach higher up rivers at high tide, and therefore provide a larger subsidiary area than at low tide.

Fortunately there is no ambiguity in the provision that islands located within the bay will be counted as part of the area of the bay.

The Convention also provides that if a bay has a mouth wider than 24 nautical miles the closing line may be set within the bay where it narrows to that critical distance. In such a case there is no need to draw the baseline between prominent points; they can be fixed on smooth coasts.

In a Convention where many of the articles mean all things to all men the rules about bays are fairly clear. Unfortunately the force of this clear language is undermined by the disclaimer that the rules do not apply to historic bays. It would not be so damaging if there was a general understanding of the definition of historic bays, but that is the only place such features are mentioned in the Convention. Strohl (1963, 269) suggests that the earliest use of the term historic bay occurred in 1910, when Drago dissented from the North Atlantic Coast Fisheries Arbitration. The concept has caused much debate amongst international jurists, and the best accounts of the various legal issues are provided by Strohl (1963) and

Bouchez (1964). It is not proposed to delve into the legal niceties of the debate in this book; rather attention will be focused on the practical significance of the concept.

Recourse to proclamations of authority over historic bays allows states to escape from the provisions concerning the drawing of closing lines and defining legal bays. This escape is simplified by the lack of codification of international law regarding historic bays. This means that there is no bay which cannot be claimed by one of these two available means. The importance of this situation rests on the fact that the waters of historic bays form part of the internal waters of the state, and the right of innocent passage does not exist unless it can be demonstrated that the waters were not previously considered to be internal. Because one of the conditions generally associated with claims to historic bays is that the state has exercised jurisdiction for a long time, it is open to any state to assert that it has believed for a long time that the waters were internal waters as part of an historic bay. The other two conditions are that a formal claim is made and that other countries acquiesce in the exercise of that authority. There are many lists which purport to name historic bays which have been claimed or which could be claimed (Strohl 1963, 253–68; Bouchez 1964, 215–37; and United Nations 1958, vol. 1, 3–8), but they are not very useful for two reasons. First, some states have closed alleged historic bays with straight lines without any reference to their historic status. Second, a larger number of states have made no move to proclaim the bays listed against their name as historic bays. For example, the Portuguese, French and Swedish baselines enclosed Sado, Laholm, and Granville Bays respectively without any mention of their possible historic status. In contrast, although there are seventeen bays listed as possible historic bays of Australia not one has been proclaimed.

With the exception of the Gulf of Panama, all the historic bays which appear on the various lists would directly affect only traffic to or from the coastal state concerned. This is not surprising if it is recalled that acquiescence by other states is usually considered to be one of the requirements for successful claims to historic bays.

The concept of historic bays has spawned the concept of historic waters as a modern legal claim, although the idea that certain areas of waters were subject to states is not new. A recent claim to rights over historic waters was made by India and Sri Lanka on 8 July 1974. The claim was made in a proclamation defining a boundary separating the waters, islands and seabed of Palk Strait. Palk Strait has the characteristics of a shallow bay lying between the east coast of Ramana-thapuram in India and the west coast of Northern Province in Sri Lanka. The southern end of the strait is almost closed by a line of small islands called Adam's Bridge. These waters have been used by fishermen from both shores for thousands of years, without challenge by alien states. Further, in 1903–4 in the Madras High Court it was held that Palk Strait was not part of the normal sea because it was landlocked by British territory for eight-ninths of its circumference (Jessup 1927, 14–16). The Convention does not deal with historic waters, but the precedent established by India and Sri Lanka will make it easier for other countries, singly or in concert, to follow a similar course.

Ports and roadsteads

The third local situation which permits straight lines to replace the low-water mark is found in ports and roadsteads. The outermost permanent harbour works are considered as part of the baseline from which the territorial sea, and therefore other zones, is measured, and presumably the harbour can be closed by a straight line, although this is not explicitly stated. However, this would not be a matter of great moment since the artificial mouth of a harbour between breakwaters would normally be less than a mile, so there would be negligible influence on the extent of territorial waters claimed. However, most states would probably prefer that their harbours should be classed as internal waters, and that can only be done if the mouth is closed by a straight line. Roadsteads, where vessels either wait to enter harbour or are unloaded by lighters, may also be included in the territorial sea. It is not explained how this is done if the roadsteads lie outside the territorial waters claimed from the coast. It would be necessary either to consider the roadstead as an outlier of territorial waters, almost certainly bounded by straight lines, or it would be necessary to extend the territorial waters to cover the roadstead by drawing a straight baseline which would achieve that purpose.

Low-tide elevations

Before proceeding to consideration of the regional circumstances which permit the use of straight baselines, it is necessary to comment briefly on the role of low-tide elevations. These were mentioned in the discussion of the definition of the low-water mark, and the rule specified in the Convention (Article 13) is crystal clear. If the low-tide elevation lies within the territorial waters claimed from the coast of the mainland or an island, it generates a further claim to territorial waters. When the low-tide elevation lies beyond the width of the territorial sea from the mainland or an island it may not be used to claim territorial waters. The Convention does not make it clear whether a low-tide elevation which falls within the territorial waters drawn around a rock can be used to generate further claims. In the absence of any specific prohibition, it is safe to predict that states will use low-tide elevations lying within the territorial seas of rocks as points on the baseline from which the territorial seas are measured, whenever it suits them. However, the Convention (Article 7 [4]) does prohibit the use of low-tide elevations as points used to define a regional straight baseline, unless they are surmounted by lighthouses or similar installations which are permanently above sea-level, or unless the use of such features for baselines has received general international recognition. There is plainly scope for the unnecessary construction of navigation aids on low-tide elevations to permit their use by countries constructing regional baselines.

Regional straight baselines

There are four situations where regional straight baselines can be constructed according to articles in the Convention. First there is the case of coasts which are deeply indented and cut into, such as the fjord coast of Chile (Convention, Article 7). Second there are the coasts which are fringed with islands in the vicinity of the coast (Convention, Article 7). The third situation in which straight baselines are appropriate involves unstable coasts which are likely to retreat. In such cases straight lines may be drawn around the furthest seaward extent of the coast, and these lines will continue to serve as the baseline for the measurement of maritime zones even if the coast retreats from the line (Convention, Article 7 [2]). Finally straight baselines are appropriate to surround the domains of archipelagic states (Convention, Article 47).

The short quotation which introduced this chapter, which draws attention to the lack of mathematical precision of a justified rule, refers to the requirement that straight baselines must not depart to any appreciable extent from the general direction of the coast. It is an unfortunate fact that apart from the rules for drawing archipelagic baselines, the rules for drawing straight baselines lack any kind of mathematical precision. In the following quotation from the Convention (Article 7), terms capable of significantly different interpretations have been printed in italics.

1. In localities where the coastline is *deeply indented* and *cut into*, or if there is *a fringe of islands along the coast* in its *immediate vicinity*, the method of straight baselines joining appropriate points may be employed. . . .

2. Where because of the presence of a delta and *other natural conditions* the coastline is *highly unstable*, the appropriate points may be selected along the furthest seaward extent of the low-water line and, notwithstanding subsequent regression of the low-water line, such baselines shall remain effective. . . .

3. The drawing of such baselines must not depart *to any appreciable extent* from *the general direction of the coast*, and the sea areas lying within the lines must be *sufficiently closely linked to the land domain* to be subject to the regime of internal waters.

4. Straight baselines shall not be drawn to and from low-tide elevations, unless lighthouses or *similar installations* which are permanently above sea level have been built on them or except in instances where the drawing of baselines to and from such elevations has received *general international recognition*.

5. When the method of straight baselines is applicable under paragraph 1 account may be taken, in determining particular baselines, of *economic interests peculiar to the region concerned, the reality and the importance of which are clearly evidenced by a long usage.*

There is no point in making an exhaustive analysis of the range of meanings which can be attached to the terms emphasized in this quotation, because there is not the slightest evidence that the majority of governments of coastal states is interested in more precise definition of any of these terms. Agreement on the rules quoted was reached very early in the United Nations Conference on the Law of the Sea. That is not surprising because the imprecise language would allow any coastal country, anywhere in the world, to draw straight baselines along its coast. Various studies of specific baselines by The Geographer have included the obvious criticisms that such baselines contravene existing regulations, but that seems to have been the sole effort to hold the line against the indiscriminate declaration of baselines. Nor would it be necessary for countries to introduce some enterprising, new interpretation of the debatable terms to justify the selection of a baseline, because existing baselines provide all the justification which any country could need, as the following examples show.

It would be very difficult to find smoother sections of coast than exist in Senegal north and south of The Gambia. This fact did not prevent the Senegalese authorities from proclaiming straight baselines between Pointe Rouge and Pointe de Sangomar north of The Gambia, and between the southern boundary of The Gambia and the tower at the entrance of the Casamance River; the two systems are 54.6 and 33 nautical miles long respectively. The decree giving effect to the proclamation was dated 5 July 1972 (The Geographer 1973b). It requires a vivid imagination to believe that the coast of Guinea is either deeply cut into or fringed with islands, yet on 1 July 1964 the Guinean government proclaimed a straight baseline 120 nautical miles long joining Sene and Tamara Islands. A curious feature of this straight baseline is that it is not tied to the mainland, and therefore sailing along the coast it would be possible to find oneself in Guinea's internal waters without ever having crossed a Guinean baseline. But at least Guinea did link two pieces of territory over which it had sovereignty. By its declaration of 10 July 1968 Venezuela created a single baseline closing the Orinoco River which measures 99 nautical miles. The eastern terminus is situated on the coast of Guyana, and is 18 nautical miles beyond the terminus of the boundary which separates the two countries. Venezuela presumably thought its territorial claim against Guyana justified this use of a basepoint on the Guyanan coast. Three years later, on 28 June 1971, the government of Ecuador took a leaf out of Venezuela's book and added a new development. Ecuador drew a baseline measuring 345 nautical miles (figure 3.8). The northern terminus is Punta Manglares, which is in Colombia, and the southern terminus is a point in the sea 52 nautical miles from the coast. There is only one part of Ecuador's coast which could be considered to be indented, and that is in the Gulf of Guayaquil in the extreme south, yet along this section the baseline deviates from the general direction of the coast by 60°. But it required Bangladesh in 1974 to free baselines from the need to be attached at any point to territory. Bangladesh's baseline which measures about 140 nautical miles connects two points on the surface of the sea and generally follows the alignment of the 10 fathom isobath. As in the case of Guinea, because the baseline is not attached to the mainland it would be possible to sail along the coast, into Bangladesh's internal waters, without having passed across that country's baseline.

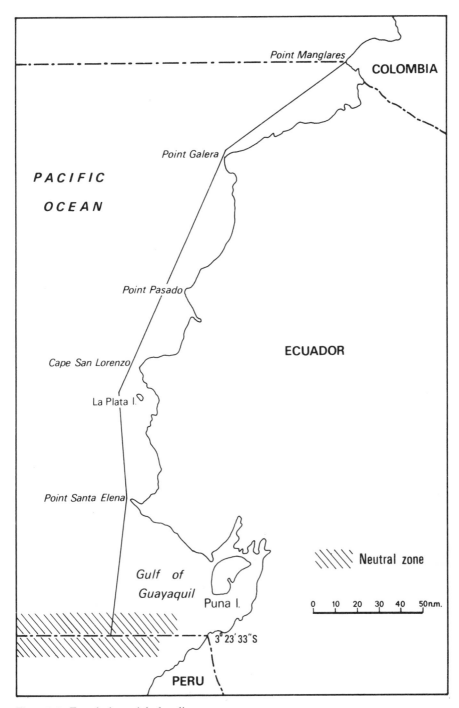

Figure 3.8 Ecuador's straight baselines

Table 3.2 records information about the straight baselines of twenty-eight countries. It was compiled in an effort to discover if there was any objective way of determining which baselines conformed to the spirit of the Convention and which seemed to breach that spirit. Of course it could be argued that all these baselines

Table 3.2 Some proclaimed straight baselines, excluding archipelagos

	Number of segments	Number of legs	Average length of legs (nautical miles)	Longest leg (nautical miles)	Maximum distance between baseline and nearest coast (nautical miles)
Indented coasts					
Chile	8	67	20.2	64.9	30
Finland	1	179	4.4	8	6
France	11	77	9.1	39	20
Iceland	2	36	21.8	74.1	24
Ireland	6	44	10.8	25.2	10
Sweden	7	95	10.4	30	10
Turkey	2	119	5.2	23.5	9
United Kingdom	1	25	11.3	40.3	10
Fringing islands					
Denmark	19	72	4.9	17.8	7
East Germany	3	7	11	22.8	7
Guinea-Bissau	1	11	13.9	29	9
Mozambique	5	23	19.7	60.4	10
South Korea	4	19	23.4	60.3	53
Thailand (islands of Phuket and Chang)	2	30	7.4	19.7	10
West Germany	6	18	5.2	21.5	17
Yugoslavia	3	26	9.4	22.5	6.6
Uncertain basis					
Albania	1	7	12.5	21.2	6
Burma	1	21	39.3	222.3	75
Cuba	1	124	11.1	70	25
Ecuador	1	4	86.2	136	52
Guinea	1	1	120	120	17
Haiti	1	10	37.2	111	40
Madagascar	1	37	42.7	123.1	25
Mauritania	1	1	89	89	34.2
Mexico	10	22	16.2	39.4	13
Portugal	1	2	26.4	31.25	21
Senegal	5	15	9.3	22	5
Thailand (Phangan I)	1	15	8.4	33.75	33
Venezuela	1	1	98.9	98.9	22

Figure 3.9 Albania's straight baselines

were proclaimed before the Convention was completed, but they all follow the conclusion of the 1958 Convention on the Territorial Sea and Contiguous Zone, the rules of which were adopted with some additions for inclusion in the Convention. So while it is true that some countries did not adhere to the 1958 Convention, no government can have been unaware of the rules which were accepted by several governments for the construction of baselines, and no country has renounced any straight baselines when it became apparent that they were contrary to the spirit of the Convention in draft form, as it existed in 1975. After a careful examination of each column and combination of columns it was concluded that there is no objective mathematical test which will distinguish genuine from spurious baselines. For example, the figures for Guinea-Bissau and Albania are similar, yet there can be no doubt that the straight baseline is appropriate in the case of Guinea-Bissau, with its multitude of islands in the Arquipelago dos Bijagos, which mask over two-thirds of the coast, while a straight baseline is quite inappropriate along Albania's uncomplicated coast (figure 3.9).

The Geographer in various studies has calculated the ratio of land to sea between the coast and the straight baseline for particular countries, and the computations has yielded ratios of 1:3.5 for Britain and Norway and 1:50 for Burma. Such an index is a useful guide, because it is generally true that baselines which create a high value will be of doubtful validity. Unfortunately this is a very laborious index to calculate, especially in the case of countries such as Finland and Yugoslavia. Further, in many cases it is unnecessary to make the calculation to demonstrate that there has been an obvious breach of the spirit of the rules.

Another index which could be calculated is the extent to which the use of straight baselines increases the area of territorial waters over the zone which could be claimed by using the low-water mark of the coast and closing lines for river mouths and bays. This calculation must be made for a standard width of territorial waters. For example, when the present claim of Ecuador to territorial seas of 200 nautical miles is plotted, and the area compared with the area which would result from the use of the low-water marks of the coast, it transpires that Ecuador has gained 1569 square nautical miles, which have been subtracted from the area of high seas. If Ecuador had claimed a territorial sea 12 nautical miles wide, the additional areas resulting from the use of the straight baseline would have been 4485 square nautical miles. Similar calculations were made for another eight countries, and the answer was then divided by the length of the baseline, so that the index expresses the additional areas of territorial waters in square nautical miles for each nautical mile of straight baseline. The results are shown in table 3.3. This index is fairly easy to calculate and it appears that a high value suggests that the baseline has been constructed in contravention of the Convention's spirit. However, the index will not detect those countries which have drawn inappropriate baselines but which do not gain these by any substantial increase in the area of territorial waters. For example, the very low figure for Senegal results from the baseline being drawn along, and very close to, a smooth coast. Of course it is not baselines such as those proclaimed by Senegal and Albania which cause concern

Table 3.3   Index to show the increase in the
area of territorial waters as a
result of the use of straight baselines. The method of calculation
is described in the text

Country	Index
Senegal	0.5
Guinea-Bissau	1
Thailand (Chang Island)	1
Thailand (Phangan Island)	4.5
Portugal	4.9
West Germany	6.8
Guinea	9.6
Haiti	10.6
Venezuela	10.6
Ecuador	13

to trading and fishing countries; it ought to be the baselines such as those proclaimed by Bangladesh, Burma and Ecuador, which significantly increase the
area falling within internal and territorial waters.

However, while there is no objective mathematical test which will establish the
extent to which particular straight baselines conform to the terms of the Convention, it is possible to describe a general profile of proper and improper straight
baselines. Proper straight baselines usually have a number of segments, each composed of several legs, interspersed with sections of the low-water mark of island
and mainland coasts. These are necessary qualifications if the line conforms to the
general direction of the coast. The length of individual legs is short and the baseline is rarely more than 24 nautical miles from an exposed coast. These baselines
do not usually enclose a high proportion of water to land, and they do not extend
the outer limit of territorial waters far into the contiguous zone or the exclusive
economic zone. By contrast improper straight baselines generally have few
segments composed of a few legs, and are rarely interspersed with sections of low-
water mark. Individual legs may be very long, and the centres of such long legs
might be distant from the exposed coast. Such baselines often enclose a high ratio
of water to land, and cause the conversion of large areas of contiguous zone or
exclusive economic zone into territorial waters.

In some cases countries proclaim straight baselines which, like the curate's egg,
are good in parts. For example, while the Irish baseline proclaimed on 20 October
1959 is certainly justified along the west coast from Scart Rocks near Malin Head
in the north to the Old Head of Kinsale in the south, the south coast east of the
Old Head of Kinsale seems too smooth to justify the extension of the straight
baseline. It would have been more appropriate for the Irish authorities in this area
to rely on the low-water mark and closing lines across Youghal Bay, and Dungar-
van and Waterford Harbours. On 12 June 1970 Thailand proclaimed straight
baselines around three sections of the coast fringed with islands. It would be

impossible to find fault with the segments proclaimed around Ko Kut and Ko Chang in the northeast of the Gulf of Thailand, and around the islands at the north end of Malacca Strait. However, the authorities seem to have stretched the concept of fringing islands out of shape by founding a baseline on Ko Phangan in the western part of the Gulf of Thailand.

There does not appear to be any case where a country has established a straight baseline around an unstable coast because the coast had that character. The Convention (Article 7 [2]) specifically mentions deltas. When baselines in the vicinity of deltas are inspected it appears that in at least three major cases the countries concerned have more than anticipated the concessions contained in the Convention. Burma and Venezuela have drawn baselines well in advance of the deltas of the Irrawaddy and Orinoco Rivers respectively, and Bangladesh has drawn a floating baseline some distance seawards of the delta of the River Ganges. It is possible that the baseline drawn around the mud islands fringing the coast of Guinea-Bissau will prove to be an unwitting application of this section of the Convention. The islands, formed from sediment discharged by the Geba and Corubal Rivers, do change their shape and suffer periods of growth and retreat. If a general retreat occurred the authorities would be able to maintain the baseline at the location established in August 1966, when the territory was still a Portuguese colony.

Archipelagic baselines

The Convention (Article 46) defines an archipelagic state as one constituted wholly by one or more archipelagos, although it may include other islands. The rules defining the construction of these baselines try to be precise and stand in sharp contrast to the rules established for drawing straight baselines along mainland coasts. There are four conditions which must be met. First, the ratio of water to land within the baselines must lie between the values of 1:1 and 9:1. This provision excludes widely scattered archipelagos, such as Tonga, and archipelagos such as Britain, Japan and New Zealand, which consist of a few large islands close together. Second, no leg of the baseline may exceed 125 nautical miles in length. This provision also acts against the scattered archipelagos. The third rule is that only 3 per cent of the legs of the baseline may exceed 100 nautical miles in length, and the final requirement is that the baselines must conform to the general configuration of the archipelago.

These tests vary in the certainty and consistency with which they can be interpreted. The requirement that only 3 per cent of segments may measure more than 100 nautical miles has a superficial exactness. It is a simple matter to calculate that baseline systems with 2–33 segments would not be entitled to any segments in excess of 100 nautical miles, while a system with 167–200 segments would be entitled to five long segments. However, there is no rule which stipulates how many segments a state must draw in any archipelagic system. Therefore once a state has decided how many segments are needed in excess of 100 nautical miles, it is a simple matter for the state to adjust the number of segments to satisfy this test.

If a country had a larger number of very small segments than seemed reasonable there might be suspicions that they had been drawn to permit certain segments over 100 nautical miles in length to be created. But this would be a suspicion which was impossible to verify because the state concerned could simply assert that it was faithfully following the requirement which prohibits baselines from departing from the general configuration of the archipelago.

This requirement about baselines conforming to the shape of the archipelago is highly subjective. It corresponds to the condition in Article 7 that straight baselines of continental states must not depart to any appreciable extent from the general direction of the coast. It is only necessary to examine baselines drawn by states such as Burma, Ecuador and Venezuela to gather examples of baselines which have departed to a measurable extent from the general direction of the coast. Since archipelagic states are empowered to draw baselines around the outermost points of the outermost islands and drying reefs, it is probable that in the case of any scattered island groups that different cartographers would select different lines to represent the general configuration of the archipelago. It is possible to generalize that the systems which reflect the shape of archipelagos most closely will have many short segments sometimes connected by segments along the low-water line.

The test which establishes the ratio of water to land will be easy to apply in an objective manner if there is no doubt about what is land and what is water. A section of this provision qualifies the rule by permitting water within fringing reefs to be counted as land. There is no clear statement about how complete the reef fringe must be to enable this exception to be applied. There is another provision which it is generally believed was inserted for the benefit of the Bahamas. It stipulates that waters lying over steep-sided oceanic plateaus, which are enclosed or nearly enclosed by a peripheral chain of limestone islands and drying reefs, may be counted as land for the purposes of calculating the ratio of water to land. It would need a detailed study of the structure and geology of other archipelagos to discover whether any other countries could avail themselves of this advantage.

The rule which appears to be capable of objective and consistent application requires that no segment should measure more than 125 nautical miles in length. The only problem concerns the nature of the basepoints which are connected. Archipelagic states, as noted earlier, are authorized to draw baselines connecting the outermost islands and drying reefs. Later in the same article states are instructed that baselines may only be drawn to low-tide elevations which lie within the normal territorial sea measured from dry land, or, if they are outside that range, if they are surmounted by lighthouses or similar installations. Now a low-tide elevation is described in Article 13 as a naturally formed area of land surrounded by and above water at low tide and submerged at high tide. This description exactly fits a drying reef. This use of two different terms may provide a loophole which would enable states to draw baselines to their outermost drying reefs irrespective of their distance from land and whether or not they are surmounted by a lighthouse or similar installation. In any case it is not clear what is meant by similar installations. Perhaps a radar reflector, or a fog horn, or an automatic light on a pole would be deemed to satisfy the requirement.

In recent years some archipelagic states in the southwest Pacific Ocean have designated more than one set of archipelagic baselines. The Solomon Islands, Fiji and Papua New Guinea have done so. The Convention is silent on whether this is a proper or an improper interpretation of the rules. Since there is no specific prohibition there seems every likelihood that the practice will continue. It is then a nice question whether each set of baselines in a particular system must meet all the rules of length and ratio, and general configuration. The answer seems to be that each individual system must meet the specific requirements, and that is how the countries concerned have interpreted the provisions.

It should be recorded that if the ability of archipelagic states to draw multiple sets of baselines is generally accepted, then there will be renewed agitation by continental states such as India and Ecuador, with offshore archipelagos, that they should be allowed to surround them with systems of straight baselines. It would be agitation which would be very difficult to refute on logical grounds.

It seems to follow that if archipelagic states can draw more than one set of baselines, that it is also open to archipelagic states to draw baselines around only those parts of their islands which satisfy the various rules. For example, Fiji, Papua New Guinea, Seychelles, Solomon Islands, and Tonga have remote islands which could not be included in the baseline system, but they have other groups which could easily satisfy all the requirements of Article 47. Vanuatu would also fall into this category if its claim to Matthew and Hunter islands succeeded. Conversely, if Vanuatu's claim to these islands lapsed then it would be one of twelve countries which could draw archipelagic baselines around their entire territory. The other members of this group are Antigua, Bahamas, Cape Verde, Comoros, Grenada, Indonesia, Jamaica, Maldives, Philippines, Saint Vincent and the Grenadines, and São Tomé and Príncipe.

Islands and rocks

Before turning to consideration of the continental margin it is necessary to examine the provisions in Part VIII of the Convention. This Part deals with the regime of islands. After describing an island as a naturally formed area of land surrounded by water and above water at high tide, it is observed that islands may be used to claim the entire suite of maritime claims, including territorial waters, contiguous zone, exclusive economic zone and continental shelf. Then comes the part of the regime which is difficult to interpret.

The final paragraph of Part VIII establishes that rocks which cannot sustain habitation or economic life of their own shall not be used to claim exclusive economic zones or continental shelves. There are two problems in any attempt to decipher this sentence. First, it is necessary to discover how rocks can be distinguished from islands; second, it is essential to understand the minimum requirements for sustaining habitation or an economic life.

It requires very little research to establish that there is no sure rule for distinguishing rocks from islands. The name 'rock' or 'island' is not a reliable guide, because those responsible for naming them, whether discoverers or boards of geographical names, follow no consistent rules. However, it is probably safe to conclude that any country which possesses a feature called an island will resist all efforts to persuade it that the structure is only a rock. It will be equally safe to assume that some countries which own features called 'rocks' will reserve the right to consider them to be islands.

There is probably general agreement that rocks must consist of solid parts of the continental crust. Sand islands or cays could never be construed to fall under the terms of the provision about rocks, even though they may be incapable of sustaining habitation or any economic life of their own.

Efforts to distinguish rocks from islands on the basis of size must fail, despite the valiant efforts of Hodgson (1974) and Hodgson and Smith (1976). It would be possible to arrange insular features on a continuum from the smallest rock to the island of New Guinea, and the decision to draw the line which separated rocks from islands would always be arbitrary. Nor could the absence or presence of vegetation be a guide to insular features. Some sand islands in the Spratlys are devoid of vegetation, while some rocks, such as Sail Rock in Saint Vincent and the Grenadines, possess shrubs and grasses.

Even if it was possible to secure agreement that one particular feature was a rock, it could not be disqualified for use as a base for claims to an exclusive economic zone and continental shelf until it was ascertained that it could not sustain habitation or an economic life of its own. This first requirement could be interpreted to mean that the rock had to be large enough to permit a shelter to be built, or that the rock had also to provide all the necessities of life. While the first interpretation seems to be sensible the second seems to be too restrictive. It is not required anywhere in the Convention that coastlands should provide all the necessities of life, so why should rocks large enough to support a shelter be treated differently?

The Convention offers no guide about the level of economic activity necessary to enable a rock to qualify as a basepoint for the complete range of maritime claims. Presumably if the rock was used regularly for the collection of guano then it would qualify. It is less clear that the use of the rock for the collection of weather data, or as the site for a navigation aid, would allow the rock to qualify as one with an economic life of its own. Allowance would also have to be made for the subsistence use of the rock by traditional societies. Aborigines in northern Australia use isolated rocks for the collection of shellfish and birds' eggs. Larger rocks in other areas where traditional societies survive might be used as shelters during extended fishing trips. It would certainly be unreasonable to require that the economic life was of a commercial nature.

It would also be a nice question to decide if a rock had an economic life of its own because it was a tourist attraction and people were engaged in the regular activity of transporting groups to the rock, either to take photographs or to collect shells. It is possible that the aim of this requirement was to prevent rocks like Rockall from being used for extended maritime claims. In that case the section is not very important because there are very few such oceanic rocks around the world. However, it is anomalous that while rocks cannot be used as basepoints if they cannot sustain habitation or an economic life, low-tide elevations can be so used if they have a lighthouse or similar installation on them. It seems to be an anomaly in the Convention that there is no mention of rocks in the sections dealing with baselines for either coastal or archipelagic states.

Brown has shown that the problem just analysed is an old one. In 1923 the British Empire sought to produce general agreement on the basis of maritime claims, and concluded that they should only be made from territory capable of use or habitation. The report then continued:

> It is recognised that these criteria will in many cases admit of argument, but nothing more definite could be arrived at in view of the many divergent considerations involved. It is thought that no criteria could be selected that would not be open to some form of criticism.   (Brown 1978, 206)

The outer edge of the continental margin

The 1958 definition of the continental shelf stated that countries could claim the adjoining submarine area to a water depth of 200 metres, or beyond that to depths where natural resources could be exploited. Plainly as a country gains technical skills it will be able to extend its claims seawards. This was not considered to be important at the time, although some countries, notably Yugoslavia and India, sought to establish definite limits which could not be extended.

At the third United Nations Conference on the Law of the Sea the precise definition of the outer edge of the continental margin became a matter of great importance for three reasons. First, the decision to establish international super-vision of mining on the deep seabed meant that the outer edge of the continental margin marked the boundary between national sovereignty and international control. Second, exploration of the margin and improved mining techniques had convinced the countries which possessed wide shelves that the distant parts of the margin might contain useful mineral resources, and that the techniques for extracting them would be available in the foreseeable future. Third, countries with narrow shelves, or which were landlocked, were determined to restrict national control of wide shelves so that these areas could be exploited by the inter-national community, from which they would derive special consideration. As early as the second session in Geneva, during the first half of 1975, it was clear that there were three options to solve this disagreement between the states which wanted to be able to claim the entire shelf and those which wanted to restrict those claims. The first two options were that one group would carry the argument; either states would be able to claim the entire margin no matter how wide it was, or no state would be able to claim a continental margin wider than 200 nautical

miles. This latter option would mean that the continental shelf claim was sub-
sumed in the claim to an exclusive economic zone. The third option was that
states should be allowed to claim to the edge of wide margins, but required to pay
a fee or rent for the rights, which would form a fund to be shared by other
countries. The inability of either major group to convert the other to its point of
view left the third option as the only realistic alternative. Accordingly the Convention (Article 82) makes provision for states which generate revenue from the
shelf beyond 200 nautical miles to make payments to the international authority
which governs mining of the deep seabed. That authority is responsible for dis-
bursing the accrued funds according to equitable principles which take into
account the interests and needs of developing states and particularly the least
developed and landlocked members of that group.

This compromise did not avoid the need to define precisely the outer edge of
the continental margin. This proved to be a complex matter as far as the delegates
to the conference were concerned, and to the single paragraph of Article 76 or the
1977 draft of the Convention there has been added a further nine paragraphs,
which still leave room for different interpretations.

It is not proposed, at this stage, to consider the difficulty of interpreting the rule
which permits states to claim 'the natural prolongation' of their land territory.
This is a matter which will be raised when the settlement of international boundaries is considered in the next chapter.

Before discussing the rules set out in the Convention (Article 76) it is necessary
to note that the article uses the term continental shelf as a synonym for continental
margin, as well as using the term in its strict sense as a special part of the continental margin. The general use of the term continental shelf to mean the
continental margin was inherited from the 1958 Convention which dealt with a
legal concept rather than a specific physical feature. Most continental submarine
margins consist of a gently sloping continental shelf which is bounded seawards
by a steep continental slope, which in turn is linked to the deep seabed by a continental rise, which consists of an apron of debris masking the junction of the continental slope and the deep seabed. Unfortunately for persons wishing to determine
maritime boundaries, the outstanding characteristic of the margin's morphology
is its wide variation. The width of the shelf varies from 700 nautical miles in the
Barents Sea to less than 20 nautical miles west of the Niger Delta. The depth of
water at the break between shelf and slope varies from 11 fathoms to 300 fathoms,
and the break in gradient may occur over 1 to 5 nautical miles. The gradient of the
continental slope varies from 1° off the coast of northwest Australia to 45° off
Santiago, where the slope descends into the Bartlett Trough. The width of the
slope varies from 10 to 20 nautical miles. Finally, continental rises are not present
where there are troughs, and elsewhere this mantle of debris may extend as much
as 400 nautical miles seaward from the base of the continental slope, as it does off
Dakar in West Africa. In the following discussion the term continental margin
will be used when the three individual elements are considered in association.

The Convention (Article 76) distinguishes between margins which are wider or narrower than 200 nautical miles. States which possess margins narrower than this distance may claim out to 200 nautical miles, effectively duplicating the claim to the exclusive economic zone. Countries which possess margins wider than 200 nautical miles may define the outer edge of the margin in one of two ways, both of which are subject to absolute restriction.

The first method permits the state to draw its continental margin boundary between those points seaward of the foot of the continental slope where the thickness of sedimentary rocks is at least 1 per cent of the shortest distance between such points and the foot of the continental slope. The foot of the continental slope is assumed to be the point of maximum change in gradient of its base. This proposal is known as the Irish formula, and it has been known for students grappling with its complexity to smile knowingly when told of its origin.

The second method permits states to draw boundaries not more than 60 nautical miles seaward of the foot of the continental slope. This proposal was first made by Hedberg (1973), but it is now considered by some delegates to be of Irish origin since it was part of the two-fold concept for boundary delimitation advanced by the Irish representatives at the Law of the Sea Conference in 1976. Whichever of these two methods is used the state must ensure that the straight lines forming the boundary consists of segments not more than 60 nautical miles long.

Hedberg (1976a and 1976b) has been the most severe critic of the use of sediment thickness for boundary definition, and he concluded that 'this proposal would be too impracticable in application to deserve serious consideration, even if other conceptually undesirable aspects were ignored' (Hedberg 1976b, 62). It is astonishing that despite the case which he raised against the adoption of this proposal it has been incorporated in the Convention.

Hedberg (1976a, 8) says it is not possible to define the thickness of sediments sufficiently precisely for the determination of boundaries. This is because there is a margin of error in seismic determination supported by a few drill holes, which is too large for survey purposes. Drummond (1978) has observed that errors in establishing boundaries on the seabed could cost as much as one million dollars per metre. In addition it is assumed that the thickness of sediment is measured above the acoustic basement, but Hedberg points out that in the contact zone between continental and oceanic crusts, there may be interdigitations of sedimentary and igneous rocks which will give a false acoustic basement. To produce a chart showing a boundary based on this method would require many trial-and-error drill holes. It is also true that sedimentary thicknesses can show sharp changes over quite short distances, and a boundary based on this system could be highly irregular in configuration.

One of the conceptual objections which Hedberg raises to this method is that an attempt will be made by the coastal states to ensure that all sediments of sufficient thickness to bear hydrocarbon deposits were included in their domain, leaving none for the international community.

In 1978 the Secretariat of the Law of the Sea Conference produced a map showing various limits of the continental margin. These limits included a line 200 nautical miles from coasts, the outer edge of the continental margin, and boundaries according to the twin Irish proposals. It was not specified how the outer edge of the margin was obtained, but the line bears a close resemblance to the outer edge of the continental slopes and rises shown on a map prepared by The Geographer (1973a). That is probably a correct interpretation since the Convention defines the margin as consisting of 'the shelf, the slope and the rise' (Convention, Article 76). A careful inspection of this map reveals the following main points. First, there are many areas off Antarctica, New Zealand, northeast Brazil, the west coast of Africa and western Canada where the Irish proposals create lines which are less than 200 nautical miles from the coast, while the margin is wider than 200 nautical miles. This creates the silly situation that because the margins are wider than 200 nautical miles one of the Irish proposals must be used, but either method will produce a line which is landward of the 200 nautical mile limit.

Second, there are only a few areas when a boundary drawn according to the thickness of sediment lies seaward of the boundary 60 nautical miles from the foot of the slope. This is scarcely surprising, because for this to happen the sediments 61 nautical miles from the foot of the slope must be at least 1130 metres (3708 feet) thick. The regions where thick sediments produce a boundary more than 60 nautical miles from the foot of the slope are off Dronning Maud Land and the eastern shores of the Antarctic Peninsula, off Montivideo and Oranjemund, and at the heads of the Arabian Sea and the Bay of Bengal. After measuring the distance between the sediment boundary in the Bay of Bengal and the foot of the slope it is possible to calculate that the sediments must be at least 2095 metres (6870 feet) thick.

Third, there are some locations where the boundaries based on the Irish formulae lie seawards of the outer edge of the margin. This situation occurs southwest of the Sandwich Islands near the Antarctic Peninsula, south of Heard Island, north of South Georgia, south of Macquarie Island, in the Tasman Sea, in the Kermadec and Tonga Trenches and west of the Marianas. While it is easy to imagine that a boundary 60 miles seaward of the foot of the continental slope will be located on the deep seabed where there is no rise, it is difficult to understand how it is possible to make a calculation of sediment thickness in such situations, especially since the Convention (Article 76) stipulates that the margin does not include the deep ocean floor.

It might be wondered why developed countries aware of the difficulties of applying the formula based on sediment thickness supported its inclusion. The explanation is probably found in the fact that the formula offers an opportunity in certain circumstances of extending national claims to the continental margin. There is no downside risk in including this formula since it can never be used to restrict a national claim. Further, the characteristics which make it difficult to apply also make it very difficult to verify and that would be considered an advantage by countries seeking the widest possible claim to the continental margin.

As mentioned earlier both parts of the Irish formula are subject to one of two absolute limits. Either the limits shall not exceed 350 nautical miles from the state's baselines, or they shall not exceed 100 nautical miles seaward of the 2500 metre (1366 fathoms) isobath. In the case of submarine ridges the absolute limit which must be used is 350 nautical miles from the baseline of the coastal state. The Convention does not define submarine ridges, although since oceanic ridges are excluded from claims to the margin, it is clear that the submarine ridges are not the features in the middle of the oceans. The matter is confused by the proviso that this rule about submarine ridges does not apply to 'plateaux, rises, caps, banks and spurs' (Convention, Article 76). These terms are not defined, so presumably it is up to individual states to decide whether they have submarine ridges or spurs.

While there is no agreement amongst geomorphologists about a precise meaning for each of the terms 'plateaux, rises, caps, banks and spurs', it is some help that the Convention describes them as natural components of the continental margin. This means that they must be composed of continental rather than oceanic crust. If they are attached to the continental margin then they will be treated in the normal way which has already been described. However, there appears to be no absolute requirement that such features should be attached to the continental margin. If that view is correct then it is necessary to decide whether there is any critical level of detachment which would prevent the coastal state from establishing a claim. Separation from the margin could be caused by downfaulting, folding or volcanic activity.

The question can be tackled from two positions. First, it could be assumed that only the margin which is continuous with the mainland can generate a line along the foot of the slope. In that case the detached feature could certainly be claimed if it lay within 60 nautical miles of the foot of the slope. It could also be claimed if the thickness of sediments exceeded one per cent of the distance to the foot of the slope. If this rule was applied the assumption would have to be made that it was possible for the thickness of sediments between the drill site and the foot of the slope to be thinner than at the drill site. There appears to be no provision in the Convention which would prevent that assumption being ruled to be valid.

The second position would argue from the assumption that the detached fragments of the margin could also generate lines along the foot of the local continental slope. Thus if the feature was a detached plateau, then it would be surrounded by continental slopes, and perhaps by continental rises. In that case it would be possible for the coastal state to measure seawards from the foot of the slope of the margin contiguous with the continent, and landwards and seawards from the detached feature. If the zone claimed seawards from the continent overlapped the zone claimed landwards from the detached plateau, then the claims would be continuous.

Since countries will be able to select the rules which favour them and to use different rules for different sections of the margin, the following course is recommended. First construct charts showing lines which are 350 nautical miles from baselines and 100 nautical miles seawards of the 2500 metre isobath. Second, locate the foot of the continental slope and mark in a boundary 60 nautical miles seawards of that feature. If this line falls short of the most distant absolute line already shown, then begin to gather information to allow the sediment formula to be used, providing that formula will produce a line closer to the most distant absolute limit. If the most distant absolute line is 100 nautical miles seawards from the isobath, prepare evidence to show that no related sections of the margin could be considered to be a submarine ridge. The evidence will have to be carefully collected because it must satisfy the Commission on the Limits of the Continental Shelf which is established by the Convention.

Conclusions

Coastal states can claim five maritime zones. Proceeding seawards from the coast they are internal waters, territorial seas, the contiguous zone, the exclusive economic zone and the continental shelf. Those states which are composed of archipelagos may also claim archipelagic waters, which have some of the characteristics of territorial waters.

The rights of the coastal state and aliens vary in these maritime zones, and do so in an inverse manner. Thus aliens have more rights concerned with communication involving navigation, overflight and the laying of submarine cables than they have with fishing and the conduct of marine scientific research, but they have no rights at all in respect of mining the continental margin.

Exactly how real these rights are for both parties remains to be tested. It is possible that some coastal states may be able to restrict alien rights by adopting one interpretation of the terms of the Convention rather than another. It is also possible that powerful countries may be able to insist on a generous interpretation of their rights in the maritime zones of a weaker state.

The construction of maritime boundaries involves three processes: they are the selection of a baseline, the determination of the outer edge of the continental margin, and the negotiation of international boundaries with neighbouring countries. Only the first two processes have been considered in this chapter; the third is the subject of the next chapter.

Countries will tend to adopt the low-water mark for which data are available along those sections of coast where such a baseline is appropriate. The considerable expense involved in deriving a new, lower datum would only be justified when it gave control over waters considered important for strategic reasons. The rules for drawing local and regional baselines are sufficiently vague to enable countries which want to draw such baselines to do so. This activity has been simplified by the precedent for liberal interpretation of the rules, created by several regional baselines which have been drawn by some states and accepted by others. The requirements for archipelagic baselines, especially the absolute limit of 125 nautical miles for individual legs and the insistence that the water-to-land ratio should lie within the range 1:1 and 9:1, are the most precise of the rules for the construction of regional baselines. So far no country has claimed a baseline on the ground that the coastline is unstable, but it will be surprising if such claims are not made in the future.

The section of the Convention defining the means by which the outer edge of the continental margin should be defined is very unsatisfactory. Imprecise terms are used and the information on which the thickness of sediment formula can be applied is both difficult to obtain and confirm. The only map published by the United Nations Secretariat indicates some anomalies, and it seems certain that if they are evident on a small-scale world map they will loom larger when the detailed charts required by the Convention are constructed by each coastal state.

References

Beazley, P. B. (1978) 'Maritime limits and baselines: a guide to their delineation', special publication 2, *The Hydrographic Society*, London.

Bird, E. F. C. (1976) *Coasts*, 2nd edn, Canberra.

Bouchez, L. J. (1964) *The Regime of Bays in International Law*, Leyden.

Brown, E. D. (1978) 'Rockall and the limits of national jurisdiction of the United Kingdom', *Marine Policy*, 2, 181–211.

Drummond, S. (1978) 'The nautical chart – friend or foe', *Marine Geodesy Journal*, 1 (3), 207–15.

Fairbridge, R. W. (1950) 'Recent and pleistocene coral reefs of Australia', *Journal of Geology*, 58, 330–401.

Hedberg, H. D. (1973) 'The national–international jurisdictional boundary on the ocean floor', *Ocean Management*, 1, 83–118.

Hedberg, H. D. (1976a) 'Ocean boundaries for the law of the sea', *Marine Technology Society Journal*, 10 (5), 6–11.

Hedberg, H. D. (1976b) 'Relation of political boundaries on the ocean floor to the continental margin', *Virginia Journal of International Law*, 17 (1).

Hodgson, R. D. (1974) 'Islands: normal and special circumstances', in Gamble, J. K. and Pontecorvo, G. (eds) *Law of the Sea: Emerging Regime of the Oceans*, Cambridge, Mass.

Hodgson, R. D. and Smith, R. W. (1976) 'The Informal Single Negotiating Text (Committee II): a geographical perspective', *Ocean Development and International Law*, 3, 225–59.

International Court of Justice (1951) *Fisheries Case – Judgement of 18 December 1951*, Reports of Judgements, Advisory Opinions and Orders, Leyden.

Jessup, P. C. (1927) *The Law of Territorial Waters and Maritime Jurisdiction*, New York.

New China News (1973) Melbourne, 4 April.

Raptis (A.) and Son v. *South Australia, 1977*, Commonwealth Law Report, 138, 346–98.

Shalowitz, A. L. (1962) *Shore and Sea Boundaries*, vol. 1, Washington.

Strohl, M. P. (1963) *The International Law of Bays*, The Hague.

The Geographer (1973a) *Composite Theoretical Division of the Seabed* (map), Washington, DC.

The Geographer (1973b) *Straight Baselines: Senegal*, 'Limits in the Seas' series, no. 54, Washington, DC.

United Nations (1956) *Report of the International Law Commission, General Assembly, 11th Session*, supplement No. 9 (*A/3159*), New York.

United Nations (1958) *Conference on the Law of the Sea*, New York, 1.

United States v. *Louisiana, 1969*, 394, US, 11–88.

4
International maritime boundaries

Since January 15, the Saigon authorities in south Viet Nam have brazenly sent warships and airplanes to intrude into China's territorial waters and air space around and over the Hshisha Islands, forcibly occupy Chinese islands and open fire on Chinese fishermen engaged in production and Chinese naval vessels on normal patrol duty. They have thus flagrantly infringed on China's territorial integrity and sovereignty and made frantic provocations against the Chinese people.

(*Peking Review* 1974, 4)

The fourth Meeting between the officials' Delegations of Indonesia and Australia on maritime boundaries delimitations was held in Jakarta on 27–29 October 1981. . . . The meeting made progress and a Memorandum of Understanding concerning the implementation of a provisional fisheries surveillance and enforcement arrangement was signed on 29 October 1981.

(Australian Department of Foreign Affairs 1981, III–IV)

After an exchange of correspondence and informal contacts which took place in 1964 and 1965, the Parties opened negotiations in October 1970 concerning the delimitation of their respective continental shelves. Since these negotiations, which continued until the beginning of 1974, were unsuccessful, the heads of the two Governments agreed in principle, during discussions held in Paris on 19 July 1974, to submit their dispute to an arbitral tribunal.   (Court of Arbitration 1977, 4)

The three quotations have been selected to illustrate the three main processes by which international maritime boundaries have been created; they are unilateral action, bilateral negotiation and arbitration. This chapter begins with an examination of these processes, then proceeds to an examination of the circumstances which make the creation of international maritime boundaries difficult, and concludes by considering ways in which states try to mitigate the problems which are sometimes created when international lines are drawn.

Processes of international maritime boundary evolution

One of the important differences between international limits on land and sea is that the colonial powers were almost solely responsible for the land boundaries which today surround the states which emerged as empires disappeared. While the limits inherited by the new countries were not universally free from ambiguities, which sometimes created serious problems, there was a fairly complete network of lines. Very few new countries have inherited sea boundaries from the colonial period. However, some maritime boundaries were drawn by colonial powers, and more lines of convenience have been elevated to the status of maritime boundaries by some of the new countries.

On 3 August 1928 the Sultan of Johore and the British authorities agreed on a boundary to separate the territorial waters of Singapore and Johore. The boundary followed an imaginary line following the centre of the deep-water channel of Johore Strait (Prescott 1975, 415–17). While it might be legally argued that this was a bilateral treaty, such argument would discount totally the dominant political position of Britain. In 1958 a British Order in Council defined continental shelf boundaries separating the offshore areas of Brunei from Sabah and Sarawak (Prescott 1981, 41). It appears, from a map published by the Malaysian authorities, that this British boundary has been accepted by Malaysia (Directorate of National Mapping 1979). In rare cases colonial powers have negotiated maritime boundaries on behalf of colonies which have either become independent or wish to become independent. For example, in 1971 and 1973 Australia and Indonesia created a maritime boundary south of New Guinea, which was accepted by Papua New Guinea when it achieved independence. More recently, in January 1982 France and Australia agreed on a maritime boundary separating claims from Australia and New Caledonia, a territory where some groups have been pressing for independence. Fortunately the negotiated boundary seems to satisfy all reasonable claims from New Caledonia.

In several cases some new countries have tried to base their maritime claims on lines which colonial powers drew on the seas, even though such claims are inappropriate. It was a common technique in the Pacific Ocean, where there are so many small islands, for colonial powers to use straight lines surrounding groups as a form of geographical shorthand, to avoid the need to name every feature which was claimed. Thus in June 1867 the United States of America and Russia separated their territories in the Bering Strait and Sea by a series of straight lines. In 1879 Britain defined the islands annexed to Queensland by a line drawn through the northern part of Torres Strait, which meant that there was no need to name the myriad of islands. Britain and Germany divided the Solomon Islands in 1899 by straight lines; a year before, Spain and the United States had indicated the Philippine islands transferred to the latter by a frame of meridians and parallels. Some of these lines of reference have now been claimed as historic maritime boundaries. Thus the Philippines has claimed as territorial waters all seas between its archipelagic baselines and the Spanish-American treaty limits of 1898. This results in territorial waters 294 nautical miles wide in the northeast and less than 1 nautical mile wide in the southwest. Vietnam has claimed that the Sino-French treaty of 1887, which drew the land boundary between China and the former French colony, also settled the sea limit through the Gulf of Tonkin. This preposterous claim is based on the fact that the treaty allocated islands to the two countries according to whether they lay east or west of meridian 108° 3′ east. There is no indication of where this meridian ceases to act as a maritime limit, and that is important, because if it is projected southwards it intersects the Vietnamese coast between Hue and Da Nang.

Fortunately such remarkable claims are rare, and the comparatively recent emergence of wide claims to the seabed and overlying waters has meant that most independent states have had to negotiate their own boundaries rather than accept inherited boundaries from the colonial period.

The need to draw an international maritime boundary arises when two states make claims to waters or seabed which overlap. When two states share a coastline there will always be the need to project a maritime limit seawards, from the terminus of the land boundary. The length of that boundary will depend on the types of zones claimed. The shortest line will be drawn when both sides claim only territorial seas, although if there are offshore islands it is possible that a comparatively long line will be needed to separate territorial waters. For example, the Greek islands of Kerkira and Erikousa off the terminus of the land boundary with Albania will eventually require those two countries to draw a common territorial sea boundary 43 nautical miles long. The longest boundary for adjacent states would be needed when they both claimed the continental shelf, and when that continental margin was wider than 200 nautical miles. For example, the margin extending northwards from Varangerfjorden, which is shared by Norway and the Soviet Union, is shown on some maps to have a width in excess of 600 nautical miles. The need for maritime boundaries between opposite states will be determined by the width of seas between them and the zones which they claim. For example, if the waters are less than 24 nautical miles wide it will be necessary to draw a boundary separating territorial seas; if the waters are in the range of 48 to 400 nautical miles it will be necessary to draw a boundary separating exclusive economic zones; and finally, if the waters are more than 400 nautical miles wide, and are underlain by a continuous continental margin, it will be necessary to draw a continental shelf line.

Thus the process of boundary formation normally begins when two countries make claims which overlap. Usually they would not make claims simultaneously, and quite often a claim by one state will prompt a claim by an adjacent or opposite country which wishes to protect its interests. Thus in the Gulf of Thailand the claim to the continental shelf by South Vietnam on 9 June 1971 was followed by a Cambodian claim on 1 July 1972 and a Thai claim on 18 May 1973. In each case the states defined their claim by specific boundaries, all of which eventually overlapped. Frequently states make claims to an exclusive economic zone, or the continental shelf, without specifying the exact limits of the claimed zone, and with the caveat that where such claims overlap claims by neighbouring states, the division will be made by consultation between the two parties.

Bilateral action

Once overlapping claims have been made the situation can develop in two distinct ways, which are represented in figure 4.1 as unilateral and bilateral action. It is proposed to consider bilateral action first. States will often engage in preliminary correspondence and informal contacts in order to make an estimate of the difficulties concerned. When issues have been clarified delegations will then engage in discussions to discover whether grounds exist for an agreement. At this stage it is usual for technical officers with skills in surveying, geology, mining and law to be in attendance, so that expert evidence on these points is available. Indeed, it is possible that if the political masters decide that no great matters of principle and national interest are concerned, they will turn over the problem of defining a proposed line to some of these technical officers. Of course the final agreement must always be reached by those with political authority, and this is frequently the foreign ministers of each country. If agreement is reached then a boundary is likely to result. In some cases, such as the agreement between Poland and Russia on 18 March 1958, the boundary will separate single zones; this agreement was concerned only with territorial waters (The Geographer 1973, 1–2). In other cases

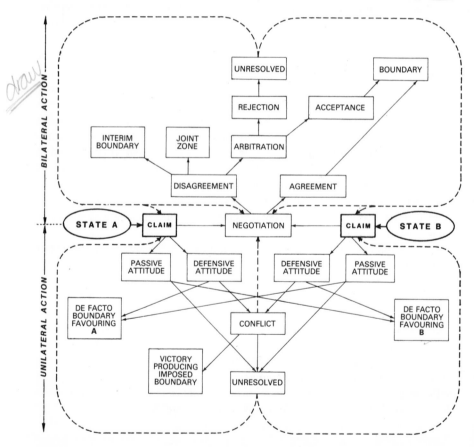

Figure 4.1 Procedures in the negotiations of maritime boundaries

a single boundary will separate multiple zones. Thus the treaty between Colombia and Ecuador signed on 23 August 1975 limits their respective marine and submarine areas; in a similar fashion the Australian-French agreement of January 1982 produced a single line which separated the French economic zone from the Australian fishing zone, and the continental shelves over which each state exercised sovereign rights. It is common for boundary agreements to specify the authorities which will be consulted to determine the survey data by which the location of the boundary will be described, and to make provision for the boundary to be marked on large-scale charts. While the path from claims, through negotiations, to agreement and a boundary appears direct in figure 4.1 it must be recognized that the negotiations may be long and sometimes they will be interrupted because the way appears impassable.

If the parties are unable to reach agreement, then, as the diagram shows, a number of different results might ensue. First, the matter might be left unresolved and the states might resort to unilateral action to obtain the aims which they regard as just. Second, the governments might decide to refer the matter for settlement to a tribunal. Such a tribunal would be the International Court of Justice, or representatives of a group of states drawn from the region in which the dispute is situated. Plainly for this course to be attractive to both sides it is essential that they should have confidence in the objectivity of the tribunal, and confidence that the presentation of their case will result in a satisfactory line. Arbitration has been the course adopted successfully by West Germany, the Netherlands and Denmark, the United Kingdom and France, and Libya and Tunisia when they could not agree on continental shelf boundaries off their coasts. Argentina and Chile resorted to a tribunal appointed by Queen Elizabeth II to settle ambiguities in the description of their land boundary of 1881. In making its judgement the tribunal also announced a maritime division of adjacent sea areas.

Arbitration was often used by the colonial powers when faced with a particularly difficult land boundary. Thus in 1909 King Alphonso XIII of Spain was asked to adjudicate on the disputed boundaries of Walvis Bay, between Britain and Germany; in 1897 Paul Honore Vigliani, former Chief President of the Court of Cassation of Florence, handed down a judgement on the difficult question of the proper location of the Anglo-Portuguese boundary in Manicaland, which today has been inherited by Mozambique and Zimbabwe. This is a technique which has been used by modern states to settle difficult problems. India and Pakistan used a tribunal in 1968 to produce a boundary in the Rann of Kutch, and six years earlier Cambodia and Thailand had allowed the International Court of Justice to pronounce on the ownership of the temple of Preah Vihear. In many arbitrations it has appeared that the learned judges have been aware of the need for a political solution which was acceptable to both sides. So it is comparatively rare for one side to enjoy complete victory, although Germany at Walvis Bay, Thailand at the temple of Preah Vihear, and Argentina in the Beagle Channel were all left empty-handed. While the joint decision to refer the matter to a tribunal will often contain an explicit statement that both sides will accept the judgement, that does not always happen. Thus Argentina decided not to accept the award of the tribunal which conferred ownership of disputed islands in the Beagle Channel to Chile. If the arbitration does not resolve the matter then states might decide to engage in further negotiations, or resort to unilateral action to secure their aims.

The third and fourth courses following disagreement in negotiations produce temporary compromises. The first compromise results in the creation of an interim boundary. This is a comparatively rare development, perhaps for the excellent reason that interim boundaries have the ability to become fossilized and immovable. Australia and Indonesia agreed on a provisional line to separate their fisheries surveillance and enforcement activities, on 29 October 1981. The line has been drawn so that Indonesia secures provisional control over more than half of the area which lies between the conflicting claims of the two countries. Although the agreement notes that the line is without prejudice to the location of the permanent fisheries boundary still to be agreed, it will be remarkable if Australia gains a much larger area than is available south of the present line.

The second compromise following disagreement on the location of a final boundary results in the construction of a joint zone. This solution was adopted by Saudi Arabia and Bahrain in February 1958, by Korea and Japan in June 1978, and by Malaysia and Thailand in February 1979. Joint zones are generally less satisfactory than a single line, the special administrative arrangements they require are often inconvenient and expensive, but they are certainly preferable to unfriendly relations which might otherwise fester because of an unresolved dispute over seas and seabed.

It ought to follow that these compromises will eventually be succeeded by a single permanent boundary, selected after further rounds of negotiations, but unless there is serious friction in the joint zone or along the provisional boundary, they might last for a long time. The Malaysian–Thai agreement on their joint zone realistically has an original life of fifty years, and if the boundary is not settled in that time the existing arrangements will continue!

Unilateral action

Turning now to unilateral action by states when overlapping claims occur, there are again a number of possible developments. They will be determined by the attitude which the two states adopt towards the claims, and to simplify the discussion it is suggested that states will either adopt a passive or a defensive attitude. By adopting a passive attitude it is understood that the state will avoid conflict in the overlapping area. For example, it will refuse to be provoked if its nationals are prevented from fishing or exploring the seabed in the zone claimed by both sides, and it will not take punitive action against aliens who operate in the disputed area. In contrast the adoption of a defensive posture implies that the state will protect its nationals who operate in the area claimed by both states, and will actively prevent or discourage aliens from undertaking economic ventures in the same area.

Since each state has a choice of two attitudes there are four possible situations. If both countries take a passive position then the issue of competing claims will remain unresolved. Problems would arise if nationals from each state created difficulties for each other while engaged in competitive fishing or mining; in such cases the national administrations might be reluctantly involved, and perhaps negotiations would be encouraged.

If one state took a passive role while the other state defended its claim then a *de facto* boundary would result, favouring the defensive state. The fourth situation would occur if both states adopted defensive attitudes, in which case conflict would result. This conflict could end in one of three outcomes. First, the sides could end the conflict before a decisive result was achieved and engage in negotiations, thus pursuing the courses available through bilateral action. Second, the conflict could simply peter out without either side winning, in which case the boundary issue would be unresolved. Third, one side could emerge victorious and force a boundary on the defeated state. It is an interesting and encouraging fact that maritime boundaries do not seem to have resulted from the assertion of superior force by one party to a dispute. There has been friction, but it does not seem to have produced a decisive result from one side. Much of the friction which has occurred has not been concerned over boundaries between the maritime zones of two adjacent or opposite states, but over the outer limits of littoral states; thus the limit in dispute separates one country's fishing or exclusive economic zone from the high seas. The Anglo-Icelandic cod wars and the occasions when tuna boats registered in the United States have been arrested in the Pacific by South American or Pacific Island countries have provided the most obvious examples.

Existing agreements

At the end of March 1983 there were seventy-eight ratified maritime boundary agreements, which is only a small fraction of the potential maritime boundaries which states might decide to draw by agreement or unilateral action. There are two striking characteristics of existing treaties. First, fifty-seven agreements relate to the continental shelf. This demonstrates that there has been a major concern with securing control over defined areas of the seabed, presumably because of the hope that these areas might contain fields of petroleum or natural gas. It is also true that continental shelf boundaries are easier to draw because their surveillance is a comparatively simple matter. Any intruder wishing to explore or exploit the seabed would soon be detected and could be dealt with. On the other hand the surveillance of territorial sea boundaries is a much more demanding matter; vessels which appear to be engaged in innocent passage could quite easily be carrying contraband or illegal immigrants, or, inadvertently, plant and animal diseases. For this reason and because territorial sea boundaries are drawn close to land, where there is normally a greater density of activity than over the distant continental shelf, states seem to take a long time to reach agreement on boundaries separating territorial seas.

The second striking characteristic of the agreed boundaries is that fifty-one are located in enclosed or semi-enclosed seas, including the North Sea, the Baltic Sea, the Caribbean, the Mediterranean, the Persian Gulf, the Black Sea and the seas enclosed by the islands of southeast Asia. If the agreements applying to the south-west Pacific Ocean, where there is a multitude of island states, were added, the total would reach fifty-nine out of seventy-eight agreements. It appears that the close proximity of opposite neighbours in these regions encourages the settlement of maritime limits by co-operative action.

Each maritime boundary occupies a unique location, and its selection in bilateral negotiations will be based on a unique set of circumstances. Those circumstances, which might be related to politics, geography or economics, will occur in a variety of combinations; some of those combinations will make agreements harder to reach than others. The next section explores these circumstances and records the difficulties they present.

Circumstances which complicate maritime boundary negotiations

The settlement of any international maritime boundary faces the basic problem that there are no precise rules governing the manner in which negotiations should be conducted, and no definite principles to guide the parties. The Convention treats negotiations about territorial waters and other zones separately. Article 15 deals with the delimitation of territorial waters between opposite and adjacent states. It reproduces the exact sense, and almost the exact wording, of Article 12 of the *Convention on the Territorial Sea and Contiguous Zone*, which was agreed in 1958 at the United Nations conference. In the absence of agreement neither state is entitled to extend its claim beyond the equidistant line, except where historic title or other special circumstance require this provision to be varied. Since there is no definition of how historic title is established or which special circumstances would be properly invoked under this Article, there is no restriction on any country to oppose the use of the equidistant line to settle the issue.

Figure 4.2 shows the construction of a median line between two imaginary countries, Sandringham and Brighton. The land boundary terminates at Lucas Point, and the first point (1) on the line of equidistance is located at equal distances from Lucas Point and Point Margaret and Cape Philip. Lucas Point is common to both countries and the other features represent the closest features of Sandringham and Brighton respectively. The boundary is then extended on a course equidistant from Point Margaret and Cape Philip without regard to Lucas Point. It proceeds through the next point (2) until a fresh turning point (3) is reached, which is equidistant from those features and from Allen Island, which belong to Brighton. Now Cape Philip drops out of consideration and the boundary is drawn with reference to Allen Island and Cape Margaret. Eventually a point (5) will be reached when Cape Ponsonby must be considered, and thereafter the boundary will be drawn without reference to Point Margaret. Figure 4.2

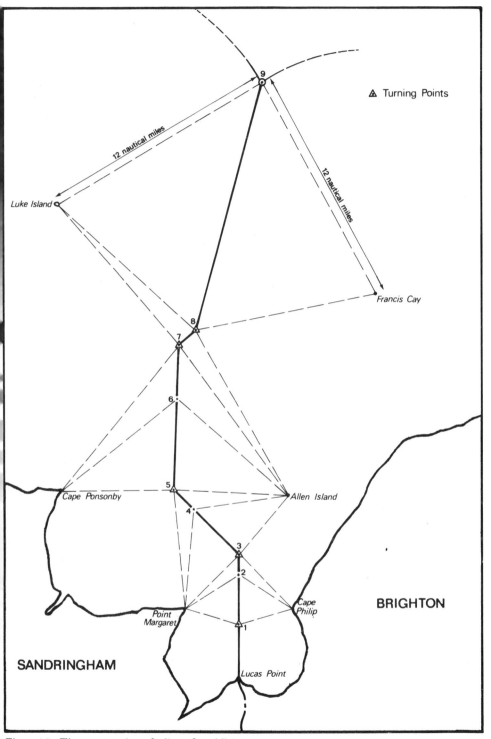

Figure 4.2 The construction of a line of equidistance

shows how the extension of the boundary will continue, using Luke Island and Francis Cay in turn, until a point (9) is reached at the intersection of territorial seas 12 nautical miles wide, which are measured from the outermost islands.

The Convention makes no stipulation about how boundaries separating contiguous zones should be selected. Until the resumed tenth session in August 1981 the language of Articles 74 and 83, which dealt with the division of exclusive economic zones and continental shelves between adjacent or opposite states, presented the choice of equidistant or equitable boundaries. The delimitation had to be in accord with international law, and should be based on equitable principles, using the median line where appropriate and taking account of all prevailing circumstances. In view of the fact that there has never been any definition of equitable principles, or prevailing circumstances, it might have been assumed that all states could accept this article secure in the knowledge that it does not exclude the introduction of any consideration into boundary negotiations. The assumption would have been wrong. The Convention (Articles 74 and 83) now requires the delimitation of these maritime boundaries to be based on international law, as referred to in Article 38 of the Statute of the International Court of Justice, in order to achieve an equitable solution. Alas, Article 38 does not provide much help. It enjoins the Court to reach decisions by applying international conventions expressly recognized by the contesting states; by international custom; by the general principles of law recognized by civilized nations, which *en passant* surely implies that there are uncivilized nations; and by judicial decisions and the teachings of the most highly qualified publicists (Rosenne 1957, 538). Conversations with several international lawyers suggest that there is nothing in this prescription to prevent any state from raising any matter it wants in support of a particular boundary alignment which will suit it.

It is this lack of restriction on arguments which might be raised that accounts for the wide range of circumstances which *might* create complications for boundary negotiators. The emphasis is necessary because this is not a discussion of immutable laws. There is no guarantee that if a particular circumstance exists difficulties will attend the negotiations. The critical circumstance will always be the relations between governments engaging in the negotiations. If relations are cordial and governments are determined to reach a fair solution, then the chances are excellent that such a result will be achieved no matter what other circumstances exist. Having noted that good relations will probably promote a fair and prompt solution the converse must also be stated. If relations between governments are poor and clouded with distrust or hostility, it would be a simple matter to raise difficulties in negotiations over maritime issues. In the following discussion the circumstances which might complicate boundary negotiations have been grouped into three categories labelled political, geographical and economic.

Political circumstances
Dealing first with political circumstances it is plain that the lack of formal relations between countries, or poor relations, will probably prevent the start of

negotiations. For example, it is unthinkable that Jordan would discuss maritime limits with Israel, or that China would discuss maritime boundaries with Taiwan. The resolution of Iraq's maritime boundaries at the head of the Persian Gulf, where it suffers from a zone-locked condition, will have to await the improvement in relations with Iran and Kuwait.

The next most important political circumstance concerns conflicting claims to territory from which maritime zones may be claimed. In the South China Sea the plethora of claims to the Spratly Islands by China, Vietnam, Taiwan, the Philippines and Malaysia ensures that no early settlement of maritime limits in this region is likely. Venezuela's claim to western Guyana, the claims by Bahrain and Qatar to the Huwar Islands, and the Anglo-Irish dispute over the status of Rockall mean that those pairs of countries cannot begin to draw their maritime boundary until the sovereignty question is settled. Conflicting claims to territory are always a fruitful source of dissension and ill will, and the difficulties are exacerbated when the disputed territory would allow a successful claimant to make claims to potentially valuable seas and seabed.

There will also be occasions when a government is obsessed with domestic problems and feels unable to conduct negotiations about maritime limits. At the beginning of 1982 that was probably the situation in Cambodia, El Salvador, Lebanon and Poland. It is also possible that neighbours will be reluctant to enter into negotiations with unstable governments which might be replaced, in case the new administration rejects any progress made by its predecessor.

The declaration by one country of baselines which breached the spirit and letter of existing and proposed rules might cause serious difficulties if the country concerned then insisted that the baseline must be considered in any selection of a median line. A definite case concerned Iceland, when certain baselines pushed the outer limit of its exclusive economic zone seawards, at the expense of the high seas and to the detriment of British and other fishing fleets. There are many baselines around the world which would fall into the unreasonable category, but it is hard to find any evidence that they have caused difficulties in boundary negotiations. It seems probable that if a country felt disadvantaged by such baselines it would simply construct its own to offset any gains which would fall to its neighbours. This appears to have happened when Malaysia and Indonesia negotiated their seabed boundary in 1969. The line appears to follow a median course between the Indonesian archipelagic baselines in the Strait of Malacca and some undeclared baselines belonging to Malaysia. The existence of these baselines appears to be confirmed by a map issued by the Malaysian authorities (Directorate of National Mapping 1979). The inferred baselines can be identified by measuring a line parallel to the outer edge of Malaysia's claimed territorial sea and 12 nautical miles distant. Such a line passes through Pulau Perak and Pulau Jarak, which are quite inappropriate as points on a straight baseline. Since Bangladesh proclaimed a straight baseline in April 1974 which closely follows the alignment of the 10 fathom isobath, it could be argued that any coastal state anywhere could proclaim a straight baseline!

Negotiations can be complicated if one of the parties holds an historic view which limits its scope for compromise. The resolution of differences over islands in the Beagle Channel between Argentina and Chile has been delayed because of Argentina's traditional perspective that the Atlantic Ocean coasts and islands belong to Argentina and the Pacific Ocean coasts and islands to Chile (Republic of Chile 1977, 142). In the South China Sea, China's insistence that all the Nansha or Spratly Islands and associated submerged banks have belonged to China from time immemorial, will make it very difficult for any country to negotiate with China. In the same area the Philippines' reliance on the historical virtue of the 1898 American–Spanish peace agreement could create difficulties in negotiating with Taiwan, Indonesia and any states which make good their claims to some or all of the Spratly Islands.

Difficulties can arise if negotiations produce only part of the boundary system needed and if there is a change of attitude before the negotiations are resumed. The best example of this is provided by the Australian–Indonesian seabed negotiations. In 1971 and 1972 Australia and Indonesia agreed on seabed boundaries. In the Arafura Sea, east of Portuguese Timor, the boundary lay close to the line of equidistance as it crossed the continuous continental shelf that linked the two countries. West of Portuguese Timor, where the deep Timor Trench divided the margin into two distinct parts, Australia was able to persuade Indonesia that the boundary should lie north of the line of equidistance, on the ground that the Australian shelf was much wider than the Indonesian shelf. After Indonesia had acquired Portuguese Timor it became necessary for the two countries to negotiate again to fill the gap south of the former Portuguese colony. By now the official Indonesian view was that they had been 'taken to the cleaners' last time and that the section of boundary linking the agreed sections must follow a line of equidistance. This boundary had, at the time of writing, proved impossible to settle. A similar problem could arise if two countries settle a seabed boundary in a location other than the median position without at the same time negotiating a boundary to distinguish control over the waters above the seabed. Because the basis on which waters and seabed are claimed is different, it is open to the state which was awarded the smaller area by the seabed boundary to argue in favour of an equidistant line to separate the waters. In the event of the proposal being successful it would mean that one country would own an area of sea while another country owned the underlying seabed. Such an arrangement has been created by the agreement between Australia and Papua New Guinea of 1978. It is comparatively rare, and obviously will create potential problems of friction between those parties exploring and exploiting the seabed, and fishermen, who will probably be obliged to give production platforms a wide berth and who might tear their nets on the debris of mining, which often accumulates on the sea floor.

Geographical circumstances
Turning now to consideration of the geographical circumstances which might make negotiations difficult, the first two situations relate to islands. First, there is the difficulty of deciding when a feature standing above high tide ceases to be a

rock and can be considered an island. Second, there is the problem associated with the location of islands, which can sometimes be very inconvenient for one of the parties. Article 121 of the Convention stipulates that an island is a naturally formed area of land surrounded by water, which is above water at high tide. The article also confirms that states may claim all maritime zones from such features. The final part of the article provides that rocks which cannot sustain human habitation or economic life of their own may only be used to claim territorial waters. There is no other indication of how to distinguish rocks from islands. Hodgson (1973) proposed categories of rocks, islets, isles and islands based on area, but there is no evidence that his sensible views attracted wide support or commitment from governments. It is apparent that decisions about the status of features which might be rocks or islands will have to be thrashed out between negotiators. But, even if there is no question that a feature is a rock, there is still the thorny problem of deciding whether it can sustain human habitation or has an economic life of its own. It might prove impossible to separate the economic life of a rock from the low-tide reef on which it stands. It is not certain that fishing on and around the reef would be considered to be part of the economic life of the rocks which surmount it. Nor is it clear whether it would be reasonable to claim that a rock had economic life of its own if fishermen collected birds eggs and turtles from the feature, or if other persons scraped guano off the rocks, as some South Africans do from features off the coast of Namibia. There is scope for disagreement on this point concerning rocks which have an important position in terms of maritime claims.

Some islands have an ephemeral nature and it is not clear whether this is a matter of any importance. Cays are low islands built of sand and coral rubble by wave action on reefs which are awash (Bird 1970, 206–7). Sometimes these features are stabilized by vegetation which promotes the accumulation of further sand and debris. Sometimes beach rock is formed by the deposition of calcium carbonate in the zone of repeated wetting and drying, and this offers greater resistance to erosion than the unconsolidated material. But cays can be destroyed by exceptional waves in severe storms, and it must be asked whether a state's claim to maritime zones disappears when the cay vanishes. This particular problem might bedevil the vexed territorial questions in the Spratly Islands of the South China Sea. There is also the problem of claiming new islands which are formed. In 1970, after cyclonic activity, a new island was formed in the Bay of Bengal off the western terminus of the boundary between India and Bangladesh. The two countries respectively call it New Moore Island and South Talpatty Island. Both countries have claimed it and the dispute has caused some friction between them. Chiu (1977) has discussed the possibility that China's claims to submerged banks in the South China Sea may be partly designed to pre-empt any other claims to islands which may form on these features in the future.

For some countries, such as Turkey, the inconvenient location of alien islands is the most serious adverse circumstance to the settlement of maritime limits. Because islands act as national outposts from which maritime claims can be made, their fortunate location, close to the shores of another country, can augment the claim of the state which owns the island and confine the claim of the opposite or adjacent state. This circumstance was the crux of the problem between Australia and Papua New Guinea in Torres Strait; some Australian islands, annexed in 1879, lay within a few hundred yards of the coast of Papua. There are other cases where similar circumstances apply. The presence of Greek islands close to the Turkish coast has already been mentioned; in addition French islands off New-foundland, the Spanish island of Chafarinas close to Morocco, Britain's Channel Islands near the French coast, and Thai and Vietnamese islands off Cambodia's coast all provide situations which either called for careful negotiations or presently form the cause of disputes between states (Bowett 1978, 41–4).

If the alien island is small and very close to a foreign coast, the maritime zones claimed from it could form an enclave within the zones claimed from the main-land. That is the situation with Karaman Island in the Red Sea, which belongs to South Yemen but lies off the shore of Yemen. Rather that would be the case if South Yemen was able to regain its island, which was seized by its neighbour during fighting in October 1972. If South Africa insisted on maintaining its legiti-mate maritime claims from the guano islands along the coast of Namibia, some of them would be enclaves within zones attached to the Skeleton Coast (Prescott 1977, 224). It will generally be found that when a state is seriously disadvantaged by the presence of an alien island, a request will be made during negotiations that the full effect of the island should be discounted. It is in such situations that the disagreement about the suitability of an equidistant boundary is most obvious and often most bitter. However, there are also other circumstances where this debate arises. While the Convention employs a very narrow definition of states with special geographical characteristics, the term will be much more widely inter-preted by states seeking to oppose lines of equidistance. The Convention (Article 70) deems states to have special geographical characteristics, which need redress, when they are dependent on the exploitation of living resources in the exclusive economic zones of neighbours, or when they can claim no exclusive economic zone. Some states which do not satisfy these strict criteria might still consider themselves very unfortunate when their maritime claims are curtailed because they possess only a short coast, or because of the configuration of their coast, or because of the nearness of neighbouring territory. This last point has already been considered. Countries with short coasts are usually only able to claim compara-tively small sea areas. This would be true of Zaire, with its narrow corridor between the two parts of Angola; Iraq, which is closed in at the head of the Persian Gulf by Warbah and Bubiyan Islands, which belong to Kuwait; Jordan; and Guatemala's eastern coast on the Golfo de Honduras. States with concave coast-lines face a disadvantage because they are unable to claim an area commensurate with the length of their coastline. This was one of the strong arguments used by West Germany in its case against the Netherlands and Denmark. Other countries which possess concave coastlines include Cameroon, Panama and Thailand.

Thus those countries which are restricted by alien islands, or which have only short coasts or concave coasts, or which are closely surrounded by neighbours, are likely to argue strongly against the use of equidistant lines as maritime boundaries. The apparent difficulty between proponents of lines of equidistance and limits founded on equitable principles has been finessed by the reference to Article 38 of the Statute of the International Court of Justice. The emphasis is now on an equitable solution. This new emphasis follows the judgement of the tribunal which dealt with the case concerning the Channel Islands. That judgement found that the rule of equidistance and the rule relating to special circumstances had the same aim, which is the delimitation of a boundary in accord with equitable principles (Court of Arbitration 1977, 85).

In theoretical terms the new formulation reduces the concept of equidistance to an equal status with other considerations which might be used to produce an equitable solution. In practical terms the concept of the equidistant line will always be accorded a higher rank by a number of countries, and in many negotiations the nub of the disagreement will continue to be the use of an equidistant line versus the use of a boundary based on some other principles. Plainly the firm adherence of two sides during negotiations to these different bases for boundary construction will make it harder to reach a solution than if both sides agree on one of them. But even if both sides agree that an equidistant line is inappropriate, it might still be hard for them to agree which circumstances should be considered in producing an equitable boundary. Oxman (1980) claims that discussion of equitable principles at the Law of the Sea Conference is understood to refer to the criteria listed by the International Court of Justice in the North Sea case. They are the general configuration of the coasts as well as the presence of any special features; the physical and geological structure of the continental shelf, together with the nature of natural resources which are known or readily ascertainable; and a degree of proportionality linking the area of shelf and the length of coastlines measured in the general direction of the coast (International Court of Justice 1969, 54). Oxman's view might be correct, but this falls short of guaranteeing that states engaged in a dispute will restrict themselves to those three elements. The tribunal in the Channel Islands case noted that the judgement in the North Sea case contained the assertion that there is no legal limit on the considerations which states can urge in order to ensure equitable procedures apply (Court of Arbitration 1977, 92). Brown (1971, 50) has picked up this point in his usually effective way and asked why the judges in the North Sea case did not consider population size, *per capita* income, dependence of industry on shelf resources, and the relative poverty of land resources. Nor will some states accept the view of these two international tribunals that it is not the purpose of an equitable solution to create a situation of complete equity when geography and nature have established an inequity (International Court of Justice 1969, 50; Court of Arbitration 1977, 218). It is all very well for international judges to argue that equity calls for a suitable abatement of disproportionate effects of special geographical circumstances; for politicians with electorates to satisfy equity is likely to mean at least equality.

Since there is no restriction on the range of issues which can be introduced into the debate about an equitable solution, that debate might be very long, especially when there is a marked discrepancy between the two antagonists. It was noticeable that despite the apparent soundness of a legal claim to most of Torres Strait, Australian governments seemed to be placed continually on the defensive when Papua New Guinea raised the issue of its comparative poverty.

The next geographical circumstance which might complicate maritime boundary negotiations concerns the nature of the seabed shared by two adjacent or opposite states. The Convention permits states to claim the seabed which extends throughout the natural prolongation of its land territory, without providing any guidance on how that natural prolongation will be determined. The continental shelf of the Convention is a legal abstraction which does not reflect the complexity of the world's continental margins. There are three obvious features which might be examined in an effort to determine the direction and extent of the natural prolongation of a state's territory. First, the gradient of the seabed could be considered. Since the general tendency of continental margins is to decline in elevation from the coast to the abyssal plain, some states might argue that so long as the gradient is downwards from their shore, a claim to the margin should succeed. Second, the structure of the seabed could be investigated to discover whether it was formed and deformed by the same processes and forces which moulded the coastal regions. If the faulting or folding evident on shore was duplicated in the offshore zones, that might provide a strong argument for claiming the similar area as a natural prolongation. Finally, the geology of the coast and seabed could be compared to reveal whether there are continuities between the two zones. It is a matter for speculation, which would probably never be conclusive, how much weight should be attached to each of these characteristics, or to combinations of them.

While it is a comparatively simple task to identify the factors which might be taken into account in debates about natural prolongation, it is a more difficult duty to discover the circumstances in which that debate is appropriate. To assist the discussion on this question a geographical classification of claims to the continental margin has been prepared; it appears in table 4.1.

The first major category concerns only a single country. In such cases natural prolongation will only be an issue when the margin is wider than 200 nautical miles, and any debate on the matter will be between the coastal state and the Commission on the Limits of the Continental Shelf, which must approve national limits on wide margins.

The second category concerns countries with opposite coasts, and there are two basic situations. In the first the countries are less than 400 nautical miles apart, in the second they are separated by more than this distance.

Dealing with countries which are less than 400 nautical miles apart, it is first necessary to consider cases where the margins are separated by areas of the deep seabed. If neither of the margins extends across the median line then there can be no question of natural prolongation being an issue. That issue might arise,

Table 4.1 A geographical classification of claims to the continental margin

---

[A] Only one country is involved
    1 The margin is narrower than 200 nautical miles.
    2 The margin is wider than 200 nautical miles.*
[B] Two opposite countries are involved
    1 The countries are less than 400 nautical miles apart.
      (i) The margins are separated by the deep seabed.
        a Neither margin extends across the median line.
        b One margin extends across the median line.*
      (ii) There is a continuous margin between the two countries.
        a The margin is undifferentiated.
        b The margin is differentiated by a zone which does not include the median
          line.*
    2 The countries are more than 400 nautical miles apart.
      (i) The margins are separated by the deep seabed. This situation is the same as
        in [A], providing neither margin approaches within 200 nautical miles of the
        other mainland. The situation would be the same as in [B] 1 (i) b if either of
        the margins approached within 200 nautical miles of the opposite mainland.
      (ii) There is a continuous margin between the two countries.
        a The margin is undifferentiated.
        b The margin is differentiated by a zone which does not coincide with the
          median line.* There are two possible situations in this case. In one the
          differentiation zone will lie more than 200 nautical miles from each coast;
          in the other it will lie within 200 nautical miles of one mainland.
[C] Two adjacent countries are involved
    1 The margin is narrower than 200 nautical miles.
      (i) The margin is undifferentiated.
      (ii) The margin is differentiated by a zone which does not include the median
        line.*
    2 The margin is wider than 200 nautical miles.
      (i) The margin is undifferentiated.
      (ii) The margin is differentiated by a zone which does not include the median
        line.*
      (iii) A spur from the continental margin of one country passes in front of the
        continental margin of its neighbour.*

Note:
* In these cases it might be possible to make use of arguments about natural prolongation.
Source: Author's research.

however, if one of the margins does project across the median line. Such a case is shown in figure 4.3a, where a deep trench divides two margins of sharply contrasting widths. In such cases it is possible that the country with the wider margin would argue, on grounds of natural prolongation, that the proper location for the boundary separating their shelves is the axis of the deep trough.

If the margins are continuous, questions of natural prolongation could only arise if the margin was differentiated on structural or geological grounds by a zone which did not encompass the median line. Such a situation is shown in figure 4.3b, when it would be to the advantage of one country to argue in favour of locating the boundary in the zone of differentiation.

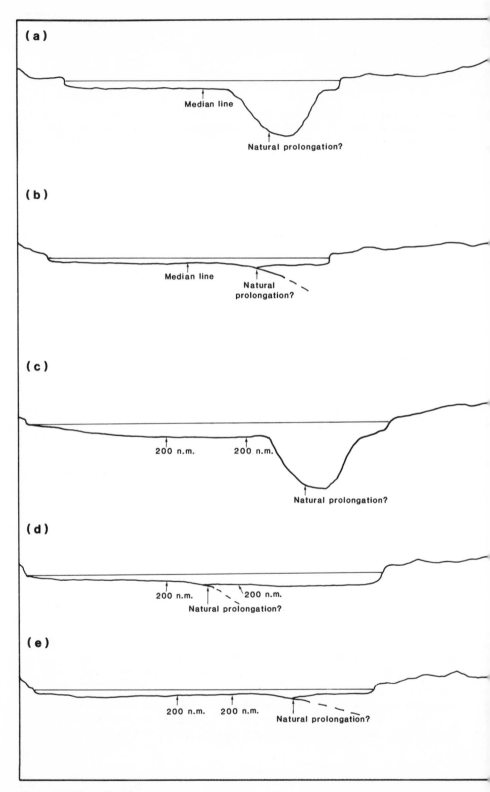

Figure 4.3 Natural prolongation

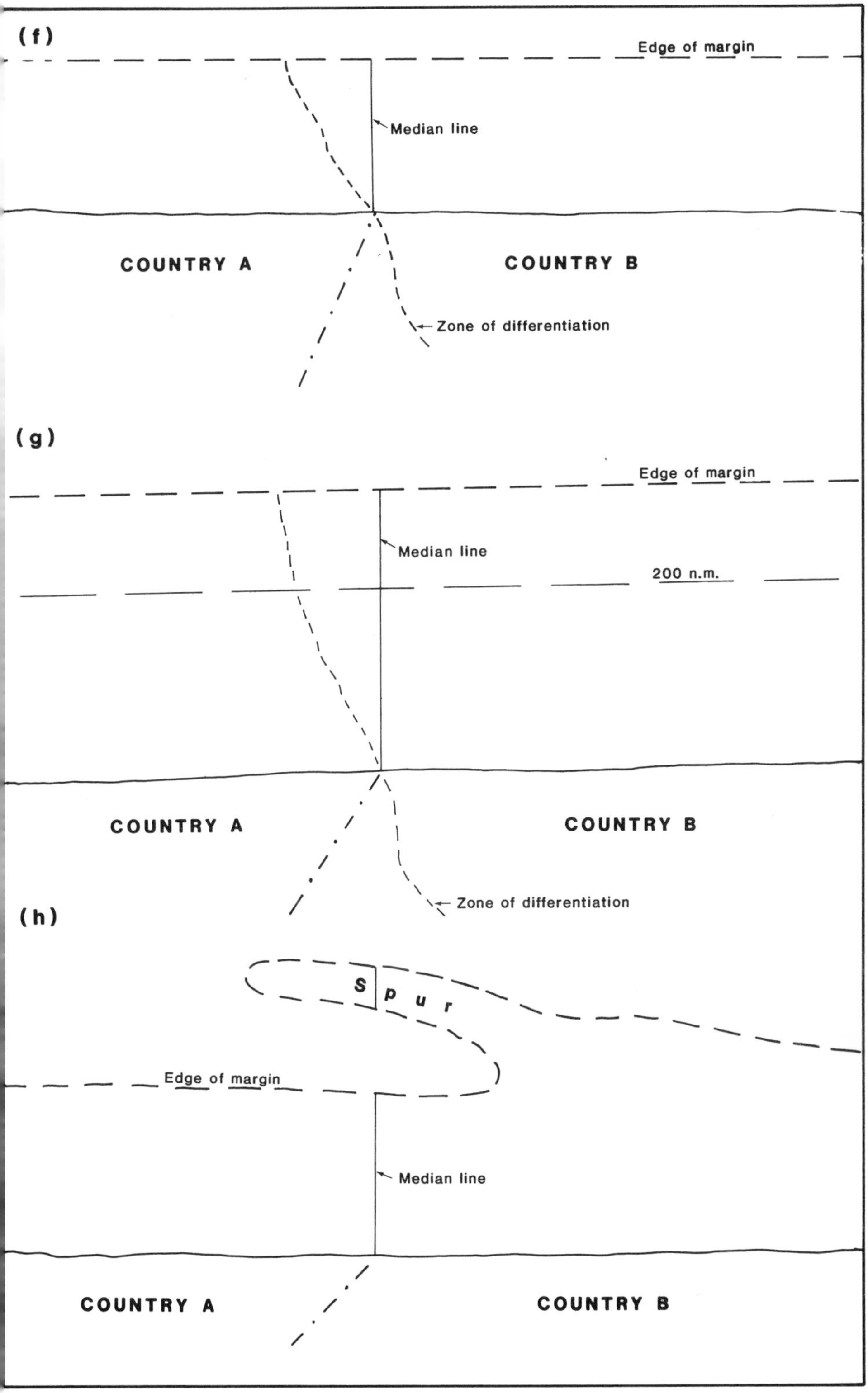

(f)

Edge of margin

Median line

COUNTRY A   COUNTRY B

Zone of differentiation

(g)

Edge of margin

Median line

200 n.m.

COUNTRY A   COUNTRY B

Zone of differentiation

(h)

S p u r

Edge of margin

Median line

COUNTRY A   COUNTRY B

Turning now to countries which are more than 400 nautical miles apart, once again the first case to be considered concerns margins which are separated by areas of deep seabed. Providing neither margin reaches closer than 200 nautical miles to the opposite shore, there do not need to be any negotiations about shelf boundaries. Each country will be able to make a unilateral claim as in the first category. However, if one of the margins did approach within 200 nautical miles of the opposite coast, the situation would reproduce that shown in figure 4.3a at a different scale. The revised diagram is shown in figure 4.3c, and it would appear to be open to the country with the wider margin to argue in favour of the concept of natural prolongation, in an effort to secure the largest area.

If the countries which are more than 400 nautical miles apart are linked by a continuous continental shelf, there will be no room for arguments about natural prolongation if that margin is undifferentiated. However, if the margin is differentiated by a zone which does not include the median line, it is possible that the issue of natural prolongation will be raised by the country which is apparently favoured. There are two possible cases in this general situation. In the first the zone of differentiation would lie more than 200 nautical miles from each coast; in the second the zone would lie within 200 nautical miles of one of the coasts. These circumstances are shown in figures 4.3d and 4.3e. The few cases in this category are listed in table 4.2.

The third main category concerns states which share adjacent coasts, and in this case the prime subdivision is based on whether their margins are less than 200 nautical miles wide or more than this distance. If the margin is narrower than 200 nautical miles and undifferentiated then there can be no question of natural prolongation being an issue. However, if there is a differentiation which appears to link the margin in front of one country to the neighbouring state, on geological or structural grounds, then questions of natural prolongation might be raised. A possible situation is shown in figure 4.3f.

If the margin adjoining neighbouring states is wider than 200 nautical miles there appear to be three possible situations. First, if the margin is undifferentiated there can be no question of raising arguments about natural prolongation. If there is a zone of differentiation and it does not coincide with the median line, it will be a nice question to decide whether arguments about natural prolongation can be directed to the entire margin or only to those parts beyond 200 nautical miles from the coast. The problem is shown in figure 4.3g.

The third case involves the existence of a spur projecting from the margin of one country in front of the coast of the neighbouring state. The situation is shown in figure 4.3h. The question which must be asked is whether the country on whose margin the spur originates may claim all the spur on grounds of natural prolongation.

This classification has avoided the complication of offshore islands and coasts of irregular configuration because the number of cases would have been multiplied many times and the classification would become unwieldy. Nor has this discussion addressed the question of whether a state which appears to be at a dis-

Table 4.2 Opposite states which are separated by a continuous
continental margin more than 400 nautical miles wide,
which can be entirely claimed

Australia (Heard Island) and Antarctica[1]
United Kingdom (Falkland Island Dependencies) and Antarctica[2]
Sri Lanka and India
Australia (Lord Howe Island) and New Zealand
Australia and France (New Caledonia)
Fiji and Vanuatu or France (New Caledonia)[3]
United Kingdom and Iceland
India and Oman
Denmark (Greenland) and the Soviet Union[4]
Canada and the Soviet Union[4]

Notes:
1 This boundary would only be necessary if Australia's claim to Antarctica
   was not sustained.
2 This boundary would only be required if Britain's claim to Antarctica
   was not sustained.
3 The uncertainty recorded here results from a dispute between France
   and Vanuatu over the ownership of Hunter and Matthew Islands.
4 It is not clear whether claims to Lomonosov Ridge would be excluded by
   the Convention.

Source: Author's research.

advantage in respect of the facts of natural prolongation can simply refuse to
discuss shelf boundaries, and insist instead on all discussions being related to the
delimitation of exclusive economic zones. A survey of fifty-seven shelf boundaries
reveals only three where it appears that natural prolongation has been a factor.
Two concern West Germany's boundaries with the Netherlands and Denmark
after Germany's successful case before the International Court of Justice. The
third involves Australia and Indonesia. In the Timor Sea the boundary was fixed
on the Indonesian side of the median line, presumably because of the existence of
the deep Timor Trough.

In February 1982 the International Court of Justice handed down a judgement
in the case concerning the continental shelf adjoining Libya and Tunisia
(International Court of Justice 1982). Both countries based their main arguments
on details concerned with natural prolongation. For Libya, natural prolongation
was viewed in a continental perspective, and it therefore followed that the natural
prolongation of north Africa was northwards towards the edge of the African
plate. Attention was drawn to the Permian hingeline, which passed through the
Jeffara coastal plain of southern Tunisia and northern Libya. Tunisia was also
concerned with the processes of plate tectonics, but specifically focused on the
orogeny which followed the collision of the African and Eurasian plates and
which resulted in the erection of northern Tunisia from folded thick sediments.
The grain of these structures in northern Tunisia can be found in the seabed east
of Tunisia, as it declines towards the Ionian abyssal plain.

Here then was a classical confrontation between a continental and regional natural prolongation. Unfortunately for the *aficionados* of natural prolongation the Court discounted the structural, geological and morphological evidence and manufactured a curious line which was very properly and very severely criticized in three dissenting opinions by André Gros, Shigeru Oda and Jens Evensen.

A careful reading of the separate and dissenting opinions attached to the judgement makes the following points clear. First, natural prolongation is a basis for claim only in respect of those continental margins which are wider than 200 nautical miles. As Jiménez de Arechaga points out in his separate opinion, the second alternative definition of the continental shelf in Article 76 (1) is independent of the criterion of natural prolongation (International Court of Justice 1982, 15). This alternative permits claims to a width of 200 nautical miles where the margin does not extend that far. This sound conclusion leads him to the belief that in respect of shelves narrower than 200 nautical miles at least the notion of the continental shelf is being incorporated in that of the exclusive economic zone (International Court of Justice 1982, 16).

Oda does not restrict the confusion between the regimes of the continental shelf and the exclusive economic zone to those cases where the margin is narrower than 200 nautical miles.

> At all events, the sovereign rights to be exercised by the coastal State for the purpose of exploring and exploiting the mineral resources of submerged submarine areas have been expressly subsumed under both the regime of the continental shelf and the regime of the exclusive economic zone. Any concrete issue that may arise concerning the exploitation of mineral resources within the 200-mile limit will thus, for the time being, be cloaked in legal ambiguity, for it will not arise bearing the label 'continental shelf' or 'made in the exclusive economic zone'.   (International Court of Justice 1982, 81)

This is a view which Evensen shares when he remarks that when the exclusive economic zone concept deals with resources of the seabed it is in practice a continental shelf concept (International Court of Justice 1982, 10). Both Oda and Evensen raise serious doubts about the wisdom of drawing separate lines to divide the continental shelves and exclusive economic zones of adjacent countries, although such boundaries already exist in the areas divided between Australia and Papua New Guinea and Australia and Indonesia. Oda very sensibly notes that in his view the question before the Court could equally well have concerned the exclusive economic zone as the continental shelf. It is difficult to reach any other conclusion than that the insistence of both parties on the continental shelf concept resulted from their convictions that each had an unanswerable argument on the issue of natural prolongation.

Articles 186–191 provide for the creation of a Sea-Bed Disputes Chamber of eleven members. This Chamber may consider disputes between countries and between countries and the Authority and it shall give urgent advisory opinions on legal questions requested by the Assembly or the Council.

Economic circumstances

Two economic circumstances might complicate negotiations. First, if there is a marked disparity in wealth and resources between two states, the poorer state may argue for the lion's share of the disputed zone, or at the very least the poorer country might try to persuade the richer state to discount part of its claim. Second, negotiations might be made more difficult if the economic potential of a disputed area is high, or is totally unknown. If the overlap formed by two claims is known to be valuable in terms of fields of petroleum or natural gas, both countries will be reluctant to compromise until each has fully tested the resolve of the other state. Conversely, if the value of the disputed zone is totally unknown, the uncertainty about what is at stake will encourage countries to try to strike the hardest bargain possible. An example of the first situation is found south of east Timor, in the gap between the boundaries agreed by Indonesia and Australia in 1972 and 1973. There are two promising structures in that zone and at the beginning of 1984 both countries seemed equally determined to secure them exclusively.

It is comparatively easy to list for any maritime dispute the circumstances which complicate its solution. However, it would be unwise to seek to attach to any listing a mathematical precision in comparing the difficulty of various disputes. In every case the critical element is always the attitude of states towards the question. If governments approach the issue in a spirit of conciliation, then the apparently serious difficulties associated with near-by alien offshore islands, or with potentially rich continental margins, will be readily overcome. Conversely, if governments approach the matter with a determination to secure their preferred solution, then even trivial difficulties can be magnified into apparently impassable obstacles.

Boundaries on land and sea

This section must be concluded by drawing comparisons between international boundaries on land and sea. The period of drawing land boundaries, which occupied the colonial powers during the second half of the nineteenth century, is now being matched by the intense activity of the myriad of coastal states around the world. Further, the motive for drawing both sets of boundaries is the same. Countries were concerned to avoid the risk of conflict with neighbours over uncertainty about the extent of national jurisdiction, and at the same time wanted acknowledged rights to areas which they valued for the security they offered or the resources they contained; and the same preoccupations spark their interest in modern maritime limits.

Both sets of boundaries are usually fashioned by bilateral negotiations, although arbitration is also common to both. To the present no maritime boundaries have been forced on a state by a more powerful adversary, as has happened in the case of some land boundaries, but there is no reason why this development should not take place eventually. However, there are important differences in the bases of claims made to land and sea. National cases for the ownership of land were supported by arguments which included reference to geography, distribution of people, historical association, exploration, language and religion. By contrast arguments in favour of national maritime claims invariably proceed from a measure of propinquity; there must always be a coast from which the waters are claimed. Arguments of historical use are employed to claim seas, but they are always subordinate to the original argument on a degree of adjacency.

Some might assert that an important difference is to be found in the fact that there is now a single code of rules for claiming maritime regions, whereas there was never such a code for territorial ambitions. While that is strictly true, this text has demonstrated that no country would be inhibited by the text alone from making the widest claims it felt to be desirable. Therefore this is not a significant difference between the evolution of land and sea boundaries.

Geographers have identified four stages through which the evolution of land boundaries may proceed (Prescott 1978, 63); they are allocation, delimitation, demarcation and administration. The first three stages result in the line being progressively more closely defined and eventually marked in the landscape. This gradual approach to a final line is not evident in the evolution of maritime limits; they generally emerge immediately in their final form, and of course they are rarely demarcated. Demarcation only usually occurs near the coast and in navigable waterways, when buoys may be placed, or markers on land might indicate the location of the line.

In most cases the maritime boundaries are marked on large-scale charts which both sides regard as accurate, and it is now normal for boundary agreements to specify that the actual location of boundary turning points at sea and on the seabed will be determined by surveyors who have mutually agreed on a reliable method. In many cases the various boundary segments are defined as straight lines, and there is no indication of which type of straight line is meant. There are four common straight lines at sea. First there is the great circle arc, which is a circle around the surface of the globe which is drawn so that its plane passes through the centre of the earth. All meridians and the equator are great circles. A small circle arc is distinguished from such lines by possessing a plane which does not pass through the earth's centre. A rhumb line is one which crosses all meridians at a constant angle as it spirals towards the north or south pole. Finally, a geodesic is the shortest straight line between any two points at sea. The appearance of these lines on charts will vary as the projection varies. For example, a rhumb line will appear as a straight line on the Mercator projection, on which great circle courses will appear as curved lines, unless they are meridians or the equator. Thamsborg (1977) has shown that the area bounded by a rhumb line and a geodesic linking two points separated by 4 degrees of latitude and 10 degrees of longitude would be about 2000 square nautical miles. Fortunately most maritime boundaries would have shorter segments, and surveyors are aware of the possibility of confusion. Well-qualified surveyors and hydrographers will also be aware of the value of each country adopting a common spheroid and a uniform geodetic datum. A spheroid is the mathematically defined surface of the earth, and some determinations differ in the length of the major axis and the degree of polar flattening. The geodetic datum is the reference point, either in terms of horizontal position or vertical elevation, from which other points can be determined. If countries fixing an agreed maritime boundary are operating on the basis of different spheroids and different geodetic datums, problems could arise in certain circumstances and it would be sensible to avoid any risk, especially if the divided area is known to contain hydrocarbon deposits.

The mitigation of problems associated with international maritime boundaries

When countries draw land boundaries separating their territories, it is usual for special provision to be made for those inhabitants who live close to the boundary and who might wish to cross it fairly frequently in connection with their work or social contacts. While that particular problem does not arise often in respect of maritime boundaries, there are occasions when the strict enforcement of rules up to the boundary would create difficulties. For example, it is now general for countries which draw a boundary through a common continental shelf, to agree that if any field of hydrocarbons extends across the boundary, they will consult about the most effective way to exploit the structure and apportion the revenue derived from it. A particular problem arose in the Timor Sea as Australia began to make moves to extend its fishing zone. For many years Indonesian fishermen had been travelling in sailing boats to fish around Australian islands such as Ashmore, Cartier and Browse, and catching fish by traditional methods. The fish were then dried in the rigging for the return journey. The strict application of Australian rules would have prevented this activity, and to avoid that difficulty a Memorandum of Understanding was agreed. Under its terms the fishermen were permitted to continue their traditional activities subject to prohibitions on taking turtles and some other sedentary species, and the requirements that landings would only take place at specified points and that modern fishing techniques would not be introduced. The Indonesian fishermen have continued to operate in those northern Australian waters and there do not appear to have been any serious problems in this reasonable arrangement.

At the beginning of 1982, Indonesia and Malaysia agreed on a formal arrangement which will guarantee Malaysia transit rights through Indonesia's archipelagic waters in the vicinity of the Natuna islands. Those waters lie across the direct route between peninsular Malaysia and Sarawak and Sabah. Concern about this situation led Malaysia to lead a drive to include subsection 6 in Article 47 of the Convention; it provides that if archipelagic waters lie between two parts of an immediately adjacent neighbouring state, the traditional rights of the divided state will continue and be respected.

It is to be expected that as more maritime boundaries are drawn, and problems similar to those described arise, innovative solutions will be found to avoid unnecessary dislocation to traditional activities which will not adversely affect the sovereign state if they are continued.

Conclusions

The process of constructing maritime international boundaries normally begins when two states make overlapping claims from adjacent or opposite positions. In most cases the problems which have been solved have disappeared during the course of bilateral negotiations. In some cases the parties have resorted to arbitration, and this is a solution which might be used more often. Fortunately no disputes have been settled by force, although it is not impossible that this course will prove attractive to some country in the future.

In some cases, when the negotiations proved inconclusive it was decided to create a joint zone or an interim line, which would allow continued use or development of known resources to continue.

While several political, geographical, economic and technical circumstances can complicate negotiations over maritime boundaries, it appears that the nature of relations between the states is the critical factor. The most important geographical factor to the present has been the location of alien offshore islands close to the coast of a neighbouring state. However, it is possible that a greater reliance on the concept of natural prolongation will result in some bitter quarrels over the structure, geology and gradient of shared continental margins.

A start has been made to mitigate the adverse consequences of a strict application of rules in the vicinity of maritime boundaries. It is to be expected that this trend will continue.

References

Australian Department of Foreign Affairs (1981) 'Australia/Indonesia: maritime delimitation negotiations', *Backgrounder*, 308, III–VI.

Bird, E. C. F. (1970) *Coasts*, Cambridge, Mass.

Bowett, D. W. (1978) *The Legal Regime of Islands in International Law*, New York.

Brown, E. D. (1971) *The Legal Regime of Hydrospace*, London.

Chiu, H. (1977) *China's Attitude towards Continental Shelf and its Implication on Delimiting Seabed in Southeast Asia*, Occasional Papers/Reprints Series in Contemporary Asian Studies, 1, University of Maryland.

Court of Arbitration (1977) *The United Kingdom of Great Britain and Northern Ireland and the French Republic: Delimitation of the Continental Shelf*, The Hague.

Directorate of National Mapping (1979) *Map Showing Territorial Waters and Continental Shelf Boundaries of Malaysia*, 2 sheets, scale 1:1.5 M, Kuala Lumpur.

Hodgson, R. D. (1973) *Islands: Normal and Special Circumstances*, Research Study Bureau of Intelligence and Research, Washington, DC.

International Court of Justice (1969) *The North Sea Continental Shelf Cases*, Reports of Judgements, Advisory Opinions and Orders, The Hague.

International Court of Justice (1982) *Case Concerning the Continental Shelf (Tunisia/Libyan Arab Jamahiriya): Judgement*, The Hague.

Oxman, B. H. (1980) 'The Third United Nations Conference on the Law of the Sea: the eighth session (1979)', *American Journal of International Law*, 74, 1–47.

Peking Review (1974) 'Saigon authorities invade China's Hsisha Islands and provoke armed conflicts', 17 (4), 4.

Prescott, J. R. V. (1975) *Map of Mainland Asia by Treaty*, Melbourne.

Prescott, J. R. V. (1977) 'Mining the seabed and the law of the sea', *Optima*, 26 (4), 222–40.

Prescott, J. R. V. (1978) *Boundaries and Frontiers*, London.

Prescott, J. R. V. (1981) *Maritime Jurisdiction in Southeast Asia: A Commentary and a Map*, EAPI Research Report no. 2, East–West Center, Honolulu.

Republic of Chile (1977) *Canal Beagle: Laudo-Award*, Geneva.

Rosenne, S. (1957) *The International Court of Justice*, Leyden.

Thamsborg, M. (1977) 'Geodetic hydrography as related to maritime boundary problems', *International Hydrographic Review*, 51 (1), 157–73.

The Geographer (1973) '*Territorial Sea and Continental Shelf Boundaries: Poland–Soviet Union*', 'Limits in the Seas' series, no. 55, Washington, DC.

5

International maritime zones

That the persons of our citizens shall be safe in freely traversing the ocean, that the transportation of our own produce, in our own vessels, to the markets of our own choice, and the return to us of the articles we want for our own use, shall be unmolested, I hold to be fundamental, and the gauntlet that must be hurled at him who questions it.   (Jefferson 1904–5, 14, 301)

But thus much is certain: that he that commands the sea is at great liberty, and may take as much and as little of the war as he will.
                    (Bacon, 'Essay of the true greatness of kingdoms and estates')

Now I would give a thousand furlongs of sea for an acre of barren ground: long heath, broom, furze, anything.   (Shakespeare, *The Tempest*, I, i)

The quotations from the writings of Jefferson and Bacon refer to the two enduring uses of the high seas for trade and war. The third important use, for discovering new lands, ended in the nineteenth century. Those who thought that the era when naval power was important had ended must have reviewed their opinions in the wake of the war between Argentina and Britain over the Falkland Islands and their dependencies. The despairing cry of Gonzalo, which ends the first scene of *The Tempest*, might well have represented the opinion of most landsmen until recent years. The high seas appeared to have no intrinsic economic worth, except for the relatively small catches of fish. But that is no longer the view of governments, whose representatives engaged in a protracted debate over the regulations which would govern the mining of manganese nodules on the deep seabed, which lies beneath most of the high seas. It was dissatisfaction with the sections of the Convention dealing with this subject which led the United States to vote against its adoption in 1982.

This chapter deals with three international maritime zones. The first two have already been mentioned; they are the high seas and the deep seabed beyond national control. The third zone consists of the waters surrounding Antarctica. At present this zone would be viewed in different ways by different countries. The members of the Antarctic Treaty have carefully created a special regime for the economic use of these waters, and generally observe the terms of that regime. Some countries, which are not members of the Antarctic Treaty, refuse to recognize its authority or relevance and therefore regard the waters which surround Antarctica as part of the high seas, and the underlying seabed as being beyond national jurisdiction and therefore part of The Area.

These three zones possess different characteristics. The concept of the high seas is very old and the rights in it have been clearly defined for a long time, by practice if not by conventions or treaties. These rights have been widely used by most countries, whether coastal or landlocked, and the rights of others have been generally respected. At the various sessions of the conference which produced the Convention, issues connected with the high seas were settled rather easily. The most contentious point concerned the deletion of the exclusive economic zone from the high seas, but even this matter failed to become a stumbling block.

The regime dealing with the deep seabed proved the most contentious of the Third United Nations Conference on the Law of the Sea. Its critical nature is attested by the length and complexity of the articles in the Convention dealing with The Area; by the host of papers and chapters written on the subject; by the attention it has received in newspapers; and by the fact that concern about the interpretation of the relevant articles persuaded the United States to vote against the adoption of the Convention, and a number of other countries to abstain. The concept of the deep seabed being the common heritage of mankind was first proposed in 1967 (Pardo 1978, 9), and while much expensive research has been conducted into the techniques for finding, mining and processing manganese nodules, the industry has not been established on a commercial footing. The strong contrary positions adopted by various countries to the issue of mining the deep seabed means that it is possible that serious international friction will develop, as some states seek to operate outside the terms of the Convention.

While determination of national rights in the high seas and of the rules which have been devised for mining the deep seabed involved most of the countries in the international community, the total membership of the Antarctic Treaty is thirty-one, of which sixteen are Consultative Parties. These sixteen countries have the dominant influence in determining policy under the terms of the Antarctic Treaty. The Treaty came into force in 1961, and during its life a number of important decisions have been taken which have led to agreements on the manner in which research and economic activities south of parallel 60° south should be conducted. Questions over the status of the seas about Antarctica were not raised at the Law of the Sea Conference because of the certainty that such questions would seriously impair the chances of reaching a final Convention. Nine months after the Convention was signed in Jamaica in December 1982, the subject of Antarctica was being inscribed on the agenda of the United Nations at the request of Malaysia and some other countries.

The high seas

In the 1958 Convention on the High Seas the first article defined them as all parts of the sea that are not included in the territorial or internal waters of states. This declaration codified what had long been state practice. The 1982 Convention, in Article 86, adds the exclusive economic zone and archipelagic waters to the list of maritime zones not considered to be high seas. Since it is now generally accepted

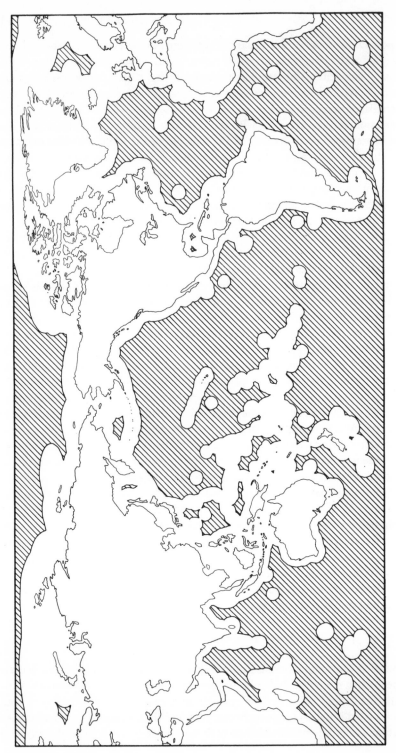

Figure 5.1 The high seas

that coastal states will claim exclusive economic zones 200 nautical miles wide, it follows that the area of the high seas has been considerably reduced by the application of the new definition. The reference to archipelagic waters is not significant in terms of eroding the high seas directly, since where states proclaim archipelagic waters in accordance with the provisions of the Convention, those waters would in any event have formed part of any claim to an exclusive economic zone. However, it is possible that when states measure their exclusive economic zone from archipelagic baselines rather than from the islands they connect, small areas of ocean that would have otherwise been high seas may be removed from that category of waters. Providing the baselines are drawn to preserve the general configuration of the archipelago, in accordance with the Convention, these reductions in the area of the high seas will be very small.

The distribution of high seas
The extent of high seas is shown in figure 5.1. In constructing this map it has been assumed that all countries will claim an exclusive economic zone 200 nautical miles wide, and that countries will observe the rules carefully in drawing straight baselines and archipelagic baselines. The map shows that there are sixteen areas of high seas. The largest consists of vast expanses of the Atlantic, Pacific and Indian Oceans, which are connected south of Africa, Australia and South America. While the connecting passages south of Australia and Africa are wide, that which lies south of South America would be restricted to a width of 40 nautical miles if national claims were permitted from Antarctica. In all the oceans there are isolated islands or island groups which are surrounded by national waters. The largest reduction in the area of high seas occurs in the Pacific Ocean, where the nations of the southwest Pacific reduce the high seas in the vicinity of Easter Island to a narrow waist linking the wider northern and southern sections. The same groups of islands also produce marked culs-de-sac of high seas between Lord Howe and Norfolk Islands, between the central and western island groups of Kiribati, and west of the Kermadec Islands of New Zealand.

The second largest area of high seas is found in the Arctic Ocean. It is hemmed in by claims to exclusive economic zones by Canada, Denmark, Norway and the Soviet Union. There is no direct link between these high seas and those found in more temperate oceans, as figure 5.2 shows.

The remaining fourteen areas of high seas are also enclaves surrounded by national waters, but they are all much smaller than the high seas of the Arctic Ocean. Only four of these small enclaves of high seas are found outside the Pacific Ocean. In the Norwegian Sea, between the Norwegian mainland and Iceland, Jan Mayen and Greenland there is an elongated area of high seas, which overlies the deepest parts of the Norwegian and Greenland Basins. To the east of this area a smaller enclave of high seas is located in the Barents Sea between Svalbard and Novaya Zemlya; it overlies a comparatively shallow section of the continental margin stretching north of Europe.

Figure 5.2   High seas in the Arctic Ocean

Two very small enclaves of high seas are found in the Gulf of Mexico, overlying waters with a depth of 3000 metres; they are bounded by national claims of Mexico and the United States.

The ten enclaves of high seas in the Pacific Ocean are all on the western margin. Starting in the south, a tiny enclave is found embedded in the exclusive economic zone which surrounds New Zealand and its offshore islands. It is found between the Auckland and Antipodes Islands. In the eastern Coral Sea there is another small enclave; it is bounded by national claims to seas 200 nautical miles wide from Papua New Guinea's Cape Deliverance, Solomon Islands' Indispensable Reefs and Australia's Mellish Reef. The seabed in this area lies more than 2000 metres below the surface. The most easterly enclave of high seas in the Pacific

Ocean lies between the Society Islands of French Polynesia and the Cook Islands; the water depth in this region is in excess of 5000 metres. In the Fiji Basin, bounded by claims from Solomon Islands, Fiji and Vanuatu, there is an enclave of about 18,000 square nautical miles, overlying a seabed more than 3000 metres below. To the north of this zone there is a corridor, stretching for 1200 nautical miles to the northwest, between the claims of Solomon Islands and Papua New Guinea on the southwest and Tuvalu, Kiribati, Nauru and the Trust Territory of the Pacific Islands on the northeast. An extension of the corridor westwards is located west of Kapingamurangi Island. The extension continues for about 900 nautical miles astride parallel 3° north and separates the claims of Indonesia and Papua New Guinea to the south from those of the Trust Territory of the Pacific Islands to the north. The waters in this enclave are more than 4000 metres deep.

A large, irregular enclave of high seas is found east of the Philippines. It is bounded on the south by the Trust Territory of the Pacific Islands, on the east by the Marianas and on the north by Parece Vela, which is a small coral reef owned by Japan. To the north of this small reef lies a rectangular enclave of high seas measuring about 360 nautical miles from north to south and about 120 nautical miles from east to west. This zone, which consists of waters with depths to 6000 metres, is entirely bounded by Japanese claims; the Okinawa Islands lie to the west and Ogasawara Gunto to the east.

In the Sea of Okhotsk there is a narrow strip of high seas about 300 nautical miles long and 50 nautical miles wide; it is entirely surrounded by Russian claims with depths generally less than 2000 metres. The last enclave is found in the Bering Sea. It is triangular in shape, with the base, following the alignment of the Aleutian Islands, about 400 nautical miles long, and the apex 300 nautical miles distant. The depths of this enclave of high seas is more than 2000 metres.

The significance of these enclaves of high seas is that they provide an excuse to be in the area for vessels belonging to countries other than those whose claims adjoin the enclave. Plainly to reach those enclaves vessels will have to pass through zones claimed by adjoining states. In the southwest Pacific Ocean this is an advantage which is known to be exploited by people poaching fish. The presence of enclaves of high seas increases the difficulties of fisheries officers of the island states of Micronesia, Melanesia and Polynesia. There may be circumstances when for strategic reasons, major powers might also find it convenient to have the excuse that they are entitled to use some of these enclaves of high seas for navigation, overflight and research. It seems certain that any suggestion that the small enclaves, excluding the Arctic Ocean, should be absorbed into surrounding national claims would be resisted by many countries, including those which are landlocked and geographically disadvantaged.

To conclude this section describing the distribution of high seas it is only necessary to record that high seas have been totally eliminated in all the enclosed and semi-enclosed seas apart from the Arctic Ocean and the Gulf of Mexico. Thus there are no high seas in the Mediterranean, Baltic, North, Black, Red, Yellow, South China and East China Seas, the Persian Gulf and the Sea of Japan.

Freedoms of the high seas

The 1958 Convention on the High Seas conferred four freedoms; they were the freedoms of navigation, fishing and overflight, and the freedom to lay submarine cables and pipelines. The Convention has added two other freedoms in Article 87. They are the freedoms to conduct scientific research and to construct artificial islands and other installations. While scientists will cherish the freedom to conduct research in view of the dwindling opportunities for marine investigation, countries regard the freedoms of navigation, overflight, and fishing as the most important.

The freedoms of movement are most important for all countries in terms of trade; to a few countries these freedoms are also important in a strategic sense. If it was possible to measure the number of people who travelled by sea, it is likely that the vast majority would travel within national waters, because the major movements would be across the enclosed and semi-enclosed seas such as the North Sea, the Mediterranean Sea and the seas of southeast Asia. If the calculation of tonnes of cargo moved by seas could be made it is probable that more than half would move entirely within national waters. When the major sea lanes are examined for their passage through high seas, it is evident that many include long sections through national waters. The Geographer (1973) produced a map showing sea lanes and waters within 200 nautical miles of land (see figure 5.3). The map reveals that vessels plying between Australia and Japan rarely sail through areas of high seas; that tankers sailing from the Persian Gulf to Europe generally only enter the high seas after turning the Cape of Good Hope and setting course for Cape Vert near Dakar; and that many routes across the Atlantic Ocean pass through national waters surrounding St Helena and Ascension Islands and the Azores.

The heaviest density of major shipping lanes in the high seas is found in the Atlantic Ocean between parallels 5° south and 45° north. It is across these waters that vessels ply their trade between the major population and production centres of Europe, north America and the south American states of Brazil and Venezuela. By comparison, the pattern of major shipping lanes in the high seas of the Pacific Ocean is formed by a few connections between Japan and Chile, Peru and the United States.

Figure 5.3 also shows that apart from minor routes to Prudhoe Bay in Alaska, Narvik in northern Norway, and Arkhangel'sk in Russia, shipping routes through the high seas lie between parallels 45° south and 65° north.

Jefferson's concern with the fundamental nature of freedom of navigation on the high seas seems to be shared by modern political leaders, for there is no evidence that this freedom has been impaired in recent years. The problems for captains of vessels on the high seas are mainly presented by the elements and failures of machinery; they do not have to worry about hostile political actions by countries other than the flag state.

Most coastal states possess at least armed coastguard vessels to protect their shores and to ensure that illegal acts within claimed maritime zones are prevented

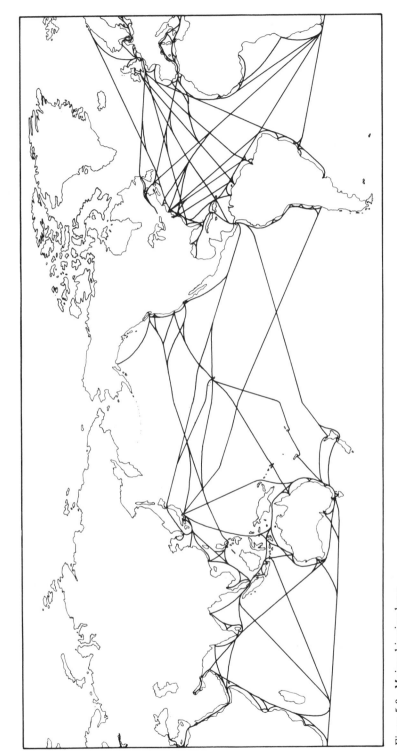

Figure 5.3 Major shipping lanes

or detected and punished. Many coastal states have a navy, but in most cases that navy will only operate within 200 nautical miles of the state's territory. The five permanent members of the Security Council, China, France, the Soviet Union, the United Kingdom and the United States of America, possess large navies by comparison with the rest of the world, and while the Chinese navy generally stays close to Chinese maritime zones, the other four navies send vessels to distant regions across the high seas.

Navies are powerful instruments of government policy in both war and peace. The importance in war is self-evident to any student of world history. The significance of naval power in times of war is most graphically shown by Pemsel (1975), who published an atlas showing naval battles during the four ages, which he called the age of the galleys, the age of sail, the age of iron and steel and the nuclear age. The age of the galleys began in 1210 BC when the fleets of the Hittites and Cypriots fought off Cyprus; it ended on 17 July 1657 when the Venetian and Turkish forces clashed in the second battle of the Dardanelles. The age of sail overlapped the age of galleys, for the first battle of sailing ships was in 1508 when a Gujerati-Egyptian force surprised the Portuguese fleet in the eastern Mediterranean Sea. However, Pemsel gives 1582 as the true beginning of the age of sail; he ends it in 1840, which was the year when Vice-Admiral Stopford captured St Jean d'Acre. The last battle between sailing ships occurred on 5 July 1833, when British ships engaged the Miguelite faction from Portugal. The first battle of the age of iron and steel was between Turkish and Russian fleets off Sinop, on the southern shore of the Black Sea in 1853. Pemsel begins the nuclear age in 1945, and the events off the Falkland Islands in June 1982 confirm that we are still in that age. Summary maps of the four ages of naval battles according to Pemsel are shown in figures 5.4–5.7. What all the diagrams show, and it is not surprising, is that with few exceptions all the major naval battles throughout history have occurred close to land, and certainly within waters which today fall under some form of national control.

Gunboat diplomacy

The use of the navy in peacetime must now be considered. Most countries would certainly use their navy at some time as a maritime police force to supervise the activities of aliens in national waters. Indeed that is the major use of the navies of most countries. However, navies, especially those of the United States and Britain still have a role in what is popularly called gunboat diplomacy. Many modern commentators and editors when they use that phrase do so in a disparaging manner, and infer that while such actions may have been common in the colonial period, they now belong to an antiquated view of international politics. Cable (1971) and Luttwak (1974) have shown that gunboat diplomacy is still a tool of modern politics, which is available to those countries with comparatively large fleets. Cable (1971, 175) defines gunboat diplomacy as the use or threat of limited naval force, otherwise than as an act of war, in order to gain advantage, or to avert loss, either in the conduct of international relations or against foreign nationals in

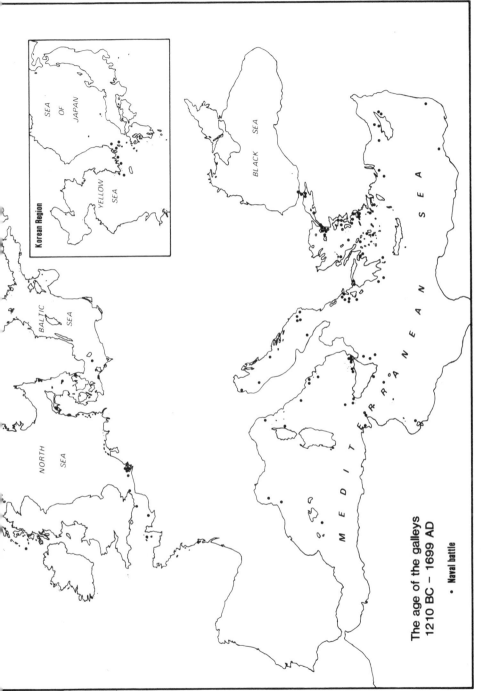

Korean Region

SEA OF JAPAN

YELLOW SEA

BLACK SEA

MEDITERRANEAN SEA

BALTIC SEA

NORTH SEA

The age of the galleys
1210 BC – 1699 AD

• Naval battle

Figure 5.4 Sea battles in the age of the galleys

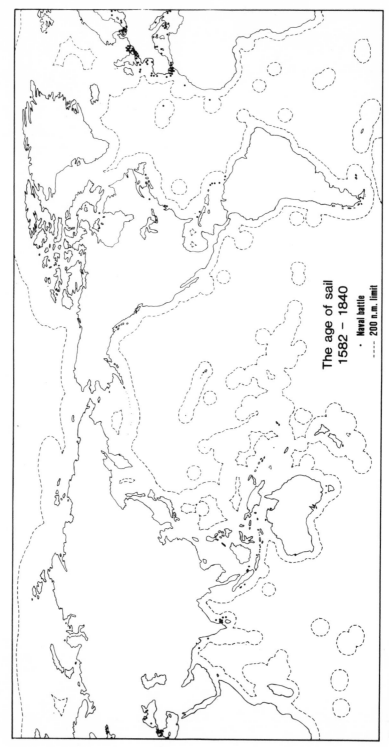

The age of sail
1582 – 1840

• Naval battle
--- 200 n.m. limit

Figure 5.5 Sea battles in the age of sail

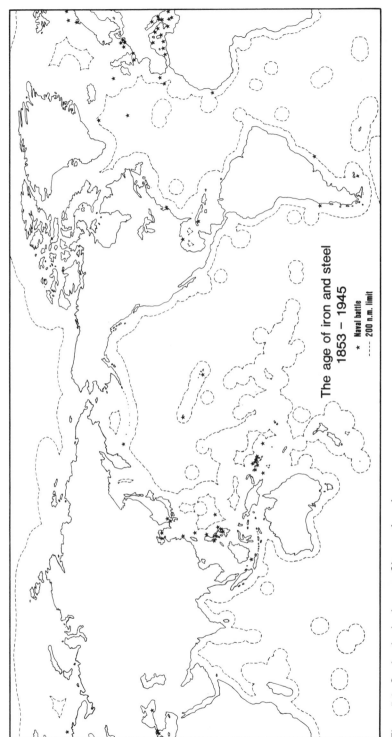

The age of iron and steel
1853 – 1945

★ Naval battle
--- 200 n.m. limit

Figure 5.6   Sea battles in the age of iron and steel

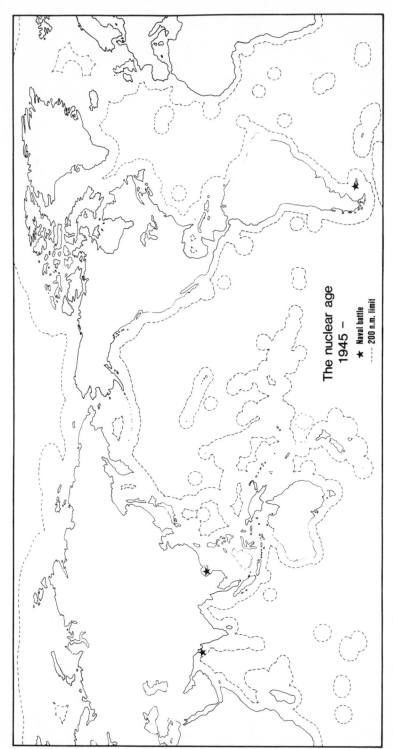

The nuclear age
1945 –

★ Naval battle
---- 200 n.m. limit

Figure 5.7 Sea battles in the nuclear age

their own territory. Cable then proceeds to classify acts of this nature into four categories. First there is definitive naval force, which is an action seeking clearly defined aims, preferably by presenting a *fait accompli*. For example, in November 1921 HMS *Glowworm* embarked the former Emperor Karl of Austria-Hungary after his unsuccessful attempt to regain his throne. The ship took him from Baja, on the middle reaches of the River Danube, to Romania, whence he was trans-ferred to another ship HMS *Cardiff*, which took the former Emperor to Madeira. This action was taken on behalf of the European allies to ensure that he was not rescued by his supporters, or captured by his opponents, during his voyage to exile. Thus a definitive action removes the cause of the dispute as far as the assailant is concerned. Of course, it is possible that such force will produce reper-cussions, as the victim of the gunboat diplomacy reacts. For example, on 5 April 1960 the Netherlands government announced that it was sending the aircraft carrier *Karel Doorman* and two destroyers to West Irian to deter attacks by Indonesia on this remaining Dutch territory. Indonesia retaliated against Dutch nationals and property and broke diplomatic relations.

Second there is purposeful naval force, which is designed to exert pressure so that some other authority takes the action required to redress the situation. For example, on 18 August 1921 the United States embarked 400 marines on USS *Pennsylvania* to induce Panama to accept an American decision about a boundary dispute which Panama had with Costa Rica. The implied threat of the embar-kation of this force was sufficient to persuade Panama to accept the American decision. Almost exactly four years later, when the United States sent USS *Denver* to Corinto and USS *Tulsa* to Bluefields, which are on the Pacific and Caribbean coasts of Nicaragua respectively, in order to prevent a *coup d'état*, the rebels were not overawed and the government was dislodged.

Third there is catalytic naval force. This is speculative activity where the intention is not always precise and the outcome is often uncertain. For example, in December 1965 Britain posted the aircraft carrier HMS *Eagle* off the coast of Tanzania in order to reassure the Zambian authorities who were worried about air attacks from Rhodesia, which had declared itself independent in the previous month.

Fourth there is expressive naval force, which simply emphasizes the particular attitude of a country. In July 1967 a Soviet naval squadron visited Alexandria and Port Said, and it was announced that Russia was ready to co-operate with Egypt in repelling aggression. In December 1938, in order to underline his country's independent foreign policy, the foreign minister of Argentina arrived at Lima for a Pan-American conference on board the cruiser *La Argentina*. This was a technique which Argentina had learned from President Roosevelt a year earlier, when he arrived at Buenos Aires on the cruiser *Indianapolis*, accompanied by the USS *Chester*, to register disapproval of Argentinian policy prohibiting inter-vention in the affairs of other countries.

In an appendix, Cable (1971, 175–229) lists occurrences of gunboat diplomacy during fifty years beginning in 1920. An examination of those events shows that the United States and Britain were the countries which most frequently employed gunboat diplomacy. The United States was involved in sixty cases and Britain in fifty-five. The country with the third largest involvement was France, with twelve cases. The other two countries with major navies, the Soviet Union and China, resorted to gunboat diplomacy on five and two occasions respectively. A total of twenty-four states engaged in 181 acts of gunboat diplomacy against fifty countries. Some countries, such as Britain, the United States, Russia, China, France and Turkey, appeared on the lists of aggressors and victims, but the country which was the victim most frequently was China, which had gunboat diplomacy applied against it on twenty-three occasions.

Having stated the reliable opinion that gunboat diplomacy is still a weapon used by some countries in international relations, it is difficult to proceed to generalizations with any confidence. However, while it is impossible to construct a working model of states which will resort to gunboat diplomacy, or their likely targets, or the circumstances in which this option will be employed, the following very general comments can be made. Gunboat diplomacy is usually employed by a country which either has superiority in the particular theatre concerned or can act quickly before being detected by a stronger force. It is easier for countries such as Britain, the United States and Russia to move their fleets so that they can achieve a dominant position in remote areas and make use of gunboat diplomacy. Other countries tend to operate only close to home ports. Thus Iraq's prohibition in 1961 on Iranian shipping using the Shatt el Arab, Cuba's raid on refugees in the Bahamas in August 1963, and various Turkish actions near Cyprus were all undertaken in situations where the aggressor operated along short lines of communication. Except in three cases all occurrences of gunboat diplomacy in recent years have been directed against coastal states. The three exceptions involve Austria in 1921 and Rhodesia in 1965 and 1966. Generally the forces exerting pressure remain off the coast and do not enter narrow waterways. The epic events associated with the incursion up the Yangtze River by HMS *Amethyst* in April 1949 show the risks of naval vessels entering rivers of hostile countries. Countries in a state of internal turmoil appear to be perceived by strong countries as being vulnerable to gunboat diplomacy. Pressure against China, Nicaragua, Lebanon and Zaire was exerted when these states were passing through major political disturbances. Such states are probably more vulnerable when they lack powerful allies, which might be prepared to protect them.

There seems to be no reason to doubt that gunboat diplomacy will continue to be used by countries when it suits them. However, only the major powers such as Britain, China, France, Russia and the United States seem likely to send their fleets across the high seas to engage in such activities; other countries are likely to restrict their forays into this activity to adjacent areas of national waters.

O'Connell (1975) made an interesting study on the influence of law on seapower. In his characteristically perceptive way he noted that navies afforded governments the means of exerting pressure in ways which were stronger than diplomacy but which did not involve the unpredictable risks of war, and he identified the freedom of the seas as the mechanism which made the forces available, without committing them. He also observed that the only safe prediction about the relationship between law and seapower was that the element of law would be more predominant at lower levels of conflict, in localized situations with restricted objectives. As the conflict increases in area and intensity so law assumes a reduced role in influencing the application of naval power.

Fishing on the high seas

It is impossible to obtain accurate estimates of the amount of fish taken in the high seas. Alexander and Hodgson (1975, 586) provide a figure of 10 per cent of the weight of fish caught in all waters. There is no doubt that the great part of fish harvested are taken within 200 nautical miles of the world's coasts.

The Convention refers in a number of articles to fish in the high seas. The right to fish in the high seas, which is accorded to all states in Article 116, is qualified in a number of general ways. For example, Article 117 notes that all states have the duty to co-operate with other states in taking measures to conserve the living resources of the high seas, and the point is repeated in the next two articles. They refer to the establishment of regional fisheries where appropriate, and outline the actions which states should take in compiling accurate statistics, exchanging information and calculating the maximum sustainable yield.

There are further qualifications to the freedom to fish in the high seas in the articles dealing with the exclusive economic zone. Where fish stocks overlap the exclusive economic zone and the adjacent high seas the nations concerned in harvesting the resource should agree on measures necessary for the conservation of those stocks. Article 64 calls on nations which harvest high migratory species, which pass through the exclusive economic zones of several states and extensive areas of the high seas, to co-operate to promote optimum use of such species. They are listed in an annex, and are mainly tuna, pomfrets, sailfish, swordfish, sauries, dolphin and sharks. Anadromous stocks, which live in saltwater and breed in freshwater, are the subject of Article 66. The state in whose waters the fish breed is given the responsibility for ensuring the conservation of these stocks, and fishing is restricted to the exclusive economic zone of such states, except where this rule would cause economic dislocation to another state. Where fishing occurs in the high seas for anadromous stocks there should be agreement between the states concerned and the state where the stocks originate. The salmon is the main fish of this type, and much of the international negotiation on fishing has been concerned with the Atlantic and Pacific salmon fisheries (Crutchfield and Pontecorvo, 1969). Catadromous stocks, which live in freshwater and breed in saltwater, are dealt with in Article 67. Again the state of origin is charged with regulating this fishery, which is restricted to exclusive economic zones. When these stocks, which are principally eels, pass through the exclusive economic zones of two states they are enjoined to co-operate in establishing rules for their use.

Bardach and Matsuda (1980) have provided a useful account of the biology and economics of tuna fisheries. Their map of fishing grounds and exclusive economic zones indicates that the fish can be caught in the high seas of the tropical Pacific Ocean, and in three of the enclaves of high seas described earlier. The tuna family of fish is the most important highly migratory species, and it is obviously going to be very difficult to reconcile the interests of countries such as Japan, Taiwan, South Korea and the United States, which have large tuna fleets, the Philippines and Indonesia, which possess waters where many tuna spawn, and the island states of the southwest Pacific Ocean, which control waters through which major tuna shoals pass.

Driver (1980, 39–44) provides a useful account of international fisheries organizations. He distinguishes commissions dealing with a single species, such as the International Pacific Halibut Commission, from regional commissions such as the International Commission for Northwest Atlantic Fisheries. He concludes that the system does not appear to have worked very well because of inadequate enforcement measures and the existence of loopholes which enables members to dissent. He also observes that it has proved very difficult, for national and international political reasons, to secure the agreement of members for reductions in quotas, even when that course was founded on reliable scientific evidence. Finally Driver draws attention to the unlimited entry to the fishery by non-member states which can undermine carefully prepared conservation measures.

Driver (1980, 44) and Bardach and Matsuda (1980, 477) comment on the high costs of research into fisheries in the high seas, and of surveillance of measures designed to conserve those stocks.

The fact that there is such a sharp contrast between the general statements in the Convention about the regulation of international fisheries and the very detailed rules about the mining of the deep seabed, suggests that the negotiators realized there was no chance of securing agreement about an activity which had been undertaken by so many countries for such a long time. The prospect of recurring difficulties about international fisheries is unfortunately excellent, and it will involve developed countries in the north Atlantic and Pacific Oceans, and developed and developing countries in the central Pacific Ocean.

The deep seabed

In the Convention the deep seabed is named as 'The Area', and it is defined as the seabed and its sub-soil which is beyond national jurisdiction. This means that before the precise area of the deep seabed is known it will be necessary for each coastal state to fix the limits of its national claims to the continental margin. However, where the margin is narrower than 200 nautical miles, then it can be assumed that the minimum boundary of the deep seabed will lie 200 nautical miles from the appropriate state baseline.

The distribution of the deep seabed

The sixteen areas of high seas described earlier do not overlie sixteen areas of deep seabed, because some areas of high seas cover parts of the continental margin which can be claimed by coastal states such as the Soviet Union and New Zealand. However, ten of the areas of high seas will have corresponding areas of deep seabed, but only in three cases will the limits of the high seas and deep seabed correspond exactly; in the other cases the deep seabed underlies only part of the high seas.

The very large area of the deep seabed underlying the Pacific, Indian and Atlantic Oceans is not continuous south of South America. Claims to that part of the continental margin called the Scotia Ridge, from the Antarctic Peninsula and the Falkland Island Dependencies, would overlap and separate the deep seabed in the south Atlantic from that in the south Pacific Ocean. The limits of the deep seabed would be fairly easy to establish in the Pacific Ocean, where most of the coastal states would only be able to claim shelves 200 nautical miles wide. The only areas of uncertainty would occur in the southwest, near New Zealand and Australia, and in the east, between the Galapagos Islands and the mainland of Ecuador. In the Indian and Atlantic Oceans the wide shelves would mean that final definition of the deep seabed would have to await national claims from countries such as Sri Lanka, India, the Seychelles, the United Kingdom, Ireland, Canada, the United States and Argentina.

The deep seabed in the Arctic Ocean would be reduced by wide shelf claims by Russia and divided into two parts by claims to the Lomonosov Ridge. There would be no deep seabed under the high seas in the Barents Sea, and the area of deep seabed under the high seas in the Norwegian Sea would be reduced by claims to wide shelves by Norway and Iceland. The areas of high seas in the Gulf of Mexico would be underlain by shelf claims by Mexico and the United States of America.

In the Pacific Ocean, the enclaves of high seas which cover wide shelves are those in the Sea of Okhotsk, the Coral Sea and the sea south of New Zealand. The three areas of high seas in the vicinity of parallels 5° south to 15° south correspond exactly to underlying areas of deep seabed. The other areas of high seas in the western Pacific Ocean, stretching from the Bering Sea in the north via the Philippines Sea to the Fiji Basin in the south, would all overlie smaller areas of deep seabed, because of claims to wide shelves by countries such as Russia, the United States, Japan and Fiji.

Deep seabed resources

The chief resources which are hoped to be obtained from the deep seabed in the foreseeable future are found in manganese nodules. The prospects for finding hydrocarbon reserves are poor. First, there are the mid-oceanic ridges, which occupy about one-third of the area of the deep seabed, where the presence of basalt flows underlain by massed igneous dykes offer no chance of finding oil or gas (Kent 1980, 63). On the abyssal plain linking the mid-ocean ridges with the continental margins there are some considerable thicknesses of sedimentary material where hydrocarbons might have accumulated and been trapped. The problem of such reserves surviving is related to the high temperature gradients found in these sediments. It is likely that the high temperatures will have cracked the petroleum and metamorphosed gas to its constituent elements (Kent 1980, 64). The best chance would be associated with what Kent (1980, 64) calls microcontinents, which are massive submerged blocks of continental material, such as are found off the Seychelles and the Kerguelen Islands. While it is impossible to be certain, it seems possible that such areas will be subject to national claims, rather than being left as part of the deep seabed.

McKelvey (1980, 467) and Earney (1980, 166–7) have described the possible formation of mineral lodes in the deep seabed. In the various magmatic chambers under the seabed it is possible that magmatic segregation concentrates minerals producing significant deposits of chromium, nickel, platinum and copper. However, the size of the deposit would be directly related to the size of the chamber since the slow cooling associated with large chambers would be necessary for comprehensive magmatic differentiation.

Along the mid-ocean ridges the permeability of the seabed will permit the penetration of seawater and the establishment of a convection system which will leach minerals out of the rocks and deposit them at or near the surface, as sulphides. In view of the high costs of collecting nodules from the surface of the seabed, it is safe to predict that the costs associated with mining lodes under the seabed would prevent competition with land-based mines at present.

The best map of the world distribution of nodules was prepared by Rawson and Ryan (1978). If it is assumed that the richest deposits are those where the nickel content is more than 25 per cent, and where the nodules cover more than half the seabed in the vicinity of the site, it is possible to find five sites. The most important, because it covers a wide area and is based on the analysis of several samples, is found along parallel 15° north to the east of the meridian which passes through Hawaii. This is the region of the renowned Clipperton Fracture. The other sites are found south of the Islas Galápagos; on the Tasmanian Ridge; south of Perth in Western Australia; and in the region of the Cape of Good Hope. Rawson and Ryan (1978) record only a few sites in the Atlantic Ocean, but only the site off the tip of southern Africa has the high nickel content and the high density of nodules. It seems likely that other sites of high quality exist. Indeed, it is probable that some have been found and their whereabouts kept as an important commercial secret.

Uncertainties facing nodule miners
There are two major uncertainties about the mining of nodules from the deep seabed. The first concerns the profitability of mining, if it was allowed to take place subject only to free market forces. The second uncertainty relates to the possible impact of the regulations contained in the Convention on the profitability of deep-seabed mining.

There have been many attempts to construct models which would allow the profitability of nodule mining to be calculated under different assumptions about the richness of the deposit, its distance from the processing factory, the methods of collection and refining, the level of world mineral prices, and tax regulations. The only point which appears to be universally agreed is that it would require the investment of large capital sums to find, assess, mine and process nodules. One of the most detailed assessments was prepared by Flipse (1981), who divides the costs into eight sectors.

First, there is the sector dealing with research and development of a mining, transport and processing system, which will require scale tests. While this is proceeding the search for a suitable deposit can continue. Flipse calculates that these two activities will cost about $US 172 millions. The second set of costs is associated with the mining of the nodules. It is estimated that the cost of two new ships, with all the necessary mining gear, would be about $US 294 millions, and that the operating costs of these ships would be $US 68 millions each year.

Once the nodules have been collected it is necessary to transport them to the shore, and the cost of the vessels and the support equipment such as helicopters which will be necessary for this activity amounts to $US 174 millions, with an annual operating cost of $US 21 millions. The port facilities which will be necessary to allow the discharge of the cargo and its storing when necessary are estimated to cost $US 30 millions with annual operating charges of $US 3 millions. The transport system will need to be extended on land to convey the nodules to the processing plant, and Flipse estimates that such a system will cost about $US 40 millions, with recurring annual charges of $US 7 millions.

The construction of the plant to extract the minerals from the nodules would involve an investment of $US 458 millions, and the running costs each year would amount to $US 100 millions. The seventh set of charges is concerned with environmental costs. Quite clearly the extraction plant is going to generate large volumes of waste material. Whether this material is returned to the sea or used as landfill there are going to be charges. Flipse assesses the cost of disposing of waste on land as $US 22 millions in terms of capital cost, with recurring annual charges of $US 7 millions. Finally, under the heading of additional support charges it is estimated that a further capital cost of $US 1 million with recurring annual charges of $US 16 millions will be incurred.

These calculations result in a total capital cost, once a site has been discovered and proved, of about $US 1 billion, with annual recurring charges of $US 229 millions. It has seemed worthwhile to detail these charges to demonstrate beyond doubt that the investment required will be high. It is not proposed to explain in detail the different calculations on returns, or levels of taxation, because it is much harder to make reasonable predictions about metal prices or the policies of national treasurers. But if it is accepted that it will take at least five years, once a site has been proved, to establish the systems necessary to mine, transport and process the nodules, it is clear that there is an element of risk in the investment. It is the conclusion of Flipse (1981, 28) that on the basis of his calculations nodule mining will not be undertaken by commercial interests, unless the process involves a metal which is critical to the major product of the investing company. Reynolds (1982, 3), who is associated with a major mining company in Australia, made the assessment that with the current state of the technology for seabed mining, it cannot compete economically with production from mines on land.

While Flipse (1981, 28) lists the developments which might improve the profitability of seabed mining, so that the return on investment increases the attractiveness of the activity, Reynolds (1982, 8) notes that some governments might encourage uneconomic mining of the deep seabed for reasons of prestige or strategy.

Turning now to the uncertainty attached to the operation of the terms of the Convention, it is not proposed to examine all the many regulations governing mining of The Area in minute detail. It seems more important to emphasize the simple message that the chief thrust of the present Convention seems to be that nodule mining is not an activity which should be readily encouraged. The Convention's terms and regulations will discourage deep-seabed mining in a number of ways.

First, international control of nodule mining will increase the cost of each operation. The investments and running costs assessed by Flipse did not take into account these additional costs because their scale cannot be accurately computed; however, the types of additional costs can be outlined. Applicants seeking to mine the deep seabed will have to provide details either of two equivalent sites, or of one site which can be divided to support two mining operations. One of the sites will be reserved by the international authority for its own purposes. This means that each applicant has to expend much more money than would otherwise be required if it only had to prove a single mine site.

There is also a complex provision which would disallow an application in the following circumstances.

> [If] the proposed plan of work has been submitted or sponsored by a State party which already holds:
> (i) plans of work for exploration and exploitation of polymetallic nodules in non-reserved areas that, together with either part of the area covered by the application for a plan of work, exceed in size 30 per cent of a circular area of 400,000 square kilometres surrounding the centre of either part of the area covered by the proposed plan of work.   (Convention, Annex III, Article 6)

The aim of this provision is to prevent a single consortium from gaining a monopoly over a series of mine sites close together. Its operation can be seen through examining figure 5.8.

A consortium proves two sites named Area A and Area B, one of which will be reserved by the Authority. Both sites have an area of 60,000 square kilometres. The consortium also holds two other areas C and D, which each have an area of 60,000 square kilometres. Now a circle with an area of 400,000 square kilometres will have a radius of 356.9 kilometres, and a circle of that radius has been

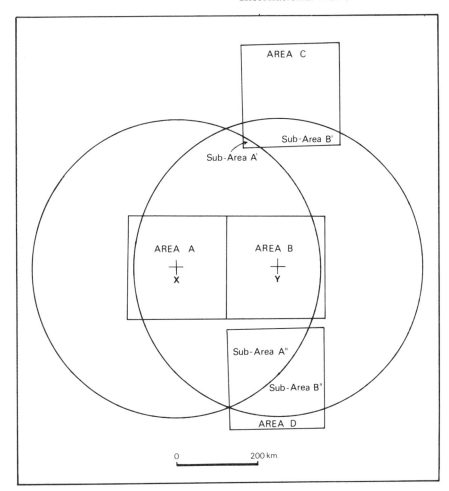

Figure 5.8   Anti-monopoly provisions for deep-seabed mining

described about point X, which is the centre of Area A. It will be seen that this circle encloses a small area of Area C, labelled Sub-Area A′, and a larger area of Area D, which is labelled Sub-Area A″. The party making the application would automatically be refused permission if the total area of Area A and Sub-Areas A′ and A″ exceeded 30 per cent of 400,000 square kilometres, which is 120,000 square kilometres.

Area A	60,000 square kilometres
Sub-Area A′	993 square kilometres
Sub-Area A″	23,570 square kilometres
Total	84,563 square kilometres

So the application would pass the test in respect of Area A. If the same exercise was carried out for Area B a different result would be obtained. The circle with a radius of 367 kilometres described about point Y now cuts off Sub-Areas A' and B' in Area C and Sub-Areas A" and B" in Area D.

Area B	60,000 square kilometres
Sub-Areas A' and B'	15,611 square kilometres
Sub-Areas A" and B"	46,442 square kilometres
Total	122,053 square kilometres

This combined area is larger than 120,000 square kilometres so the application would fail in respect of Area B.

It would be possible for the applicant to reduce the area and the boundaries of the proposed sites so that both satisfied this rule.

The second rule which would bring automatic disqualification also is designed to avoid monopolies. No party may apply for a site which would bring its total holding to more than 2 per cent of the total seabed which has not been reserved by the Authority. By taking the area of the world's oceans and subtracting the area which lies within 200 nautical miles of land, an approximate extent for The Area can be obtained. The figure would be 291,959,200 square kilometres. This would be a slight exaggeration because some countries would claim beyond 200 nautical miles to the edge of the margin. If the Authority reserved one-quarter of the deep seabed then 2 per cent of the remainder would be 4,379,388 square kilometres; if it reserved half The Area then 2 per cent of the remainder would amount to 2,919,592 square kilometres; and if the Authority reserved three-quarters of the deep seabed then 2 per cent of the remainder would amount to 1,459,796 square kilometres. This smallest figure would still be equivalent to eighteen mine sites of 80,000 square kilometres each.

Applicants will have to pay the cost of having their application processed, and the fee is expected to be about $US 500,000; refunds will be made if the costs prove to be less than that figure. Successful companies will have to pay an annual fixed fee of $US 1 million. Once mining starts the miners must make annual payments, either by paying a production charge or by paying a combination of production charge and a share of net proceeds. In the first case the production charge will be 5 per cent of the market value of the processed metals in the first ten years, and 12 per cent for the remaining years of operation. When combination charges are paid the production charges will be 2 per cent for the first ten years and 4 per cent thereafter. The share of net proceeds will depend on the investment return yielded by the operation. When the return is less than 10 per cent the Authority will take 35 per cent of the return in the first ten years and 40 per cent thereafter. When the return is greater than 20 per cent the Authority will take 50 per cent in the first decade and 70 per cent thereafter. Any potential applicant will beware once he reads in Article 13 of Annex III to the Convention, that in making rules and regulations regarding the financial terms of contracts, the Authority shall be guided by the objective of ensuring optimum revenue for the Authority from the proceeds of commercial exploitation. Other objectives are listed, but none detracts from that principal aim.

There is no doubt that the Authority will need a lot of money, because it will be creating a large bureaucracy which, if the experience of the United Nations is any guide, will be expensive to run. The Assembly is the supreme organ of the Authority, and it will meet at least once a year, and its membership will consist of representatives of all states which are signatories to the Convention. The Council is the executive organ of the Authority; it will consist of thirty-six members and will meet at least three times each year. It will have two subsidiary organs. The first is the Economic Planning Commission; it will consist of fifteen members who are expert either in mining or in international trade or international economics. This Commission will be responsible for devising mechanisms by which the policies of the Authority or Council can be implemented, especially with regard to control of production and the payment of appropriate compensation to developing countries which are adversely affected by deep-seabed mining. The Legal and Technical Commission also consists of fifteen members expert in mining, oceanography, protection of the marine environment, or economic aspects of mineral production. The main task of this Commission will be to review proposals for mining and to make recommendations to the Council. It will also have to take account of possible ecological damage to the marine environment, and to calculate production ceilings. There will also be a Secretariat consisting of a Secretary General and such staff as he needs.

The Authority will also need large sums of money because the Convention appears to envisage it as a mechanism by which developing states will benefit financially. Again and again throughout the various articles dealing with deep-seabed mining there are references to developing countries, and they cover such subjects as being favoured in any division of surplus funds generated by the Authority; benefiting from any joint schemes with the Enterprise, which is the mining arm of the Authority; having its nationals trained in the techniques of deep-seabed mining; and being protected against any adverse economic effects on their production from mines on land.

The second way in which the Convention will discourage mining of the deep seabed is because it permits the Authority to control the level of production. The production levels will be set for nickel, and they will operate for twenty years in the following way. The annual ceiling of nickel production will be the sum of two values. The first value will be the difference in nickel consumption in the year before the first commercial mining and the year five years earlier. Actual values will not be used; instead the annual value will be determined by means of a trend line derived from a linear regression of the logarithms of actual nickel consumption for the previous fifteen years. Thus if the first year of commercial production was 1989, it would be necessary to draw trend lines through actual nickel consumption for the periods 1974–88 and 1969–83. Then by comparing the trend line values for 1983 and 1988 the first value in the calculation would be derived.

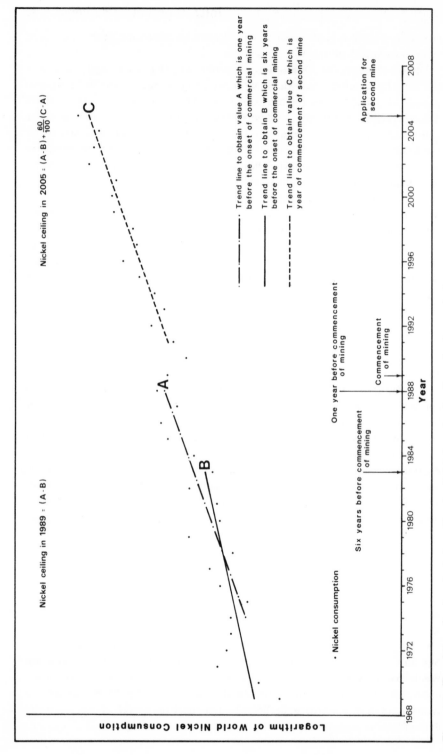

Figure 5.9 Trend lines for the calculation of levels of nickel production from the deep seabed

The second value is 60 per cent of the difference between nickel consumption in the year for which the production permit is applied and the year immediately prior to the first year of commercial production from the deep seabed. Once again the values compared would be those derived from trend lines over fifteen-year periods. Thus, if the permit application was for 2005, it would be necessary to construct trend lines for the periods 1974–88 and 1991–2005. These lines would give values for 1988 and 2005, and 60 per cent of that difference would provide the second value. This means that the first value will only need to be calculated once; the second value will have to be calculated for each year a new mining application is submitted (figure 5.9).

Nickel was selected rather than copper or cobalt because seabed copper production would not be significant, while cobalt seabed production would be very significant. Reynolds (1982, 5) asserts that the best mine sites could increase the world's cobalt supply by one-quarter, and that if production levels had been tied to cobalt, seabed mining would have been effectively blocked. Some African countries, including Zaire, suggested that production should be related to cobalt, but countries from other regions rejected this concept.

There are also provisions in the Convention which would prevent miners who discovered that their site had a greater extent than envisaged from being able to continue their production into the newly discovered adjacent areas.

The Convention will also discourage deep-seabed mining because it provides for the establishment of the Enterprise, which will mine the seabed on behalf of the Authority and therefore the world community. The Enterprise will have signal commercial advantages over other seabed miners. For example, it will be able to use half the mine sites which the commercial applicants are required to prove; so it will save on exploration costs. The Enterprise has the right to acquire technology used in seabed mining on fair and reasonable terms from the successful mining applicants. The Authority will reserve 38,000 metric tonnes of nickel production from the annual total of permitted production for the Enterprise. Capital will be provided to the Enterprise without conditions relating to the ability of the Enterprise to operate profitably, and some of the capital will be free of interest. The Enterprise is unlikely to be taxed on any profits it might make, and it will not have to spend risk capital on the development of technology. Lastly, the Enterprise will benefit by having its staff trained very cheaply by the other miners.

While the three discouragements to mining which have been described are serious, it is possible that the main discouragement lies in the fact that the operation of the rules in the Convention are uncertain. This means that applicants for exploration or mining rights cannot be confident that they have foreseen all the difficulties and delays. For example, it is quite evident that the Legal and Technical Commission is required to take into account questions relating to the protection of the marine environment and the avoidance of pollution. There is no evidence in the literature that definitive studies have been made of the risks which seabed mining pose in terms of pollution and damage to marine ecology. Anyone who has followed the contests, in countries such as Australia and the United States, between groups wishing to develop mineral resources and groups wishing to prevent or curtail that development, will be aware that conservation issues can drag on for a long time, causing the postponement of the onset of mining. There would be considerable scope for conservationists to insist that a long period of expensive research was necessary before any commercial mining of the deep seabed should be authorized.

Eskin (1981, 6) in describing some of the considerations which persuaded President Reagan to order a review of the Law of the Sea Conference and American interests, noted that the Authority seems to have broad discretion which could lead to changes in the terms and conditions of mining rights, and that this introduced uncertainty into the American industry. Eskin also observed that there was no permanent or guaranteed place for the United States on the Council. This would mean that the United States, which could expect to be a major contributor to the funds levied for the Authority, and United States companies, which are in the forefront of seabed mining technology, would have no guaranteed voice except in the Assembly, where every country has an equal voice. Indeed, it is not possible to predict the composition of any of the Authority's organs except the Assembly. The Council consists of thirty-six members, who will be elected by the Assembly members. These elections will be for different groups representing various economic and geographical interests. Four members will be elected from those countries which during the previous five years have imported or consumed more than 2 per cent of the world's total imports or consumption of the commodities produced from categories of minerals derived from the deep seabed. In any case one of those members must be from socialist Eastern Europe. The countries which might be eligible in this group include the United States, Japan, Britain, West Germany, France, Italy, the Netherlands and the Soviet Union. Four other members will be selected from the eight countries which have the largest investment in preparation for and in the conduct of activities in seabed mining. Once again one of these members must be from socialist Eastern Europe. The other countries probably eligible for elections would be the United States, Japan, West Germany, France and the United Kingdom. Four members will be elected from the states which are the major net exporters of the categories of minerals derived from the deep seabed. It is stipulated that such exports must be derived from territory under the control of the state. It is a fine point whether only countries which produce and are major net exporters of all the minerals mined on the seabed can represent this group. If that is the correct interpretation then possible representatives would be Chile, Canada, Australia, Brazil, Zambia and Zaire. In any case two of the representatives from this group must be developing states who rely heavily for their economic prosperity on mineral exports. Six members will be elected to represent the developing countries, including those with large populations, those that are landlocked, major importers of minerals, and those which are potential producers of minerals which can be mined on the seabed. The remaining eighteen members will be elected to ensure an equitable geographical distribution of seats on the Council as a whole, and there must be at least one member from Africa, Asia, socialist Eastern Europe, Latin America and 'Western Europe and Others'. Apart from the arguments of where Africa ends and Asia begins, and whether Papua New Guinea is part of Asia, the region styled 'Western Europe and Others' is a curious one. Presumably it includes all those areas not specifically included elsewhere. So it would comprehend Western Europe, probably with Greece and Turkey, North America but not the non-Latin Caribbean, Australia, New Zealand and the countries of the southwest Pacific Ocean. If the various groups based on economic interests or geography can agree on the nominations to the Assembly, they will be elected, otherwise there appears to be no objection to the Assembly selecting any country in the group which is prepared to stand for election.

It would be very difficult to predict which states would be elected to the Council, and even harder to predict how the states with differing interests might combine in favour of particular policies. In view of the majorities which are specified for deciding certain substantive issues, it appears that each of the main groups are confident of winning at least a quarter or one-third of the seats. It is not clear on what that confidence is based as far as those countries with an interest in mining the deep seabed as soon as possible are concerned. Further, the Council appoints the members to the Economic Planning Commission and the Legal and Technical Commission, two bodies which will play a very important role in influencing the development of deep-seabed mining.

Finally, a long-term uncertainty is introduced by the provision in the Convention that a review conference will be held fifteen years after commercial mining of the deep seabed begins. The review conference will examine whether the Convention has achieved its aim to make deep-seabed mining benefit mankind as a whole; whether reserved areas available for the Enterprise, and unreserved areas used by other miners, have been developed and exploited in a balanced manner; whether seabed mining has been undertaken in a manner which fosters the healthy development of world trade and the international economy; whether monopolies have been prevented; and whether the benefits derived from The Area have been shared equitably, taking into particular consideration the interests and needs of developing states. The conference will reach decisions by consensus, but if that course fails to produce results within five years, the conference can decide by the support of three-quarters of the members to change the Convention, and those changes will be binding on all parties once two-thirds of those parties have ratified them.

Major attitudes to seabed mining
This provision plainly alarmed the government of the United States, and it is predictable that it will exercise the minds of planners and investors interested in the long-term operation of seabed mines. The long contest over the regulations governing mining on the deep seabed, which occupied parts of every session of the Law of the Sea Conference, was between two broad philosophies which were

supported by different groups of states for different reasons. The first philosophy considers the minerals of the seabed to be a resource which technology has now made available and which should be exploited without delay with the minimum of necessary international supervision. The second philosophy believes that these resources belong to a special world category which should be used so that the poor countries benefit most, and so that there is the minimum interference to the orderly marketing of existing supplies of minerals from mines on land. While as a general rule the developed countries favoured the first approach and developing countries preferred the second, the correlation was not perfect and within each group there were differences on how the aims of each group should be achieved.

Countries supported the early development of nodule mining for three reasons, which sometimes operated singly and sometimes in combinations. For some states the prime consideration centred on the financial benefits which it expected to secure from nodule mining. These countries usually contained companies with the technical and financial capacity to harvest these minerals and process them. Such activities would promote economic activity within shipyards and engineering workshops; generate employment opportunities; and ultimately provide taxes to the government. The main consortiums of companies conducting research into nodule mining are the Kennecott Group, with contributions from American, British, Canadian and Japanese companies; Ocean Mining Associates, with participation by American, Belgian and Italian companies; Ocean Minerals Company with involvement by American and Dutch companies; and Ocean Management Incorporated which includes American, Canadian, West German and Japanese companies. In addition to these groups the French government has a major interest in Association Française pour l'Etude et la Recherche des Nodules, and the Japanese authorities are deeply involved in the Deep Ocean Minerals Association, which includes thirty-nine companies covering trade, shipbuilding, steel-making, mining and electrical products.

Some countries favoured the early start to nodule mining because they needed to import nickel and cobalt. Where these minerals could be produced from the deep seabed by domestic companies it would mean that the country would save foreign exchange and improve its balance-of-payments position. Where alien companies would be the producers the importers could at least hope for reduced or stable prices for these commodities, and that would be particularly true for imports of cobalt. Some developed countries, which experienced discomfort during the 1970s when pressure was exerted by petroleum producers, would welcome any development which ensured that the production of important minerals was widely spread amongst the world community. The involvement of more countries in nickel and cobalt production at the same time offers opportunities for spreading purchases, and makes it harder for co-operative action amongst the producers for economic or political gain.

Countries which sought, and secured, strict controls over mining of the deep seabed were responding to a variety of motives. Some countries, lacking companies with the skills and funds to undertake research and mining, were determined to protect some areas of the seabed so that resources would still be available to exploit, if they should ever be able to participate in seabed mining. Some others were hopeful that their depressed economic circumstances could be alleviated with funds generated by the international authority. For this to happen it is clearly necessary for the activities of the miners to be carefully supervised by a body representing the interests of developing countries, and capable of enforcing the rules and collecting the royalties and taxes.

Some states insisted on strict production controls for seabed mining because they were fearful that their production of the same minerals on land would become less profitable. These countries not only sought to avoid any sharp increase in the supply of these minerals, they also demanded that they would be insured against loss by compensation payments for any damage caused to their export trade. Although few states would admit it, some countries wanted to restrict the incidence of seabed mining on the ideological grounds that it would probably benefit the developed countries most.

Possible future strategies

It is impossible to predict whether mining of the deep seabed will proceed in the foreseeable future. There seem to be three possibilities. The first is that some companies will be prepared to make a proposal to the Authority for exploration and mining rights in the belief that the first applicants will be most favourably treated. After all the Authority has a vested interest in there being applicants who will provide work for the bureaucracy; will provide the Enterprise with proven sites; will start paying fees and royalties to help fund the operations of the Authority and its various organs; and will transfer technology to the Enterprise so that it can have the chance to begin mining. Such companies might be encouraged by their national authorities either for reasons of national prestige or because it is considered to be a strategically useful activity. The strategic benefits might be found in securing domestic supplies of nickel or cobalt; or in exploiting an area of seabed which would otherwise fall to a competing country; or in the development of deep-water technologies which would have defence applications.

The second possibility is that some companies, encouraged by their national governments for strategic reasons, might be prepared to mine the deep seabed outside the framework of the Convention. The uncertainty of the response of the Authority or the United Nations, and the impossibility of knowing the outcome of any possible legal actions in international courts, would mean that any company set on this course would want very definite assurances from its national government.

The third possibility is that no companies will offer to work within the rules of the Convention, and none will be prepared to operate outside them, and it is left to the Enterprise to initiate mining of the deep seabed. That is probably the least likely development, because the Enterprise would not be able to compel the transfer of technology and would have to incur considerable expense in exploring and proving sites. Further, it is unlikely that the countries which have companies engaged in seabed mining research would be prepared to contribute the large share of levies to fund the Authority, if much of that money was to be used by the Enterprise. It seems more probable that if the Enterprise decides to give impetus to seabed mining it will do so by proposing a joint venture with some group on terms favourable to the group.

Unless such a joint venture is established, or unless countries decide for strategic reasons to encourage companies operated by their nationals to mine within or outside the Convention's framework, it appears unlikely that seabed mining for nodules will occur in The Area in the near future. However, it is possible that nodule mining will occur within the exclusive economic zones of some states. In the southwest Pacific Ocean there are a number of island states which consist of fragments of territory which rise steeply from the abyssal plain. Such territories include considerable areas of abyssal plain on which nodules may be found. The best example of such a territory is provided by French Polynesia which can claim an exclusive economic zone measuring 1,385,200 square nautical miles, most of which would consist of abyssal plain. Nodule harvesting in such an area would fall outside the scope of the Authority and would be subject only to bilateral agreements between the company and country concerned.

So far in the discussion attention has been focused on the terms of the Convention. It is now necessary to turn to a resolution which was passed by the Conference on the Law of the Sea at the same time as it adopted the Convention. This resolution governs preparatory investment in pioneer activities relating to polymetallic nodules. One of the express aims of this resolution is to make provision for investment by states or companies in relation to seabed mining during the period before the Convention enters into force.

Under the terms of this resolution the following countries are designated as being eligible to apply for pioneer status: France, Japan, India, Russia, Belgium, Canada, West Germany, Italy, Britain, the Netherlands and the United States of America. This eligibility rests on the countries, or companies within their territory, being engaged in activities concerned with discovery of nodule fields, and techniques for harvesting, transporting and processing the nodules, to the extent that they had spent at least $US 30 millions in these activities before 1 January 1983. Further, at least $US 3 millions had to be spent in the area for which a mining application is made.

Once the Preparatory Commission begins to function states may apply for pioneer status on behalf of themselves or companies owned by their nationals, and such application must be accompanied by a certificate of the level of expenditure. The application must also include details of a site not exceeding 300,000 square kilometres in area. The area shall be capable of supporting two equivalent mines, and the Commission will designate which area it will reserve for the Enterprise and which is available as the pioneer area.

Within six months of the Convention entering into force the applicant with pioneer status must submit a plan of work in accordance with the terms of the Convention. Those plans will be approved and when production quotas are authorized the pioneer companies and states will have priority over all other applicants.

In return for this privileged status the entities with pioneer ranking must fulfil the following additional conditions. First, a registration fee of $US 250,000 must be paid when the application for pioneer status is made, and a further equal amount must be paid when the plan of work is submitted. Second, the applicant must relinquish 20 per cent of the pioneer area three years after the date of allocation; a further 10 per cent of the area must be relinquished after five years; and finally, after another three years, an additional 20 per cent must be released to the Authority. Third, every registered pioneer investor shall carry out exploration in the reserved area, at the request of the Preparatory Commission, on the understanding that the costs incurred, plus 10 per cent of that figure, will be reimbursed. In addition the investor must provide training for all personnel designated by the Commission and undertake to transfer technology according to the terms of the Convention.

It remains to be seen whether these provisions are sufficiently attractive to persuade the countries concerned to seek the benefits and incur the responsibilities outlined. The only point which is clear at present is that the Soviet Union decided not to vote in favour of the adoption of the Convention precisely because this resolution was drafted. It is the view of the Soviet authorities that this resolution places it at a disadvantage. While Russia is likely to operate alone, the companies of other countries will often co-operate. Since only signatories to the Convention can sponsor pioneer applications Russia would have to be a signatory to obtain the benefits of this provision. However, a United States firm could be in association with a Japanese company, and providing Japan was a signatory, it could sponsor the joint American–Japanese application even though the United States did not adhere to the Convention.

The seas and seabed surrounding Antarctica

These areas have been included in the consideration of international maritime zones for reasons which distinguish them from the high seas and the deep seabed. The latter are unquestionably international maritime zones in existing international law and state practice. In contrast the status of waters and seabed around Antarctica is uncertain because of the following circumstances.

First, there are some claims to the territory of Antarctica, and while three of the claims overlap, there is one segment of the continent which is not claimed by any country. No maritime claims are enforced from the claimed sectors of Antarctica, and no baselines have been proclaimed around any of these coasts, where there are serious technical problems about identifying baselines in the terms of the Convention.

Second, the areas of seas and seabed are the subject of part of the Antarctic Treaty, to which a small number of countries adhere. Within the context of the

Antarctic Treaty conventions have been agreed, again by a few states, which apply to the economic use of living resources in the seas, and attempts are now being made to produce a convention dealing with the exploitation of mineral resources on and near the continent. The Antarctic Treaty is of uncertain duration, although it would be expected to last until at least 1995, and it adopts a completely neutral position to the question of national claims to Antarctic territory.

Third, some countries which are not members of the Antarctic Treaty take the view that national claims to parts of the continent will never gain popular international recognition, and that the present structure of the Antarctic Treaty is unsatisfactory for the future supervision of an area which like the deep seabed should be part of the common heritage of mankind.

It is now necessary to examine each of these circumstances in more detail, so that the unique complexity of these areas about Antarctica can be understood.

National claims in Antarctica

Seven states have laid claim to parts of Antarctica; they are Argentina, Australia, Britain, Chile, France, New Zealand and Norway. In chronological order the first formal claim was by Britain on 21 July 1908, when the Governor of the Falkland Islands was also appointed as Governor over South Georgia, the South Orkneys, the South Shetlands, the South Sandwich Islands and Graham's Land (Christie 1951, 301–2). These territories were defined as being bounded by the meridians 20° west and 80° west, and south of parallel 50° south. These lines on a map enclose part of the tip of South America, although the text made it clear that there was no claim in this direction. However, a correction was made in a new proclamation made on 28 March 1917; the area was defined as lying south of parallel 50° south between meridians 20° west and 50° west, and south of parallel 58° south between meridians 50° west and 80° west. On 26 February 1962 Britain detached those areas south of 60° south to form the British Antarctic Territory.

The boundaries of the Ross Dependency were created on 30 July 1923. For some years the Colonial Office in London had been seeking ways to extend British control over various regions of Antarctica, and it was decided to issue an Order in Council, under the British Settlements Act of 1887, and place the area under the authority of New Zealand. The limits of the Ross Dependency were set at 160° east and 150° west, and they have not been altered.

The limits of Australia's Antarctic Territory were fixed by another Order in Council dated 7 February 1933. This claim was located between 45° east and 160° east except for France's Adélie Land. Australia could not provide the precise meridians which separated Australia's claim from Adélie Land, because France had never announced what they were. Bush (1982, 481) has provided the most useful information concerning the evolution of the precise limits of Adelie Land. After enquiring on 20 December 1911 whether France claimed part of Antarctica, Britain was told quite firmly that France maintained its claim to Adélie Land. The French reply of 16 April 1912 noted that Commandant d'Urville's voyage and claims had been reported in various newspapers, including the *Sydney Morning Herald* of 13 March 1840.

A year later, on 29 March 1913, Britain advised France that it intended naming it King George V Land. The co-ordinates were given, and Britain noted that the area did not impinge on Adélie Land, which Britain understood to extend from 136° east to 147° east. Wisely, the French did not reply to this claim.

When the time came to define the boundary with Adélie Land there were three versions which Britain and Australia had considered. The 1913 letter set the limits at 136° east and 147° east. A report to the Imperial Conference of 1926 had left a gap in the proposed British claims between 135.5° east and 142° east. Mawson had claimed Australian territory during 1931 which left a French gap between 138° east and 142° east.

When the French declared the limits of Adélie Land for the first time, in a letter dated 24 October 1934 (Bush 1982, 498), they had selected 136° east and 147° east. This proposal was rejected by Britain which proposed 136.5° east and 142° east. They cited an official French chart of 1840 for this proposal. The French letter in reply on 5 October 1936 tried to trump the French chart with the British letter of 1913! It was pointed out that the chart had existed for seventy years before Sir Francis Bertie wrote his letter in 1913, and France was at a loss to understand the new interpretation. France proposed that the western boundary should be 136° east while the eastern boundary should be drawn between 142° east and 147° east.

The leisurely pace of the correspondence continued with a British reply on 13 October 1937. The French claim for territory east of 142° east was rejected, and the British authorities pointed out that Lord Bertie had relied on the *Sydney Morning Herald* of 13 March 1840, when 147° had appeared as a misprint for 142°. The Sydney report was based on a French report in a Tasmanian newspaper, and the French report had the correct co-ordinates. The French accepted the British suggestion and fixed the limits of Adélie Land between 136° east and 142° east on 1 April 1938.

Norway's first formal claim in the Antarctic was made on 23 January 1938, when a Royal Decree asserted sovereignty over Bouvet Island. On 1 May 1931 a similar claim was made to Peter I Island. Although Norwegian explorers were active in the area between British and Australian claims in the period 1926 to 1937, no formal claim to territory was made. That situation changed in 1938 when Germany sent the *Schwabenland*, commanded by Alfred Ritscher, to stake a claim in the vicinity of the Greenwich meridian. In a week planes were used to photograph 350,000 square kilometres of territory, on flights totalling 12,000 kilometres, during which the German flag was dropped every 25 kilometres. After receiving a recommendation from the Foreign Ministry on 14 January 1939, the Norwegian king, on the same day, proclaimed Norwegian sovereignty over the area between the British and Australian claims. Norway did not claim a sector of the continent because similar claims by the Soviet Union in the Arctic would act against Norway's interests.

After a long history of exchanges with Argentina, Chile declared the limits of its Antarctic territory on 9 November 1940. A claim was made to all lands, islets, reefs of rock and pack ice within the meridians 90° west and 53° west. The eastern boundary encompasses the South Shetland Islands which Chile asserted were discovered from Chile and formed part of its colonial forerunner.

When Argentina was advised of this claim it responded on 12 November 1940. The Argentinian note observed that Argentina could also make unilateral claims, but it did not think that such actions augmented incontestable rights. However, Argentina did not persist with this view and a map published by the Instituto Geográfico Militar in 1940 showed a claim to Antarctica south of parallel 60° south between meridians 75° west and 25° west. In a note to the British authorities on 15 February 1943 Argentina announced its limits, and the western boundary had been withdrawn to meridian 68° 34' west, which is the meridian nominated in the agreement with Chile of 23 July 1881 to divide the island of Tierra del Fuego.

In November 1946 Argentina signalled another change in its western boundary by producing another map under the authorship of the Instituto Geográfico Militar. The new western limit was meridian 74° west. This claim was expressed formally in an act to re-establish Argentina's national territory on 28 February 1957. The new boundary is close to the meridian which passes through the mountain Cerro Bertrand, which is the most westerly point in Argentina. The seven national claims, the zone claimed by Britain, Argentina and Chile, and the unclaimed zone between meridians 90° west and 150° west are shown in figure 5.10.

None of the seven claimant states has proclaimed baselines around any part of the coast of Antarctica. The Convention gives no guide to the construction of baselines around ice-bound coasts. The only reference to areas covered by ice is contained in Section 8 of Part XII which deals with the protection and preservation of the marine environment. Article 234, which constitutes Section 8, provides that coastal states have the right to enforce non-discriminatory measures to avoid pollution in ice-covered areas of the exclusive economic zone, where the severe climatic conditions cause hazards for navigation. The article goes on to justify this right because of the severe risks to marine ecology in cold regions. There is no generally agreed rule for drawing maritime boundaries around ice-bound coasts. In 1911 the Russian claim to territorial waters was measured from the line of the lowest ebb tide, or from the extremity of coastal standing ice (Jessup 1970, 27–8). While Fauchille (1925, 203–4) raised the question he did not attempt to provide the answer.

There is no simple answer, and there is little doubt that along any ice-bound coast, different scientists, lawyers, politicians and fishermen would propose different baselines. The suggestions would include limits of shelf and pack ice at different times of the year, and the line at which sea-level intersects rocks on the continent. None of these lines would be satisfactory because all would be difficult to determine. The limit of shelf ice around Antarctica is probably the most

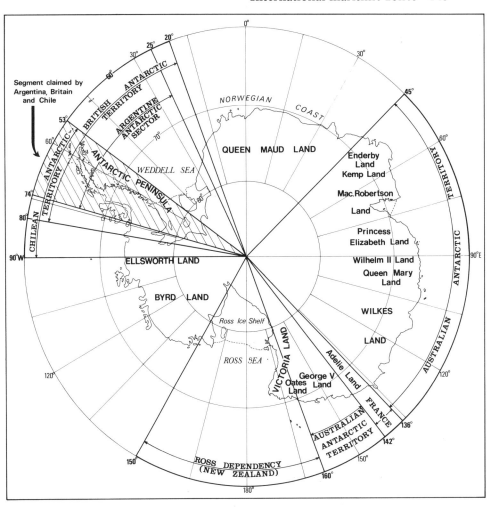

Figure 5.10   National claims in Antarctica

constant, but when icebergs are calved from the ice-edge it can cause a retreat of some kilometres. The outer edge of the pack ice would show wide seasonal variations in a single year and between comparable periods in different years. The line along which the contemporary sea-level intersects the continental rock structure can be identified, but it is an arbitrary line without any reasonable merit. If the rock coast was to be exposed by the removal of the ice then it is certain that the sea-level would be affected by the considerable increase in the volume of melt-water, and by the isostatic adjustment of the continent following the reduction in weight.

It has been suggested (Lovering and Prescott 1979, 193) that an answer to the problem might be found by examining the purpose of the maritime zones which are to be declared. Territorial waters designed to give the state protection from

spies, smugglers and illegal immigrants do not appear to be of any great significance in Antarctica, because the continent is hard to reach; there is no permanent
population to defend; it is not a potential haven for illegal immigrants whose act
of trespass would be fairly easily detected; and it does not represent a market
where contraband would yield high profits. By contrast the exclusive economic
zone about Antarctica could be valuable, especially in terms of living resources in
the sea. It is therefore important that the baseline should be positioned so that the
exclusive economic zone can be used by fishing vessels for a sufficient part of the
year. This means that the exclusive economic zone must include waters which are
free or comparatively free of ice during the summer months. Thus it would seem
sensible for coastal states in Antarctica to collect data about ice conditions on a
seasonal basis, and about the size and migration of fish stocks, so that the baseline
can be drawn in a location which gives fishing fleets access to extensive areas of
the exclusive economic zone.

In respect of claims to the continental margin, it appears that there would be
very few cases where states would need or wish to use the absolute limit of 350
nautical miles seaward of the baseline in assessing whether to select lines in
accordance with the two formulae based on distance and sediment thickness.
Generally, these formulae will produce limits which lie within 350 nautical miles
of the coast, or within 100 nautical miles of the 2500 metre isobath.

Although all seven states which claim sovereignty in Antarctica have declared
territorial waters, or exclusive economic zones, or fishing zones 200 nautical miles
wide around their metropolitan territory, and around detached possessions in
temperate areas, none has enforced such limits around Antarctica.

It is interesting to speculate on possible claims to the area lying between the
Chilean and New Zealand claims. The bases of sovereignty used by the seven
existing claimants include discovery, exploration, acts of annexation, and awards
by a fifteenth-century pope! In terms of discovery and exploration the United
States has the basis for a claim. Ellsworth and Hollick-Kenyon flew over part of
this area in 1935 and landed four times en route. Ellsworth claimed the sector
between meridians 80° west and 120° west for the United States at his first
landing, about 79° 15' south and 102° 35' west (Ellsworth 1937, 201). It is also
possible that Russia would consider making a claim. When the Soviet Union
accepted an American invitation to attend a conference which ultimately led to
the conclusion of the Antarctic Treaty, the formal reply noted that Russia
reserved all rights based on discoveries and explorations by Russian navigators
and scientists, including the right to present appropriate territorial claims on the
Antarctic (Hanessian 1960, 460). So long as there is no definite rule in international law about the basis on which territorial claims can be made, it is easy to
agree with Archdale (1958, 247) that Antarctica is no exception to the rule that
powers as well as individuals tend to support the law that suits their case. There
seems little doubt that if the United States or Soviet Union decided to make a
claim to part of Antarctica that an apparently impressive case could be presented
by either country.

The Antarctic Treaty

The intense competition for national control of the Antarctic Peninsula amongst Argentina, Chile and Britain prompted American initiatives to solve the difficulties, in 1947 and 1948. There were various proposals about placing the continent under a United Nations trusteeship agreement or an international condominium of interested states. The competitors gave different responses to the proposals and probably the most useful suggestion was made by Chile in the Escudero Declaration. It was proposed that territorial claims should be held in abeyance for five years, during which period international scientific co-operation should be encouraged.

During the debate which followed these proposals the Chilean idea was refined to include the provision that during the five years of scientific co-operation the establishment of bases would have no bearing on territorial claims. The Korean war distracted attention from this question, and then the International Geophysical Year gave impetus to its re-examination. In 1958 the United States started the process which led in December 1959 to the conclusion of the Antarctic Treaty; and it came into effect in 1961.

The provisions of this treaty apply to the area south of parallel 60° south including all ice shelves, but they do not infringe the rights which countries possess on the high seas. The main articles of the Antarctic Treaty deal with freedom of scientific enquiry and the exchange of information amongst scientists; the prohibition of using Antarctica for military purposes or nuclear explosions; the observation of the activities of one country by another state; and the accession of parties to the treaty.

The preamble to the treaty names twelve countries which are usually described as the consultative states. They are Argentina, Chile, Belgium, Britain, France, Japan, New Zealand, Norway, Australia, South Africa, the Soviet Union and the United States of America. These countries have the right to take part in consultative meetings which are held approximately every two years. Other countries can accede to the treaty, but they may only send observers to the consultative meetings, unless, by virtue of substantial scientific activity in Antarctica, they are raised to full membership of the treaty. While East Germany, Czechoslovakia, Romania, Denmark and the Netherlands have acceded to the treaty, Brazil, India, Poland and West Germany have become consultative members, on the strength of their substantial research activities on the continent.

Article IV deals with the issue of territorial claims, and it provides that the treaty cannot be interpreted as diminishing any territorial claim or prejudicing the attitude of any country to recognition of territorial claims. The article further stipulates that no activities during the life of the treaty can be used to substantiate or enlarge existing claims, to deny any sovereign claims, or to provide a basis for new claims.

In the various consultative meetings since 1961 the members of the Antarctic Treaty have fashioned a number of arrangements to govern co-operation over communications on the continent, to protect and preserve the environment, and to regulate the use of Antarctica and the surrounding seas for economic purposes. It is to this last matter that attention must now be directed.

In 1968 a working group prepared a draft convention for the regulation of pelagic sealing. It was a detailed document and followed precise recommendations of the Scientific Committee on Antarctic Research (*Polar Record* 1969, 670–5). When the matter was raised at a subsequent meeting of the consultative parties, it was decided that the conservation of seals in the sea did not fall within the terms of the Antarctic Treaty (*Polar Record* 1971, 730). The members then decided to organize a conference in London to deal with this question, and the Convention for the Conservation of Antarctic Seals (Treaty series, 1978) entered into force on 11 March 1978. This Convention followed earlier drafts very closely and specified total permissible catches in each year as 175,000 crabeater seals *Lobodon carcinophagus*; 12,000 Leopard seals *Hydrurga leptonyx*; and 5000 Weddell seals *Leptonychotes weddelli*. A total prohibition was placed on the killing of Ross seals *Ommatophoca rossi*; Southern elephant seals *Mirounga leonina*; and fur seals of the genus *Arctcephalus*. The closed season was set from 1 March to 31 August, except for Weddell seals older than one year, when the closed season was extended to 31 January. Three zones were designated as reserves within which the taking of seals was prohibited. These areas were found around the South Orkney Islands between parallels 60° 20′ south and 60° 56′ south, and meridians 44° 5′ west and 46° 25′ west; in the southwest Ross Sea south of parallel 76° south and west of meridian 170° east; and the area of Edisto Inlet, south and west of a line joining Cape Hallett and Helm Point.

Six zones for sealing were designated; they were between meridians 0° and 70° east; 70° east and 130° east; 130° east and 170° west; 170° west and 120° west; 120° west and 60° west; and 60° west to 0°. This last zone also included that part of the Weddell Sea lying west of meridian 60° west. Each of the zones will be closed, in turn, for one open season; this means that at such times the zone will be closed from 1 March to 31 August the following year. Members whose nationals engage in sealing are required to provide statistical details of number of vessels, size of crews, numbers of days′ operations, numbers of adult and pup seals of each species taken, and biological information about those seals.

After the reduction in whaling in waters around Antarctica it was evident that commercial fishing in the region was becoming increasingly important. At the same time fears emerged that the harvesting of krill, which is a red shrimp-like crustacean, and which occupies a central position in the marine food chain, might threaten the marine ecosystem. The Ninth Antarctic Treaty Consultative Meeting in 1977 approved a proposal that rules should be devised to protect and conserve marine living resources in Antarctic waters. The Convention for the Conservation of Antarctic Marine Living Resources was agreed at a meeting in Canberra in May 1980, and it came into force on 7 April 1982 after being ratified by Australia, Japan, the Soviet Union, Chile, South Africa, the United Kingdom, the United States and New Zealand.

The Convention applies to the waters covered by the Antarctic Treaty, that is those seas south of 60° south, and to the waters between this parallel and the Antarctic Convergence. This important marine border occurs when the northward flowing cold Antarctic water meets and sinks under the warmer, southward moving sub-Antarctic waters (Lovering and Prescott 1979, 32). The Convention defines the location of the Convergence by a series of parallels and meridians, which are shown in figure 5.11. In fact the location of the Antarctic Convergence will vary with seasonal conditions, and at different times the defined lines will include some waters lying north of the Antarctic Convergence, and exclude some lying south of that border.

The conservation principles on which the Convention is based seek to prevent any decrease in the size of any harvested population to levels below those which ensure its stable recruitment; to maintain the ecological relationships between harvested, dependent and related species; and to prevent changes in the marine ecosystem which are not reversible within twenty or thirty years. It is the task of a Commission established by the Convention to oversee the operation of these principles. It is empowered to designate quotas of species which may be harvested, to declare open and closed seasons, and to set aside special areas for scientific study on conservation. Such actions must be taken in the light of data which the Commission is empowered to collect, and of scientific advice from the scientific committee for which the Convention also provides. It was clearly understood during the negotiations that in setting quotas for harvestable species the Commission was required to take into account the possible effects on the natural predators of the species (Australian Department of Foreign Affairs 1981, 16). By the time the permanent secretariat to support the Commission had been established in Hobart, Tasmania, in August 1982, East and West Germany and Argentina had also ratified the Convention.

The Final Act of the conference which settled the details of the Convention included a statement relating to islands, included within the area covered by the Convention, over which the existence of state sovereignty is recognized by all members. The statement specifically dealt with the Kerguelen and Crozet Islands, and noted that conservation measures adopted by France before the Convention entered into force would continue to apply, until modified by France. This stipulation would also presumably apply to Australia's Heard and McDonald Islands, South Africa's Prince Edward and Marion Islands, and Norway's Bouvet and Peter I Islands. Because Britain's claim to the Falkland Island Dependencies is challenged by Argentina, it may be presumed that this provision does not apply in those cases.

The question of developing a system to supervise mining was raised at the meeting of members of the Antarctic Treaty in Buenos Aires in 1981. A recommendation was then made to the governments concerned dealing with mineral resources in Antarctica. The representatives were plainly concerned that while at present there are no viable economic mineral deposits on the continent or its surrounding continental shelf, there was a possibility that exploration and exploitation in the future might damage the spirit of international co-operation and the

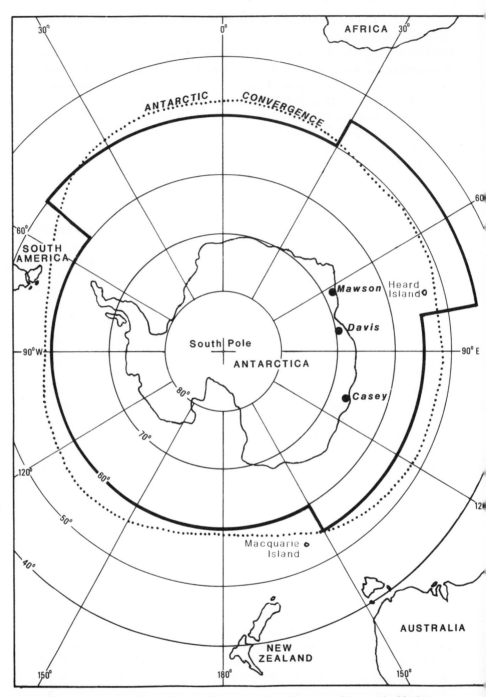

Figure 5.11 Area to which the Convention on the Conservation of Antarctic Marine Living Resources applies

environment. The recommendations stressed the unity of the continent and its offshore areas; affirmed that the protection of the Antarctic environment and its dependent ecosystem was a basic consideration; and asserted that the regime developed must be acceptable to the claimant and non-claimant states, without prejudicing the interests of all mankind. The main requirements of the regime which were set out included means for assessing the impact of mining on the environment; for determining whether such mining would be acceptable; and for governing the ecological, technological, political, legal and economic aspects of acceptable activities. There is plenty of evidence that it will take a long time to fashion an effective set of rules, to the satisfaction of both claimant and non-claimant states. Fortunately there is no evidence that mining on the continental shelf of Antarctica is likely to occur in the next decade. It seems likely that before that time passes, critical questions will be posed about the future of the continent and its surrounding seas by the countries which are not members of the Antarctic Treaty.

It has proved difficult to decide the boundary within which the minerals regime should apply. Before considering the alternatives it is necessary to note one fundamental point. Some countries believe that the offshore areas of Antarctica form part of The Area under the terms of the Convention. They argue that since there are no coastal states in Antarctica with recognized sovereignty, there can be no offshore areas subject to national jurisdiction. In that case The Area extends to the shores of Antarctica.

There are two objections to this view. First, it is well known that the subject of Antarctica was never raised at the Conference on the Law of the Sea, because of the conviction that such considerations would distract the delegates and prevent any satisfactory conclusion from being reached. Thus the Convention cannot possibly deal with Antarctica and its offshore areas since the subject was deliberately excluded from examination. The second objection rests on the fact that the Convention describes only one situation when exclusive economic zones and continental shelves may not be claimed from land. This exception concerns rocks which cannot sustain habitation or an economic life of their own. This exception clearly does not apply to Antarctica.

If the Treaty survives and the minerals regime is created then one of the following boundaries might be selected. First, the boundary could be claimed that would be appropriate if national claims were made from Antarctica. Such a boundary would be chosen by the application of one of the formulae related to the foot of the continental slope.

Second, the minerals regime could be applied south of 60° south, but this parallel would encompass areas of the seabed which would fall to The Area if national claims were made from Antarctica. It would also enclose submarine areas which could be claimed from the South Sandwich Islands and Heard and McDonald Islands. Third, the boundary could simply be defined as a line connecting fixed points in the manner of the boundary enclosing the area for conserving living resources.

The uncertain political future

It seems that before the end of this century the most critical question about the politics of Antarctica must be faced and answered. That question is whether parts of the continent and adjoining offshore waters and seabed will be reserved for national control or use, or whether the entire continent and its offshore areas will be subject to international supervision by a body wholly representative of the world community. The chance that these two possibilities are not mutually exclusive is discounted. It is inconceivable that national claims by Chile and New Zealand, recognized by the world community, should be separated by an international area occupying Marie Byrd Land. Nor is it possible to imagine a continent divided into national territories washed by international waters, or an international continent surrounded by segments of waters where individual states have exclusive economic rights.

It is not possible to predict how or when the question will be answered. Perhaps a rising level of demands by countries outside the Antarctic Treaty for the continent to become part of the common heritage of mankind will cause serious rifts between groups within the Treaty. Perhaps the growing conviction that the resources of Antarctica and its offshore areas are very valuable will lead some of the claimant states to assert exclusive rights in a forceful manner. Equally, it is possible that firm conclusions about the poverty of Antarctic resources, or the certainty that they will never be economically exploited, might lead most of the claimant states to abandon positions of sovereignty. Possibly a majority of members of the Assembly or the Council created to supervise the deep seabed beyond national control will pre-empt the debate by insisting that the area under its jurisdiction extends to the coast of Antarctica, since those submarine areas are beyond national control.

It is possible to be more definite about the political problems which will be faced by the assertion of national or international control over Antarctica.

The most difficult problem involved in the assertion of national sovereignty will concern the disputed claims of Argentina, Britain and Chile. The events in the Falkland Islands and their dependencies in 1982 make it apparent that these claims are resolutely held and defended. Further, the bitter wrangling between Argentina and Chile over islands in the Beagle Channel gives no promise of an early settlement to their conflicting claims to the Antarctic Peninsula.

The technical problem of drawing baselines has been mentioned. Once that problem was solved there would be the serious political problem of settling limits between national maritime claims. This would first involve careful charting of all the features around the coast from which maritime claims could be made. Obviously the simplest solution would be to extend the meridians, which define the national sectors, seawards. Otherwise it would be necessary to negotiate either equidistant or equitable boundaries seawards. That would take much longer and in some cases the area available for particular states would not be increased over allocations secured by using meridians. For example, lines of equidistance between French and Australian claims are both deflected east of the bounding meridians, by approximately the same angle. In the same manner, what New Zealand gains at the expense of Australia because of the Balleny Islands, it loses because of the alignment of the coast of King Edward VII Land.

Any country which succeeded in making good its claim to part of Antarctica and the offshore areas would then face the difficulty of designing rules for the exploitation of the surrounding waters, so that the ecosystem was protected and pollution of the region avoided. Plainly there would also be more difficult logistic problems than usual in supervising economic activities by nationals and aliens in these remote waters.

Some indication of the problems which would face attempts to convert the Antarctic Treaty into a more widely based international authority is provided by the difficulties which attended the negotiation of the rules dealing with the deep seabed beyond national control. The following topics are only the most important which would be raised in debates designed to fashion international control of Antarctica.

First, should economic exploitation be permitted? Nations would divide in different ways depending on whether biological or mineral resources were being considered. There would be some countries with strong conservation lobbies, which would urge that no economic exploitation on land or sea should be permitted. Other developed countries, such as Japan and the Soviet Union, might well favour fishing, in which they are already engaged, but oppose mining. Developing countries, especially those which are very poor, might strongly support the maximum economic use of the region, providing the distribution of benefits was weighted heavily in favour of landlocked and geographically disadvantaged states. Oil-producing countries might well oppose drilling for petroleum and natural gas around Antarctica because of the impact any finds might have on international oil prices. If they were unable to sustain their opposition they might seek controls over levels of production, or the maintenance of minimum prices, or financial compensation for any proved losses to export income.

If it was eventually decided that some economic use should be permitted, it would be necessary to decide who should be allowed to harvest or mine the resources. It seems probable that the parallel solution adopted in the Convention would also be applied here. This would mean that exploitation could be undertaken by national entities as well as by the international authority. The issue of the price to be paid for rights to exploit these waters would also cause some disagreements. Those countries without skills and ability would try to set the price as high as possible, while the developed countries wanting fishing or mining leases would seek to discount the price because of the difficult environment, the need to spend large sums on research, and the risks to which capital investment was exposed. It is certain that any agreement reached on this matter would include a section on the transfer of technology from developed to developing countries.

A wrangle would seem unavoidable over the question of voting rights in the executive organ of the international authority. Blocs of states sharing common interests would try to ensure that they held voting strengths which enabled them to veto any proposals which were against their interests. The kinds of blocs which might emerge would include developed states with the desire to exploit resources; countries concerned to protect the environment of Antarctica against significant change; landlocked and geographically disadvantaged states; oil-producing countries; and fish-exporting states.

Perhaps the existing structure of the Antarctic Treaty might provide a basis for negotiating a new arrangement which will win wide acceptance from the world community, although the provisions dealing with sovereignty would have to be deleted. An additional problem would be presented by South Africa's full membership of the treaty. This situation would be regarded as unsatisfactory by a number of Third World countries. In any case, if a new comprehensive international treaty was adopted by consensus for Antarctica and the surrounding waters there would be the problem of the status of sub-Antarctic islands owned by Australia, Britain, Norway, France and New Zealand. If the countries concerned insisted on maintaining their control over such islands there would be the need to harmonize conservation regulations in the waters claimed from them, and in the waters around the continent. In the case of the Balleny Islands, Heard and McDonald Islands, the South Orkney Islands and Peter I Island, it will be necessary for boundaries to be determined around the outer edge of their maritime claims. In respect of the Australian islands it would only be necessary to fix a continental shelf boundary; the other islands are less than 400 nautical miles from the mainland and thus the limits of their exclusive economic zone would need to be fixed. Presumably the countries concerned would have to negotiate with the international authority.

Conclusions

When statesmen consider the three international maritime zones of the high seas, the deep seabed, and the waters around Antarctica, they must have a declining level of certainty about the rights of nations in these areas and the political problems which they will engender.

The rights to sail and fish in the high seas, and the details about the way in which these activities should be conducted, have been settled for a comparatively long time. There is a body of case law to which reference can be made in complex situations. The rules about the deep seabed have been agreed only recently and there is no certainty about the manner in which these rules will be interpreted, or about which states will decide to observe them. While the Antarctic Treaty has existed for more than twenty years only a few countries have adhered to it.

Since the Second World War the area of the high seas, which are those seas beyond national claims, has been greatly reduced by claims to fishing zones, territorial seas and exclusive economic zones 200 nautical miles wide. The remaining area consists of a number of enclaves, and there are some deep culs-de-sac of high seas between national claims. This pattern of high seas creates problems for states with adjoining national claims, which seek to control alien activities.

The area of the deep seabed is smaller than the extent of the high seas, because the latter overlap some national claims to the continental margin. There is great uncertainty about the extent to which those companies with the skill and resources to mine manganese nodules will respond to the rules contained in the Convention. There is probably equal uncertainty about the manner in which these rules will be interpreted by the organs of the Authority. In this respect the attitudes of the United States, West Germany and Japan will be critical, although it seems possible that the present economics of seabed mining will discourage early ventures into this field.

Antarctica is now coming into clearer international focus. It was not a major issue when the Law of the Sea was being debated, but the conclusion of that debate frees diplomatic energies to examine Antarctica and at the same time provides arguments favouring a wider international approach to the continent. Since the high seas and deep seabed are those areas beyond national control, it would not be unreasonable to argue that they both extend to the coast of Antarctica. The Indian expedition which landed on the continent on 9 January 1982 is only the most recent, visible demonstration of the Third World in the southern continent. The only certain prediction seems to be that this interest will continue to grow.

References

Alexander, L. M. and Hodgson, R. D. (1975) 'The impact of the 200-mile Economic Zone on the Law of the Sea', *San Diego Law Review*, 12, 569–99.

Archdale, H. E. (1958) 'Claims in the Antarctic', *Yearbook of World Affairs*, 12, 242–63.

Australian Department of Foreign Affairs (1981) *Special Antarctic Treaty Consultative Meeting and the Conference on the Conservation of Antarctic Marine Living Resources*, Canberra.

Bacon, F. (1857) 'Essay of the true greatness of kingdoms and estates', in Whately, R. (ed.) *Bacon's Essays* with annotations, London, 286–95.

Bardach, J. E. and Matsuda, Y. (1980) 'Fish, fishing and sea boundaries: tuna stocks and fishing policies in Southeast Asia and the South Pacific', *GeoJournal*, 4–5, 467–78.

Bush, W. M. (1982) *Antarctica and International Law*, 3 vols, London.

Cable, J. (1971) *Gunboat Diplomacy: Political Applications of Limited Naval Force*, London.

Christie, E. W. H. (1951) *The Antarctic Problem*, London.

Crutchfield, J. and Pontecorvo, G. (1969) *The Pacific Salmon Fisheries: A Study of Irrational Conservation*, Baltimore.

Driver, P. A. (1980) 'International fisheries', in Barston, R. P. and Birnie, P. (eds) *The Maritime Dimension*, London, 27–53.

Earney, F. C. F. (1980) *Petroleum and Hard Minerals from the Sea*, London.

Ellsworth, L. (1937) 'The first crossing of Antarctica', *Geographical Journal*, 84, 193–213.

Eskin, O. E. (1981) 'Statement by the Director of Ocean Law and Policy for Oceans and International Environmental and Scientific Affairs', presented to the 15th Annual Conference of the Law of the Sea Institute, 6 October 1981, Honolulu.

Fauchille, P. (1925) *Traité de droit international public* [Treatise on public international law], Paris.

Flipse, J. E. (1981) 'The economic viability of deep ocean mining', unpublished paper presented to the 15th annual conference of the Law of the Sea Institute, 6 October 1981, Honolulu.

Hanessian, J. (1960) 'The Antarctic Treaty 1959', *International and Comparative Law Quarterly*, 9, 436–80.

Jefferson, T. (1904–5) *The Writings of Thomas Jefferson*, ed. A. A. Lipscomb, 20 vols, London.

Jessup, P. (1970) *The Law of Territorial Waters and Maritime Jurisdiction*, New York.

Kent, Sir P. (1980) *Minerals from the Marine Environment*, with contributions from N. C. Fleming, London.

Lovering, J. F. and Prescott, J. R. V. (1979) *Last of Lands: Antarctica*, Melbourne.

Luttwak, E. N. (1974) *The Political Uses of Seapower*, Baltimore.

McKelvey, V. E. (1980) 'Seabed minerals and the law of the sea', *Science*, 209, 464–72.

O'Connell, D. P. (1975) *The Influences of Law on Seapower*, Manchester.

Pardo, A. (1978) 'The evolving law of the sea: a critique of the Informal Composite Negotiating Text (1977)', in Borgese, E. M. and Ginsburg, N. (eds) *Ocean Yearbook I*, Chicago, 9–37.

Pemsel, H. (1975) *A History of the War at Sea: An Atlas and Chronology of Conflict at Sea from Earliest Times to the Present*, Annapolis, Md.

Polar Record (1969) 'Report of the fifth Antarctic Treaty Consultative meeting, Paris 1968', 14, 663–75.

Polar Record (1971) 'Report of the sixth Antarctic Treaty Consultative meeting, Tokyo 1970', 15, 729–43.

Rawson, M. D. and Ryan, W. B. F. (1978) *Ocean Floor Sediments and Polymetallic Nodules*, a world map, equatorial scale 1:23 M, US Department of State, Washington, DC.

Reynolds, J. O. (1982) 'Deep sea mining and the regime of the new Convention', unpublished paper presented to a seminar on the Law of the Sea organized by the Australian Branch of the International Law Association and the University of New South Wales School of Law, Sydney, 19 June 1982.

The Geographer (1973) *World Shipping Lanes*, equatorial scale 1:41.5 M, Washington, DC.

6

The Indian Ocean

The Indian Ocean has become a British lake.   (Bowman 1928, 44)

Since the opening of the twentieth century, the Atlantic and Pacific Oceans have been the primary theatres of history for the people of the United States. Two world wars and lesser conflicts have been fought on those oceans and on the continents they separate. As we approach the final quarter of the twentieth century, however, it is increasingly clear that the Indian Ocean is becoming the new arena of political conflict.   (Harrigan 1975, 19)

The Indian Ocean conference of left-wing movements in April 1978, which had focussed on demilitarising the Indian Ocean, had provoked the wrath of the super powers bent on dominating the region. And imperialism proceeded to recruit counter revolutionaries to plot an overthrow of the progressive government of President René (Seychelles). Their aim is to create puppet regimes throughout the Indian Ocean.   (*Africa Research Bulletin* 1978, 4852)

Decolonization of the shores of the Indian Ocean proceeded at a slower pace than in the other oceans. Now, apart from some of the debris of empires, such as the French islands in the Mozambique Channel and the British Indian Ocean Territory in the Chagos Archipelago, the shores belong to independent countries. Further, the Indian Ocean is distinguished by the fact that its shores are occupied by developing countries to a greater extent than any other ocean.

If the Indian Ocean is considered to lie north of the Antarctic Convergence, it has a maximum west–east extent of 4200 nautical miles and a maximum north–south extent of 3700 nautical miles. While the main body of water scarcely extends north of the Tropic of Cancer, the extensions provided by the Red Sea and the Persian Gulf reach to 30° north.

Tchernia (1980, 202) notes that the Indian Ocean may be divided into two parts to the north and south on the grounds of meteorological conditions, general circulation and hydrology. The monsoon regime, which is characterized by a reversal of wind direction, dominates the climate of the Indian Ocean north of 10° south. This system is generated by the extensive regions of Eurasia and influenced in its effect by the proximity of the African continent. The alternation of northeast winds in January and southwest winds in June in the northern region makes it the only extensive oceanic area which experiences a seasonal reversal of surface currents to match the changes in wind direction. The salinity of the northern region is less uniform than in the southern region because the Arabian Sea is made more saline by the outflow of water from the concentration basins provided by the Red Sea and the Persian Gulf, where there is an excess of evaporation over precipitation, and because the Bay of Bengal and the waters between Australia and Indonesia are made less saline by heavy precipitation, by the discharge of the Ganges and Irrawaddy Rivers, and by intermixing with waters from the Pacific Ocean with a lower level of salinity. The offshore winds provided by the monsoon regime produces the upwelling of cold waters rich in nutrients off the coasts of southeast Arabia, Somalia and western India. This activity promotes the growth of exceptional blooms of plankton, which can sometimes be so extensive that they deprive the water of oxygen and cause the death of fish.

The southern region falls mainly under the influence of the sub-tropical high pressure belt which is centred about 27° south in June and about 35° south in January. This more consistent pressure pattern is matched by a fairly constant wind pattern which produces a system of surface circulation which varies only slightly throughout the year. The levels of salinity in the southern zone increase gradually towards the Antarctic, and the southern seas generally have a higher content of dissolved oxygen and a lower concentration of nutrients.

When the submarine morphology of the Indian Ocean is considered the major apparent division is into east and west regions. In the vicinity of meridian 70° east there is a mid-ocean ridge which is extended northwards by the Chagos-Laccadive Plateau. To the east of this prime feature there are three major basins. The Central Indian Basin is encountered first and is bounded by the Ninety East Ridge, which takes its name from the meridian with which it coincides. Between the Ninety East Ridge and the Java Trench is located the Wharton Basin, and south of Australia lies the South Australian Basin. In the western region there is a more complex pattern of basins. Proceeding from north to south there are the Red Sea Basin, the Arabian Sea Basin, the Somali Basin, the Mascarene Basin off the east coast of Madagascar, the Madagascar Basin to the southeast of that island, the Crozet Basin, the Mozambique Basin and the Aghulas Basin off southeast South Africa. Although the division of sediments on the seabed does not correspond exactly with the mid-ocean ridge, the eastern seabed is generally covered with red clay, while globigerina ooze occupies most of the western area.

The more complex submarine topography in the western Indian Ocean compared with the eastern zone is also reflected in the number of islands in the two regions. If the island chains in Indonesia which mark the northeastern edge of the Indian Ocean are discounted, then it is plain that the largest number of islands *in* the Indian Ocean are located in the western sector. The archipelagos of the Maldives, Laccadives, Mauritius, Seychelles, Comoros and Madagascar, together with the southern islands belonging to South Africa, France and Australia, outnumber by a considerable margin the Andaman and Nicobar Islands, Sri Lanka, and Cocos and Christmas Islands.

This structural division into eastern and western regions is reinforced when the political nature of the littoral states is examined. First, around the western zone there are twenty-seven littoral countries, compared with seven bounding the eastern zone. Also, in the western zone are all the territories still owned by European powers or in special association with them. France owns islands in the Mozambique Channel, as well as Réunion, Amsterdam and St Paul Islands, and the Crozet and Kerguelen Groups. In addition, Djibouti and Mayotte are in a special relationship with France. Britain's possessions are now restricted to the islands comprising the Chagos Archipelago.

Second, there is a much higher level of political conflict in the western than in the eastern region. The civil wars in Afghanistan and Ethiopia; the international conflict between Iran and Iraq, the periodic disturbances in the Middle East and along the Somali–Ethiopian border, and the general hostility directed against South Africa find no equivalent in the eastern region now that India and China seem prepared to talk about their territorial and other problems. Also in the western region there are disputes over the ownership of islands involving Britain and Mauritius, Iran and the United Arab Emirates, Iraq and Kuwait, Bahrain and Qatar, the two Yemens, France and Mauritius, France and the Comoros, and France and Madagascar. The only possible dispute over ownership in the eastern region would concern Narcondam Island, which Burma sometimes appears to covet from its neighbour India.

While the Indian Ocean is bordered by wide continental margins on either side of the Indian subcontinent, south of Madagascar and northwest of Australia the continental shelves form only a small part of those margins. Off northwest Australia there is an extensive continental slope, while in the other localities named there is a wide continental rise. The continental margins are particularly narrow off the coasts of southeast Arabia.

The three quotations at the head of this chapter illustrate that while Britain once briefly dominated the Indian Ocean, it is now an arena for international competition and sometimes conflict. That competition exists both between the Soviet Union and the United States, and between some countries in the region. As the third quotation illustrates there are also traces of competition between developed and developing countries.

The main strategic interest of the great powers in the Indian Ocean centres upon the productive oilfields of the Persian Gulf. This important energy region for developed countries was forced into sharp focus during the rapid rises in oil prices in 1973, and a concern was generated which persisted through the partial glut of oil in the early 1980s. The western world, led by the United States, has a vested strategic interest in ensuring that this prime oil region does not fall under the control of states potentially hostile to their continued progress. Equally, the western powers must ensure that the movement of petroleum across the oceans will not be hindered. Therefore there has been concern with those sections of the Indian Ocean where international straits are located. The Straits of Hormuz, Bab al Mandab and Malacca, and the Mozambique Channel, are zones where the seaways narrow to a degree which would make them targets for hostile naval action. The decline in importance of the Suez Canal as a route used by oil tankers has made the Strait of Bab Al Mandab less important. The development of large tankers occurred during the period 1967–75 when the Suez Canal was closed and vessels had to make a detour around the Cape of Good Hope, which added 4850 nautical miles to the journey to Europe and 3300 nautical miles to the journey to the east coast of North America. These longer voyages encouraged the development of very large tankers. The Egyptian government is trying to regain some of the lost tanker traffic by widening and deepening the canal. By 1978 the depth of 19.5 metres (64 feet) allowed the passage of loaded vessels up to 150,000 deadweight tonnes. Further, in the four years from 1982 it is intended to increase the width of the canal by 70 metres (229 feet) and its depth by 4 metres (13 feet) to allow vessels of 260,000 deadweight tonnes to sail through. If these efforts are successful then the Strait of Bab al Mandab will become more important in the strategic planning of major powers.

Claims to maritime zones

Table 6.1 lists littoral states according to the suite of maritime zones which they claim. This table deals only with the territorial seas, contiguous zones and fishing or exclusive economic zones, which are all measured from a common baseline. Claims to the continental margin are considered separately. The thirty-six states and dependent territories form fourteen groups when classed according to their maritime claims.

Bahrain, Jordan and Qatar claim only the minimum territorial seas 3 nautical miles wide. While there would be little practical point in Jordan claiming any wider zones from its extremely narrow coast on the Gulf of Aqaba, facing the opposite Egyptian and Israeli coast not more than 8 nautical miles distant, there seems to be no obvious reason why the other two states should continue to persist with the claim inherited from Britain. The British Indian Ocean Territory forms a group by itself; to the territorial seas 3 nautical miles wide has been added a fishing zone measuring 12 nautical miles. The lack of population on the Chagos Archipelago might be the reason for this modest claim to an economic zone. These islands are still claimed by Mauritius, although the importance of the Anglo-American base on Diego Garcia suggests that the claim will not be fulfilled. The islands were detached from the territory administered from Mauritius in 1965, three years before Mauritius became independent. The disagreement between Britain and Mauritius has been sharpened since the election of a new government in Mauritius in 1982. Although this government has accepted the compensation offered by Britain to the resettled islanders, it has reserved its position on the question of sovereignty.

Israel is also the solitary member of a group since it claims only a territorial sea 6 nautical miles wide. When Israel made this claim in 1956 it did so because most states in the Mediterranean claimed such seas. Indeed Turkey still claims 6 nautical miles along its Mediterranean coast and 12 nautical miles along its

Table 6.1 Maritime claims in the Indian Ocean

Countries	Territorial sea	Contiguous zone	Exclusive economic or fishing zone
Group 1	3	—	—
Bahrain			
Jordan			
Qatar			
Group 2	3	—	12
British Indian			
Ocean Territory			
Group 3	3	—	200
Australia			
United Arab Emirates			
Group 4	6	—	—
Israel			
Group 5	12	—	—
Ethiopia			
Iraq			
Kuwait			
Group 6	12	18	—
Egypt			
Saudi Arabia			
Sudan			
Yemen (Sana'a)			
Group 7	12	—	50
Iran			
Group 8	12	—	200
Comoros			
France			
Indonesia			
Kenya			
Mauritius			
Mozambique			
Oman			
Pakistan			
Seychelles			
South Africa			
Thailand			
Group 9	12	18	200
Bangladesh			
Group 10	12	24	200
Burma			
Djibouti			
India			
Sri Lanka			
Yemen (Aden)			
Group 11	50	—	—
Tanzania			
Group 12	50	—	150
Madagascar			
Group 13	200	—	—
Somalia			
Group 14		Irregular	
Maldives			

Source: Author's research.

Black Sea shores. By the end of 1982 Greece was the only other state in the Mediterranean claiming this width.

Australia and the United Arab Emirates both claim territorial seas 3 nautical miles wide and a fishing or exclusive economic zone 200 nautical miles wide. The United Arab Emirates would only be able to claim the full economic zone from the coast of Dhufar on the Arabian Sea.

Ethiopia, Iraq and Kuwait compose a group which claims only a territorial sea 12 nautical miles wide. These countries are located on narrow seas where wider claims would be unrealistic. The sixth group consists of four states in the northern part of the Red Sea; Egypt, Saudi Arabia, Sudan and Yemen (Sana'a) claim territorial seas 12 nautical miles wide and a contiguous zone which extends for 18 nautical miles from the baseline. This means that the contiguous zone forms a band 6 nautical miles wide outside the territorial seas. The Egyptian and Saudi claims were made in 1958 and Yemen (Sana'a) and Sudan followed suit in 1967 and 1970 respectively. In fact the Saudi and Egyptian proclamations, on 16 and 17 February respectively, anticipated and exceeded the proposals contained in the Convention on the Territorial Sea and the Contiguous Zone, which was agreed in April 1958. This Convention only permitted claims to a contiguous zone measuring 12 nautical miles from the baseline; thus any state claiming territorial seas 12 nautical miles wide was effectively prevented by the Convention from claiming any contiguous zone. Iran, with a claim to territorial seas of 12 nautical miles and to a fishing zone in the Gulf of Oman 50 nautical miles wide, forms a separate group.

The next three groups share the common claims of territorial waters 12 nautical miles wide and economic zones 200 nautical miles wide; they differ in claims to a contiguous zone. The largest group, consisting of the Comoros, France, Indonesia, Kenya, Mauritius, Mozambique, Oman, Pakistan, Seychelles, South Africa and Thailand, do not claim any contiguous zone. Bangladesh is the only state in the group which claims a contiguous zone 18 nautical miles wide. The other five states, Burma, Djibouti, India, Sri Lanka and Yemen (Aden) make the orthodox claims according to the Convention. To the territorial seas of 12 nautical miles and the economic zone of 200 nautical miles has been added a contiguous zone of 24 nautical miles, which is the maximum permitted.

The remaining four groups each consist of a single member. On 24 August 1973 Tanzania increased its claim to territorial seas from 12 nautical miles to 50 nautical miles. On the same day an economic zone of the same width was announced; this means that effectively Tanzania has only a single zone 50 nautical miles wide. One month after Tanzania's declaration Madagascar also increased its territorial sea from 12 to 50 nautical miles. It also simultaneously proclaimed an economic zone, but this measured 150 nautical miles wide. Somalia is one of fourteen countries which claims territorial seas 200 nautical miles wide; this proclamation was made on 10 September 1972, and, perhaps not surprisingly, no other maritime zones are claimed.

The final group is represented by the Maldives, and its claims can only be described as irregular. Rather than treat the claims of the Maldives here and refer later in this chapter to other aspects such as baselines and overlaps with claims from the British Indian Ocean Territory, it is proposed to consider the general question of the Maldives maritime zones now. There are three problems associated with the maritime boundaries delimited by authorities in the Maldives. The first concerns the status of the constitutional rectangle; the second deals with the definition of the outer edge of the exclusive economic zone; and the third relates to apparently disputed waters between the Maldives and the British Indian Ocean Territory.

In the 1964 constitution, the territory of the Maldives was defined as the islands and the air and sea surrounding and in between the islands, contained within a rectangle formed by meridians and parallels. In 1972 the rectangle was amended so that the meridians were 72° 30′ 30″ east and 73° 48′ east, and the parallels 7° 9′ 30″ north and 0° 45′ 15″ south. At no point does the constitutional rectangle touch any of the territory of the Maldives (The Geographer 1978). As figure 6.1 shows, the northern limit passes within 1 nautical mile of the reef surrounding Ihavandiffulu Atoll, while the eastern boundary lies within a similar distance of Felidu Atoll. It is not known whether the authorities consider this frame to be a floating baseline, although the definition of a fishing zone in February 1969 and of territorial waters and a fishing zone in December 1970, and of an exclusive economic zone in December 1976, produced limits which were parallel to the edges of the constitutional rectangle. There is no evident historic justification for these meridians and parallels, which on the west and east respectively pass 52 and 38 nautical miles from the nearest land. The Maldives would be able to draw archipelagic baselines. The ratio requirement would be satisfied by the provision in the Convention which allows waters within fringing reefs of atolls to be counted as land. However, the use of archipelagic baselines would give little advantage to the Maldives because of the linear arrangement of the islands.

It appears that the outer edge of the exclusive economic zone has been drawn by measuring 200 nautical miles due east and west of the meridians which bound the constitutional rectangle. In the south the parallel line is set at a distance of 197 nautical miles. The novel development is simply to project these lines until they meet, so that the constitutional rectangle is surrounded by an exclusive economic rectangle, except in the north where a boundary has been negotiated with India. This means that the corners of the outer boundary, in the southwest and southeast, are 280 nautical miles from the nearest points on the constitutional rectangle and 310 nautical miles from the nearest land.

Although the Maldives has apparently claimed only 197 rather than 200 nautical miles in the south, the claim still impinges on areas which are closer to the northern territory of the British Indian Ocean Territory. The total area involved is 21,600 square nautical miles. So long as Britain uses the territory for strategic purposes only it may not trouble to contest this area. A different situation would occur if Mauritius ever regained the Chagos Archipelago and decided to colonize it in order to reduce pressure on restricted land in the present territory of Mauritius.

There are seven groups of states when claims to the continental margin are

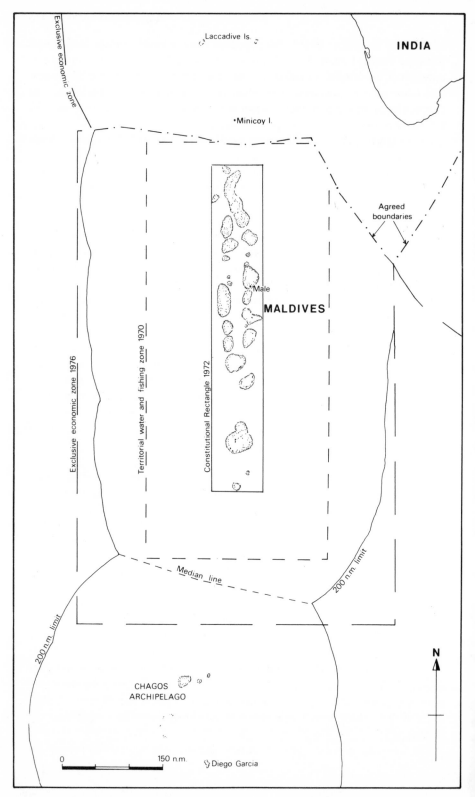

Figure 6.1 The Maldives' maritime claims

considered. Australia, Egypt, Madagascar, Oman, South Africa, Sudan and Thailand have all made their claims in terms of the 1958 Convention on the Continental Shelf. The limits set in that document were either the 200 metre isobath or such depths as would permit the exploitation of natural resources. Egypt, Oman and Sudan adopted this standard without adhering to the 1958 Convention.

Yemen (Sana'a) and Pakistan adopted only part of the 1958 definition. Yemen (Sana'a) set its claim at the 200 metre isobath, which Pakistan interpreted as the 100 fathom line. Meanwhile two countries, Indonesia and Israel, adopted the second part of the 1958 Convention and claimed the continental margin out to the limit of exploitability.

The limit of 200 nautical miles or the edge of the continental margin, specified in the Convention, has been used by Burma, India, Mauritius, Seychelles, Sri Lanka and Yemen (Aden). Bangladesh since April 1974 has claimed the continental margin to the outer limits of the continental margin bordering on the ocean basin or the abyssal floor.

Nine countries have made claims to the continental margin which are not specific; they are the seven countries around the Persian Gulf other than Oman, and Kenya and Tanzania. The remaining nine states or territories make no specific claim to the continental margin, but seven of them have claimed 200 nautical mile exclusive economic zones which would comprehend all the available continental margin off their coasts. The other two, Ethiopia and Jordan, face narrow seas or gulfs where continental shelf claims would not be appropriate.

The use of straight baselines

The possibility that the Maldives authorities are using the constitutional rectangle as straight baselines has been noted, but there are ten other states which have definitely employed straight baselines along all or part of their coast. They are Australia, Bangladesh, Burma, Djibouti, Ethiopia, Indonesia, Kenya, Madagascar, Mozambique and Thailand. Where the scale permits these baselines are shown in figure 6.2. The baselines of most of the countries are completely orthodox and conform to the spirit and the letter of the 1958 Convention on the Territorial Seas and Contiguous Zone, and the new Convention. Mozambique inherited a set of conservative baselines drawn by the Portuguese colonial authorities in August 1966. The Australian baselines were not drawn until 1982 because of delays in negotiations between the federal and Commonwealth governments. The Indonesian baselines, drawn in February 1960, are the only archipelagic baselines in the Indian Ocean. Although they were drawn long before the rules for such baselines were codified in the Convention, they satisfy the rules, which could almost have been designed from the Indonesian model.

Three baselines must be distinguished for special comment. In April 1974 Bangladesh proclaimed a set of straight baselines measuring 221 nautical miles.

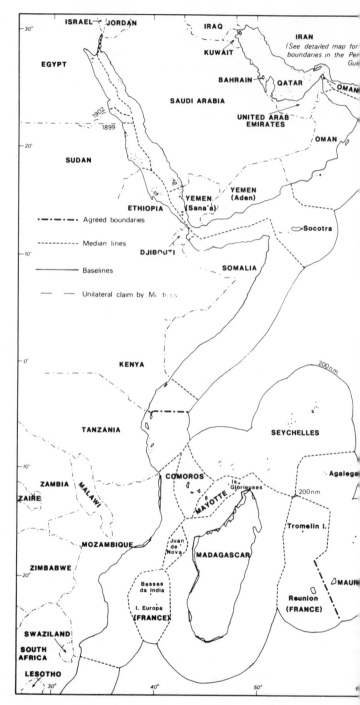

Figure 6.2 Agreed and potential boundaries in the Indian Ocean

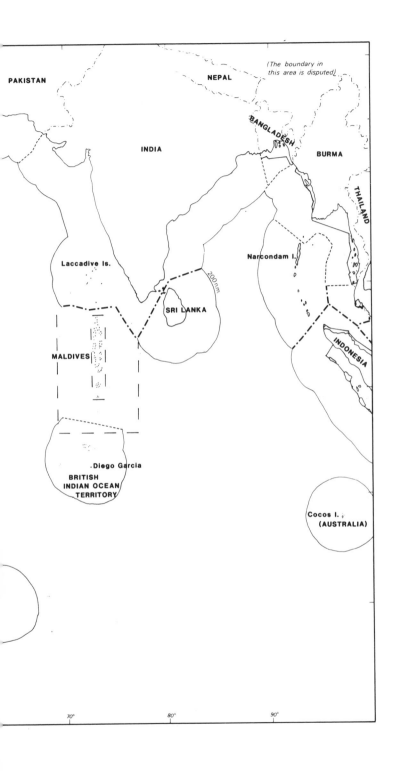

PAKISTAN

NEPAL

(The boundary in
this area is disputed)

BANGLADESH

INDIA

BURMA

THAILAND

Laccadive Is.

Narcondam I.

200 nm

SRI LANKA

INDONESIA

MALDIVES

.Diego Garcia

BRITISH
INDIAN OCEAN
TERRITORY

Cocos I.
(AUSTRALIA)

70°   80°   90°

None of the eight points which define these baselines is located on land. The line appears to follow the course of the 10 fathom line, except west of Cox's Bazar where there is a deep landward indentation of this isobath. No justification seems possible for this baseline. Even if the coast of the Ganges delta was considered to be unstable and liable to retreat, that is no justification for fixing the baseline as much as 50 nautical miles seaward of the nearest land. Because this baseline is not anchored to the coast it would be technically possible to sail into the internal waters of Bangladesh without crossing the straight baseline.

The representative of Bangladesh circulated a letter to the eleventh session of the Conference on the Law of the Sea in which he drew attention to the peculiar geomorphological conditions off the shore of the Ganges delta. He noted that wide fluctuations in the low-water mark and extensive areas of shallow water meant that the area could not be charted in the usual way. It was further observed that apart from the channels leading to the ports of Chalna and Chittagong the area was not navigable. In letters circulated two days later, on 30 April 1982, the Burmese and Indian delegations rejected this defence of its actions by Bangladesh. This reaction seems quite reasonable, because acceptance of the baselines would mean that lateral boundaries between Bangladesh and its neighbours were deflected in favour of Bangladesh. By claiming this baseline Bangladesh has sought to convert 6200 square nautical miles of potential exclusive economic zone into territorial and internal waters.

The Burmese baseline, proclaimed in November 1968, extends along the entire coast of the country. In 1977 it was amended slightly to include West Canister Island as a turning point instead of Cabusa Island. The baseline was justified by reason of the geographical conditions prevailing along the coast and to safeguard vital economic interests. While Burma has not adhered to the 1958 conventions, parts of its baselines are apparently against the letter and spirit of the new Convention. First, the closing line for the Gulf of Martaban is 222 nautical miles long, which is nearly ten times the accepted closing distance for a bay. It is possible that the Gulf of Martaban could be claimed as an historic bay, but the Burmese declaration did not use this option. Second, while there are fringing islands along the Tenasserim Coast it is evident that the guiding principle on which the baselines were drawn was to connect the outermost islands. This view is strengthened by the fact that West Canister Island was the only one seaward of the baselines when they were first proclaimed. In drawing these baselines, especially between Great Western Torres and the Haycock, it appears that no thought was given to satisfying the requirement that the seas lying within the lines must be sufficiently closely linked to the land domain to be subject to the regime of internal waters.

Ethiopia drew baselines around the Danlac Archipelago in September 1952, six years before the 1958 Convention on the Territorial Sea was devised. If the baselines simply tie the archipelago to the Eritrean coast there is no difficulty. However, if it surrounds the archipelago then it may be in breach of the new Convention.

Six countries in the Indian Ocean have proclaimed legislation which would permit the construction of straight baselines, without actually defining any line. They are Egypt, Mauritius, Oman, Saudi Arabia, Somalia and Sudan. As a general rule these proclamations follow the 1958 Convention fairly closely, but there is a less restrictive interpretation of bays which may be closed, and certainly the Saudi and Oman statements would permit submerged shoals and banks to be used as points in a baseline system.

The other countries in the region have not proclaimed straight baselines, and perhaps that fact reflects the generally smooth coasts around the Indian Ocean. It appears from inspection that only the Comoros could draw archipelagic baselines. Three lines could connect Grand Comore, Anjouan and Moheli; the longest would measure 76 nautical miles and the ratio of water to land would be 1:3.9. The islands of Réunion, Seychelles and Mauritius are too widely scattered to produce a ratio of water to land less than 9:1, and Madagascar is too big to produce a ratio of water to land in excess of 1:1.

Agreed international maritime boundaries

There are no agreed international maritime boundaries in the Red Sea, and in the following discussion the agreements in the Indian Ocean and the Persian Gulf are treated separately.

Since April 1971, when Australia and Indonesia agreed on a continental shelf boundary, there have been eighteen international agreements concerning the delimitation of maritime boundaries in the Indian Ocean. They have involved only eleven countries. Indonesia has been most active, being a party to ten of the agreements, followed by India and Thailand, which are parties to eight and six agreements respectively. In some cases a single boundary has been the subject of more than one agreement; thus there are three agreements dealing with the continental shelf boundary between Australia and Indonesia, and a further three dealing with India's continental shelf boundary with Indonesia. Ten of the agreements deal with the continental shelf, while others deal with historic waters, economic zones and territorial waters.

When the location of the agreed boundaries is inspected it is evident that the east–west political dichotomy, which was mentioned earlier, is once again evident. Sixteen of the eighteen agreements are located in the eastern part of the Indian Ocean. In the western sector the only agreements separate the economic zones of Réunion and Mauritius and the various maritime zones of Kenya and Tanzania.

These boundary segments have not been constructed according to a single principle. Some, such as the continental shelf boundary between India and Indonesia and the boundary separating the maritime zones of Burma and Thailand, follow a median course, so that each country secures the waters and sea-bed which are closer to its territory than the territory of any other state. Six of the agreements are based entirely on the principle of equidistance; they concerned India's boundaries with Sri Lanka and the Maldives, Réunion's boundary with

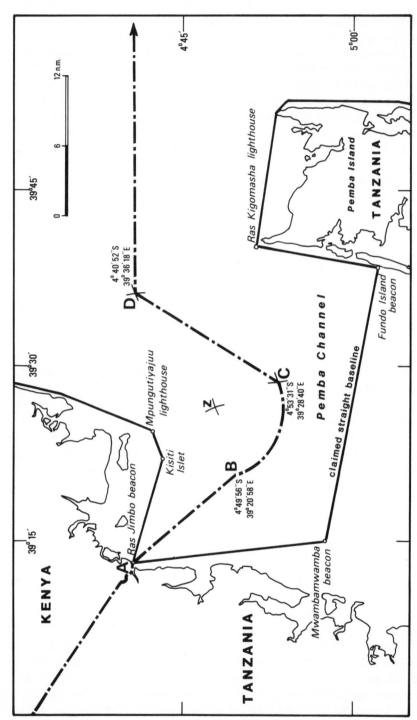

Figure 6.3 The maritime boundary between Kenya and Tanzania

Mauritius, and the two boundaries already mentioned. The other agreements produced marine boundaries which connected some equidistant points and some which were closer to one of the states than the other. The boundary between Kenya and Tanzania is typical of this category of boundary, as figure 6.3 shows.

The two countries agreed on a boundary which separates their various maritime zones on 9 July 1976, when Tanzania replied to an earlier note from Kenya dated 17 December 1975 (The Geographer 1981, 1). This boundary consists of four parts. The first section A–B is a median line drawn between the Tanzanian base-line between Ras Jimbo beacon and Mwambamwamba beacon and the Kenyan baseline linking Ras Jimbo beacon and Kisiti Islet. The third section, which must be constructed before the second section can be identified, is a straight line joining the two intersections of arcs with a radius of 12 nautical miles described from Mpungutiyajuu lighthouse and Ras Kigomasha lighthouse, which belong to Kenya and Tanzania respectively. This third section is shown by the points C and D. The second section joining points B and C is an arc of a circle with a radius of 6 nautical miles. The centre of this arc is shown as point Z, and it is obtained by finding the northernmost intersection of circles with a radius of 6 nautical miles described about points B and C. The fourth section of the line is coincident with the latitude of point D. The completed boundary, which terminates at the outermost limit of the national jurisdiction of the two states, thus consists of two equidistant sectors, A–B and C–D, and two sectors which favour Kenya, B–C and the line east of D.

There are seven agreed boundaries in the Persian Gulf and they all separate areas of the continental margin. Saudi Arabia and Bahrain agreed on a boundary to separate their continental margins in an agreement signed February 1958. The boundary is defined by fourteen points, some of which are equidistant, and measures 99 nautical miles. An unusual feature of this agreement is the Fasht Bu Saafa Hexagon, which measures 358 square nautical miles. This is a zone which is managed by Saudi Arabia, which then makes half of any revenue derived available for Bahrain. An agreement was reached between Saudi Arabia and Iran on 24 October 1968; it defined their continental shelf boundary for 139 nautical miles. Some of the points were equidistant, but offshore islands were generally dis-counted. Soon afterwards Qatar and Abu Dhabi drew a continental shelf boundary on 20 March 1969 without using any equidistant points. Dayyinah Island, which belongs to Abu Dhabi, was not given full effect, and the two countries agreed to share the revenue derived from the al Bunduq field which lies close to the boundary between Dayyinah and Das Islands (figure 6.4); Abu Dhabi has the responsibility of supervising this field.

Qatar signed another agreement, this time with Iran, on 20 September 1969. The short boundary was defined by five equidistant points which were drawn with reference to the mainlands of each state; offshore islands were ignored. As in a number of similar cases the terminus of the line in the west could not be decreed, because it forms a trijunction with claims from Bahrain. The bearing of the most westerly segment of the Iran–Qatar line was specified. When Iran and Bahrain

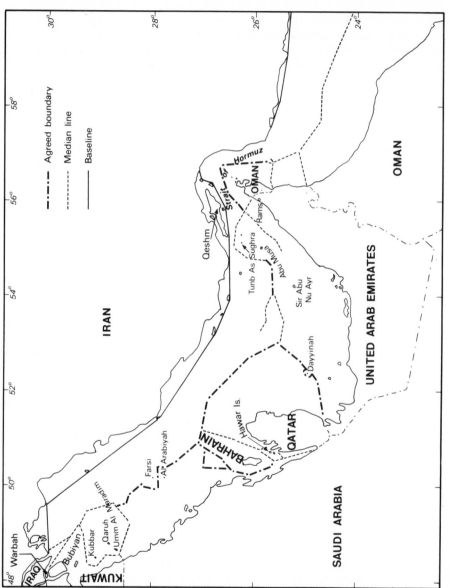

Figure 6.4 Agreed and potential boundaries in the Persian Gulf

agreed on a shelf boundary on 17 June 1971 it was still impossible to fix the trijunction in the absence of agreement between Bahrain and Qatar. However, the second agreement repeated the same alignment for the most easterly segment as Iran and Qatar used, so the trijunction is now simply a matter for Bahrain and Qatar to decide. Iran continued its efforts to fix all its limits, and on 25 July 1974 an agreement with Oman was announced which drew a boundary for 125 nautical miles; twenty-one points, most of which were equidistant, defined the line. The termini were simply defined as points along a bearing from the most eastern and western points. The former will depend on the Oman–Ras Al Kaymah boundary and the latter on the Oman–Sharjah lateral line. Only a month later, on 31 August 1974, Iran agreed on a shelf boundary with the United Arab Emirates, in the sector belonging to Dubai. This boundary measures 39 nautical miles which appears to be equidistant from the mainlands. Curiously the boundary is closer to Sharjah's island Sir Abu Nu Ayr than to any territory of Dubai.

In all these agreements the parties agreed that there would be consultation regarding the exploitation of any petroleum or gas field which straddled the boundary drawn on the continental shelf. This is a sensible precaution which most continental shelf agreements appear to include.

Actual and potential maritime boundary problems in the Persian Gulf

Five characteristics of the Persian Gulf influence the construction of maritime boundaries. First, the waters are shallow and the seabed contains many proved and more suspected gas and petroleum fields. The maximum depth of 60 fathoms presents no problems to modern drilling and production technology, but this accessible nature of the seabed means that fringing states are anxious to secure their full entitlement to the continental shelf. Second, the Persian Gulf is fairly narrow, with a maximum width of 150 nautical miles along the meridian which passes through Hendorabi, and a minimum width of 28 nautical miles in the Strait of Hormuz. This means that no state can claim an economic zone of 200 nautical miles without impinging on claims from an opposite state. Further, the presence of islands in the Gulf will require some territorial sea boundaries to be negotiated.

The third relevant characteristic is that the coast of the Persian Gulf, which stretches for about 2300 nautical miles, is comparatively smooth. There are few bays which satisfy the tests for closing lines; those which exist are found mainly on the coast of Saudi Arabia between parallels 26° and 28° north. Only two sections of coast could be described as deeply cut into or indented and they are located on the west coast of Qatar and around the Musandam peninsula, which forms part of Oman south of the Strait of Hormuz. The fourth characteristic is that while there are many islands in the Persian Gulf they tend to be small and located close to the coast. The islands of Bahrain and Qeshm are the largest in the Gulf. The small size of the islands and their low density means that there are few locations where islands could be considered to fringe the coast in its immediate vicinity. Thus the construction of baselines tying islands to the coast is probably only appropriate for the United Arab Emirates, west of Abu Dhabi, and for Iran on the northern edge of the Strait of Hormuz. Only a few islands are near the middle of the Gulf. North of Bahrain the islands called Farsi and Al Arabiyah, which belong respectively to Iran and Saudi Arabia, are distant from the coast; east of Qatar, as the Gulf narrows towards the Strait of Hormuz, there are a number of small islands close to the middle of the Gulf which belong to Iran and the United Arab Emirates. Some of the islands close to the coast cause boundary complications because they are claimed by two adjacent states, or because they deflect the median boundary in favour of one state.

The last characteristic concerns the political division of the littoral around the Persian Gulf. There is a sharp contrast between the north coast, which is occupied entirely by Iran, and the south coast which is divided amongst seven states. This arrangement means that the pattern of boundaries consists of a single central limit separating Iran's claims from all the others, and then five transverse boundaries linking the southern coast and the central line, and separating the adjacent claims of the seven southern states.

There are four disputes related to rival claims to islands in the Persian Gulf. At the head of the Gulf there is a disagreement between Iraq and Kuwait over the ownership of islands called Bubiyan and Warbah. These flat islands with swampy shores have been formed by alluvial deposition; Bubiyan Island is 44 kilometres long and 21 kilometres wide, while Warbah Island is 11 kilometres long and 3 kilometres wide. This latter island is located only 2 kilometres off the coast of Iraq. Before Kuwait became independent in 1961 Iraq claimed the entire territory of Kuwait, and two years passed before Iraq recognized the independence of its neighbour, without abandoning its claim to the islands. There would be clear advantages for Iraq if it possessed these islands. It would be less shelf-locked than it is at present, and it would have areas where oil terminals and other facilities could be constructed. Iraq is reported to have requested a long lease of the islands in exchange for recognition of Kuwait's ownership of them, but the matter is still unresolved.

The islands called Kubbar, Qaruh and Umm Al Maradim are disputed by Kuwait and Saudi Arabia. These three islands lie off the coast of the former neutral zone which formed part of the border between the two countries. When the zone was divided in 1965, and that dividing line modified in 1973, no provision was made to divide ownership over the islands. The three islands command about 2000 square nautical miles if lines of equidistance are drawn around them. It is possible that the solution will not be for one state to succeed entirely in its claim, but for the islands to be divided, or for the area attached to them to be controlled jointly by Kuwait and Saudi Arabia.

Bahrain and Qatar have a disagreement over which state owns the Hawar Islands, which lie close to the west coast of Qatar. There is one large and twenty small islands. The dispute was raised in 1936 when Bahrain was in the process of negotiating oil concessions. The British Resident of the time supported Bahrain's view that the islands and islanders had always been subject to the ruler of Bahrain. Qatar contested the claim, mainly on grounds of proximity, but Britain judged in 1939 that the islands belonged to Bahrain. This opinion, and a similar one in 1947, also by Britain, were rejected by Qatar and the matter is still unsettled. Saudi Arabia has made some efforts to arbitrate in this dispute, which does not seem to have impaired relations between the two claimants.

The fourth dispute over islands arose in 1971 when Iran annexed the islands called Tunb As Sughra, Tunb Al Kubra and Abu Musa, which had previously been regarded as part of Sharjah, a member of the United Arab Emirates. Sharjah's objections to this annexation have failed to restore authority over the islands and although Iraq has championed Sharjah's cause the islands remain firmly under Iranian control. The area which would fall to the islands if lines of equidistance were drawn is about 1500 square nautical miles.

There is also a dispute between Oman and Ras el Khaymah, which is one of the United Arab Emirates. Oman claimed a stretch of the Gulf coast 17 kilometres wide, which extends to the village of Rams and includes the port of Khawr Khuwayr.

Another point of dispute concerns the terminus of the Iraq–Iran boundary, from which their common marine boundary will be constructed. In 1981 and 1982 the two countries fought an intermittent war over the question of the alignment of their boundary. According to the second Treaty of Erzurum in 1847, Turkey, which then controlled the area occupied today by Iraq, secured control of the Shatt Al Arab which is formed by the confluence of the Euphrates and Tigris Rivers. Persia, the other party to the treaty, secured the towns of Abadan and Khorramshahr. With the assistance of British and Russian cartographers the two countries agreed on a closer definition of the boundary by 1914, when a Protocol signed in Constantinople confirmed that the boundary was along the Persian bank of the river, except in the vicinity of Khorramshahr. In 1934, after some disagreements over the rights of passage for Iranian ships, the boundary was also shifted from the bank to the median line in the vicinity of Abadan.

In June 1975, with the assistance of mediation by President Boumédienne of Algeria, Iraq and Iran signed a new Protocol which moved the boundary to a median line, drawn when the water level is at the lowest level to permit navigation. This Protocol defined the seaward terminus as 29° 51.20' north and 48° 48.68' east (The Geographer 1978, 7). The matter was thrown into fresh doubt in September 1980 when Iraq abrogated this latest agreement and war broke out.

Potential problems in the Red Sea

The structure of the Red Sea makes it less attractive as a target for oil and natural gas exploration. The faulted structure of both littorals, which extends to the seabed, does create some structural traps but also creates avenues by which hydrocarbon deposits can leak away. This is a zone of active tectonic movement as

Africa and Arabia appear to be diverging around the hinge of Suez. While the deep axial trough in the Red Sea contains some rich metallic brines, the technology to extract these metals, at a price which will compete with mines on land, is not yet available.

There are three potential problems concerning marine boundaries in the Red Sea and they all involve islands. The first concerns Egypt and the Sudan. The Anglo-Egyptian Agreement of 19 January 1899 fixed the eastern boundary between the two territories as parallel 22° north. On 4 November 1902 an Arrêté created an administrative arrangement whereby the Egyptian authorities governed some tribes south of the parallel 22° north in the Nile valley, while the authorities in the Sudan controlled certain coastal tribes north of the same parallel. This administrative boundary reaches the Red Sea 100 nautical miles northwest of the point where the parallel 22° north intersects the shore. It is not clear which of these two termini should be the starting point for any common maritime boundary. Nor is it clear what the status of islands off this section of coast would be if the northern terminus was selected. Egypt might argue that while the administrative boundary had now been accepted on the mainland, at no stage did it deal with the offshore areas.

Further north, in the mouth of the Gulf of Aqaba, lie two islands called Tiran and Sinafir, which used to form part of the Ottoman Empire. In 1950 Egypt, apparently with Saudi Arabia's agreement, occupied the islands. In 1957 Saudi Arabia informed the government of the United States of America that it claimed the islands. In 1967 Israel's forces occupied the islands, and the Camp David agreement required the return of the islands to Egypt as part of Zone C. This is the zone which will be supervised by Egyptian police and United Nations forces.

Karaman Island is located off the coast of Yemen (Sana'a); it is 22 kilometres long and 10 kilometres wide, and except on the east coast, where there is a harbour, the island is ringed with reefs. During the sixteenth century the island was the centre of Portuguese activities in the Red Sea, then it passed to the Turks, who lost it to Britain in 1915. As a British possession it was administered as part of the Colony of Aden, and it remained with that territory when it became independent in 1976, as Yemen (Aden). Unfortunately for that state forces from Yemen (Sana'a) have occupied Karaman Island and refuse to relinquish their control. If Yemen (Aden) ever secures the return of the island and settles boundaries with Yemen (Sana'a), the waters around Karaman will stand as an enclave set in the maritime zone of Yemen (Sana'a).

Potential and actual problems in the Indian Ocean

There are four problems concerning the ownership of islands apart from the claim by Mauritius to the Chagos Archipelago. In the Mozambique Channel there are a number of French islands which are coveted by Madagascar and the Comoros.

The Mozambique Channel is about 900 nautical miles long, with a narrowest width of 230 nautical miles, and there are islands spaced regularly throughout its length. In the northern mouth are the Comoros, the Aldabra Group of the Seychelles, and the French territories of Mayotte and Iles Glorieuses. At the southern end are Bassas da India and Ile Europa, which both belong to France, and in the middle of the Channel is Juan de Nova, another French possession. The problems of drawing maritime boundaries in the Mozambique Channel are complicated by a number of factors. First, the Channel is used extensively by large tankers plying from the Persian Gulf to Europe and North America. Second, Madagascar has claimed the French islands of Iles Glorieuses, Ile Europa, Bassas da India and Juan de Nova. Third, the decision of Mayotte to secede from the Comoros, because the citizens wished to preserve a special relationship with France, was unpopular with many African leaders. Finally, some of the best fishing grounds are located between Madagascar and Mayotte.

If the boundaries were drawn as lines of equidistance according to the present pattern of ownership, Madagascar and Mozambique would share a common line for only 60 nautical miles. Elsewhere the central part of the Channel would fall to the various island groups. This arrangement would be unsatisfactory to Madagascar at least, which claims Iles Glorieuses, Ile Europa, Bassas da India and Juan de Nova. These islands have no permanent residents but weather stations are located on them and the crews are rotated on a regular basis. The authorities in Madagascar argue that these four islands form an integral part of Madagascar on grounds of geographical proximity, history and law, and many Third World countries have found these arguments sufficiently persuasive to give support to United Nations General Assembly resolution (34/91). According to this resolution France is invited to initiate negotiations with Madagascar for the reintegration of the four islands with Madagascar. France takes the view that these four islands were unoccupied territory when acquired by France, and were administered from Madagascar for reasons of convenience until that territory became independent. Furthermore, the French government believes that consideration of this matter by the United Nations constitutes interference in its internal affairs and therefore is contrary to the Charter of the United Nations.

East of Madagascar another French island is claimed, this time by Mauritius. Ile Tromelin, which measures only 1 square kilometre, is situated north of Réunion, from which it is administered. Mauritius claims the island on the grounds that it was part of the territory administered by Britain from Mauritius. According to Mauritius, the French obtained permission from Britain in 1954 to build an airstrip and a weather station on the island, but this agreement did not transfer sovereignty. The weather station still has a French crew which is regularly changed. It is interesting that in the agreement between Mauritius and France, which settled the seabed boundary between Mauritius and Réunion in April 1980, the northern terminus of the line is a point which is equidistant from Réunion, Mauritius and Ile Tromelin (The Geographer 1982, 4). It seems certain that Mauritius refused to allow any northward extension of the boundary pending settlement of the disputed status of Ile Tromelin.

A problem has arisen between India and Bangladesh over a new island which was formed off the Ganges River delta. It is about 5 nautical miles offshore and was first noted in 1971 by the Indian navy. The island, which is in the shape of a letter U, had an area in 1978 of about 3 square nautical miles, but it appeared possible that it would grow larger. The problem arises because the island is off the mouth of the Harinbhanga River, which marks the boundary between the two countries. According to the Award by Lord Radcliffe in 1947 the boundary follows the district boundary between Khulna and 24-Parganas (Prescott 1975, 321). India claims the island on the grounds that the flow of the Harinbhanga River is to the east of the island, and that the island lies on the natural prolongation of Indian territory. Bangladesh replies that the river flows to the west of the island and that it is not possible to distinguish the natural prolongation of India and the natural prolongation of Bangladesh. In the view of the authorities in Bangladesh it is only possible to speak of the natural prolongation of the Ganges River Delta. This island is called New Moore or Purbasha by Indian sources, and South Talpatty by those in Bangladesh. It appears that the ownership of the island is a matter of greater importance for Bangladesh than India. If the island fell to India, any line of equidistance which took account of the island would erode the area previously considered available for Bangladesh, to a greater extent than the Indian claim would be eroded if the island fell to Bangladesh. Plainly the effect on Bangladesh, which is partially zone-locked at the head of the Bay of Bangal, would be more serious than on India which has extensive areas which can be claimed from its coasts and outlying possessions.

The final problem concerns Narcondam Island, which is a possession of India in the Andaman Sea. This island is a craterless volcano with an area of 7 square kilometres, which stands 710 metres above sea-level and is bounded by cliffs 100 metres in height. The island is occupied by a small detachment of police and two wireless operators. As figure 6.5 shows, if India insists that any boundary negotiated with Burma gives full effect to Narcondam Island, the Indian claim will cover part of the continental shelf of the Irrawaddy River delta. The area concerned would depend on whether the line of equidistance was based on the Burmese coastline or the Burmese baseline which closes the Gulf of Martaban. In the first case the area would be 1175 square nautical miles; in the second case the area measures 580 square nautical miles. On a number of occasions the Burmese authorities have claimed Narcondam Island, but India has shown a determination to defend its sovereignty in this matter. There is plenty of scope in other parts of the Andaman Sea for the two countries to negotiate a compromise; the particular problem would only be intractable if one side took an inflexible position. Burma would presumably argue that on grounds of natural prolongation no claim to part of the continental shelf of the Irrawaddy River delta could be made from Narcondam Island. However, there are two counter-arguments against this view. First, there is a submarine ridge linking the island with the continental margin off the delta. Second, questions of natural prolongation need not arise where states are less than 400 nautical miles apart. India could simply make its claim to an

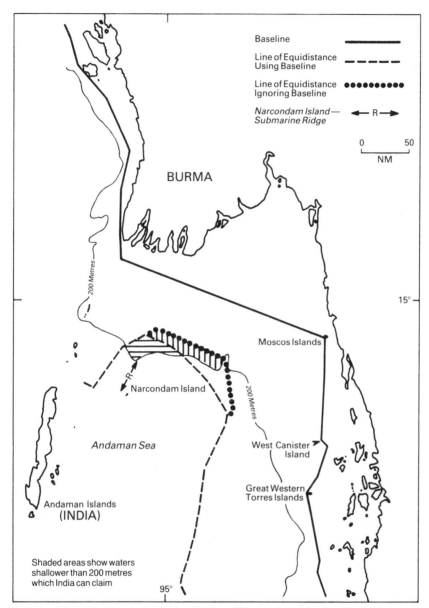

Figure 6.5 Possible boundaries in the vicinity of Narcondam Island in the Andaman Sea

exclusive economic zone and refuse to discuss questions of continental shelves separately.

The remaining problem, concerning Australia and Indonesia, does not involve rival claims to islands. In 1971 and 1972 Australia and Indonesia agreed on two segments of boundary dividing their continental shelf. The eastern section, which extended from about meridian 133° east to Papua New Guinea, followed an equidistant course, reflecting the continuous and uniform shelf which separates the two countries. The western segment was divided into two distinct sections because of the existence, at that time, of Portuguese Timor. These two sectors lay north of the median line, and reflected the existence of the deep Timor Trough which distinguishes the Australian margin from the margin of Timor. However, the boundary did not follow the axis of the trough, as Australian authorities had hoped; instead it occupied a location between the axis of the trough and the median line.

Australia was unable to reach any agreement with Portugal to close the gap in its northern boundary before 1975, when Indonesia annexed Portuguese Timor. After some delay the Australian authorities recognized this annexation and began talks with Indonesia to close the gap in the line. Indonesia now argued in favour of the median line, which would create a pronounced Indonesian salient on the Australian margin. The Australian representatives maintain that the gap should be closed by a straight line so that the disputed area of about 9000 square nautical miles belongs to Australia. Since the area is considered to have excellent hydrocarbon prospects, it is unlikely that either side will yield the entire area.

Conclusions

The Indian Ocean exists as a coherent political concept only in the rhetoric of politicians. Discussion of nuclear-free zones in the Indian Ocean, or the Soviet-American competition for Indian Ocean supremacy, mask the important divisions which exist within this major basin.

These differences can be directly traced to the varied interests of the littoral states and the configuration of the Ocean. For example, India appears to be the only country, which is sufficiently strong and with a central location, with the capacity to aim for a major regional role in the Indian Ocean. In that respect India contrasts sharply with the Sudan, which is remote, Yemen (Sana'a), which is small, and Bangladesh which is impoverished. Most of the littoral states are concerned with their immediate location, with the problems of securing a fair share of the available resources of the adjacent seas. The main extra-regional interest for most will be unimpeded transit through international straits for their exports and strategic imports such as petroleum.

There are important political sub-regions within the Indian Ocean. The Persian Gulf and the Mozambique Channel are zones within which serious political problems might develop. The former region is clearly more complex because of the number of countries involved and the concentration of oil production there. Serious political problems will only arise in the Mozambique Channel if France is determined to preserve sovereignty over its island possessions.

While Russia and the United States have Indian Ocean fleets their major concerns deal with comparatively small areas of the Ocean and its littoral. The Persian Gulf and Red Sea with their narrow exits are of major interest, and there is slighter though comparable concern with the approaches to the Strait of Malacca. It appears to be beyond the hope of both powers to form exclusive alliances with all or even the major littoral states, just as it appears to be impossible for each to prevent the other from obtaining bases where supplies can be stored, repairs made and crews refreshed.

Attention has been drawn to the contrast between the east and west of this ocean in respect of the settlement of maritime boundaries. The process of boundary construction is well advanced in the east, and the outstanding problems involving Burma and India, and India and Bangladesh do not seem to be hindering exploration for offshore resources. Only in the Persian Gulf is boundary-making advanced in the west, but even here there are important gaps in the network which might be hard to fill because of the potential intrinsic worth of the areas of seabed. Elsewhere maritime boundaries seem unimportant compared with more pressing domestic problems, for example along the African littoral, or are impossible to negotiate because of the state of relations between neighbours, such as India and Pakistan and Oman and Yemen (Aden).

As a laboratory of case studies the Indian Ocean is well equipped with proper and extravagant baselines and claims to maritime zones; with sensible international agreements based on equidistance and equity; and with potential conflicts based on competition for territory and the varied interpretation of the terms of the Convention.

References

Africa Research Bulletin, Political, Social and Cultural Series (1978) 15, Exeter.

Bowman, I. (1928) *The New World: Problems in Political Geography*, 4th edn, New York.

Harrigan, A. (1975) 'Security interests in the Persian Gulf and Western Indian Ocean', in Wall, P. (ed.) *The Indian Ocean and the Threat to the West*, London, 19–36.

Prescott, J. R. V. (1975) *Map of Mainland Asia by Treaty*, Melbourne.

Tchernia, P. (1980) *Descriptive Regional Oceanography*, transl. D. Densmore, Exeter.

The Geographer (1978) *Maritime Boundary: India–Maldives and Maldives' Claimed 'Economic Zone'*, 'Limits in the Seas' series, no. 78, Washington, DC.

The Geographer (1981) *Maritime Boundary: Kenya–Tanzania*, 'Limits in the Seas' series, no. 92, Washington, DC.

7

The south Pacific Ocean

'Is your news certain?'
'Yes,' replied the Indian, 'I had it at Punta Arenas.'
And the Kaw-djer asked:
'All the islands to the south of the Beagle Channel belong to Chile?'
'All of them.'
'Including Nueva?'
'Yes.'
'This was unavoidable,' murmured the Kaw-djer. His voice was charged with deep feeling. He then returned to his house and locked himself in his room.   (Verne 1909)

But on a hundred windswept lone Pacific isles,
The terraces of crude white crosses,
Do not stir.   (Auslander 1946)

For whole generations of Americans the names of Guadalcanal and the Coral Sea have precise geographical meanings which are not shared by the names Vanuatu and Kiribati. In similar fashion Bolivians know about Arica, the coastal area lost to Chile one hundred years ago, while being ignorant about Tuvalu. The south Pacific Ocean has experienced a violent history which is recorded in dusty volumes and oral traditions. There have been battles and diplomatic clashes over the ownership of territory. Happily, since the Second World War the region has entered into a period which matches the ocean's name, and there is probably a lower level of super-power and local-power rivalry in this region than in any other oceanic region.

This chapter is organized into five sections. After an introduction which justifies the division of the south Pacific Ocean into two distinct regions there are three sections dealing with the southwest Pacific Ocean. These three sections deal with unilateral maritime boundaries established in the region; the bilateral boundaries which have been negotiated or which remain to be settled; and the major maritime issues in the region. The final section deals with the littoral of South America, which is the smaller of the two regions in the south Pacific Ocean.

Introduction

The northern limit has been set in the vicinity of the equator, in order to avoid consideration of the majority of Pacific territories of the United States of America.

These islands are more sensibly considered as part of the north Pacific Ocean which includes an American littoral. The southern limit has been set at 60° south latitude since that marks the northern boundary of the zone subject to the Antarctic Treaty. Within this wide area, bounded by Australia in the west and South America in the east, there are two regions distinguished by geography and history.

The dividing line coincides with meridian 120° west. It separates the multitude of islands to the west from the uncluttered seas to the east. It divides the areas of early Spanish colonization from the later colonies of Britain, Germany and France. It distinguishes the eastern zone, where decolonization ended in the middle of the nineteenth century, from the western region where decolonization is both recent and incomplete.

The most persistent climatic element in the south Pacific Ocean is the large anticyclonic circulation in the east. This system is centred on Easter Island during August and south of that island during February. The strong anti-clockwise wind system produces winds that blow from the south and parallel to the South American coast north of 38° south. This alignment of winds and coast, together with cold offshore currents, ensures that precipitation does not exceeed 750 millimetres, yielding desert conditions along much of the Chilean and Peruvian coast. In contrast the alternation of cyclonic and anticyclonic circulations in the western region, in the vicinity of Australia, provides a confused, often weak circulation in the summer months and steadier southeast trade winds in winter. Precipitation in this region is generally in excess of 1200 millimetres, and in some tropical regions such as Papua New Guinea exceeds 3000 millimetres. The triangle of low precipitation in the east is bounded by the South American coast, the equator, and a line passing through Phoenix and Malden Islands, the Marquesas and Easter Island.

In structural terms there is also an important division between the two regions in the vicinity of 120° west. Just to the east of that meridian lies the Pacific–Antarctic Ridge, which marks the line of ocean floor spreading. The smaller area to the east is distinguished by clusters of seamounts, associated with the Chile Rise and the Easter Island Fracture Zone, but there are comparatively few islands in this region. The main representatives are Islas Juan Fernandez, the Easter Island Group and Islas Galapagos. The collision coast along the South American littoral is marked by the deep Chile–Peru Trench, which has the effect of making the continental margin very narrow. The Carnegie Ridge which terminates in the Islas Galapagos, and the Nazca Ridge, located southwest of Lima, are the two most prominent submarine elevations.

In the west the trenches which correspond to the Chile–Peru Trench are found stretching northwards from New Zealand. The Kermadec and Tonga Trenches trend northeastwards, and then there is an abrupt change in direction as the Vityaz, New Hebrides and New Britain Trenches trend west-northwest. Between these trenches and the mid-oceanic ridge there is a multitude of individual submarine elevations which are crowned with a profusion of islands. West of the Kermadec and Tonga Trenches there is a series of plateaus and rises, such as the Campbell and Fiji Plateaus and the Lord Howe and Solomon Rises. Around eastern Australia, Papua New Guinea, New Zealand, and to a lesser extent Fiji and New Caledonia, there are wider continental margins than are found in the eastern region along the south American littoral.

The division between east and west in the south Pacific Ocean is not reflected in the distribution of tuna stocks. This valuable resource occurs in wide bands across the Pacific in waters which rarely have temperatures less than 21° Celsius. However the stocks tend to be found further south in the western extremities of the south Pacific Ocean (Bardach and Matsuda 1980).

In the eastern region there are three continental states: Chile, Peru and Ecuador. In the west there are nineteen insular territories which fall into three groups. First there are eleven independent states; they are Australia, Fiji, Kiribati, Nauru, New Zealand, Papua New Guinea, Solomon Islands, Tonga, Tuvalu, Vanuatu and Western Samoa. Four territories have a special relationship with a metropolitan power. The Cook Islands, Niue and Tokelau have special relationships with New Zealand, and American Samoa is an unincorporated territory of the United States. The remaining territories are colonies; Pitcairn is British while France controls French Polynesia, Wallis and Futuna and New Caledonia.

Unilateral maritime boundaries in the southwest Pacific Ocean

This section examines those maritime boundaries which countries can proclaim without reference to any other state. First, all countries can proclaim baselines from which their maritime zones are measured. If neighbours are sufficiently distant it is then a mechanical task to fix the outer boundaries of territorial seas, contiguous zones, and exclusive economic zone. The task of fixing the outer edge of continental margins wider than 200 nautical miles is not a mechanical one, and any boundary selected would have to be approved by the commission created by the Convention.

Only Papua New Guinea shares an island with another country, and therefore has an adjacent neighbour. In every other case territories do not share islands and therefore they only have opposite neighbours.

No countries in the southwest Pacific Ocean claim contiguous zones, perhaps because such claims do not have to be made in order to secure the rights such zones confer. All countries claim 200 nautical miles as a fishing or exclusive economic zone, or have foreshadowed such a claim. Further, with the exception of Australia, Tuvalu and American Samoa, each territory claims territorial seas 12 nautical miles wide. It would probably be safe to assume that the 3 nautical miles claimed by the three exceptions will eventually be increased to 12 nautical miles.

This pattern of claims means that states will be able to fix the outer edge of their territorial seas when their nearest neighbours are more than 24 nautical miles distant. The outer edge of fishing or exclusive economic zones will only be capable of unilateral determination when neighbours are more than 400 nautical miles away.

The claimed baselines fall into three groups. First, Australia since 14 February 1983 has proclaimed a set of straight baselines around the coast of the mainland and Tasmania. Second, Papua New Guinea, Fiji, Vanuatu and Solomon Islands have proclaimed archipelagic baselines. Third, most of the remaining countries have announced the principles on which baselines will be drawn without specifying any precise lines.

The proclamation of Australia's baselines was the final step in a complex set of constitutional arrangements by which federal authorities transferred to the States and Territories control over the territorial seas and the underlying seabed for certain purposes. The federal government retains control over defence, security and other essential functions. It was stipulated in the arrangements that if the territorial seas were increased to 12 nautical miles in width that the area vested in the States and Territories would not be increased beyond the present 3 nautical miles. Three weeks after the proclamation there was a change of government in Canberra and the Labor administration has threatened to rescind the offshore constitutional arrangements. However, it is unlikely that any such action would alter the baselines which have been proclaimed.

The baseline proclamation is a complex document. It does not name the legal bays which have been closed, it will be left to navigators around the coast to decide, according to the rules set out, whether a particular bay has been closed by a straight line or not. There are then three schedules which deal with mainland Australia, Tasmania and offshore groups of islands. There are 297 segments of straight baselines around the mainland (figure 7.1). Most of the baselines appear to conform with the spirit and letter of Article 4 of the 1958 Convention, although in some cases the meaning of part of that article seems to have been stretched to breaking point. For example, it is straining credibility to regard Mooroongga Island as a fringing island which permits Castlereagh Bay in the Northern Territory to be closed, especially when Howard, Banyan and Millingimbi Islands, closer to the coast, have the configuration of classical fringing islands.

The Australian authorities eschewed the obvious baseline along the outer edge of the Great Barrier Reef in Queensland. It is generally believed that this apparent modesty was based on political pragmatism. The federal government did not wish to transfer the entire reef to Queensland because this was perceived to be electorally unpopular amongst significant sections of the Australian community.

The baselines around Tasmania seem to be unexceptional, but the same cannot be said of the third schedule which draws baselines around Macquarie Island and the Houtman Abrolhos Group. While the Macquarie baselines are orthodox, those surrounding the Houtman Abrolhos Group must be based on an original interpretation of Article 4. It has been widely assumed that baselines could not be drawn to enclose offshore archipelagos of continental states. It was such a belief which led Canada, India and Ecuador, amongst others, to argue for the retention of an article in the Convention which specifically permitted such baselines.

There is a final part of the proclamation which defines the boundaries marking the outer edge of the territorial seas around some islands in Torres Strait. These

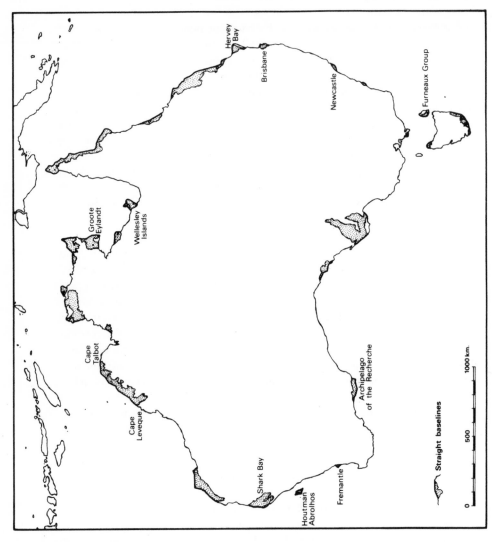

Figure 7.1 Australia's baselines

definitions are part of the 1978 agreement between Australia and Papua New Guinea; inspection of these limits reveals that Australia has used the outer edge of surrounding reefs rather than any straight baselines.

Where straight baselines have not been drawn and where closing lines are not appropriate in the case of rivers or bays, the normal Australian baseline is the lowest astronomic tide. This is the lowest tide which will be recorded in a full cycle of 18.6 years under normal atmospheric conditions. This is a difficult line to find, and it is likely that the only areas where this level will push the baseline significantly further seawards than the spring low-water mark will occur along coasts already enclosed by straight baselines.

If Vanuatu allowed its claim to Matthew and Hunter Islands to lapse, it would be the only country in the region which could proclaim archipelagic baselines around its entire territory. In fact such baselines were proclaimed on 11 October 1982. The system consists of twenty-one segments connecting two sections of the low-water mark. The longest section is 90 nautical miles and the land-to-water ratio within the baselines is 1:4.7. If Vanuatu was able to secure Matthew and Hunter Islands from France, it would not be able to incorporate them into the archipelagic baselines because they are more than 125 nautical miles from the nearest part of the main group of islands, called Aneityum.

By the National Seas Act, 1977, which was certified on 28 February 1977, Papua New Guinea made an interim delimitation of archipelagic waters. Baselines were defined by eighty-four turning points; the longest segment measures 120 nautical miles and the ratio of land to water is 1:1.3. Two island groups called Tauu and Nukumanu were left outside the baseline system, although they were defined as archipelagos, and it was noted that their internal waters might form part of the archipelagic waters of Papua New Guinea. The baselines around these two groups are defined as continuous lines between the outermost points of islands, shoals, rocks and reefs. It is possible to argue that these areas were designated as archipelagos so that their inhabitants would not feel neglected by a government in Port Moresby, which had struggled with the sensitivities of some of the citizens of Bougainville. In fact the Tauu islands could be incorporated into the archipelagic baselines without breaking any of the rules, although some might try to argue that such an inclusion would not preserve the general configuration of the archipelago. Such criticism could be countered by reference to the Convention, which authorizes archipelagic states to draw their baselines around the outermost points of the outermost islands. Nukumanu is more than 125 nautical miles from Tauu, so it could not be included in the baseline system.

Fiji's archipelagic baselines were contained in the Marine Spaces Act, 1977, which received royal assent on 21 April 1977. The act excluded Rotuma Island and its dependencies and Ceva-i-Ra from the baselines; they are located respectively 245 nautical miles to the north and 270 nautical miles to the southwest of the main group. However, the statement by which Fiji made this declaration public contained the observation that an amendment would be introduced to allow an archipelagic regime to be established for Rotuma Island and its dependencies.

The Marine Spaces (Amendment) Act, 1978, received royal assent on 5 October 1978, and it contained the change that the phrase 'seas of the Fiji archipelago and the Rotuma archipelago' should be substituted for the phrase 'the sea of the Fiji archipelago'. However, there is no evidence that archipelagic baselines have been proclaimed around Rotuma. By the Marine Spaces (Territorial Seas) (Rotuma and its Dependencies) Order, 1981, dated 19 November 1981, the innermost limits of the territorial waters of Rotuma Island and its dependencies were declared; they are shown in figure 7.2. The baselines are defined by nineteen turning points located on the outermost islands and reefs. If the waters were claimed as archipelagic waters they would pass the tests in the Convention. The longest segment measures 7.7 nautical miles and the land-to-water ratio is 1:1.1.

Fiji has also declared internal waters within its main archipelagic baselines. This is permitted in Article 50 of the Convention, but only in respect of bays, the mouths of rivers and harbours. Fiji appears to have drawn lines to delimit the outer edge of internal waters along the edge of surrounding reefs. This is not permitted according to Article 50. However, it would seem unreasonable to object to the practice, since Fiji, if it wanted, could have counted the waters within the fringing reefs as land for the purpose of making the calculation of the ratio of land to water. Such a revised calculation would still fall within the required span.

Solomon Islands declared archipelagic waters around five groups of islands in 1978, but the baselines fell short of the maximum possible claim and the authorities are designing new lines which will increase the area of archipelagic waters.

While Tonga has not declared any archipelagic waters it could do so. The Territorial Seas and Exclusive Economic Zone Act, 1978, which came into effect on 25 June 1979, describes the baselines from which these zones are measured. The baseline consists of the low-water mark along the coast or fringing reefs, and straight lines across the mouths of bays. While the Tongan islands are too widely scattered to allow a single set of baselines to be proclaimed, it would be possible to produce baselines around some of the islands, in the manner of Fiji. The Tongatapu Islands could be enclosed by baselines which would have a longest segment of 11 nautical miles and a land-to-water ratio of 1:2.3. If it could be satisfactorily argued that the Nomuka Group, 46 nautical miles to the north, is part of the Tongatapu Group then the baselines incorporating them would have a longest segment measuring 49 nautical miles and a land-to-water ratio of 1:8.9. While this ratio is close to the maximum limit, it could be reduced by considering some of the waters within fringing reefs as land, in accordance with the provisions of the Convention. The 'Uta Vava'u Group could also be surrounded with archipelagic baselines which would yield a land-to-water ratio of 1:5 and have a longest segment measuring 20 nautical miles.

If New Caledonia became an independent country it would not be possible for the administration to proclaim archipelagic baselines around all its territory. The islands in the Chesterfield and South Bellona Reefs in the west and Hunter and Matthew Islands in the east are all more than 125 nautical miles from the main

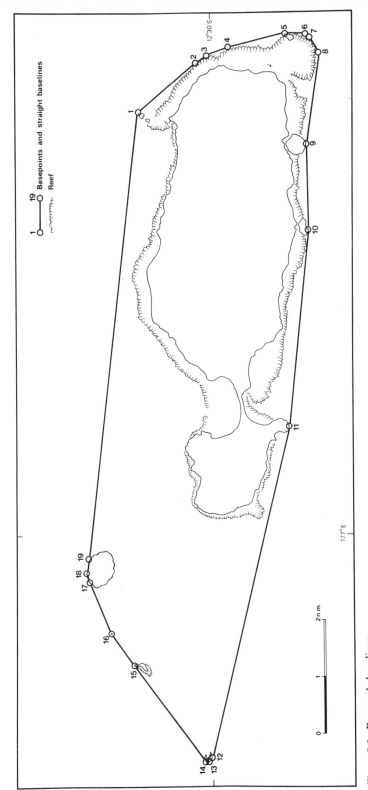

Figure 7.2 Rotuma's baselines

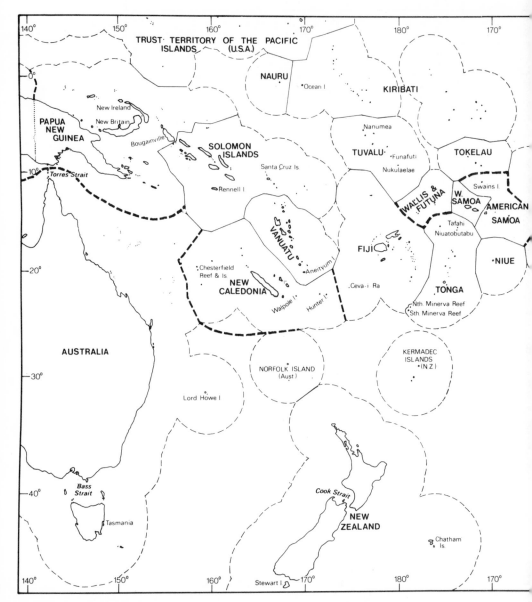

Figure 7.3 Agreed and potential boundaries in the southwest Pacific Ocean

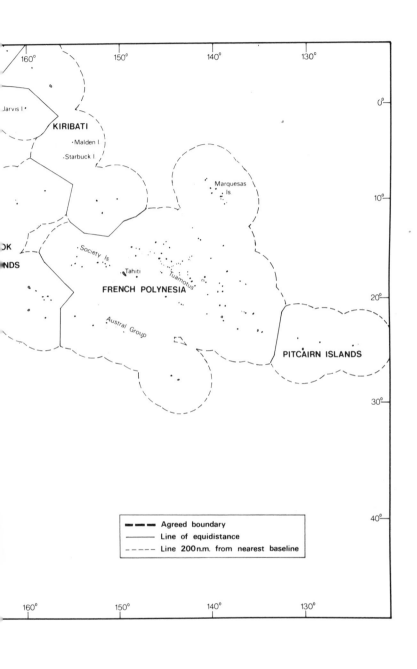

▬ ▬ ▬	Agreed boundary
——	Line of equidistance
- - - -	Line 200 n.m. from nearest baseline

group. If a baseline was drawn around the main group from Huon Island in the north to the Island of Pines in the south, the longest segment would measure 70 nautical miles, and the land-to-water ratio would be 1:3.1. If it could be established that Walpole Island was part of the main archipelago then it could be included and the longest segment would be 76 nautical miles long, while the land-to-water ratio would be raised to 1:3.6.

None of the other countries or territories has declared straight baselines. In most cases claims refer to a baseline and then stipulate that the baseline will be the low-water mark, except in the case of legal bays and rivers or where the coast is deeply indented or fringed with islands. It appears that such claims have left open the option of declaring straight baselines. One obvious location for such a system would be along the west coast of the South Island of New Zealand.

Figure 7.3 shows the extent to which countries can proclaim unilateral boundaries to the exclusive economic zones and territorial seas. Apart from the narrow waters which separate Australia and Papua New Guinea in Torres Strait, and Papua New Guinea and Solomon Islands in Bougainville Strait, all countries are sufficiently far from their neighbours to be able to make a unilateral determination of the outer edge of their territorial waters. Only American Samoa and Western Samoa are unable to draw any sector of their exclusive economic zone boundary without reference to another country. At the other end of the scale New Zealand must only agree on two short sections of its exclusive economic zone boundary with the Australian possessions of Norfolk and Macquarie Islands.

The final type of unilateral boundary concerns the outer limit of the continental margin. Figure 7.4 depicts those areas of the southwest Pacific Ocean where the margin is wider than 200 nautical miles. The main area of wide margin is south of Fiji and New Caledonia in the vicinity of Australia and New Zealand. The main locations are the Tasman Plateau south of Tasmania and the Campbell Plateau and Chatham Rise south and east of New Zealand. These areas can be claimed unilaterally by Australia and New Zealand respectively; the other wide shelves will need to be divided between various countries through bilateral negotiations.

Bilateral maritime boundaries in the southwest Pacific Ocean

There are eight maritime boundary agreements in this region. They have been concluded between Australia and Papua New Guinea; Australia and France in New Caledonia; France and Tonga; Indonesia and Papua New Guinea; Tokelau and American Samoa; American Samoa and the Cook Islands; and France and Fiji. In the latter case two segments have been agreed separating Fiji from Wallis and Futuna and New Caledonia.

Australia and Papua New Guinea reached agreement on the boundary through Torres Strait and the Coral Sea in December 1978. Papua New Guinea had argued successfully that the chain of Australian islands in Torres Strait would produce an inequitable boundary if they were given full effect. The final boundary is shown in figure 7.5. In the seas west and east of Torres Strait the boundaries separating the continental shelves and fishing zones of the two countries are coincident. In Torres Strait the two boundaries separate, with the fishing zone limit lying north of the continental shelf boundary, much closer to Papua New Guinea.

Australia made many concessions during the negotiations which led to this agreement. First, it was noted that Australia had never claimed three islands in the north of the Strait, and that Australia had no objection to Papua New Guinea acquiring these islands. Griffin (1981) has cast serious doubts on the historical evidence which justified this concession. Second, Australia waived its legitimate claim to 8800 square nautical miles of seabed and to fishing rights in 5650 square nautical miles. Third, Australia agreed that if in future it increased its territorial waters to 12 nautical miles it would not make that increase effective for those islands north of the continental shelf boundary.

This imaginative treaty also created a protected zone within the Strait which will preserve the traditional way of life for Torres Strait Islanders and inhabitants of the coast of Papua. Within this zone mineral exploration is prohibited for ten years. The western terminus of this boundary was settled by Indonesia and Australia in 1971 and inherited without any problems by Papua New Guinea when it became independent. The eastern terminus lies close to the trijunction with equidistant claims from both countries and the Solomon Islands. In fact the last few miles of the joint boundary applies only to the continental shelf, because there is a small triangle of waters around the trijunction which are more than 200 nautical miles from the nearest country.

France and Australia agreed on a maritime boundary separating claims from Australia and New Caledonia on 4 January 1982. It separates France's exclusive economic zone and seabed from Australia's fishing zone and seabed. With the exception of one segment of boundary east of Fraser Island, it appears that the line is based on the principle of equidistance. In the exceptional segment it is not possible to deduce which basepoints have been used, although it is not beyond the realms of possibility that Middleton Reef was somehow involved in the calculation, even though it does not have any features which stand above high tide. While the agreement does not specifically refer to the fact that part of the boundary only separates the seabeds claimed from the two territories, this must be the case. This conclusion is based on the fact that part of the segment east of Fraser Island lies more than 200 nautical miles from the nearest fragments of Australian and French territory.

On 11 January 1980 France and Tonga agreed on a boundary which separated the exclusive economic zones claimed from Tonga and Wallis and Futuna. This short boundary is a line of equidistance. Lines of equidistance were also used in the agreements between the United States and Tokelau and the Cook Islands. The boundary between Tokelau and American Samoa was made public on 2 December 1980, when the agreement was signed. The boundary is defined by eight points, and in a separate clause the United States recognized that the islands called Atafu, Nukunonu and Fakaofo form part of Tokelau pending an act of

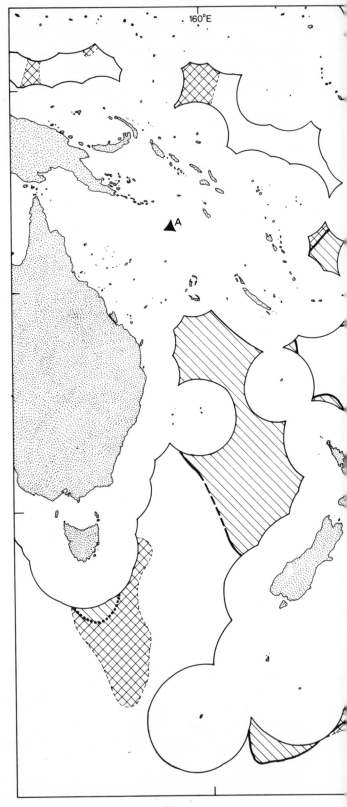

Figure 7.4 The outer edge of the continental margin in
the southwest Pacific Ocean

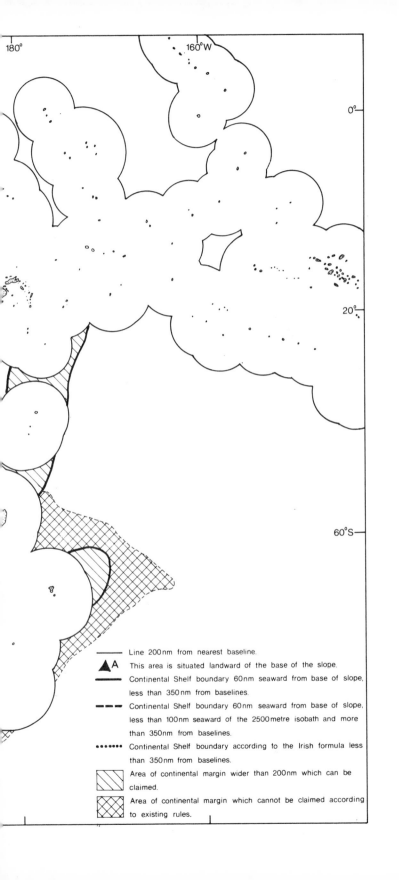

180° 160°W

0°—

20°—

60°S—

Line 200 nm from nearest baseline.

▲A This area is situated landward of the base of the slope.

Continental Shelf boundary 60 nm seaward from base of slope, less than 350 nm from baselines.

━ ━ ━ Continental Shelf boundary 60 nm seaward from base of slope, less than 100 nm seaward of the 2500 metre isobath and more than 350 nm from baselines.

•••••• Continental Shelf boundary according to the Irish formula less than 350 nm from baselines.

Area of continental margin wider than 200 nm which can be claimed.

Area of continental margin which cannot be claimed according to existing rules.

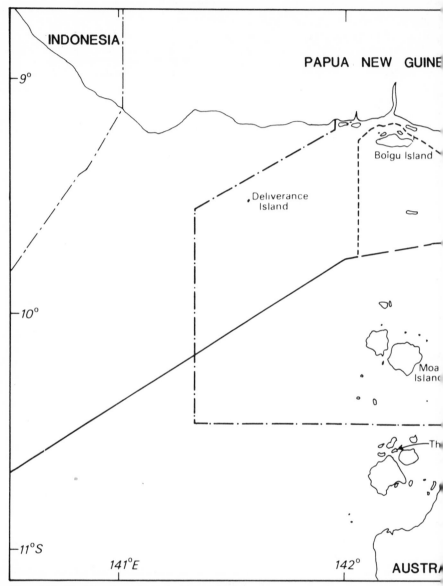

Figure 7.5 Maritime boundaries in Torres Strait

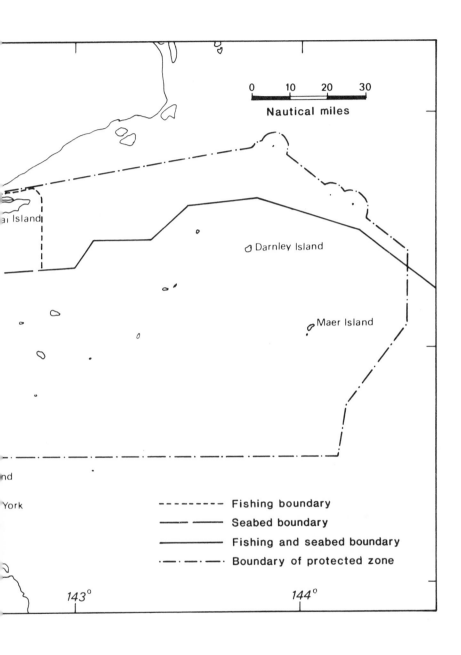

0   10   20   30

Nautical miles

ai Island

◌ Darnley Island

◌ Maer Island

ind

York

----------- Fishing boundary
———— Seabed boundary
———— Fishing and seabed boundary
—·—·—·— Boundary of protected zone

143°   *144°*

self-determination in accordance with the Charter of the United Nations. The boundary with the Cook Islands was signed on 11 June 1980; it was defined by twenty-five points. In this agreement the United States abandoned claims to islands called Manihiki, Penrhyn, Pukapuka and Rakahanga. In both these agreements full effect was given to all the islands of the parties involved.

At the beginning of 1983 France and Fiji published an agreement delimiting the boundary between the economic zones claimed from Fiji and from Wallis and Futuna and New Caledonia. Both boundary segments were based on the principle of equidistance. The most important in political terms is the boundary with New Caledonia. The line was based in part on Matthew and Hunter Islands as part of New Caledonia, and Ceva-i-Ra as part of Fiji. Matthew and Hunter Islands are also claimed by Vanuatu and France would welcome this agreement with Fiji, even though one article in the agreement specifies that it is without prejudice to sovereign rights of any neighbouring state in areas to which the agreement applies. It remains to be seen whether Vanuatu will be assured that its interests have not been seriously damaged by this agreement. The bonus for Fiji in this agreement is that Ceva-i-Ra, formerly called Conway Reef, has been recognized as an island. The reef is surmounted by a sand cay measuring about 350 metres by 70 metres and rising to a height of 2 metres.

Indonesia and Papua New Guinea ratified a boundary agreement on 9 September 1982. It extended a short maritime boundary which Australia and Indonesia had settled before Papua New Guinea became independent. The new segment of boundary passes through three points and terminates at a point which appears to be 200 nautical miles from the nearest fragments of Indonesia and Papua New Guinea.

Lines of equidistance have been drawn on figure 7.3 in those situations where there is no boundary agreement, and by measuring the areas enclosed within these lines it has been possible to compile table 7.1, which ranks the various territories on the basis of the maritime claims they can make.

The table makes it clear that there is no correlation between the area which can apparently be claimed and either the size of territory or number of citizens. Although Western Samoa has a larger area than ten other territories, and a larger population than eleven, it is only able to claim an area smaller than any other country.

If Australia is discounted, because so much of its claims lies in other seas and oceans, it is plain that the decisive factors in producing large claims are the location of the territory and the extent to which the islands which form countries are scattered or concentrated. The territories which are able to claim large areas, such as French Polynesia, Kiribati and New Zealand, have peripheral locations, and while New Zealand's territory is less scattered than the islands of French Polynesia and Kiribati, it is still more dispersed than many other territories. In contrast, the territories which claim only small areas are deficient in one or both of these qualities. For example, Western Samoa only has two islands and they are close together in a central location. The territories of Wallis and Futuna and

Table 7.1   Potential maritime claims, land area and population of territories in the south-west Pacific Ocean

Country	Potential maritime claim (square nautical miles)	Area (square nautical miles)	Population (thousands)
Australia[1]	1,854,000	2,240,771	14,615 (80)[2]
French Polynesia	1,385,200	1,145	155 (80)
New Zealand	1,058,100	78,320	3,167 (81)
Kiribati	965,000	198	58 (80)
Papua New Guinea	684,200	134,586	3,006 (80)
Cook Islands	556,100	70	18 (75)
Solomon Islands	458,400	8,682	215 (78)
Fiji	386,900	5,326	618 (79)
New Caledonia[3]	382,400	5,567	139 (80)
Pitcairn	236,900	12	—[4]
Tuvalu	211,500	7	7 (79)
Vanuatu	179,900	4,303	112 (79)
Tonga[5]	158,400	203	90 (76)
American Samoa	114,000	57	30 (77)
Nauru	92,800	6	7 (77)
Tokelau	91,300	3	1 (76)
Niue	87,300	75	3 (80)
Wallis and Futuna	71,900	80	9 (76)
Western Samoa	38,100	828	151 (76)

Notes:
1 Only part of Australia's claim is in the region.
2 Figures in parentheses indicate year of census or estimate.
3 For this table only it is assumed Hunter and Matthew Islands belong to New Caledonia.
4 The total population of Pitcairn in 1980 was 63.
5 It has been assumed that only territorial waters are claimed from Minerva Reefs.

Sources: The potential maritime claim was calculated by the author; data on area and population were taken from *The Statesman's Yearbook 1982–83*, 119th edn, London, 1982.

Tokelau are not very dispersed and are shut in by neighbouring states. Niue and Nauru have peripheral locations but consist of a single island. While it may be some consolation to the less fortunate countries that all maritime areas are not equally productive, it is nevertheless true that the larger areas give a better chance of finding valuable mineral or living resources.

There appear to be only four potentially serious maritime boundary problems in this region. This view is based on the facts that generally there is no disagreement over the ownership of islands, rocks or reefs; there is no dispute over whether features are rocks of islands; and those areas where there are continuous continental margins between two opposite states are overlain by very deep water.

Proceeding from west to east, the first potential problem might concern Pocklington Reef. This feature is located in the Solomon Sea and is deemed to belong to Papua New Guinea. The problem with Pocklington Reef is that it is capped only by some rocks; in 1977 there were also two wrecks, one was in a single piece, the other vessel had broken into two parts. If this reef is used as a basepoint in settling any boundary with the Solomon Islands, the boundary will be deflected in favour of Papua New Guinea. The question which the Solomon Islands authorities will have to ask is whether the rocks on Pocklington Reef have an economic life of their own. If Papua New Guinea is unable to answer such an enquiry with positive evidence that the area is used for fishing on a regular basis, then Solomon Islands would be entitled to argue that the reef should only be used to claim territorial waters, and that any common boundary separating exclusive economic zones should be drawn without regard to Pocklington Reef.

East of New Caledonia lie two islands called Matthew and Hunter Islands. There is a dispute over whether the islands belong to France or Vanuatu. Matthew Island was discovered by Captain Gilbert in the *Charlotte* in 1788. It is volcanic in origin and has two distinct cones which are about 430 and 550 metres in height. Ten years later Hunter Island was discovered by Captain Fearn, who named the island after his ship. It is a volcanic block with an elevation of about 910 metres and it is covered by grass; there are also some scattered trees.

In 1944 it was asserted by a reliable reference work that 'they have not been claimed by France or Britain, or by any other Power' (Naval Intelligence Division 1944, 604). The 1914 Protocol establishing the Condominium of France and Britain simply referred to the Group of the New Hebrides including the Banks and Torres Islands. These two specific groups are located north of the main archipelago.

In 1965 there was an exchange of letters between the New Hebrides Joint Court and the British and French Resident Commissioners, in which it was recorded that Britain was content with the view, expressed by the French authorities, that Matthew and Hunter Islands belonged to New Caledonia. This was also the view of the editors of the *Official Gazetteer of Place Names* published by the Survey Department of the New Hebrides in 1979.

However, Vanuatu has made a claim to the islands and on 9 March 1983 an official party from Vanuatu landed on Hunter Island. Included in the group were three Custom Chiefs from Futuna, South Tanna and Aneityum. These chiefs performed dances and sang traditional songs which they believe will make it easier for the people of Tafea to return to Hunter Island. The French plaque, erected by the crew of the patrol boat *La Bayonaisse* in December 1975, was taken back to Vanuatu; in its place the landing party left a flagpole flying the flag of Vanuatu.

The area of waters and seabed which can be claimed from Matthew and Hunter Islands amounts to 59,400 square nautical miles. France is quite firm in its resolve to keep the islands and the independence movements on New Caledonia are similarly disposed to the question of sovereignty over the islands.

There is a potential problem involving Tonga's claim to the North and South Minerva Reefs. If Tonga insisted on using these reefs as basepoints from which its exclusive economic zone is measured then this would curtail the areas available to Fiji and New Zealand.

These reefs, which are called Tele Ki Tokolau and Tele Ki Tonga respectively by the Tongan authorities, were claimed in 1972 after an independent organization called the Ocean Life Research Foundation proposed to establish the Republic of Minerva. The King of Tonga sailed to the reefs and supervised the erection of two small artificial islands. In the same year the South Pacific Forum recognized Tonga's historic association with the reefs, welcomed Tonga's continuing interest in the area and agreed that other claims would not be recognized. This means that the South Pacific Forum stopped short of recognizing Tonga's sovereignty in the reefs.

The reefs are about 18 nautical miles apart. The northern reef is circular with a radius of about 1.6 nautical miles. There is a single entrance through the fringing reef and the maximum depth over the centre of the reef is 16 fathoms. The southern reef has the shape of a figure eight, measuring 4.7 nautical miles on its long axis and 1.8 nautical miles along its widest part. There is a single entrance to the easternmost loop where the water depth does not exceed 16 fathoms. Scattered around the edge of these reefs are a few coral boulders hurled onto the reef after being broken from the outer wall of the reef by storm surges. These features are probably impermanent. For example, 'a conspicuous boulder' shown on Admiralty chart BA985, corrected to 1979, had disappeared by June 1980.

On each reef the Tongan government has built a shelter about the size of a large desk, consisting of walls of coral boulders, and the whole cavity filled with coral rubble. Lights have also been erected and on the southern reef a metal tripod with two platforms has been raised. The coral shelters would not provide protection against even moderate seas at high tide, when only the few peripheral boulders and the shelters stand above water.

North Minerva Reef is 168 nautical miles from Ata Island, which belongs to Tonga. It is 154 nautical miles from Tuvana-i-Ra, which belongs to Fiji and marks Point 14 of Fiji's archipelagic baseline. When a line of equidistance is drawn between Fiji and Tonga without any reference to Minerva Reefs, it is found to lie east of these reefs. Now according to Article 60 of the Convention, only the sovereign power can construct artificial islands within its exclusive economic zone. So Tonga's first problem is to persuade Fiji that the Minerva Reefs lie within Tonga's exclusive economic zone.

When artificial islands are constructed the state concerned has exclusive jurisdiction over issues of immigration, health, safety and finance. However, the Convention makes it quite clear that the only maritime zone which can be constructed about an artificial island is a safety zone 500 metres wide. It is particularly noted that no other maritime zones can be claimed from the artificial islands, nor can they affect the delimitation of maritime boundaries.

While Tonga cannot base its claim to extended maritime zones on the two artificial islands, it could use the rocks on the reef to make such claims if it could be demonstrated first that Tonga owned the rocks, and second that they had an economic life of their own. They are not capable of sustaining habitation on any basis. New Zealand and Fiji could be expected to resist this development if Tonga decided to press ahead with maritime claims from Minerva Reefs.

The last possible problem could involve Western Samoa's attempts to obtain some relief from its seriously disadvantaged condition. It was noted earlier that Western Samoa is zone-locked by its neighbours, to the point where it is only able to make the smallest maritime claim in the southwest Pacific Ocean. One island which seriously restricts claims from Western Samoa is Swains Island, which is 194 nautical miles north of Tutuila. This island has an area of 1.5 square nautical miles and was annexed by the United States in 1925. Ownership of this island accounts for about one-third of the maritime area which can be claimed for American Samoa. Western Samoa could not be considered greedy if it sought a more equitable boundary with American Samoa than the equidistant principle would provide. However, there can be no question that any concessions would be an act of grace on the part of the United States, since Swains Island has already been given full effect in the agreement with Tokelau.

Maritime issues in the southwest Pacific Ocean

There are two main regional organizations in the southwest Pacific Ocean. The South Pacific Commission was formed in February 1947, and its present membership consists of the independent countries of the region plus the metropolitan powers Britain, France and the United States. The Commission aims to promote the economic and social welfare and advancement of the peoples of the southwest Pacific Ocean.

The South Pacific Forum was created in August 1971. There is no written constitution and the chief activity consists of an annual meeting of heads of governments. However, there are subsidiary bodies which have a clearer structure. The South Pacific Bureau for Economic Cooperation was formed in April 1973, and it seeks to facilitate continuing co-operation and consultation amongst its members in respect of economic development, trade, transport, tourism and related matters. Two further organizations were created by the Bureau. In June 1977 the Pacific Forum Line was formed. It is designed to operate an economic shipping service with ships that are owned or chartered; to provide some special services to meet the special needs of particular areas; and to distribute profits to members. While three vessels chartered from New Zealand, Tonga and Western Samoa have been operated on a fairly continuous basis the Line has not enjoyed financial success; the problem of distributing profits has not been a serious one! Some observers believe that it will not become profitable until it has container vessels and the volume of trade in the area increases.

The South Pacific Forum Fisheries Agency was created on 10 July 1979. From its headquarters in Honiara the Agency operates to collect data about fish, especially the highly migratory species; to analyse management schemes; to disseminate economic information about fish to members; to provide technical information about licensing and surveillance of fisheries; and to establish working arrangements with other regional organizations.

The members of the Agency are Australia, Cook Islands, Fiji, Kiribati, Nauru, New Zealand, Niue, Papua New Guinea, Solomon Islands, Tonga, Tuvalu, Western Samoa, Vanuatu and the Federated States of Micronesia. Since the domestic fishing industries of these countries and territories are generally incapable of harvesting the total resource in any year, some authorities have willingly entered into financial arrangements to permit distant fishing fleets to operate in their waters. To the middle of 1983 sixty different agreements of this nature had been identified (Franklin and Duncan 1982). As many as 2000 foreign vessels operate in the area in any year.

The rental agreements employ a number of different provisions. Some require the payment of a lump sum for a specified number of vessels. This is the simplest technique and the most convenient if the coastal state has no capacity to supervise fishing activities. Some agreements call for the payment of an annual fee supplemented by a levy for each fishing trip. There are strong disagreements amongst economists on the real benefits of these agreements but they are generally inconclusive because some of the important elements in the equation can prove difficult to quantify. On the credit side, in addition to fees or levies it is necessary to add the expenditure of foreign fleets in domestic ports, the value of transferred technology, and the benefit of aid agreements which, it must be said, might not otherwise have been made available. The benefits of expenditures by fleets in the area tends to be largest in areas south of parallel 10° south. North of this line the fleets tend not to call at domestic ports for supplies.

On the debit side of the account must be set the cost of surveillance and administration, plus the adverse effect which foreign activities might have on the development of the domestic fishing industry. It seems that the governments of the area are less concerned with fine academic argument than with securing an immediate economic return.

Australia and New Zealand have the best surveillance systems, and once or twice a year it is usual for a Taiwanese trawler to be arrested by the Australian authorities. Amongst the other territories Papua New Guinea and the Solomon Islands are the most energetic in trying to monitor the activities of foreign fishing fleets. The problems of surveillance are increased by the presence of culs-de-sac and long corridors of high seas bounded by national waters. They are shown in figure 7.3 and the largest enclave of high seas is found between Solomon Islands in the southwest and Nauru and Kiribati in the northeast. Smaller enclaves are located between French Polynesia and the Cook Islands; between Fiji and Vanuatu; at the trijunction of Papua New Guinea, Solomon Islands and Australia; and between Papua New Guinea and the Federated States of Micronesia. Deep corridors of high seas are located between the three parts of Kiribati, and to the east and west of Norfolk Island. These confined areas of high seas provide legitimate excuses for fishing boats to be sailed across the exclusive economic zones of the surrounding states, and are a positive boon to poachers.

The Fishing Agency has enjoyed success in making arrangements for a regional register of foreign fishing boats. It has also provided advice to countries which are negotiating with distant fishing countries and to authorities anxious to improve their surveillance and control of fisheries.

A maritime issue which has prompted a rising level of debate concerns the dumping of nuclear waste in the Pacific Ocean. There has been widespread opposition to Japanese plans to dump 10,000 drums of liquid nuclear waste; each drum would contain 200 litres. The selected site is 460 nautical miles southeast of Tokyo, in deep water northeast of Agasawara Gunto. Kiribati and Nauru approached the organization set up by the London Dumping Convention and sought an amendment prohibiting the dumping of all radioactive waste throughout the world's oceans. At present only the dumping of high-level waste is prohibited. The amendment was referred to an expert committee, since the Convention requires that amendments must be based on scientific and technical evidence. This seemed to be an outcome which was satisfactory to the Japanese, since they are confident that the scientific evidence will endorse their proposal. The countries of the southwest Pacific Ocean have also prepared a convention for the protection and development of natural resources in their seas. The tenth article requires members to take all appropriate measures to prevent, reduce and control pollution resulting from the disposal of nuclear waste. Unfortunately there is no clear definition of the area to which the convention applies, and it appears certain that it will not apply to the area where the Japanese propose to dump their nuclear waste.

Maritime boundaries in the southeast Pacific Ocean

Compared to the complex pattern of maritime boundaries in the southwest Pacific Ocean, the pattern in the eastern region is simple. Only Ecuador and Chile have drawn straight baselines along their coasts. Ecuador's baseline was proclaimed on 28 June 1971, and it has already been mentioned (see figure 3.8). There can be no question that this baseline breaches the spirit and letter of the rules of the Convention. There are two parts to the baseline. The first part along the mainland coast consists of four segments totalling 345 nautical miles. The second part about the Islas Galápagos has eight segments totalling 542 nautical miles. The mainland baseline can be criticized because it encloses a coast which is only occasionally, in local areas, deeply indented and cut into, and which is only fringed with islands in its immediate vicinity in the area of the mouth of the Babahoja River in Golfo de Guayaquil. The segments connecting the isolated Isla de la Plata to the mainland total 192 nautical miles and are impossible to justify. It is also an unusual feature of the baseline that it terminates in the open sea. Despite the fact that a number of countries, including Iran, Denmark, Bangladesh, West Germany, Norway, Sweden and Finland have adopted the same technique, there is no provision for it in the Convention.

It has never been conclusively established that baselines may be drawn by coastal states around offshore archipelagos. It has been done by a number of countries, and if archipelagic states can draw more than one set of baselines, it would be unfair if continental states were prevented from taking similar action. The baselines drawn around the Galápagos seem to be unexceptional, although some might criticize the inclusion of Isla Darwin and Isla Wolf in the system. They are 95 nautical miles from the nearest island in the main group, but historically they appear to have been considered part of the Islas Galápagos.

Chile's straight baseline south of parallel 41° south was proclaimed on 14 July 1977. It is divided into two main parts. The first consists of thirty-five segments and includes one section of low-water mark; it terminates on the Brunswick Peninsula on the north shore of the Strait of Magellan. The second part consists of thirty-one straight segments and five segments of the low-water line. The second part lies entirely south of Magellan Strait, so that the Strait is excluded from Chile's internal waters.

Both parts of the baseline follow closely the general configuration of the coast, and with a single exception Chile's baseline could be adopted as a model straight baseline along a coast which is deeply cut into and indented. The single exception is found at the southern terminus of the southern section. It is located in the open sea, at a point fixed by the Court of Arbitration in the Beagle Channel case. It has already been noted that this is an increasing tendency which is not specifically authorized by the Convention, presumably for the very good reason that if the baseline terminates in the sea then there is no proper definition of internal waters in that area.

Maritime boundaries have been drawn between Colombia and Ecuador, Ecuador and Peru and Peru and Chile. They share the common characteristics that they coincide with the parallel of latitude which passes through the terminus of the land boundary, and that a buffer zone has been created on each side of the boundary to protect vessels of the bordering states from being prosecuted for accidental trespass.

On 18 August 1952 a Declaration on the Maritime Zone was proclaimed by Chile, Ecuador and Peru. This declaration included the provisions that each country should possess control over its adjacent waters to a distance of 200 nautical miles, and that boundaries between their maritime claims should be marked by the parallels which intersect the terminus of the land boundary.

While Ecuador and Peru claim territorial seas 200 nautical miles wide, Chile claims territorial seas 3 nautical miles wide and an economic zone of 200 nautical miles. The maritime boundary between Chile and Peru coincides with parallel 18° 23′ 3″ south, which passes through boundary pillar Number 1. This pillar lies slightly north of the final terminus of the boundary on the shore. In 1969 a joint boundary commission erected two towers almost 1 nautical mile apart on the parallel of the boundary pillar. This device enables mariners to know when they have crossed the parallel and is one of the few cases where maritime boundaries have been marked (The Geographer 1979). The maritime boundary separating the claims of Ecuador and Peru coincides with parallel 3° 23′ 34″ south.

Because of the westwards bulge in the Peruvian coast the claims to a zone 200 nautical miles from that coast terminate seawards of similar claims by Chile and Ecuador. The situation is shown for the Chile–Peru boundary in figure 7.6.

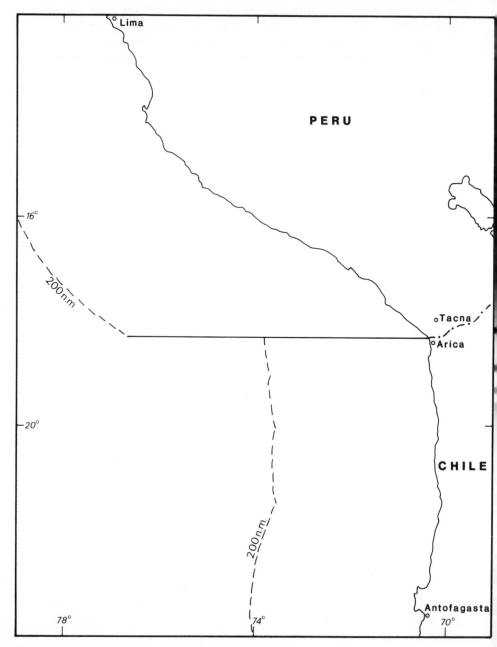

Figure 7.6   The maritime boundary between Peru and Chile

On 4 December 1954 the three countries also agreed to create buffer zones 10 nautical miles wide on either side of the boundary to avoid the risk of incidents being caused by the accidental trespass of boats from the neighbouring country across the parallel. In fact the provision applies to small vessels manned by crews with insufficient knowledge of navigation, or not equipped with the necessary equipment to determine their position accurately. It is specified that this safe-guard is not to be considered as a right to fish or hunt with intent in the buffer zone of a neighbouring state.

Ecuador was evidently able to persuade Colombia of the benefits of the system agreed by the three countries, because the boundary separating the zones of the two countries followed the same pattern (The Geographer 1976).

The maritime boundary agreement came into force on 22 December 1975, and while the parallel was not specifically identified, it must be approximately 1° 27' 24" north. As in the case of the other two agreements already considered, the buffer zone commences 12 nautical miles from the coast. There is some uncertainty whether the 12 nautical miles is measured from the coast, as mentioned in the text, or from any straight baselines which might have been drawn. It seems certain that the measurements will be from the baselines which have been substituted for the normal baseline along the low-water mark of the coast.

The only maritime boundary dispute in this region occurs at the extreme southern tip of the continent. Argentina and Chile disagree over the ownership of some islands in the Beagle Channel, and the course of the boundary which should separate their maritime claims.

The seeds of the dispute were sown in 1881 when the two countries agreed on a boundary separating their territories on the continent. Defects in the language of the treaty soon became evident and British arbitration was sought and obtained in 1896 and 1966. On these occasions Britain relied on British judges, but in 1971 when arbitration was approved for the Beagle Channel dispute, the judges were selected from Britain, the United States, France, Sweden and Nigeria. The problem was found in the third article of the 1881 treaty.

> In Tierra del Fuego a line shall be drawn, which starting from the point called Cape Espiritu Santo, in parallel 52° 40', shall be prolonged to the south along the meridian 68° 34' west of Greenwich, until it touches Beagle Channel. Tierra del Fuego, divided in this manner, shall be Chilean on the western side and Argentine on the eastern. As for the islands, to the Argentine Republic shall belong Staten Island, the small islands next to it, and the other islands there may be on the Atlantic to the east of Tierra del Fuego and of the eastern coast of Patagonia; and to Chile shall belong all the islands to the south of Beagle Channel up to Cape Horn, and those there may be to the west of Tierra del Fuego.   (United Kingdom 1977, 9)

Figure 7.7 shows the main features of the eastern Beagle Channel. In its mouth there are three islands called Lennox, Picton and Nueva, and these are the main prize in the dispute, but the concealed reward included the wide areas of sea and

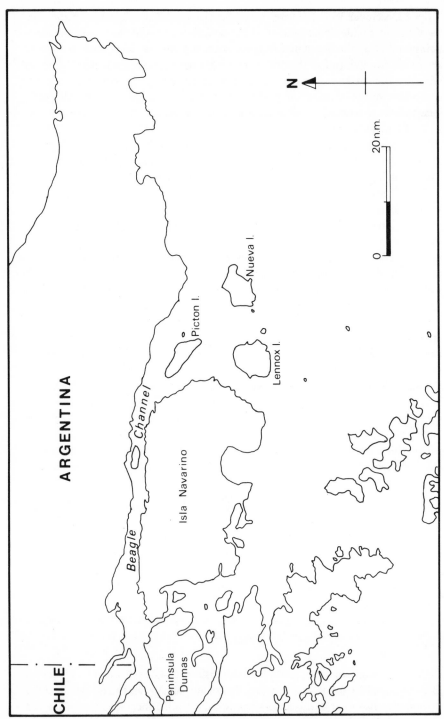

Figure 7.7 The Beagle Channel

seabed which claims from these islands would secure, and possibly useful am-
munition to fire in any debate over the ownership of the Antarctic Peninsula.

The case was concluded by a judgement on 18 February 1977; it gave the three
main islands to Chile and drew a maritime boundary through the channel to
separate the areas of both states. It generated masses of published research,
including valuable atlases of maps of the region which will prove a valuable
resource for interested scholars for a very long time.

While it would be possible to produce a detailed analysis of the arguments
which decided the case it has no place in a book concerned with maritime issues; it
is the result which is important. Unfortunately the arbitral award did not solve
the problem. Argentina, despite an agreement to the contrary, refused to accept
the judgement on 25 January 1978 (Nordquist, Lay and Simmonds
1980, 307–22). The statement which accompanied the rejection of the judgement
drew attention to serious and numerous flaws and concluded that the decision had
been handed down in violation of international rules.

The serious situation which this rejection created was avoided through bilateral
negotiations in early 1978 and the formation of a mixed Argentine–Chilean Commission. It proposed certain arrangements to avoid difficulties in the southern
border region and these were accepted by both countries (The Geographer 1980).

Consideration of the question of settling the boundary dispute passed under the
good offices of the Holy See, and there were strong rumours in late 1983 that a
compromise would be proposed which would leave the important islands to
Chile, while modifying in Argentina's favour any maritime boundary which
might result from Chile's ownership of those islands.

Conclusions

In the south Pacific Ocean there is a clear division into a smaller eastern zone and
a larger western region. The differences occur in the number of states in each
part; their insular and continental characters; the structure of the seabed; and the
colonial history of the component territories.

In the western region the multitude of island states has had two main effects.
First, it has provided a laboratory in which the rules connected with archipelagic
states are being interpreted and refined to a greater extent than anywhere else in
the world's oceans. Second, it has created the need for several segments of maritime boundaries between opposite states; indeed there is a very high density of
maritime boundaries in the region. Those which have been settled have generally
adopted the principle of equidistance.

It is a matter for congratulation that despite the plethora of boundaries there is
only one active dispute, between France and Vanuatu, and only three potential
disputes.

A beginning has been made to the establishment of regional associations
connected with maritime affairs and there is a reasonable chance that they will
increase in strength.

In the eastern region boundaries between states have been quite quickly agreed along parallels of latitude passing through the coastal termini of continental boundaries. It does not appear to have been a consideration that this system significantly curtails the area which can be claimed by Peru on the basis of the equidistance principle. The adoption of buffer zones 20 nautical miles wide, to reduce problems for small craft, is common throughout the region; a sensible arrangement which other countries might consider appropriate in their regions.

The most serious problem concerns the dispute over islands in the Beagle Channel between Chile and Argentina. Both countries have exercised restraint in the matter, but the dangers remain so long as the issue is unresolved.

One of the problems of the last century still arises from time to time. When Bolivia lost its Pacific coastline to Chile it appeared as though the countries would be enemies for ever, and as time passed it appeared that Bolivia had no chance to regain an outlet to the sea. Recently Chile has explored the possibility of providing a corridor to the sea for Bolivia. However, it wishes to avoid dividing its own territory, and therefore the corridor would have to be adjacent to Peru and consist of territory which Peru lost to Chile in the Pacific War. Peru has declined to approve such a transfer to Bolivia, and that approval is necessary under the terms of a treaty between Chile and Peru.

References

Auslander, J. (1946) 'Postscript to Iwo', *Newsweek*, 25 February.

Bardach, J. E. and Matsuda, Y. (1980) 'Fish, fishing, and sea boundaries: tuna stocks and fishing policies in southeast Asia and the south Pacific', *GeoJournal*, 4 (5), 467–78.

Franklin, P. G. and Duncan, A. (1982) 'Economic profile and evaluation of activities of distant water fishing fleets in south and western Pacific skipjack/tuna fisheries', paper presented to a workshop on the harmonization and co-ordination of fisheries regimes and access agreements, Suva.

Griffin, J. (1981) 'Territorial implications in the Torres Strait', in Boyce, P. J. and White, M. W. D. (eds) *The Torres Strait Treaty*, Canberra.

Naval Intelligence Division (1944) *Pacific Islands*, vol. III, London.

Nordquist, M., Lay, S. H. and Simmonds, K. R. (1980) *New Directions in the Law of the Sea*, vol. VII, London.

The Geographer (1976) *Maritime Boundary: Colombia–Ecuador*, 'Limits in the Seas' series, no. 69, Washington, DC.

The Geographer (1979) *Maritime Boundary: Chile–Peru*, 'Limits in the Seas' series, no. 86, Washington, DC.

The Geographer (1980) *Straight Baselines: Chile*, 'Limits in the Seas' series, no. 80 Addendum, Washington, DC.

United Kingdom (1977) *Award of Her Britannic Majesty's Government pursuant to the Agreement for Arbitration (Compromiso) of a Controversy between the Argentine Republic and the Republic of Chile Concerning the Region of the Beagle Channel*, London.

Verne, J. (1909) *Les Naufrages du Jonathon*, Paris.

8
The South China Sea

As early as the second century BC, at the time of Emperor Wu Di of the Han Dynasty, Chinese people began sailing the South China Sea. After long years of navigation, they discovered successively the Xisha and Nansha Islands.

(*New China News* 1980, 14)

Judging from the complexities of the various territorial claims to various islands in the South China Sea, territorial claims to archipelagic waters by Indonesia, the enigmatic Chinese historical claims to large portions of the South China Sea area, the various political systems among the littoral states, the various theories for delimiting maritime boundaries, and various interests involved in claiming sovereign rights over the resources of the exclusive economic zone and the continental shelf, and so on, the prospects for the solution of these problems are indeed difficult if not impossible.

(Djalal 1979)

Prospects for oil and gas appear to be favorable, as also is indicated by the intense exploration and test drilling off Borneo and in the southern part of the Gulf of Thailand by international companies. Other parts of the sediment-filled basins deserve attention as well.

(Parke, Emery, Szymankiewicz and Reynolds 1971, 723)

The three quotations which introduce this regional sea reveal that it has a long history of occupation; that it is an arena of complicated rivalry amongst the littoral states; and that there may be rich prizes to be won on the seabed.

The South China Sea is one of six marginal seas which lie between the mainland of Asia and a rampart of offshore islands. They stretch from the Indian Ocean to the Arctic Ocean, and are called the Andaman Sea, the South China Sea, the East China Sea, the Sea of Japan, the Sea of Okhotsk and the Bering Sea. While the seas share a common location there are important climatic, structural and political differences.

The South China Sea is distinguished in four important ways from the other marginal seas. First, it is the largest of the six seas; it has an area of 648,000 square nautical miles, which is more than twice the area of the Sea of Japan. Second, it is surrounded by eleven coastal states, whereas none of the other seas has more than five littoral countries. Third, the South China Sea is alone in having two important groups of islands near the middle of the sea. Fourth, the rampart of islands which forms the eastern margin of this sea contains more islands spread over a wider zone than is the case with any other of these seas peripheral to Asia. Indeed the islands of Indonesia and the Philippines which enclose the South China Sea against the mainland, themselves enclose smaller seas, such as the Sulu Sea, the Celebes Sea, the Ceram Sea, the Banda Sea, the Flores Sea and the Java Sea.

The main axis of the South China Sea stretches from Singapore in the south-west to Taiwan 1500 nautical miles away to the northeast. The shorter axis from Vietnam to Sabah measures about 480 nautical miles. On the west lie two major gulfs, the Gulf of Thailand and the Gulf of Tongking. Since the region lies athwart the main monsoon track between eastern Asia and the Indian Ocean, the South China Sea and its coasts experience an alternation of southeast winds in July and northeast winds in January. While the entire region is tropical, there is a contrast between the southern areas, which receive an annual rainfall in excess of 3000 millimetres, and the northern areas which have a rainfall in the order of 1000 millimetres.

In terms of topography the seabed can be divided into three zones. First, there is a broad, shallow continental shelf which occupies the entire Gulf of Thailand and continues southeastwards to the western tip of the island of Borneo. Second, this shelf is continued in two arms skirting the shores of the sea. The section which follows the coast of Vietnam narrows to about 30 nautical miles before broadening again to occupy the Gulf of Tongking and to measure more than 120 nautical miles in width off Hong Kong. The eastern continuation of the main continental shelf, along the north coast of Borneo, remains narrow throughout its length. The third zone occupies the main basin of the South China Sea, and this is an area of confused topography. Northeast of the main continental shelf the slope descends by a series of terraces covered with material derived from the continental shelf. This transition zone is succeeded by volcanic seamounts which are sometimes crowned by coral reefs and islands in the Spratly Group. To the northeast again, the mass of islands is replaced by an abyssal plain with depths of more than 4000 metres. Even in this zone there are more seamounts marked by the Paracel Islands.

Parke, Emery, Szymankiewicz and Reynolds (1971) have described the structure of the continental margin in the South China Sea. They have identified a major sedimentary basin, stretching from Bangkok to Singapore, lying between the Malaysian Peninsula and the Khorat-Semitau Swell which connects Mui Ca Mau and Tanjong Datu, passing just east of the Natuna Islands. East of the Khorat-Semitau Swell lies a basin which Parke and his colleagues called the Saigon–Brunei Basin. In fact the line connecting these two localities lies on the northeastern edge of this basin, which is marked by a line of seamounts which have acted as a trap behind which sediment has accumulated to a depth of 2 kilometres. This filled basin effectively extends the continental shelf off Vietnam and Borneo seawards.

North of the axis linking Ho Chi Minh City with Brunei the most important basin underlies the Gulf of Tongking. Elsewhere, in the main basin of the South China Sea the basins formed within the irregular topography of the Spratly Islands are small, with a sediment thickness not exceeding 1.5 kilometres.

The littoral states consist of China, Vietnam, Cambodia and Thailand on the continent, and Taiwan, the Philippines, Brunei and Indonesia on the adjoining islands. Malaysia is a member of both groups through its sovereignty in the Malaysian Peninsula and the northern part of Borneo. If Singapore was able to maintain its claim to Horsburgh Light, in the face of Malaysian counterclaims, then it would also be a littoral state in the extreme southwest of the South China Sea. The uncertain future of Hong Kong and Macau, and the fact that both would be zone-locked by Chinese claims, make it sensible to discount both as littoral territories in this analysis.

Baselines of states surrounding the South China Sea

The baselines proclaimed by countries around the South China Sea fall into three groups. First there are the archipelagic baselines announced by Indonesia and the Philippines; second there are the straight baseline segments proclaimed by Thailand and Vietnam; and third there are the baselines of Cambodia, China and Malaysia about which only guesses can be made.

Indonesia promulgated its archipelagic baselines on 18 February 1960. The system was defined by 195 turning points; it includes five segments longer than 100 nautical miles and two of these measure 124 nautical miles. The ratio of land to water within the archipelagos is 1:1.2. While the baselines were proclaimed more than twenty years before the principles for archipelagic baselines were finally endorsed in the Convention on the Law of the Sea, it seems evident that the Indonesian model had an important influence on determining the critical tests which were devised. Had the three mathematical tests been made stricter the Indonesian baselines would have failed them all. As it is the system passes the tests, including that requiring the baselines to conform to the general configuration of the archipelago.

The only unusual feature of the Indonesian baselines is that they have not been amended since the acquisition of Portuguese Timor as a province of Indonesia. No doubt this will be done when more urgent matters have been treated.

The archipelagic baselines of the Philippines are defined in Republic Act No. 3046 dated 17 June 1961, as amended. Eighty-one turning points define the baselines which completely surround all islands of the Republic, with the exception of those in the Spratly Group. The longest segment measures 140 nautical miles in the Gulf of Moro, but that segment could be adjusted without difficulty to reduce it to 125 nautical miles. The land-to-water ratio is 1:1.8.

Thailand claimed the Bight of Thailand as an historic bay on 22 September 1959. The closing line was defined as the parallel 12° 35' 45" north. The proclamation defined the waters inside the bay as territorial waters, when it would have been more usual to claim them as internal waters.

On 12 June 1970 Thailand proclaimed three segments of straight baselines along its coasts; two are in the Gulf of Thailand while the third is in the Strait of

Malacca. All three segments connect fringing islands and tie them to the mainland. The segments in the vicinity of Ko Kut and Ko Chang and in the Strait of Malacca are unimpeachable and conform to the spirit and letter of the existing and proposed rules for drawing baselines. However, the segment totalling 126 nautical miles which links Ko Phangan and Ko Samui appears to be based on a very liberal interpretation of the concepts of fringing islands and enclosed waters closely linked to the land domain.

Vietnam announced its baselines on 12 November 1982. The baseline extends from the Gulf of Thailand, southeast of Ko Way, to the coast of Vietnam at the entrance of the Gulf of Tongking, in latitude 17° 10' north. Sections of this baseline are plainly in breach of proposed and existing rules for drawing baselines. Since the sections concerned are not deeply indented the lines must be based on the concept of fringing islands. For example, the section joining hon Nhan and hon Khoai is 98 nautical miles in length and lies 48 nautical miles seawards of other islands nearer the coast. The section joining hon Bay Canh and hon Hai measures 163 nautical miles and lies 70 nautical miles off the mouth of the Mekong River. Finally the last section joining dao Ly Son and dao Con Co measures 145 nautical miles and passes in front of a smooth coast.

The termini of the baseline are uncertain. In the west the terminus will be selected by Cambodia and Vietnam at the point where their baselines meet. This suggests it will be located in the open sea. In the north the baseline terminates at dao Con Co and is not tied to the mainland. There is reference to a maritime boundary agreed between France and China in 1887, but even if this boundary was not a fiction, there is no indication of how the baseline proceeds from dao Con Co to the claimed boundary which lies 43' to the east.

On 1 July 1972 Cambodia announced a unilateral claim to the continental shelf. The proclamation was accompanied by a French chart, based on the prime meridian of Paris, at a scale of 1 : 1,096,000. On this chart was marked a straight baseline which started at the land terminus of the boundary with Thailand and proceeded via Ile Kusrovie and Koh Prins to Quan Phu Quoc, which was surrounded by the baseline. It is now known that Quan Phu Quoc has been confirmed as belonging to Vietnam by agreement between the two countries, which must have been reached before 28 May 1977 when a list of Cambodia's islands, published by the authorities, did not include Quan Phu Quoc (Prescott 1981, 29). Further, the Vietnamese baseline declaration was accompanied by a map which shows an area of historic waters belonging to Vietnam and Cambodia. This area is bounded on the west by a line joining Ko Way and dao Tho Chu, and on the east by the coastline of the mainland east of Quan Phu Quoc. The Vietnamese proclamation notes that the terminus of its baseline will coincide with the terminus of the Cambodian baseline, and that this common point will be located on a straight line linking Ko Way and dao Tho Chu. It is therefore reasonable to assume that Cambodia's baseline will proceed from either Koh Prins, or Koh Tang or Ilots de Sudest, to Ko Way, and from there to a point in the sea on the line linking Ko Way with dao Tho Chu. If such a line was claimed it would depend on a remarkably liberal interpretation of the concepts of fringing islands and enclosed waters linked closely to the land domain.

On 4 September 1958 China announced that its territorial sea would be measured from straight baselines connecting points on the mainland and on the outermost of the coastal islands. No map of these baselines has ever been published by the Chinese authorities. The declaration also notes that straight baselines will be drawn in respect of islands, including the Spratly and Paracel Groups, which the Chinese call Nansha and Hsisha Islands. It is known that Hainan Strait is closed by straight lines which enclose Chinese internal waters (The Geographer 1972, 3). It is not known whether the reference to baselines and offshore archipelagos refers to the whole group or to individual islands. For the Hsisha Islands to be surrounded by a single baseline it would be necessary to make an unusual interpretation of existing and proposed rules, which some countries, such as Ecuador and Australia, have already made.

While there is circumstantial evidence that Malaysia has drawn straight baselines along its coasts, there has been no proclamation about their location. The Geographer (1970, 2) mentioned that Malaysia had recently constructed baselines when discussing the 1969 agreement with Indonesia to divide the continental shelf. Later the Geographer (1973, 3) noted that 'Malaysia appears to have a system of straight baselines'. There is reference to the facts that they have never been promulgated and that the only reference to them is in the continental shelf agreement. In fact there is no mention of such baselines in the agreement, but a map attached to that agreement has not been seen and they might be shown there. Certainly the map produced by the Geographer (1970) to illustrate the analysis of the continental shelf boundary did show Malaysian baselines in the position which subsequent evidence has suggested they occupy.

The subsequent evidence is provided by two maps at a scale of 1:1.5 million (Directorate of National Mapping 1979). One map deals with peninsula Malaysia while the other covers Sabah and Sarawak. The maps show international boundaries at sea; Malaysia's territorial waters, which are coloured blue; and the limit of Malaysia's continental shelf claim, which is shown by a red line. The turning points on the shelf boundary are also listed in a table on the maps, and their coordinates are provided. The maps show no baselines, and the blue shading to represent territorial waters extends right to the coast; there is no category of internal waters.

The outer edge of Malaysia's territorial waters can be considered in two categories. First there are limits along common boundaries with Thailand, Indonesia, Singapore, Brunei and the Philippines. Second there are the other sections where the outer limit has been determined unilaterally by Malaysia. It is with these unilateral determinations that this analysis is concerned. In each case the outer limit selected by Malaysia is a straight line. Now such a pattern can only be produced by straight baselines, and those baselines can be identified by drawing parallel lines 12 nautical miles landward of the outer limit of the territorial sea. When this is done it is found that these lines pass through some islands off the coast and some headlands on the coast. They are shown in figures 8.1 and 8.2. An inspection of the assumed baselines reveals the following points. Off the east coast of peninsula Malaysia there are a number of offshore islands which could be considered to fringe the coast, and the baseline appears to connect some of the outer islands. In Malacca Strait the apparent baseline ignores the fringe of islands close to the coast in the western sector, and instead links distant islands called Perak and Jarak. The segment linking these two islands measures 125 nautical miles. The entire coast of Sarawak has been enclosed by a straight baseline system which consists of four long and two short segments. With the exception of the short segment closing the bay bounded by Tanjong Sipang and Tanjong Po, these segments lie along a coast which is not deeply indented and which does not possess a fringe of islands. The coast of Sabah on the South China Sea does have a fringe of islands and reefs, but the inferred baseline does not follow that fringe. Instead it appears to connect the islands called Labuan and Mangalum and then proceed to a point in the open sea. The effect of using these baselines, if they exist, and then considering waters within the baselines as territorial waters, is to produce claims to territorial seas 61 nautical miles wide in part of Malacca Strait and 57 nautical miles wide off northern Sabah. The apparent baselines in the Celebes Sea connect islands which could be considered to fringe the coast.

Agreed maritime boundaries in the South China Sea

There are three maritime boundaries in this region which were created in the colonial period. On 3 August 1924 Britain drew a boundary through Johore Strait and allocated islands to either Singapore or Malaysia. That channel has been surveyed recently by both countries and they are in the process of fixing the final line.

On 2 January 1930 Britain and the United States drew a boundary to separate their possessions in Sabah and the Philippines respectively. Although the line defined in that treaty served only to distinguish British and American islands, it has apparently been accepted by Malaysia and the Philippines as a boundary separating waters and seabed. The Philippines authorities have incorporated the line in their treaty limits, and the same line is shown on the Malaysian maps produced in 1979 by the symbol for an international boundary.

Malaysia was also involved in the third boundary drawn during the colonial period. In September 1958 Britain defined continental shelf boundaries separating the shelf appertaining to Sabah and Sarawak from the shelf belonging to Brunei. Those boundaries which terminated at the 100 fathom isobath, which is near the 200 metre isobath, are shown on Malaysia's maps published in 1979. It therefore appears that Malaysia has accepted them because they are also shown by the symbol standing for an international boundary. While the line between Brunei and Sabah follows a course which is almost equidistant, the western boundary between Brunei and Sarawak follows an alignment which favours Brunei to a marked extent because it lies west of a line of equidistance. The explanation of this deviation from a line of equidistance is found in the nature of

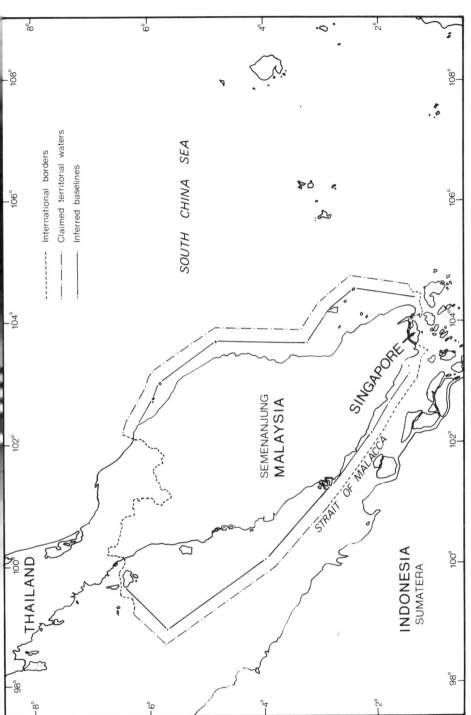

Figure 8.1 Malaysia's baselines around the mainland

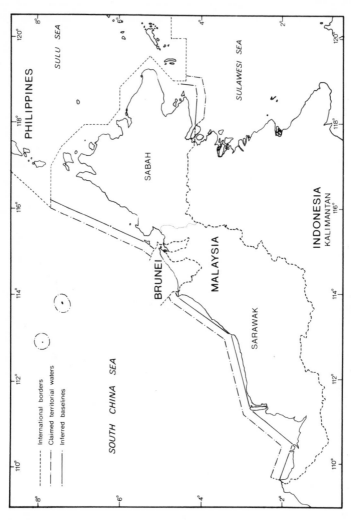

Figure 8.2 Malaysia's baselines around Sabah and Sarawak

Tanjong Baram. This headland, on the delta of the Baram River, projects rather abruptly northwestwards from an otherwise smooth coast. If a line of equidistance took full account of this headland then Brunei would have grounds for feeling aggrieved about a local, geographical accident. In fact the officer administering the government in Sarawak and the Ruler of Brunei decided to draw a true equidistant line for only a short distance, and then to continue the boundary more or less at right-angles to the general direction of the coast, ignoring Tanjong Baram.

Four maritime boundaries have been agreed since the end of the colonial period. On 7 November 1969 an agreement was ratified by Indonesia and Malaysia defining their continental shelf boundaries in Malacca Strait, in the seas between peninsular Malaysia and Indonesia's Natuna Islands, and northwards from Tanjong Datu, where the land boundary between Indonesia and Sarawak terminates. The first two segments are lines of equidistance, but the segment north of Tanjong Datu lies west of the line of equidistance and therefore favours Malaysia. On 10 March 1971 a boundary separating the territorial seas of Malaysia and Indonesia became effective. The treaty stipulates that the boundary 'shall be the line at the center drawn from baselines' of both countries. There is no indication that the Malaysian baselines are straight lines, but the alignment of the territorial sea boundary suggests that this is the case. Only the segment in Malacca Strait was drawn; other territorial sea boundaries between the two countries remain to be settled. There can be no doubt that it was the desire to settle questions of sovereignty and responsibility in this important strait which explains the priority given to this boundary segment.

Indonesia and Singapore ratified a territorial sea boundary on 29 August 1974. This boundary which extends for 25 nautical miles is defined by six points. While the three eastern points are equidistant from Singapore and Indonesia, the westerly three points lie closer to Indonesia. Indeed one of the points lies about 0.5 nautical miles inside Indonesia's archipelagic baseline system.

Finally, on 21 February 1979 Malaysia and Thailand agreed on a joint zone off the terminus of the land boundary on the coast of the Gulf of Thailand. This joint zone, which is a pentagon enclosing about 2100 square nautical miles, has been divided by a single line to distinguish areas of jurisdiction over criminal offences. It is specifically noted that this line should not be construed to indicate the alignment of the eventual boundary. A joint authority composed of equal numbers of members from each country will regulate the exploration and exploitation of the seabed, and it has been decided that the agreement will last for fifty years in the absence of any agreement about the final division of the zone. There is also a provision that the treaty will continue if no boundary has been negotiated in those fifty years.

Maritime boundary problems in the South China Sea

Because this region consists of a semi-enclosed sea the claims made by various countries overlap, and this makes it necessary for bilateral boundaries to be negotiated. There is considerable uniformity in the claims made. Seven of the littoral states claim territorial seas 12 nautical miles wide and exclusive economic zones 200 nautical miles wide. They are Brunei, Cambodia, Indonesia, Malaysia, Taiwan, Thailand and Vietnam. China and Singapore claim only territorial seas, which are respectively 12 and 3 nautical miles wide. However, it is known that Singapore will increase its claim to the conventional territorial sea of 12 nautical miles and also claim an exclusive economic zone of 200 nautical miles at the appropriate time. The Philippines claims an exclusive economic zone 200 nautical miles wide, but its claim to territorial seas results in different widths in different areas. The Philippines has claimed as territorial waters that area between its archipelagic baseline and the limits set out in treaties between the United States and Spain in 1898 and 1900 and between the United States and Britain in 1930. Because these inner and outer lines do not bear a constant relationship to each other the Philippines claims territorial seas 284 nautical miles wide in the northeast and 0.5 nautical miles wide in the southwest.

The problems of drawing maritime boundaries in the South China Sea have been made particularly difficult because some islands are claimed by more than one country, and because there is uncertainty whether some insular features are islands or rocks.

The warning 'Dangerous ground' which is written across charts of the Spratly Islands should be heeded by scholars as well as by navigators. No other part of the world possesses to the same extent the twin difficulties of a plethora of claims and a lack of precise, basic geographical information that exists there. There is no single authoritative definition of the extent of the Spratly Islands, but they are found in the southeastern part of the South China Sea. They lie south of parallel 12° north and east of meridian 112° east, but exclude all islands within the archipelagic baselines of the Philippines and those which lie within 40 nautical miles of the coast of Borneo.

An examination of various charts and pilots has revealed the certain existence of twenty-six islands or cays; they are listed in table 8.1, together with the names used by China, Vietnam, the Philippines and Malaysia. There are also seven sets of rocks which stand above high water, and they are shown in table 8.2. Because some areas have not been surveyed in detail it is probable that this list is incomplete.

All the Spratly Islands and reefs are claimed by China, Taiwan and Vietnam. The Philippines claim to an area known as Kalayaan is shown in figure 8.3; it excludes Spratly Island in the west and some reefs in the south. Malaysia claims the islands and reefs in the extreme south, and its claim is also shown in figure 8.3. It is not known which features, if any, are claimed by Brunei.

Only fourteen of the insular features in the Spratly Group are occupied. The Philippines occupy seven islands. Loaita, Thitu and Northeast Cay were occupied in 1968, and later West York Island, Flat Island, Nanshan Island and Lankiam Cay were occupied and fortified. Vietnam has forces on Spratly Island, Southwest Cay, Sin Cowe, Namyit Island and Amboyna Cay. Taiwan has

Table 8.1 Islands in the Spratly Group

	Location	Chinese	Names Vietnamese	Philippine
Alicia-Annie Reef (C)	9° 25′ N 115° 26′ E	Xian o Jiao		Arellano
Amboyna Cay (C)[1]	7° 51′ N 112° 55′ E	An Po Na Sha Zhou	An Bang	Kalantiyaw
Commodore Reef (C)[1]	8° 21′ N 115° 17′ E	Siling Jiao		Rizal
Flat Island (I)	10° 50′ N 115° 49′ E	Fei Xin Dao		Patag
Gaven Reef (C)	10° 13′ N 114° 12′ E	Nan Xun Jiao		
Grierson Reef (C)	9° 53′ N 114° 35′ E			
Irving Reef (C)	10° 53′ N 114° 56′ E			Balagtas
Itu Aba (I)	10° 23′ N 114° 21′ E	Tai Ping Dao	Thai Binh	Ligaw
Lankiam Cay (C)	10° 44′ N 114° 31′ E	Yang Xin Zhou		Panata
Landsdowne Reef (C)	9° 46′ N 114° 22′ E			
Loaita Cay (C)	10° 44′ N 114° 21′ E	Nan Yao Zhou		
Loaita Island (I)	10° 41′ N 114° 25′ E	Nan Yao Dao	Loaita	Kota
London Reef (C)	8° 53′ N 112° 15′ E	Yin Qing Qun Jiao		Quezon
Mariveles Reef (C)[1]	7° 59′ N 113° 50′ E	Han Hao Jiao		
Namyit Island (I)	10° 11′ N 114° 22′ E	Hung Ma Dao	Nam Yit	Binago
Nanshan (I)	10° 45′ N 115° 49′ E	Ha Huan Dao		Lawak
Northeast Cay (C)	11° 28′ N 114° 21′ E	Pei Zi Jiao	Song Tu Dong	Parola
Pearson Reef NE (C)	8° 58′ N 113° 39′ E	Pi Sheng Dao		Hizon
Pearson Reef SW (C)	8° 55′ N 113° 35′ E	Pi Sheng Dao		Hizon
Sin Cowe Island (I)	9° 52′ N 114° 19′ E	Jing Hong Dao	Sinh Ton	Rurok
Southwest Cay (C)	11° 26′ N 114° 20′ E	Nan Zi Dao	Song Tu Tay	Pugad
Spratly Island (I)	8° 38′ N 111° 55′ E	Nan Wei Dao	Truong Sa	Lagos
Thitu Island (I)	11° 03′ N 114° 17′ E	Zhong Ye Dao	Thi Tu	Pagasa
West York Island (I)	11° 05′ N 115° 01′ E	Xi Yue Dao		Likas
Cay (near Itu Aba) (C)	10° 23′ N 114° 28′ E			
Cay (near Thitu) (C)	11° 03′ N 114° 13′ E			

Note:
1 The Malaysian names for these features are as follows: Amboyna Cay – Kecil Amboyna; Commodore Reef – Terumbu Laksamana; Mariveles Reef – Terumbu Mantanani.

Table 8.2 Known rocks in the Spratly Group

	Location	Chinese	Names Philippine	Malaysian
Barque Canada Reef	8° 04′ N 113° 41′ E	Yin Qing Qun Jiao	Mascado	Terumbu Perahu
London (East) Reef	8° 52′ N 112° 46′ E	Yin Qing Qun Jiao	Silangan	
Fiery Cross Reef	9° 40′ N 113° E	Yung Shu Jiao	Kalingan	
Great Discovery Reef	9° 59′ N 113° 51′ E	Da Xien Dao	Paredes	
Louisa Reef	6° 20′ N 113° 14′ E	Nan Tong Jiao		Terumbu Samarang Barat Kecil
Royal Charlotte Reef	7° N 113° 35′ E	Huang Lu Jiao		Terumbu Samarang Barat Besar
Swallow Reef[1]	7° 23′ N 113° 59′ E	Dan Wan Jiao		Terumbu Layang Layang

Note:
1 It is reported by Malaysia that Swallow Reef is surmounted by an island.

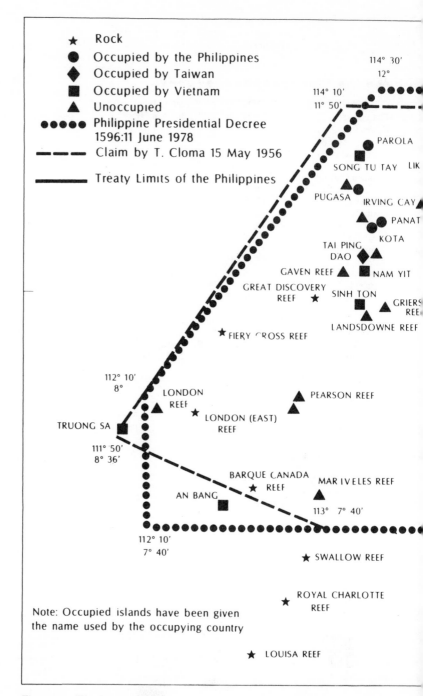

Figure 8.3 The Spratly Islands

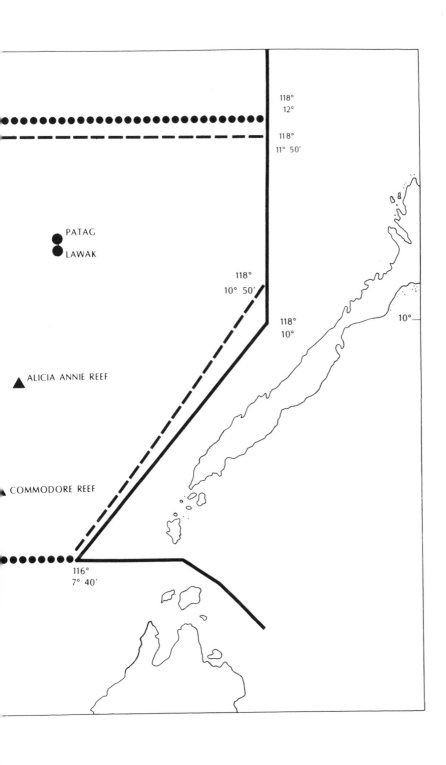

PATAG

LAWAK

ALICIA ANNIE REEF

COMMODORE REEF

118°
12°

118°
11° 50'

118°
10° 50'

118°
10°

10°

116°
7° 40'

occupied Itu Aba Island since 1956. Malaysia has built a guardhouse on Swallow Reef and it is occupied by a detachment of about twenty men. It had previously been thought that only rocks were found on this reef.

China, Taiwan and Vietnam all claim the Spratly Group on the ground that it has been part of their state from time immemorial. China and Vietnam have both been active in providing evidence of a historical nature for their claims in recent years. The palm for establishing ancient connections must be given to China, while Vietnam has been able to provide hard evidence of French acts of annexation in the 1930s. China however has also fired cartographic broadsides by drawing attention to maps produced by the Soviet Union in 1972 and 1975 which show the islands to be Chinese (Prescott 1981, 35).

The Philippines' claim on 11 June 1978 set out limits which closely followed those proclaimed by Mr Tomas Cloma in 1956. This gentleman, who owned a fishing fleet and some other commercial vessels, tried to create his own country in the Spratly Group which he called Freedomland. This attempt failed but it is interesting that the Philippines have used similar boundaries and have translated Freedomland into Kalayaan, which means 'freedom'. This claim is justified on the grounds that it was vital to the country's security and economic survival that the territory did not legally belong to any other country, that any claims by other states had been abandoned, and that the Philippines had established its sovereignty by indispensable need and effective occupation and control.

Malaysia did not make any claims to sections of the Spratly Group until 1978. It appears that the claims are based on the fact that the insular features stand on Malaysia's continental shelf. In the *New Straits Times* on 19 May 1983 the Deputy Minister in charge of Legal Matters was reported to have said that Malaysia's rights to Amboyna Cay were a simple matter of geography. Four days later the Parliamentary Secretary to the Minister of Foreign Affairs was quoted in the same newspaper as having said that Malaysia had conducted a survey of the location of Amboyna Cay and it had been found to be in Malaysian waters. If true this is a remarkable justification. It is not waters which give title to islands but islands which confer rights to waters. Despite the apparent weakness of its claims Malaysia has erected obelisks on Louisa Reef and Commodore Reef to bolster its title. It is believed that the monument on Commodore Reef was destroyed by the Philippines authorities.

There is no present indication how these conflicting claims will be resolved. While the Philippine authorities are the most active in the area, there is absolutely no indication that either China or Vietnam will relinquish their total claims. In view of the fact that Vietnam lost control of the Paracel Islands to China in 1974, it seems certain that Vietnam will not retreat from its claim to the Spratly Group. If there were only two countries involved it is possible that a joint zone might be created to allow development of resources before the claims were settled. The involvement of five countries seems to make this unlikely.

Meanwhile, the danger inherent in the political rivalry in the Spratly Islands was demonstrated when a German yacht was sunk by fire from one of the islands on 10 April 1983.

Both major gulfs on the northwest border of the South China Sea are the scene of conflicting maritime claims. The problems in the Gulf of Thailand should be easier to solve than the problems in the Spratly Group for four reasons. First, there are fewer countries involved, and none of them claims the entire area in the fashion of China and Vietnam in the South China Sea. Second, there are no islands in the middle of the Gulf and the only dispute over ownership, which formerly existed between Vietnam and Cambodia, has been solved. Third, there are far fewer islands in the Gulf of Thailand than in the South China Sea and there is no uncertainty as to whether they are islands or rocks. Finally, the structure of the seabed of the Gulf of Thailand is much simpler than the structure of the seabed in the vicinity of the Spratly Group.

The unilateral claims made by South Vietnam in June 1971, by Cambodia in July 1972, and by Thailand in May 1973 are shown in figure 8.4. It is not clear whether the present governments of Cambodia and Vietnam have preserved the claims of their predecessors, but there is no evidence that they have renounced them. An inspection of the claims shows that each country has adopted rules for drawing equidistant lines which secure the largest possible area for the claimant. Thailand has apparently ignored its own islands called Ko Kra and Ko Losin, and those of Cambodia and Vietnam called Ko Way and dao Tho Chu. Because the last-named islands are further from the coasts of Cambodia and Vietnam than the Thai islands are from the Thai coast, the line of equidistance is moved eastwards in Thailand's favour. The Cambodian and Vietnamese claims simply discount entirely the Thai islands and therefore shift the line of equidistance westwards, giving themselves a marked advantage.

It will be seen in figure 8.4 that Cambodia's claim intersects the Thai island called Ko Kut. It seems likely that this totally misguided claim results from reading the 1907 Franco-Thai boundary treaty and protocol. In the protocol it was noted that 'the boundary between French Indo-China and Siam leaves the sea at the point opposite the highest point of Koh Kut island' (Prescott 1981, 18). There was certainly no intention to continue the boundary at sea by drawing a line from the terminus on the boundary on the mainland through the highest point on Ko Kut, but that is apparently what Cambodia tried to claim in 1972.

The other lateral boundaries between Cambodia and Vietnam and between Thailand and Malaysia are still unsettled. However, both disputed zones now have a special status. Malaysia and Thailand have created a joint development area which has already been described. The area of historic waters belonging to Cambodia and Vietnam is shown on the map which illustrated the Vietnamese baselines and which was attached to the proclamation on 12 November 1982. It seems likely that Cambodia will have the greatest interest in finally resolving the problems of conflicting claims, because it has the smallest claim to the continental shelf. Its neighbours have large areas free from conflicting claims where exploration can continue; that is not the case for Cambodia.

The Gulf of Tongking, which is called Beibu Gulf by the Chinese and Bac Bo Gulf by the Vietnamese, has an area of 24,000 square nautical miles. The gulf has a maximum depth of about 80 metres and the seabed's topography is smooth. The

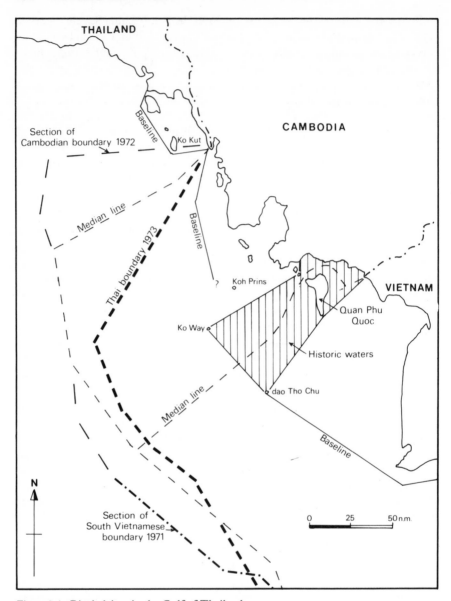

Figure 8.4 Rival claims in the Gulf of Thailand

thick Lui-chow sedimentary basin which underlies the gulf is an obvious target for oil exploration.

Chinese authorities have insisted that since 1974 there has been a disagreement between the two countries over the correct location of the maritime boundary in the gulf (*Beijing Review* 1979, 15). The Chinese assert that the matter is unresolved; the Vietnamese authorities hold the view that the maritime boundary was delimited in the Sino-French boundary agreement of 26 June 1887. This view was set out again in the third paragraph of the proclamation announcing Vietnam's baselines on 12 November 1982.

The relevant section of the Sino-French treaty, translated from the French version, contains the following provisions:

> The islands which are east of the Paris meridian of 105° 43' east [108° 3' east of Greenwich], that is to say the north-south line passing through the eastern point of Tcha's Kou or Quan-Chan [Tra Co], which forms the boundary, are also allocated to China. The island of Gotho [Kao Tao] and other islands west of this meridian belong to Annam.   (Prescott 1975, 453)

The Vietnamese authorities face four serious difficulties in persuading objective commentators that the meridian mentioned in the treaty was intended to be a maritime boundary.

First, the meridian has no termini. Boundaries invariably have a point of commencement and a point of termination. If the meridian is projected northwards it intersects the coast of China, and according to Vietnamese reasoning would award waters and seabed adjacent to the Chinese coast to Vietnam. If the meridian is projected southwards it intersects the coast of Vietnam between Hue and Da Nang; that would surely be an unwelcome development for the Vietnamese. Perhaps Vietnam would contend that the meridian should terminate southwards when it intersects the line drawn across the mouth of the Gulf of Tongking. But the 1887 treaty does not mention the gulf, and it would be very difficult to secure agreement on a single line which represents the mouth of the gulf. Different geographers would almost certainly draw it in different positions.

Second, if the meridian was the maritime boundary it would mean that Vietnam was not entitled to any territorial waters off the eastern tip of Tra Co. Surely the treaty could not have meant that, because the only zone about which there was any agreement in the 1880s was the zone of territorial waters.

Third, if this meridian was meant to be a maritime boundary, it was so far out of character with the prevailing concepts of maritime sovereignty of the period that it would have been given special mention in the text.

Fourth, there is nothing in the treaty to distinguish the use of this meridian from the use of straight lines by other colonial powers in other treaties, to separate island groups. Such lines were simply a form of geographical shorthand to avoid the need to name all the islands. This technique was used by Russia and the United States in 1867; by Britain when it allowed Queensland to annex the Torres Strait Islands in 1879; by Spain and the United States in 1898, when they defined the islands of the Philippines; by Britain and Germany when they divided the Solomon Islands in 1899; and by Britain and the United States when they distinguished their possessions in the Sulu Archipelago in 1930. There is one other example which is especially relevant. In 1939 the Governor-General of French Indo-China drew a line in the Gulf of Thailand to settle a dispute over whether certain islands belonged to Cambodia or Cochin China. The so-called Brevie Line, named after its author, was drawn at an azimuth of 126° west of true north, from the coastal terminus of the land boundary. In all its dealings with Cambodia Vietnam has insisted that this line was only designed to distinguish the ownership of islands; it has rejected any suggestion that the line should also divide the areas of seabed which attach to both countries. Presumably it takes this view because the line of equidistance lies north of the Brevie Line.

If, despite all these objections, Vietnam was able to persuade China that its view was correct there would still be two serious practical problems. It would be necessary to find the eastern end of Tra Co as it existed in June 1887, and to see whether it lay on the meridian 105° 43' east of Paris. The boundary commissioners were trying to avoid any ambiguity by providing two definitions of the same point. In doing so they fell into the same trap which has been claiming boundary architects for centuries, because if the two definitions can be interpreted to refer to different points an intractable problem is created. The second problem would involve the need to discover the termini of the meridian.

There is an inactive dispute between Singapore and Malaysia over the ownership of two islands at opposite ends of Singapore Strait. The islands are called Pulau Pisang and Pulau Batu Puteh, and they are located to the west and east of the strait respectively. In both cases the islands are surmounted by a navigation light which has been maintained by Singapore. However, the islands have been claimed by Malaysia and both lie inside Malaysia's claimed territorial waters. The claim to Pulau Batu Puteh is probably the most important for Singapore. If it was successful Singapore would have access to a lens-shaped area of sea and seabed measuring 240 square nautical miles. That might not seem to be very much, but to a zone-locked country such as Singapore it would be welcome. Such a successful claim would require renegotiation of the seabed boundary between Malaysia and Indonesia in this region. Presumably this is a problem where detailed historical research should establish the answer to which country owns the island.

Proceeding eastwards from Singapore Strait there are a number of areas where overlapping claims create difficulties. North of the Natuna Islands of Indonesia there is an area of 11,270 square nautical miles claimed by both Vietnam and Indonesia. While Indonesia claims out to the median line between the two states, giving full effect to all islands, Vietnam appears to be maintaining the continental shelf claim of South Vietnam on 6 June 1971. This claim discounts Indonesia's Natuna Islands and therefore pushes the line of equidistance southwards. Indonesia has stood firm on its claim and negotiations have continued on an irregular basis, with long intervals between short bilateral discussions.

It was noted earlier that the continental shelf boundary settled between Malaysia and Indonesia to separate claims from Kalminatan and Sarawak, deviates from the line of equidistance in Malaysia's favour. It is possible that when the boundary to separate the exclusive economic zones of the two countries is drawn in this region, north of Tanjong Datu, Indonesia will claim an equidistant line. If such a claim is accepted then Indonesia will have exclusive economic rights in the water column which overlies part of Malaysia's continental shelf. Such arrangements are not novel, but they do create the potential for friction if fishing and mining activities interfere with each other.

Eastwards along the coast of Borneo lies the small country of Brunei. On the map which Malaysia produced in 1979 to show the area of its territorial sea and continental shelf, the 1958 boundaries proclaimed by Britain in respect of Brunei are shown. While these boundaries were drawn to separate areas of the continental shelf, Malaysia has shown them as lines which also separate territorial waters.

If it is assumed that Brunei will also continue to accept the British boundaries of 1958 as defining the territorial sea out to 12 nautical miles, and the continental shelf out to the 100 fathom isobath, two problems remain. First it is necessary to delimit the boundary which marks the seaward edge of Brunei's claim to the continental shelf; and second it is necessary to fix boundaries separating the exclusive economic zones of both states.

It is uncertain whether Malaysia will be permitted to maintain its claim to the various islands and reefs in the Spratly Group, but the main problem will be the same no matter which country owns these features. The first point which will have to be clarified is which features in the Spratly Group will be used as basepoints by the country negotiating with Brunei. The cay on Mariveles Reef and Amboyna Cay are unquestionably islands, and therefore any country which owned them would be entitled to claim both the continental shelf and the exclusive economic zone towards the coast of Brunei. The median line between Brunei and those two islands is shown in figure 8.5, and that appears to be the maximum distance Brunei can claim if the equidistant principle is applied. If Malaysia or some other country insisted that there was an island on Swallow Reef, then the median line with Brunei would be moved southwards towards Brunei. If it was further argued that the rocks on Royal Charlotte and Louisa Reefs had an economic life of their own, which permitted them to be used as basepoints from which the continental shelf could be claimed, then the median line would again move southwards to the disadvantage of Brunei.

This suggests that Brunei would be wise to argue that the application of the equidistant principle would be unjust. It is possible that Brunei would argue, in the manner of West Germany in the North Sea, that it is entitled to a corridor of continental shelf reaching out into the South China Sea. For example, if the limits drawn by Britain were projected seawards, as shown in figure 8.5, they would only enclose Louisa Reef, a feature which some authorities believe is completely submerged at high tide. Such a projection would eventually reach Rifleman Bank, just beyond the present Malaysian claim. For such a claim to succeed it would be necessary for the country which owned Amboyna Cay to sacrifice its own legitimate rights.

The problem of negotiating boundaries to the exclusive economic zone could be avoided if a single set of boundaries was used to delimit all maritime zones.

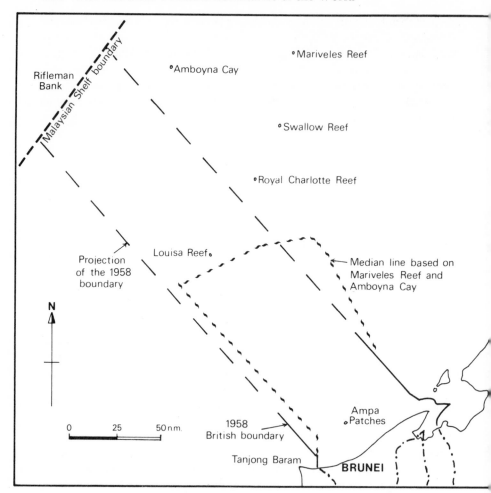

Figure 8.5   Possible maritime claims by Brunei

The British declaration of 1958 also drew boundaries between Brunei and Sarawak in Brunei Bay. Providing this line continues to be observed no new difficulties will arise, although there have been reports that Brunei claims the valley of the Limbang River which cuts the country into two parts. If such a claim is pursued then relations between Malaysia and Brunei are unlikely to be sufficiently cordial to allow Brunei to obtain concessions in the South China Sea.

In the Celebes Sea Malaysia's unilateral claims to territorial seas and the continental shelf have created a problem with Indonesia. The main difficulty concerns the ownership of the islands called Sipadan and Ligitan. These islands, which are apparently basepoints on Malaysia's system of straight baselines, lie south of the parallel which defines the last segment of the Anglo-Dutch border on Borneo. This fact provides part of Indonesia's claim to the islands. Malaysia's claim rests

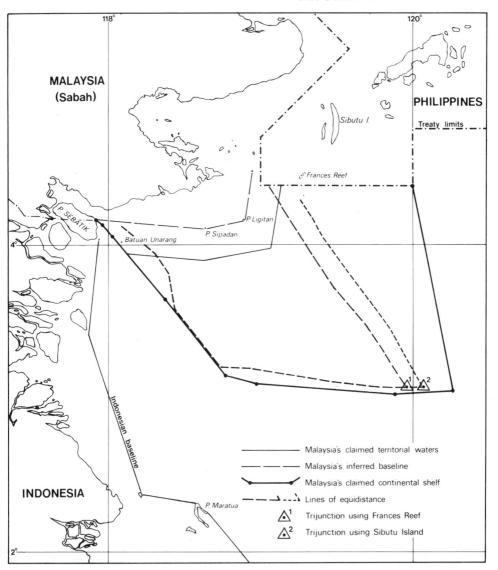

Figure 8.6   Maritime boundaries in the northwest Celebes Sea

on the fact that for many years residents of what is now Sabah have collected turtles' eggs and coconuts on the islands, and planted tapioca. An unmanned lighthouse was constructed on each island by Malaysia in the 1960s, and the area is regularly patrolled by Malaysian authorities. If Indonesia's claim succeeded Malaysia's maritime zones based on the principle of equidistance would be sharply curtailed in the Celebes Sea. Furthermore, access to Tawau would be impaired.

However, even if this disagreement was resolved in favour of Malaysia, it would still be open to Indonesia to object to Malaysia's continental shelf boundary. As figure 8.6 shows, the Malaysian claim crosses the median line in the direction of Indonesia in two places.

The Philippines has much greater grounds for complaint against Malaysia's unilateral claim to the continental shelf. Malaysia appears to have ignored both Frances Reef and Sibutu Island. While it is possible that Frances Reef might be considered to be rocks lacking an economic life of their own, it is certainly proper for the Philippines to base its claim on Sibutu Island. The area which Malaysia has claimed beyond the equidistant line based on Sibutu Island is 2180 square nautical miles.

At the northeastern entrance to the Celebes Sea lies Miangas Island. It is Point 56 in Indonesia's archipelagic baselines, but it also lies within the treaty limits agreed by Spain and the United States in 1898. The ownership of the island, then called Palmas Island, was contested by the United States and the Netherlands in 1906. The latter country claimed this feature on the basis of long and undisputed sovereignty, while the United States rested its case on the treaty with Spain. The question was referred to the Court of Arbitration at The Hague in 1925, and three years later Max Huber gave his judgement in favour of the Netherlands. Indonesia succeeded to the Dutch title when it became independent.

While the Philippines does not dispute Indonesia's sovereignty over the island the countries have not agreed on any boundary through the waters lying between Miangas Island and Mindanao. It is not expected that the negotiation of such a boundary will present any serious problems. If the line is based on the archipelagic baselines of each country, it will be gently curved. If the boundary is based on islands rather than the archipelagic baselines, it will be marked by some sharp changes in direction which will favour the Philippines.

There are other potential problems associated with any insistence by the Philippines that it is entitled to claim as territorial waters those seas which lie between the treaty limits and its archipelagic baselines. These boundaries are shown in figure 8.7. It is clear that acceptance of the treaty limits would be to the disadvantage of Taiwan. It is also certain that the Philippines has failed to win international approval for this historic claim. There were hints at the annual conference of the Philippine Society of International Law in March 1983 that the Philippine authorities might be prepared to reduce their territorial sea claim to a uniform width of 12 nautical miles when the Convention is ratified. There was also a suggestion that the claim to historic waters might be maintained in respect of those countries which do not ratify the Convention. In the statement at the signing of the Convention, the delegate of the Philippines noted that the act of signing did not affect his country's claims under the treaties of 1898 and 1930.

The statement also reiterated the Philippines claim to Kalayaan. Of all the claimants to the Spratly Islands only the Philippines could enclose them by archipelagic baselines. The islands could be linked to the existing baseline system by lines connecting Alicia Annie Reef to a point on Palawan just south of Tagbita

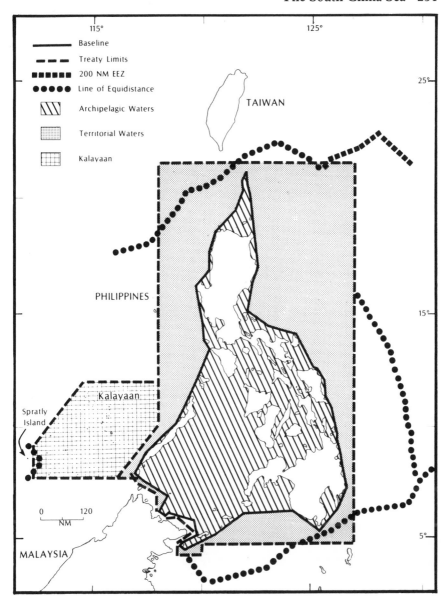

Figure 8.7 The Philippines' maritime boundaries

Bay, and connecting Commodore Reef to Ligas Point on Balbac Island. The lines would measure 117 and 102 nautical miles respectively, and the new land-to-water ratio in the expanded system would be 1:2.1. The total area of archipelagic waters added by the new baselines would measure 22,800 square nautical miles.

Conclusions

Four factors complicate the process of drawing maritime boundaries in the South China Sea. First, this semi-enclosed sea is surrounded by peripheral states which show considerable variations in size, political power and wealth. They all have some interest in securing the additional resources contained in the maritime zones off their coasts. Second, the presence of an extensive group of islands near the middle of the largest area of water, and the fact that all or some of these islands are claimed by five and possibly six countries, means that no progress can even be attempted on many bilateral boundaries.

The third factor involves the unilateral maritime claims which have been made by some countries, especially to areas of the continental shelf in the Gulf of Thailand and the southern portion of the South China Sea. Finally, the prospects for successful boundary negotiations are seriously diminished by the poor political relations which exist between some of the important participants. The antipathy between China and Vietnam; the suspicion of the members of the Association of Southeast Asian Nations towards Vietnam's intentions in Cambodia; and the refusal of most countries formally to recognize the existence of Taiwan all make the resolution of some maritime problems difficult or impossible.

There are, however, encouraging signs. First, some of the potential and actual disputes over maritime zones have been in a passive stage for years. Singapore and Malaysia, Malaysia and Indonesia, and Indonesia and the Philippines have not actively pursued rival claims and they have not allowed potential disagreements to harm their relationships. Second, Malaysia and Thailand have created a joint development area so that their determination of a common boundary can proceed at a leisurely pace, without hindering the use of seabed resources.

But perhaps the prime example of international co-operation is provided by the traffic separation scheme which was established for the Straits of Malacca and Singapore. The littoral states, Malaysia, Indonesia and Singapore, were anxious to reduce the chance of serious damage to their coasts through pollution which might follow collisions between ships or the grounding of tankers. Accidents to the Showa Maru in 1975 and the Diego Silat in 1976 encouraged this anxiety. But there were other interests. Singapore, which has become an important oil-refining centre and which has major dockyards where ships can be repaired, as well as a growing commercial fleet, was reluctant to introduce measures which might unnecessarily interfere with those activities. Major maritime nations, and especially Japan, were concerned that restrictions might make it necessary to send some vessels by a longer route, which would increase the costs for imports of fuel.

The competing interests were all satisfied by the careful re-surveying of the straits and a requirement that vessels should have a clearance under their keels of at least 3.5 metres. Japan made a very large contribution to the cost of the surveying activities and the provision of navigational aids.

Finally, it is a very satisfactory situation that despite the many problems in this region it has continued to serve as a very important route for the commercial marine traffic of much of the world, without serious difficulty.

References

Beijing Review (1979) 'Xisha and Nansha Islands belong to China', 25 May, 21, 23.

Directorate of National Mapping (1979) *Map Showing Territorial Waters and Continental Shelf Boundaries of Malaysia*, 2 sheets, scale 1 : 1.5 M, Kuala Lumpur.

Djalal, H. (1979) 'Conflicting territorial and jurisdictional claims in the South China Sea', *Indonesian Quarterly*, 3 (3), 17 pages.

New China News (1980) 'Chinese Foreign Ministry Document on Xisha and Nansha Islands', 27 February, 18 (6), 14–16.

Parke, M. L., Emery, K. O., Szymankiewicz, R. and Reynolds, L. M. (1971) 'Structural framework of continental margin in South China Sea', *The American Association of Petroleum Geologists Bulletin*, 55 (5), 723–51.

Prescott, J. R. V. (1975) *Map of Mainland Asia by Treaty*, Melbourne.

Prescott, J. R. V. (1981) *Maritime Jurisdiction in Southeast Asia: A Commentary and Map*, EAPI Research Report no. 2, East–West Center, Honolulu.

The Geographer (1970) *Continental Shelf Boundary: Indonesia–Malaysia*, 'Limits in the Seas' series, no. 1, Washington, DC.

The Geographer (1972) *Straight Baselines: People's Republic of China*, 'Limits in the Seas' series, no. 43, Washington, DC.

The Geographer (1973) *Territorial Sea Boundary: Indonesia–Malaysia*, 'Limits in the Seas' series, no. 50, Washington, DC.

9

The north Pacific Ocean

The Pacific, from the point of view of the equilibrium of the world ocean, has not the importance of the Antarctic and the Atlantic. . . . It is a sluggish ocean, with rather uniform deep water.   (Tchernia 1980, 216)

However, when one considers the Pacific Basin from a global perspective, it is possible to be distinctly sanguine about its prospects.   (Krause 1981, 11)

It can be argued that the set of maritime disputes in North-east Asia is one of the most extensive and serious to emerge with the new ocean regime. . . . On the other hand, it must be said that, although serious in law of the sea terms, these disputes are relatively minor when compared with the larger political cleavages and movements in the region.   (Buzan 1979, 199)

These quotations give the impression that the north Pacific Ocean is an expanse of water which is undistinguished in either physical characteristics or the potential to cause conflict between states. In fact, as Buzan comments, this is the only sea which is bordered by the three countries with the largest military forces, and a fourth state which occupies a very important position in world commerce. The north Pacific Ocean contains the area where the United States and the Soviet Union lie only 5 nautical miles apart, and the peninsula where the last major conventional war was fought in the 1950s. The political importance of this ocean is governed not by the actual and potential maritime disputes but by the sharp ideological differences between North and South Korea, between the Soviet Union and the United States, and between China and Japan. Thus while this chapter will describe an impressive array of maritime disputes, they play only a minor role in determining the political climate of this region.

The main characteristics of the north Pacific Ocean

The physical themes identified in the south Pacific Ocean are repeated in this region, although there are significant variations. Like its southern counterpart the north Pacific Ocean can be divided into an eastern and western sector; however the division is not marked by the East Pacific Ridge, which peters out in the vicinity of the Golfo de California. The western sector is distinguished by the multitude of islands and the semi-enclosed seas which also characterize the south-west Pacific Ocean. It is noticeable, however, that the marginal seas north of the equator, such as the Sea of Okhotsk and the Sea of Japan, are more clearly defined by surrounding continent and islands than the Tasman and Solomon Seas in the southern hemisphere. The deep trenches encountered off the island arcs in the southwest Pacific Ocean are continued northwards and become deeper and more continuous. In addition, the marginal seas in the northern hemisphere tend to be underlain more completely by continental shelves than their southern counterparts.

In the eastern regions north and south of the equator there are several seamounts, but only a few are capped by islands. The comparatively smooth coasts of Peru and Ecuador are matched by similar configurations on the coasts of the Panama Isthmus, Mexico and the United States. The fretted fjord coast of Chile is repeated in British Columbia and Alaska. However, the deep trench which defines the western border of South America is absent in the northern continent, except along the Alaska Peninsula. The broad continental rise off western Canada finds no equal in the southeastern Pacific Ocean.

Perhaps the most striking physical difference between the north and south Pacific Oceans is that the exit from the ocean northwards is via a narrow international strait. Bering Strait is 45 nautical miles wide between the continents of Asia and North America. There are two islands in the strait; Ostrov Ratmanova belongs to the Soviet Union and Little Diomede Island belongs to the United States of America. While the islands are only 2 nautical miles apart there is a channel 19 nautical miles wide between Siberia and Ostrov Ratmanova, and another, 20 nautical miles wide, between Little Diomede Island and Alaska. The fact that the two strongest countries in the world bound Bering Strait probably explains why there are no problems about transit through it. It is also true that only a small amount of traffic would normally pass between the Pacific and Arctic Oceans.

There are few political and economic similarities between the north and south Pacific Ocean. While there are only three continental countries in the south Pacific Ocean, and all in South America, compared with fourteen insular states, there is only one island country in the north Pacific Ocean and twelve continental states. Although the contrast between rich and poor countries in the south Pacific Ocean is matched by equal disparities north of the equator, the northern area does include at least four states which have an extremely important influence on political, strategic and economic developments throughout the world.

There are dependent territories in the north Pacific Ocean, just as there are in the southern hemisphere, but France is the only European power represented; it controls Clipperton Island. The United States has responsibility for other dependent territories, and indeed most of the islands which lie east of the island arcs of the Kuril Islands, Japan and the Philippines.

The various American fragments of territory enjoy varied constitutional status. The Aleutian Islands form part of the State of Alaska, and the Hawaiian Islands form a separate state in the United States. Wake, Jarvis, Johnston, Howland and Baker Islands, Kingman Reef and Palmyra Atoll are unincorporated territories of

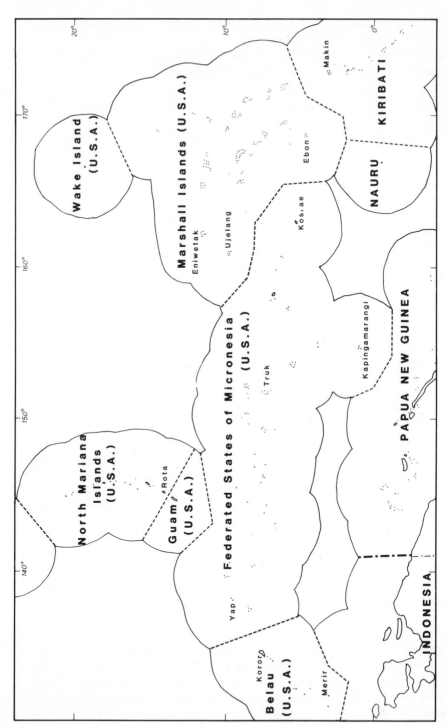

Figure 9.1 The Trust Territory of the Pacific Islands

the United States and are administered by either the Department of the Interior or the Department of Defence. Guam is an organized unincorporated territory and the Northern Mariana Islands, the Marshall Islands, the Federated States of Micronesia and Belau are United Nations Trusteeship Territories. The extent of these four territories is shown in figure 9.1. For nearly twenty years negotiations have been proceeding for the termination of the trusteeship on terms satisfactory to all parties. The Northern Marianas has decided on commonwealth status similar to that enjoyed by Puerto Rico. The other three territories have decided to pursue the path of free association, and a compact giving effect to that wish has been drafted. This compact, once it has been adopted by the Marshall Islands, Belau and the Federated States of Micronesia will enable those territories to conduct their own foreign policy and to control their marine resources. Their citizens will be able to go to the United States and work as non-immigrants, and the United States will guarantee economic assistance for fifteen years. America will also defend the territories against third parties.

Finally, a fundamental difference between the two parts of the Pacific Ocean is that the northern area has experienced periods of hostility between the major countries. The residue of suspicion which this has caused reinforces the ideological cleavages in the region, in a manner which is quite unmatched in the south Pacific Ocean.

Straight baselines

Three countries have proclaimed conventional straight baselines around the shores of the north Pacific Ocean. Mexico's straight baselines in the Golfo de California were announced on 29 August 1968. Fourteen segments of straight lines are connected by sections of the low-water mark. The effect of these combined baselines is to enclose as internal waters a fringe of sea along the east coast of Baja California, and the head of the gulf north of San Esteban Island. As figure 9.2 shows, the longest segment joins Punta Arena to Ceralbo Island. While the baselines along the east coast of Baja California might be considered to possess a fringe of islands, it is not clear how the gulf can be properly closed by the line which links the east and west coasts via San Esteban Island. It is certainly not a closing line for a legal bay. Perhaps the head of the gulf could be claimed as an historic bay, but this has not been expressly done in the Mexican proclamation. Since the decree refers to the fourth article of the 1958 Convention, which deals with drawing straight baselines along indented coasts and coasts fringed with islands, the lines must be justified by that article. There appears to have been a novel and interesting interpretation of this article by the Mexican authorities. Having noted in the proclamation that the requirement that baselines should not depart to an appreciable extent from the general direction of the coast has no mathematical precision, the Mexicans appear to have drawn two baselines along the east and west coasts of the gulf and to have discovered fortuitously that they meet at San Esteban Island!

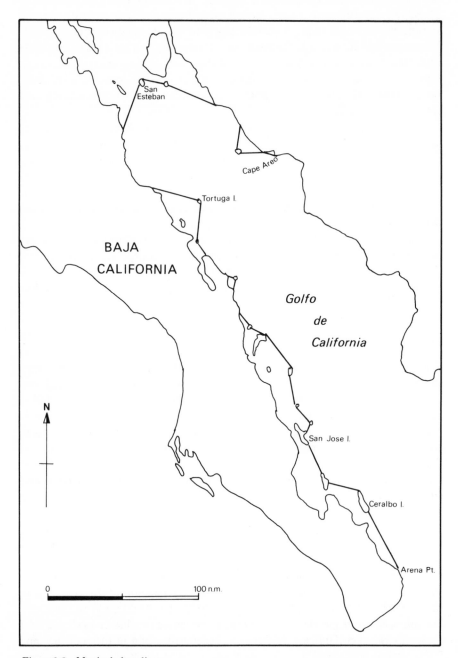

Figure 9.2 Mexico's baselines

Canada announced straight baselines along the coasts of Vancouver Island and the Queen Charlotte Islands on 29 May 1969. These coasts are certainly cut into and deeply indented and it is appropriate that straight baselines should be used. However, it is curious that the northern terminus of the Vancouver Island baseline, and both termini on the Queen Charlotte Islands baseline, are located on islands. If a baseline ends on an island then it is impossible to know the exact extent of internal waters. The baseline must terminate on the mainland, or in this case on the main island, so that the area of internal waters is completely defined.

On 20 September 1978 South Korea announced its straight baselines in four segments. Two segments in the east simply close legal bays called Yongil-man and Ulsan-man; their mouths measure 6.1 and 3.1 nautical miles wide respectively. The third segment extends for 237 nautical miles from a rock in the Korea Strait to Sohuksan-do, an island in the southwest of the country. The fourth segment extends north from the north coast of Sohuksan-do to Taeryong-do, through a series of straight sectors totalling 199 nautical miles. As in the case of Canada, the termini on the rock and on Taeryong-do mean that the exact extent of internal waters is unknown. In the Western Channel of the Korea Strait, between South Korea and Tsushima, which belongs to Japan, both countries have restricted their claims to territorial seas 3 nautical miles wide. This means that there is a corridor of sea 14 nautical miles wide separating the two bands of territorial waters.

On 2 May 1977 Japan proclaimed lines delimiting its internal waters of Seto Naikai and Osaka-wan, which lie between Honshu on the north and Shikoku and Kyushu on the south and west. These baselines, for that is how they are described, lie well inside major indentations, and therefore do not increase the area of territorial waters claimed by Japan. To avoid possible difficulties, Japan has also restricted its claims to territorial waters 3 nautical miles wide in the Soya, Tsugaru, Korea and Osumi Straits. This means that there is a corridor of seas between the territorial waters claimed from each bank of these straits.

Four countries appear to have claimed historic bays in the north Pacific Ocean. In 1947 El Salvador amended its constitution of 1886 to assert that the Gulf of Fonseca was 'a Historical Bay' shared with Honduras and Nicaragua. Problems associated with this gulf are considered in a later section. Panama announced that the Golfo de Panama consisted of historic waters on 30 January 1956. Colombia and Costa Rica, which concluded maritime boundaries with Panama in 1976 and 1980 respectively, both agreed that they would not object to the claim by Panama that the gulf was an historic bay. The Soviet Union announced on 20 July 1957 that Petra Velikogo was an historic bay; Vladivostok stands on the shores of this bay. Finally China, in declaring its general claim to territorial seas on 4 September 1958, specifically nominated the waters of Bo Hai as internal waters. There is a chain of islands across the mouth of this large bay, and the channels between these islands measure about 45 nautical miles.

North Korea has not proclaimed any straight baselines, but it is possible to deduce that such a baseline has been drawn along its east coast. On 1 August 1977

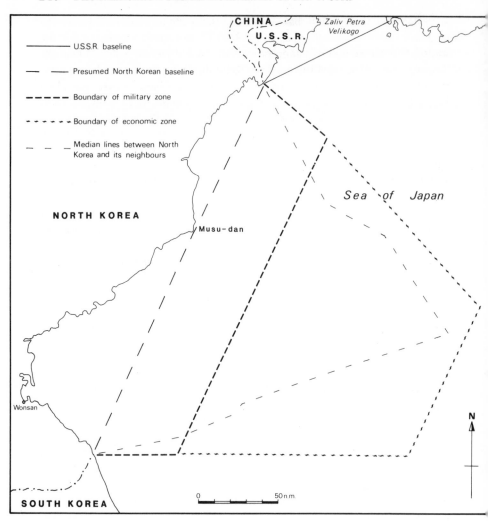

Figure 9.3 North Korea's baselines

North Korea announced the creation of an exclusive economic zone and a military zone 'to reliably safeguard the economic zone'. In the Yellow Sea the two zones were identical and extend to the median line with China. In the direction of South Korea the claims extend south of the islands controlled by the United Nations; this problem is discussed later. In the Sea of Japan the North Koreans have indicated co-ordinates for the military zone and the exclusive economic zone. The military zone is known to be 50 nautical miles wide, and it is shown in figure 9.3. When a straight line is drawn parallel to the outer limit of the military zone, and 50 nautical miles landwards, it is seen to connect the termini of North Korea's boundaries with South Korea and the Soviet Union, and to pass through Musu-dan. While there are sections of North Korea's east coast which are deeply indented, this apparent baseline cannot be justified. It does not follow the general direction of the coast, except in a most gross fashion.

Agreed international maritime boundaries and unilateral claims

There are four agreed international maritime boundaries in the north Pacific Ocean. Three lateral boundaries have been drawn in the region of central America by the United States and Mexico, and by Panama with Colombia and Costa Rica. One boundary between opposite states has been settled between South Korea and Japan.

The United States and Mexico agreed on a maritime boundary in the Pacific Ocean and the Gulf of Mexico on 23 November 1970. Both boundaries separate the 12 nautical mile territorial sea of Mexico from the 3 nautical mile territorial sea and the contiguous zone of the United States (The Geographer 1972). The only complication on the Pacific sector involved the Mexican Islas Los Coronados. This group of islands is located about 10 nautical miles southwest of the terminus of the land boundary between the two countries. The islands were given full effect, but the resulting line of equidistance was simplified into three straight segments by a mutual exchange of water and seabed. An area measuring 608,141 square metres on the Mexican side of the median line was transferred to the United States and an area 2 square metres less was transferred from the American side of the line to Mexico.

Colombia and Panama agreed on maritime boundaries in the Pacific Ocean and the Caribbean Sea on 20 November 1976, and they were ratified on 30 November 1977. The boundaries separate the marine and submarine areas of both states, regardless of the legal system which has been established over those areas. The boundary in the Pacific Ocean consists of five specified segments and another segment which has only one terminus. The boundary is described as a median line in which certain minor deviations have been ignored to simplify delimitation. For a distance of about 90 nautical miles from the coast the boundary follows the median course very closely, and is never closer to one country rather than the other by more than 1 nautical mile. However, at the final turning point the line is 20 nautical miles closer to Colombia's Isla de Malpelo than to any territory of Panama. At the final turning point, located at 5° north and 79° 52' west, the boundary then proceeds westwards along parallel 5° north until it becomes necessary to negotiate a boundary with a third country. This boundary along the line of latitude discounts Colombia's claims from Isla de Malpelo.

The maritime boundary between Costa Rica and Panama was agreed on 2 February and ratified on 11 February 1982. It consists of a single segment measuring 200 nautical miles extending from Punta Burica to a point 5° north and 84° 19' west. The line is described as a median line, and for this to be true there can only have been two basepoints considered. The first must be Punta

Burica, where the land boundary of the two countries terminates; the second must be the Panamanian island called Jicaron, which lies just south of Isla Coiba. The Isla Coco, which belongs to Costa Rica, has been discounted; it lies only 168 nautical miles from the seaward terminus of the maritime boundary. This terminus clearly also marks the end of the boundary between Panama and Colombia which was stated to follow parallel 5° north. It is not yet clear whether Colombia will agree that the terminus agreed between Costa Rica and Panama will also serve as the trijunction of the boundary, because the terminus is a few nautical miles closer to Isla Coco than to Isla de Malpelo.

On 5 February 1974 Japan and South Korea signed two agreements dealing with their common continental shelf. Disputes had first arisen in 1968 when Korea, having discovered that there were reasonable exploration prospects in the Yellow Sea, created seven mining districts which were divided amongst four petroleum exploration companies. One of those districts reached within 12 nautical miles of Kyushu and Tori-shima. Japan naturally objected and pointed out that it had already granted exploration rights in zones which overlapped the South Korean claim. South Korea took the view that Tori-shima, separated by a deep trench on the seabed from the main Japanese islands, was not entitled to claim a continental shelf. Negotiations, which were complicated by concern over the boundaries of both countries with China or Taiwan, were eventually success-ful. The first agreement created a joint development zone in the region of the overlapping claims. This zone has a lozenge shape and measures 246 nautical miles on its north–south axis and 160 nautical miles along the east–west dimen-sion. The area in the immediate vicinity of Tori-shima is excluded from the joint zone. The zone was divided into nine sub-zones which are in the process of being developed by concessionaires nominated by each country. The agreement also provides for the mineral explorers to avoid unnecessary disruption to other activities in the area, such as fishing.

The second agreement delimits a continental shelf boundary which extends from the northwest corner of the joint development zone through the Korea Strait for 420 nautical miles. This line is defined by thirty-five points and follows an equidistant course. The northeastern terminus lies about 74 nautical miles from Liancourt Rocks, which are known as Tok-do and Take-shima by the Koreans and Japanese respectively. These islands are claimed by both countries and no final decision has been made about the resolution of this dispute. Sensibly the two countries did not allow this disagreement to prevent a boundary being drawn through undisputed areas.

All countries have effectively drawn unilateral boundaries limiting various maritime zones which have been claimed, although most have noted that where such claims overlap the claims of neighbours the median line forms the limit of the reserved areas. The most common claim amongst the thirteen countries is for a territorial sea of 12 nautical miles and a fishing or exclusive economic zone of 200 nautical miles. Such claims are made by Canada, Guatemala, Honduras, Japan, Mexico, North and South Korea, and the Soviet Union. El Salvador,

Nicaragua and Panama all claim territorial seas 200 nautical miles wide and exclusive economic zones which coincide with their territorial seas. The two remaining countries are China and the United States. China claims only a territorial sea 12 nautical miles wide, while the United States claims territorial waters 3 nautical miles wide and an exclusive economic zone 200 nautical miles in width. North and South Korea are the only countries in the north Pacific Ocean which cannot claim the full width of the exclusive economic zone in at least one direction, although China will also be in that position until it regains control of Taiwan. The other countries, including the various Trust Territories, are all able to claim the full width of economic zones off long sections of their coast. The maritime boundaries of the north Pacific Ocean are shown in figures 9.4 and 9.5.

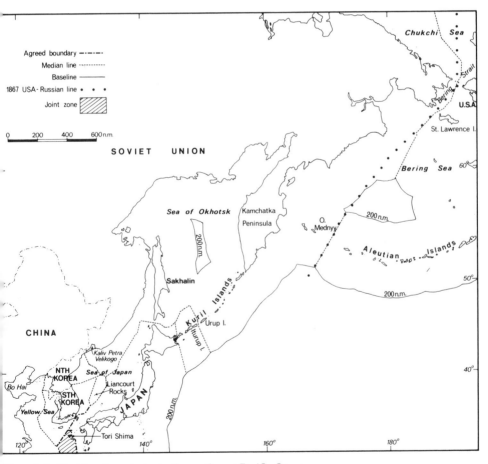

Figure 9.4 Maritime boundaries in the northwest Pacific Ocean

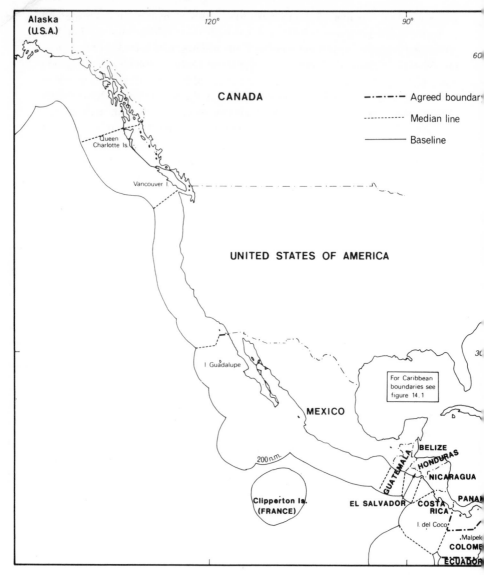

Figure 9.5   Maritime boundaries in the northeast Pacific Ocean

Actual and potential maritime boundary disputes

Most of the actual and potential maritime boundary disputes in the north Pacific Ocean are concerned with the ownership of islands. Situated about 90 nautical miles northeast of Taiwan lie the Senkaku Gunto, a group of five coral islands. They are claimed by China, Japan and Taiwan; the Chinese name for the group is

Taio Yu Tai. The principal island is called Uotsuri-shima by the Japanese and Taioyu by the Chinese; it is about 2.5 nautical miles long and 1 nautical mile wide. There is no fresh water on any of the islands, which are clothed in rattan palms and banyan trees. Possession of the islands would confer on the owner title over about 11,700 square nautical miles of the Asian continental shelf landwards of the 200 metre isobath. It is generally believed, but not yet proved, that this region could yield rich fields of crude petroleum (Tao Cheng 1974, 222).

Japan's claim to the Senkaku Gunto rests primarily on the fact that they are part of the Ryukyu Retto, which are indisputably Japanese. The Ryukyu Retto were controlled by a kingdom which paid tribute to authorities in southern Kyushu until the restoration of the Meiji in 1868. The local ruler was deposed in 1879 and the Ryukyu Retto was incorporated into the Okinawa Prefecture.

Tao Cheng (1974) has made a careful study of the arguments used by the parties to this dispute and the following account is based on his paper. Japan claims that the islands were first discovered by a Japanese in 1884, and that at that time, and subsequently in 1887 and 1892, no trace was found of Chinese concern with or control over the islands. The islands were formally annexed on 14 January 1895.

Following this development the islands were used by Mr Koga Tatsushiro to found industries concerned with collecting guano and birds' feathers and canning fish and birds. Apparently his activities failed because of rising transport costs associated with the onset of the First World War, and because of the destruction of birds by cats. However, before the islands were abandoned he had supervised the building of houses, reservoirs and docks. His son continued to hold the lease and was paid rent by the American civil administration of the Ryukyu Retto after 1958.

China asserts that one of its citizens had discovered the islands in 1719, and that the islands had been used by fishermen and pharmacists collecting herbs long before the Japanese discovery. It also points to the fact that although Japan claimed to know of the islands in 1884, no formal claim was made by that country until China had been defeated in the war of 1894 and was in no position to protest just prior to the peace treaty of Shimonoseki on 17 April 1895. In any case, the Chinese argument continues, the Senkaku Gunto were transferred to Japan by that peace treaty which described part of the transferred territory as 'the island of Formosa together with all the islands appertaining or belonging to the said island'. The islands won by this treaty were returned to China after the Second World War. In effect the Chinese argument affirms that the only time these islands were under Japanese control was from 1895, when they were ceded by the peace treaty, until 1947, when Japan was divested of territory won by conquest.

In March 1972 Japan announced that it would only deal with China on the question of the Senkaku Gunto. However, it has not seemed anxious to conclude any agreement, perhaps because of the damage it might cause to trade with Taiwan. Since Japan has also announced that it will not sanction exploration for petroleum until the matter is resolved, there is a good chance that this problem will remain dormant in the foreseeable future. However, the issue is of some importance for Japan in view of its dependence on imported supplies of pet-roleum and other fuels.

Even if the issue of the Senkaku Gunto was settled amicably in favour of China, there would still remain a potential difficulty. The equidistant line between the undisputed islands of Japan and the Chinese mainland leaves an area of 9000 square nautical miles of the Asian continental shelf landward of the 200 metre isobath, on the Japanese side of the line. The situation is similar to that which has embroiled Australia and Indonesia south of Timor. China, like Australia, claims the broad adjacent continental margin, and argues that the margin terminates at the trough with depths of 2000 metres close to Ryukyu Retto. Japan, like Indonesia, might argue that the Asian trough, like the Timor Trough, is just an incidental depression in a continuous continental margin between the two countries. Situations like these afford excellent opportunities to test the principle of natural prolongation, which would presumably find favour with China and Australia.

The second problem does not centre on the ownership of islands, but rather over what effect should be given to them. The armistice agreement of 27 July 1953 which ended the war in Korea placed five groups of islands, off the west coast of the peninsula, under the control of the Commander-in-Chief of the United Nations Command. The islands are called Paeng-yong-Do, Taechong-Do, Sochong-Do, Yonpyong-Do and U-Do, and they lie within 12 nautical miles of the coast of North Korea. The Commander of the United Nations naval force drew a Northern Limit Line between the islands and the coast of North Korea to help prevent maritime incidents in the region.

In 1973 North Korea tried to enforce its authority in the waters around these five island groups. It justified this action by asserting that the allocation of islands by the armistice agreement did not affect the maritime claims which could be made from the North Korean coast. The attempt was rebuffed, and while the claim still stands, the situation has not been forced by the authorities in North Korea. Meanwhile South Korea claims that the Northern Limit Line is the proper maritime boundary between the two countries. This does not appear to be an argument with any sound foundation, and it must be presumed that the difficulties associated with these islands is just one part of the much larger prob-lem of restoring good relations between North and South Korea.

It was noted earlier that the continental shelf boundary drawn by South Korea and Japan in 1974 stopped about 70 nautical miles from Liancourt Rocks, called Tok-do by Korea and Take-shima by Japan. Since 1952 the two countries have disputed the ownership of this island, which permits claims to about 16,600 square nautical miles of sea and seabed. There are two obvious solutions to this problem. A joint development zone could be created in the disputed area; it would match the joint development zone at the south end of the Korea Strait. Alterna-tively one side could withdraw its claim on the understanding that the island would be heavily discounted in drawing any maritime boundary through the area.

The ownership of four islands has been disputed by Japan and the Soviet Union since 1945, when the Soviet Union gained the Kuril Islands at the end of the

Second World War. The whole question turns on whether these four islands are
part of the Kuril Islands. The four islands are called Iturup, Kunashir, Shikotan
and the Habomai Group, and they are located off the west coast of Hokkaido, as
figure 9.6 shows.

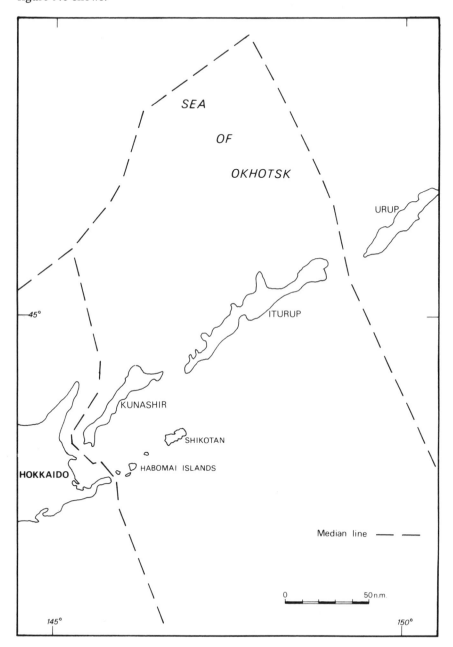

Figure 9.6 Islands disputed by Japan and the Soviet Union

There are about twenty-six islands in the volcanic chain which links Hokkaido and the Kamchatka Peninsula. In the seventeenth century Russia began exploring and occupying islands from the north, while Japan followed similar activities from the south. By 1800 Russia's influence had extended to Ostrov Urup, while Japan was dominant on Iturup, 25 nautical miles to the southwest. The Russian Imperial Ordinance of 4 September 1821 dealing with navigation and commerce in eastern Asia identified the area of Russian control as extending from Bering Strait to the southern point of Ostrov Urup. In 1855, Japan and Russia, in a treaty dealing with commerce, navigation and boundaries, set the limit between their territories in the strait separating Ostrov Urup and Iturup Island.

In 1875 Japan and Russia exchanged some territory in the region. In return for Japan's withdrawal of its claim to Sakhalin, Russia ceded its Kuril Islands. Eighteen major islands were named in the treaty; they extended from Ostrov Shumshu, just south of Kamchatka, to Ostrov Urup.

This brief account indicates that Japan had always controlled the four disputed islands until 1945. There is no way in which they could be considered to be territory 'taken by violence and greed' in the words of the Cairo Declaration of 27 November 1943. Japan has the strongest case based on history, but the Soviet Union occupies the islands. It has agreed by the terms of the Soviet–Japanese Joint Declaration of 19 October 1956 that the Habomai Islands and Shikotan would be returned to Japan when a peace treaty was signed. In 1960 the Soviet Union added a new condition for the return of those two islands; it was that all foreign troops should be withdrawn from Japan. Both countries have proclaimed exclusive economic zones about the disputed islands, but Russia controls the waters around the islands and Japanese fishermen plying their trade must secure licences to fish legally.

The Soviet Union's control of the Kuril Islands has converted the Sea of Okhotsk into a Russian lake. In addition, the islands have been fortified and some bases are used for surveillance of naval and other activities in the north Pacific Ocean. There does not appear to be any early solution in prospect, but at least the dispute has not prevented arrangements which are mutually beneficial being made in other areas.

The ratification of the Soviet–American treaty of 1867, on 20 June 1867, transferred sovereignty over Alaska and some offshore islands from Russia to the United States. The price paid by the United States for this territory was 'seven million two hundred thousand dollars in gold'. The Emperor of all the Russias ceded all the territory and dominion then possessed by the Emperor on the continent of America and the adjacent islands within two specified limits. It is the western limit which must be considered here.

The western limit within which the territories and dominion conveyed are contained, passes through a point in Behring's straits on the parallel of sixty-five degrees thirty minutes north latitude, at its intersection by the meridian which passes midway between the islands of Krusenstern, or Ignalook [Little

Diomede Island], and the island of Ratmanoff, or Noonarbook [Ostrov Ratmanova], and proceeds due north, without limitation, into the same Frozen Ocean [Arctic Ocean]. The same western limit, beginning at the same initial point, proceeds then in a course nearly southwest, through Behring's straits and Behring's sea, so as to pass midway between the northwest point of the island of St Lawrence and the southeast point of Cape Choukotski [Mys Choukotskiy], to the meridian of one hundred and seventy two west longitude; thence, from the intersection of that meridian, in a southwesterly direction, so as to pass midway between the island of Attou [Attu Island] and the Copper island [Ostrov Mednyy] of the Kormandorski couplet or group [Komandorskiye Ostrova], in the North Pacific ocean to the meridian of one hundred and ninety-three degrees west longitude, so as to include in the territory conveyed the whole of the Aleutian islands east of that meridian.   (The Geographer 1965, 1)

There are difficulties in interpreting this boundary description. Attention was drawn by a group of experts to the fact that it is not clear whether the various points defined in the description are connected by rhumb lines or arcs of great circles (The Geographer 1965, 2). They plumped for great circle lines, but do not provide the reasons for making this choice. It would be interesting to compare the location of both kinds of lines and to measure the area between them if they do not coincide. There are, however, more serious defects in this description, which was provided by Admiral Krabbe, head of the Russian Admiralty, in a memorandum to the Russian Ambassador in Washington on 24 December 1866, and accepted for inclusion in the treaty by the American side.

The first difficulty occurs because the point midway between St Lawrence Island and Mys Choukotskiy lies west of meridian 172° west. The unfortunate consequence of this circumstance is that the line cannot pass the midway point and continue to meridian 172° west. This means it is a nice issue to decide whether the turning point occurs at the midway point, or east of that location when meridian 172° west is encountered.

The second difficulty occurs in the final phrase, which conveys all the Aleutian Islands east of meridian 167° east. It then becomes important to know what was understood by the Aleutian Islands in 1867. Was Ostrov Mednyy considered part of the Aleutian chain, because it lies east of meridian 167° east? There can be no doubt that the treaty intended to leave Ostrov Mednyy with Russia, but it is careless and ambiguous descriptions such as this which create opportunities for countries which wish to be difficult during negotiations, or wish to gain a bargaining counter. The best accounts of the negotiations leading to this defective treaty are found in the studies by Davidson (1903) and Farrar (1937).

The United States announced on 7 March 1977 that where the baselines of America and the Soviet Union were less than 400 nautical miles apart, the limit of fishery jurisdiction would be the 1867 line. The Soviet Union advised the United States that it was using the same line as the outer limit of fishery enforcement (Smith 1981, 405). The United States also applies the 1867 line to the continental shelf. Figure 9.7 shows the limit and the outer edge of the fishing zones 200 nautical miles wide claimed by the two countries. This map indicates that apart from a stretch 225 nautical miles long, near the centre of the Bering Sea, the 1867 line does operate as the boundary between fishery jurisdiction.

But while the agreement to use the 1867 line as a fisheries boundary between fishing zones is welcome, there still remains the question of settling the boundary on the seabed. The Soviet Union has not agreed that the 1867 line is the continental shelf boundary and there is no reason why it should agree without very careful analysis of the benefits and disadvantages. Figure 9.7 also shows the approximate median line through the Bering Sea. The line is only approximate because it proved impossible to obtain a satisfactory large-scale chart of this sea. The median line crosses and recrosses the 1867 line, and the areas which each side would gain and lose by using the median line are not equal. The two major deviations in the Bering Sea, marked A and B, would deliver about 16,000 square nautical miles to the Soviet Union and about 7000 square nautical miles to the United States. It is the value of the seabed resources which are critical to any decision, rather than simply the area involved. It seems likely that the median line would intersect the Navarin Basin. While it has not been drilled, seismic studies suggest that the basin might contain 1.9 billion barrels of oil under waters less than 200 metres deep, and 7.5 trillion cubic feet of gas under similar water depths. In making any decision about whether to argue in favour of a line of equidistance, the Soviet Union will have to consider the extension of the 1867 line northwards into the Arctic Ocean. While the agreement refers to the line being drawn northwards 'without limit', the United States does not accept the line beyond 72° north because it does not accept the sector theory. However, it might be difficult to persuade the Soviet Union that only those parts of the 1867 definition which are satisfactory to the United States should be accepted. The intersection of the 1867 line with parallel 72° north is about 160 nautical miles from American territory and about 115 nautical miles from the nearest Russian island. If the median line was substituted in the Arctic Ocean then the United States would gain about 7700 square nautical miles in the major deviation from the 1867 line in comparatively shallow water.

It might be appropriate to argue that the 1867 line is convenient and could usefully be elevated to the status of a continental shelf boundary. It would defy reason to argue that the line must be the shelf boundary because it is described in the 1867 treaty. In that respect the American–Russian boundary is not different from the Sino-French line of 1887 in the Gulf of Tongking. Both were drawn simply to allocate islands without the need to name each one.

There are four points of coastal contact between Canada and the United States. On the coast of the Pacific Ocean Washington and British Columbia meet at the head of Juan de Fuca Strait, while to the north British Columbia and Alaska meet where the Portland Canal runs into Dixon Entrance. In the Arctic Ocean Alaska and Yukon Territory share the shore of the Beaufort Sea, and in the north Atlantic Ocean New Brunswick and Maine meet on the shores of the Bay of Fundy. Only the Pacific boundaries are considered in this chapter.

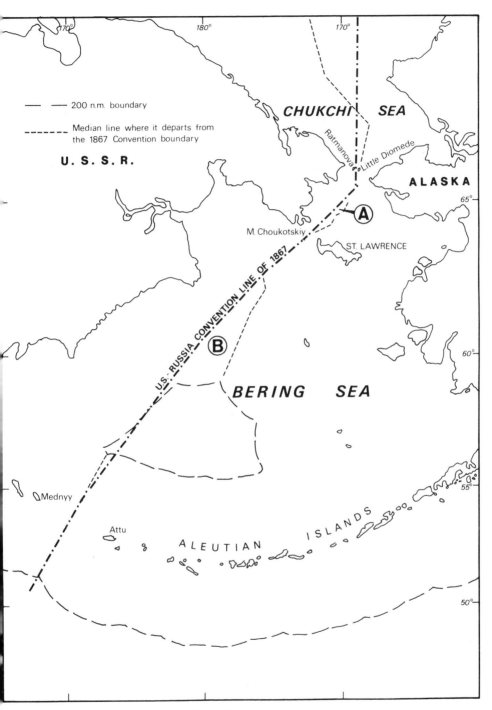

Figure 9.7 Maritime boundaries in the Bering Sea

There is no significant problem in the southern sector. The boundary treaty of 1846 and the Northwest Water Boundary Protocol of 1873 established the course of the maritime limit through Juan de Fuca Strait. The seaward projection of the boundary from the mouth of the strait has not been settled. However, there are only slight differences in the position of the Canadian and American interpretations of a median line, and they are due to technical rather than political or economic factors.

The problem in Dixon Entrance, like the problem in the Gulf of Tongking and the potential problem in the Bering Sea, involves two countries having different understandings of a line defined in an earlier document. Part of the Alaska Boundary Tribunal Award of 1903 drew a line called 'Line A–B' joining the mouth of the Portland Channel and Cape Muzon on Dall Island (Smith 1981, 400). While the United States has decided that the 1867 line in the Bering Sea is a maritime boundary, it takes the view that the 1903 limit in Dixon Entrance simply serves to allocate islands to the two countries. Canada has taken the position that Line A–B is the proper maritime boundary. When it defined its fishing zones on 25 February 1971, Dixon Channel was closed by a boundary linking Langara Island, the northernmost of the Queen Charlotte Islands, with 'Point A of Line A–B'. Figure 9.8 shows the area which is bounded by the Canadian claim and the median line which is the preferred boundary of the United States. The Canadian case is not strong because it is inconceivable that the arbitrators intended to prevent the United States having any territorial waters off the southern end of Dall Island. However, it is possible that the Canadian claim is simply designed to be a bargaining counter which can be set against American claims if the four maritime boundaries are considered as a package.

There is a potential dispute between France and Mexico over the ownership of Clipperton Island. While France's title was confirmed in an arbitral award of 1931 there has been a recent revival of Mexican interest, perhaps because of the reported concentrations of manganese nodules in the Clipperton Fracture Zone on the adjacent seabed.

Clipperton Island lies 580 nautical miles from Point Tejupan, the nearest part of the Mexican coast. It is a low atoll of elliptical shape with a largest diameter of 2 nautical miles. The surrounding reef is continuous as is the island which surmounts it; there is no channel to the central lagoon, which has depths of 55 fathoms. On the northern edge of the lagoon there are five islands called the Egg Islands because of the profusion of birds and nesting sites. At the south of the lagoon lies Clipperton Rock; this mass of phosphatized trachyte is 18 metres high and provides the most prominent landmark. There is no definite supply of fresh water on the atoll.

The island was named in 1705 after Captain Clipperton, who was an associate of Dampier. It was claimed for France on 17 November 1858 by Lieutenant Coet de Kerguelen, and this annexation was announced in the journal called *The Polynesian*, published in Honolulu, on 8 December 1858. Mexico protested but failed to take any action to press its counterclaim. Nor did Mr Lockart, who had

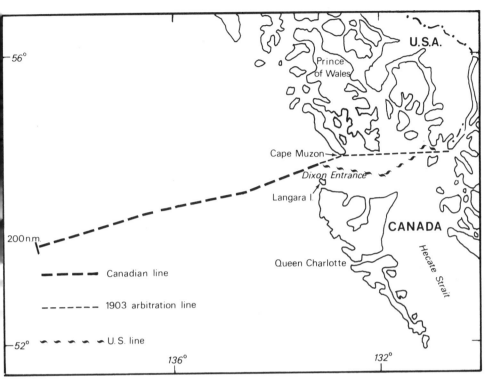

Figure 9.8 The boundary between Canada and the United States in Dixon Entrance

been given a concession to mine guano on Clipperton Island by Emperor Napoleon III, pursue this commercial opportunity. A visiting French warship on 24 November 1897 discovered three people representing the Oceanic Phosphate Company of San Francisco on the island. These worthies hoisted the American flag as the French vessel approached, and so the government of the United States was asked for an explanation. It was given on 28 January 1898; the United States had not given any mining rights and had no claims to Clipperton Island (*American Journal of International Law* 1932).

While the French were dealing with the Americans a Mexican gunboat, *La Demócrata*, visited Clipperton and landed a party of marines, who ordered the three guano miners to lower the American flag and raise the Mexican standard. Two of the miners returned to the mainland on *La Demócrata* on 15 December 1897. Three weeks later France learned of this Mexican action and reminded that country of France's title to the island.

In 1906 deposits of tribasic calcium phosphate were found, and a small garrison was sent from Mexico at the same time that a few workers began to mine this resource. In June 1914, when the island was visited by the American warship *Cleveland*, it was reported that the garrison was thriving (Naval Intelligence

Division 1943, 16). Until that time the garrison had been provisioned from Mexico every four months, but in late 1914, after the guano workers had been withdrawn, the supply ships stopped coming. Four men tried to reach the mainland in a rowboat but disappeared. Of the remaining twenty-six people, only three women and eight children were alive when the American warship *Yorktown* reached the island in July 1917.

France and Mexico agreed in March 1909 to invite His Majesty Victor Emmanuel III of Italy to act as arbiter on the question of which country owned Clipperton Island. The wheels of Italian consideration ground very slowly and the decision was not announced until 28 January 1931. The very brief decision awarded the island to France, on the basis of Lieutenant Coet de Kerguelen's act of annexation and the conviction that the fact that France had not exercised her authority in a positive manner did not imply the forfeiture 'of an acquisition already definitively perfected' (*American Journal of International Law* 1932, 394).

It would not be surprising if modern attitudes towards colonial questions and the need to help developing countries encouraged Mexico to raise this matter again in a more determined way.

There have been problems associated with the Gulf of Fonseca since 1839 when El Salvador, Honduras and Nicaragua became independent. El Salvador and Nicaragua each own one of the large headlands which define the mouth of the gulf. As figure 9.9 shows, Honduras owns much of the gulf's interior coast. The islands in the western half of the gulf are shared between El Salvador and Honduras. On 10 April 1884 El Salvador and Honduras signed a treaty which included a definition of the maritime boundary between the two countries in the Gulf of Fonseca, but that treaty was never ratified by Honduras. In 1894 Honduras and Nicaragua agreed that commissioners should settle their disputed boundary, and the joint commission produced its report in March 1900. On 5 August 1914 Nicaragua and the United States signed an agreement dealing with a canal through Nicaragua. This treaty, which was ratified on 24 June 1916, also provided for a ninety-nine year lease for an American naval base. El Salvador protested to the Central American Court of Justice, which found on 9 March 1917 that the Gulf of Fonseca was an historic bay with the characteristics of a closed sea. It also found that the gulf was the common property of the three coastal states and that the proposed naval base would violate the co-ownership of El Salvador. The United States never took up the option on the naval base and the 1914 treaty with Honduras was ended in 1971.

While Honduras still holds that the boundary with Nicaragua, drawn in 1900, is valid, El Salvador and Nicaragua argue that the waters of the gulf are indivisible. It appears that while El Salvador has always held this view, the Sandanista government has been converted recently to this opinion.

There have been problems concerning patrol vessels firing on each other and fishing vessels in the gulf, but the poor state of relations amongst the various governments has prevented any final agreement. It would seem to be in the interests of Honduras to avoid any division of the gulf because it will be closed off

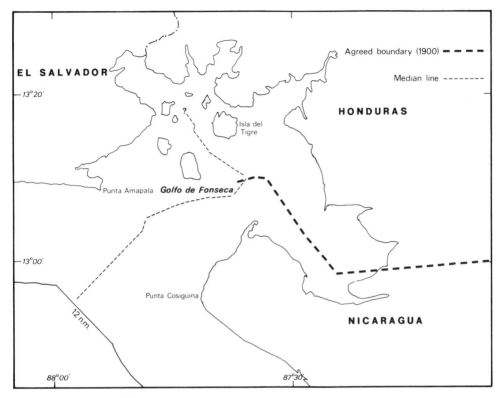

Figure 9.9 The Gulf of Fonseca

from the high seas by the claims of El Salvador and Nicaragua. However, Honduras still lays claim to certain islands in the gulf which are claimed and occupied by El Salvador. The two countries have agreed that if they have not settled this dispute by 1985 they will submit it to the International Court of Justice.

Conclusions

The north Pacific Ocean can be divided into eastern and western sectors which match the prime divisions of the south Pacific Ocean. However, the similarities of these divisions in the two hemispheres are clearer in physical terms rather than in political and economic characteristics. While there are still dependent territories in both hemispheres, it appears that the process of decolonization is proceeding more smoothly to the north of the equator. Any delays in establishing the independence of America's trusteeships owe more to domestic problems in the islands than to any reluctance on the part of the authorities in Washington. In contrast, France still has major hurdles to clear before the problems of New Caledonia and French Polynesia are solved.

Few straight baselines have been drawn in the north Pacific Ocean, and with the exception of North Korea's inferred straight baseline on its east coast, those which exist appear to conform to a reasonable degree to the existing and proposed rules for drawing straight baselines.

There are also only four international boundary agreements, and three of these are in central America. It is an indication of the problems caused by disputed islands and ideological differences that only Japan and South Korea have managed to draw an international maritime boundary in the waters of east Asia. Fortunately the problems which do exist in these waters, and between the United States and Canada on the west coast of North America, are not the dominant factor influencing state relations in the manner that the dispute over the Falkland Islands is crucial to relations between Britain and Argentina.

The problems which the United States faces in drawing maritime boundaries with Canada and the Soviet Union are not confined to the north Pacific Ocean, and it is possible that each pair of countries will devise a package of agreements to cover segments in the various oceans.

References

American Journal of International Law (1932) 'Arbitral award on the subject of the difference relative to the sovereignty over Clipperton Island', 26, 390–4.

Buzan, B. (1979) 'Maritime issues in northeast Asia', *Marine Policy*, 3, 190–200.

Davidson, G. (1903) *The Alaska Boundary*, San Francisco.

Farrar, V. J. (1937) *The Annexation of Russian America to the United States*, Washington.

Krause, L. B. (1981) 'The Pacific Basin and economic regionalism', in *Pacific Region Interdependencies*, a compendium of papers submitted to the Joint Economic Committee of the Congress of the United States of America, Washington, 11–16.

Naval Intelligence Division (1943) *Pacific Islands*, vol. III, London.

Smith, R. W. (1981) 'The maritime boundaries of the United States', *Geographical Review*, 71, 395–410.

Tao Cheng (1974) 'The Sino-Japanese dispute over Tiao-yu-tai (Senkaku) Islands and the law of territorial acquisition', *Virginian Journal of International Law*, 14 (2), 221–66.

Tchernia, P. (1980) *Descriptive Regional Oceanography*, London.

The Geographer (1965) *US–Russia Convention Line of 1867*, International Boundary Study, no. 14, revised, Washington, DC.

The Geographer (1972) *Maritime Boundary: Mexico–United States*, 'Limits in the Seas' series, no. 45, Washington, DC.

10

The Arctic Ocean and associated seas

We returned from the Pole to Cape Columbia in sixteen days . . . the exhilaration of success lent wings to our sorely battered feet. But Ootah, the Eskimo, had his own explanation. Said he: 'The devil is asleep or having trouble with his wife, or we should never have come back so easily.' (Peary 1910, 281)

It is idle to talk of freedom of the high seas with respect to an area, large parts of which are covered with ice throughout the year, other parts of which are covered with ice most of each year, and where the local inhabitants use the frozen sea as an extension of land to travel over it by dogsled and snowmobile far more than they can use it as water. (Pharand 1973, 173–4)

The offshore portion of the slope province, covering the shelf area in the Arctic Ocean and the Beaufort Sea, covers 140,000 square miles, or twice the onshore area. Because of its proximity to onshore accumulations of oil, the 20,000 square miles of the Beaufort Sea adjacent to the Arctic coast are considered a hot prospect area. (Rintoul 1975, 86)

While the Arctic environment is just as hostile today as it was in 1909 when Peary reached the North Pole, technical developments in communications and other fields have enabled parts of the region to be used for commercial, strategic and scientific purposes. However, because of its peculiar physical characteristics, this is a zone where applying the provisions of the Convention can face special difficulties.

The Arctic Ocean is the smallest of the oceans and has been considered as one of three mediterranean seas; the others are the Mediterranean and Caribbean Seas. Except in the vicinity of Canada's Queen Elizabeth Islands, the Arctic Ocean is bordered by seas. Most of these, such as the Beaufort Sea, the Chukchi Sea, the East Siberia Sea, the Laptev Sea, and the small Lincoln and Wandels Seas, do not appear to be set apart from the ocean. Only the Kara Sea has the semi-enclosed characteristics of the seas which border eastern Asia. Lying between the Arctic and Atlantic Oceans there are three more seas, which can be considered to be transitional, and which will be considered with the Arctic Ocean. These three seas are called the Greenland, Norwegian and Barents Seas. The waters within Canada's northern archipelago and in Hudson Bay and Baffin Bay are also considered in this chapter.

This polar region is separated from the Atlantic Ocean by a sill named the Wyvill Thomson Ridge which has a mean depth of 500 metres. It passes from the east coast of Greenland, via Iceland and the Faeroes to the north coast of Scotland. The Nansen Sill, which lies in a depth of about 1750 metres, distinguishes the transitional seas from the Arctic Ocean proper. This sill lies between north Greenland and Spitsbergen.

The continental margin occupies a greater extent in the Arctic Ocean and its related seas than in any other ocean. Approximately 37 per cent of the basin is occupied by the margin (Tchernia 1980, 96). The widest shelves are found off the coast of the Soviet Union, where the junction between the continental shelf and slope may lie 540 nautical miles from the coast. The shelves off the coasts of North America are generally not wider than 50 nautical miles. The deep seabed in the Arctic Ocean is divided into two major parts by the Lomonosov Ridge, which stretches from northern Greenland to Ostrova Anzhu.

The cover of sea ice varies with the seasons from 95 per cent in winter to 85 per cent in summer. The ice-free area throughout the year is the Norwegian Sea which benefits from the warmer waters of the west wind drift. This flow is augmented in summer so that Baffin Bay and the Barents Sea are generally free of ice. The warming of the continents and the discharge of major rivers, especially from Siberia, helps to free most of the coasts of Canada, the United States and the Soviet Union of ice, although the peninsula which separates the Kara and Laptev Seas is often ice-bound throughout the year. The penetration of warmer Pacific Ocean waters through Bering Strait helps to thaw sea ice in the Chukchi Sea, but this effect is less marked than the corresponding results produced by the flow from the Atlantic Ocean.

Although transport by ship is seasonal it is the prime method of moving bulk cargoes in the Arctic Ocean. The navigable route along the shores of Siberia is used by several hundred ships each year, although few make the entire journey of about 1500 nautical miles. Timber and ore from Noril'sk and Igarka in the Yenisey valley account for about half the cargoes by volume. The route from the Atlantic Ocean to the mouth of the Yenisey River is usually open from early July until the middle of December. The coastal route from the Pacific Ocean to the mouth of the Lena River is generally passable from the middle of June until the middle of October. The connection between the mouths of these two important rivers is only open for two months beginning in early August, although the season can be extended by the use of ice-breakers, some of which use nuclear fuel.

Off North America Hudson Bay is usually open from early June to mid-November, while the northern reaches of Baffin Bay allow passage between the middle of July and the middle of October. The coastal route along northern Alaska and the adjoining Yukon and Northwest Territories is only open for a short season from the beginning of August to the third week of September. The coasts between Prince Patrick Island and a point about half-way along the east coast of Greenland are rarely free of ice.

There have been major discoveries of oil and natural gas along the coasts of northern Alaska, near Prudhoe Bay; on the Canadian coast at the mouth of the Mackenzie River and Bathurst and Melville Islands; and on the coast of the Soviet Union in the Pechora Basin south of Novaya Zemlya. Offshore drilling has been in shallow water where artificial gravel islands can be used as drilling platforms. Prospective exploration has identified some promising structures off all three coasts; Denmark and Norway also have high hopes of production from the seabed off western Greenland and southeast of Svalbard respectively.

Straight baselines

With one possible exception no straight baselines have been proclaimed in the Arctic Ocean. The exception concerns two Russian straits. In an *aide-mémoire* dated 21 July 1964 the Soviet Union claimed that Proliv Sannikova and Proliv Dimitriya Lapteva in the Novosibirskiye Ostrova are internal waters. These straits could only be converted to internal waters by the construction of straight baselines, but no co-ordinates have been made public.

In contrast with the Arctic Ocean five sets of baselines have been proclaimed in the transitional seas which link the Arctic and Atlantic Oceans. The Norwegian baseline of 12 July 1935 can be considered as the origin of modern straight baselines. This system of straight lines enclosed the coast of Norway north of parallel 68° 28.8' north, as far as what was then the Finnish boundary. It was Britain's objections to this system of measuring territorial seas which led to the case before the International Court of Justice, which found in Norway's favour in 1951. Some of the language and most of the concepts displayed in the judgement found their way into Article 7 of the Convention. There were forty-seven segments in this straight baseline, and some of the points were established on rocks.

On 18 July 1952 Norway extended its straight baseline southwards from the 1935 terminus. A further seventy-five segments were added, taking the straight baseline to the Swedish boundary. If the Norwegian baseline had served as a strict model for straight baselines there could have been little complaint, but it is clear that baselines have increasingly been drawn along coasts which are not deeply indented nor fringed with islands in the manner of the Norwegian *skjaergaard*.

On 30 June 1955 Norway drew straight baselines around Jan Mayen and then completed its baseline construction by drawing straight lines around part of Svalbard on 25 September 1970. This last set of baselines does not maintain Norway's previously high standard. There can be no questions asked about the seventeen straight lines which surround Bornoya, to the south of the main group of islands. The eight baseline segments around Hopen cannot be justified in any way. The island is long and narrow with smooth coasts. Fortunately these baselines do nothing to augment Norway's area of territorial waters, and enclose only a very small area of internal waters. While the fifty-seven segments of baseline drawn around part of Vestspitsbergen can be justified because the west coast of this island is deeply indented, the same cannot be said of Edgeoya, which is linked to Vestspitsbergen by some of the segments. Further, the baseline, having started on Vestspitsbergen, then terminates on Halvmaneoya, a small island off Edgeoya. Because the baseline does not close back on to Vestspitsbergen, the area of internal waters is not clearly defined. Sailing eastwards through Freemansundet, a navigator would encounter the straight baseline on his chart and assume he was in Norway's internal waters. Sailing westwards through the same strait the navigator would not encounter any straight baseline until he was about to enter the territorial sea west of the strait! It is curious how often countries make this elementary error in drawing baselines.

Denmark drew straight baselines around the southern coast of Greenland from 70° 9' north on the west coast to 68° 28.9' north on the east coast. These baselines, and those of Chile and Norway, are classical examples of straight baselines along coasts which are both deeply indented and fringed with islands.

Iceland had modified its original straight baselines on two occasions. The straight baselines were first proclaimed on 19 March 1952. Forty-eight basepoints were used and the islands called Kolbeinsey, Hvalbakur and Gierfugladrangur were nominated as supplementary basepoints. On 22 April 1961, after negotiations between Iceland and the United Kingdom, the number of basepoints was reduced to thirty-eight on the mainland, and Kolbeinsey and Hvalbakur were also named as features from which maritime claims would be made. Finally, on 14 July 1972 seven basepoints on the mainland were eliminated. The effect of this was to move one segment of baseline, south of the island called Grimsey, seawards by 12 nautical miles, and to shift another segment west of Hvalbakur landwards by 3 nautical miles. Iceland's coast is indented on the west, north and east, but the coast on the south is generally smooth. For example, the coast between Hvalski and Medallandssandur I, which are respectively the mouth of a river and a small spit, is quite smooth and the baseline connecting them, which measures 14.5 nautical miles, cannot be justified by recourse to the concept of an indented coast, nor is there a fringe of islands. The baseline which links Medallandssandur II and Kotlutangi stretches for 20.7 nautical miles along a smooth, featureless sandy shore which is so straight that the baselines scarcely deviate from the low-water mark. Thus while the baseline is totally unnecessary along this section of coast, it does not advance Iceland's claim to maritime zones.

Two islands are used as basepoints in the southwest of the mainland. Geirfuglasker and Eldeyjardrangur lie 71 nautical miles apart, and they have been connected by a straight baseline even though there are no other islands along that sector, and even though the line at one point is 23 nautical miles distant from a smooth coastline.

The bays called Faxaflói and Breidhafjordhur are closed by straight lines measuring 73 and 40 nautical miles respectively, and it is generally believed that they are considered to be historic bays by Iceland (The Geographer 1971, 2–3). The Icelandic baselines are shown in figure 10.1.

There are also claims to historic bays by Canada and Russia. Hudson Bay was claimed by Canada as an historic bay on 13 July 1906, when fisheries Acts were amended. In 1921 the Soviet Union claimed Cheshskaya Guba and Beloye More

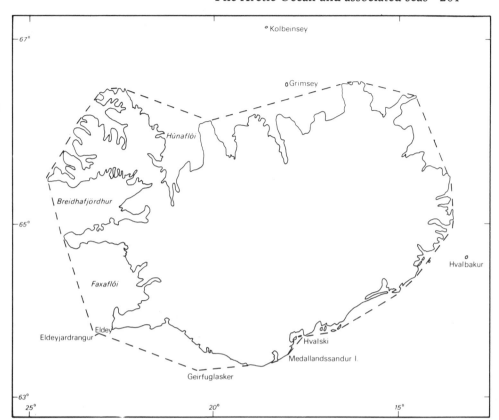

Figure 10.1 Iceland's baselines

as historic waters. These two semi-enclosed areas on the southern shore of the Barents Sea seem to have all the necessary characteristics to justify such a claim.

The most recent straight baselines were proclaimed by Denmark about the Faeroes on 21 December 1976. This new proclamation slightly altered the baselines set out on 24 April 1963. The baselines are shown in figure 10.2, and it is clear that the two longest sections do not follow the general direction of the coast. The segment linking Sudhuroy and Mykines measures 44 nautical miles and encloses the bight called Gutta Grynna. At one point this line is about 12.5 nautical miles from the nearest land. On the east of the archipelago the segment joining Fugloy and Munken measures 61 nautical miles, and at one point is 7.5 nautical miles from the nearest land.

All six countries bordering the Arctic Ocean and the associated seas claim an exclusive economic zone or fishing zone 200 nautical miles wide, and the limits of these claims are shown in figure 10.3. Claims to territorial seas do not show the same uniformity. Canada, Iceland and the Soviet Union claim 12 nautical miles.

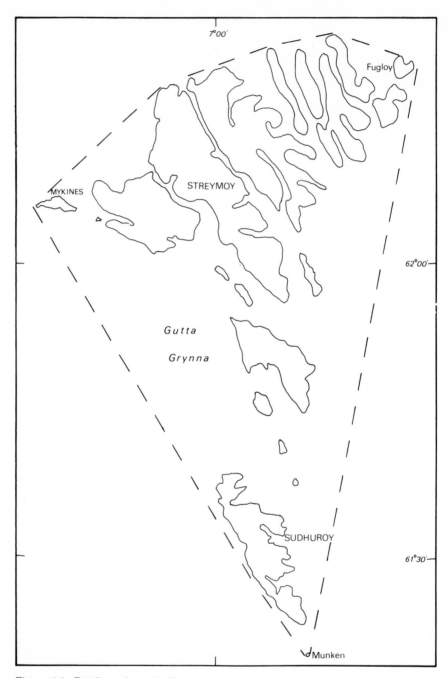

Figure 10.2 Baselines about the Faeroes

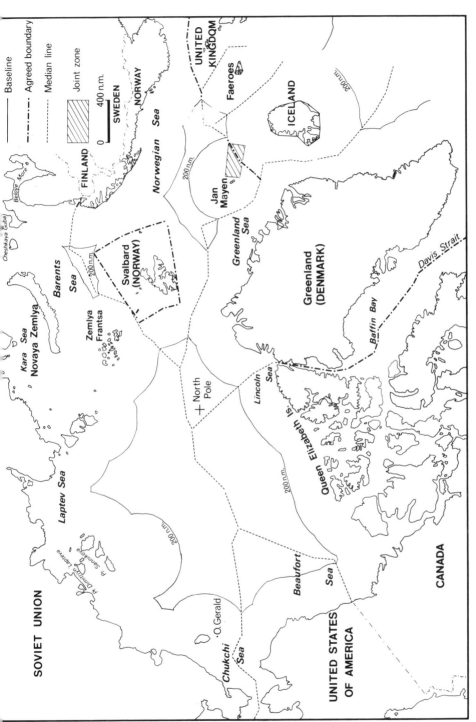

Figure 10.3 Maritime boundaries in the Arctic Ocean

Denmark and the United States claim 3 nautical miles and Norway claims the traditional Scandinavian league of 4 nautical miles.

Figure 10.3 also shows that there are three enclaves of high seas. The largest occurs in the Arctic Ocean, and the area would be covered with ice for most of the year. On the Siberian side of this ocean the area of high seas is deeply embayed because of two small islands called Zhannetta and Genriyetta, which cause a large protrusion of the Soviet Union's exclusive economic zone. There is a triangular wedge of high seas in the Barents Sea and an arcuate area in the Norwegian and Greenland Seas.

Agreed maritime boundaries

There are no agreed maritime boundaries in the Arctic Ocean. However, it is possible that the 1867 line drawn by Russia and the United States might be elevated to the status of a maritime boundary. It was noted earlier that America regards the line as a maritime boundary separating areas of fishing and seabed jurisdiction, and that the Soviet Union also observes the line as a limit to fisheries jurisdiction. Further, on 16 April 1926 the Praesidium of the Central Executive of the Soviet Union claimed all lands and islands in the Arctic Ocean between meridians 32° 4' 35" east and 168° 49' 30" west. This last meridian is defined as that which passes through the strait between Little Diomede Island and Ostrov Ratmanova. There are two problems about this line becoming an agreed maritime boundary in the Arctic Ocean. First, the United States does not accept the sector theory by which some countries make claims in the Arctic and Antarctica, and the 1867 description states that the line is continued 'without limitation' into the Frozen Ocean. So the United States would have to persuade Russia to accept a terminus short of the pole. Second, when the line of equidistance between the two countries is compared with the meridian it is clear that the United States stands to lose by allowing the meridian to be elevated to the status of maritime boundary. The area which the United States would gain from using the median line is in the Chukchi Sea; this area consists of shallow waters which are free of ice for about four months each year and which are underlain by a wide continental shelf.

In the transitional areas between the Arctic and Atlantic Oceans four bilateral maritime boundaries have been delimited. On 15 February 1957 Norway and the Soviet Union signed an agreement concerning their 'sea frontier' in Varanger-fjorden; it came into force on 24 April 1957. The limit is shown in figure 10.4. The line was defined as a single segment joining the terminus of the land boundary with intersection of the outer limits of the territorial waters claimed by each country. Norway's territorial water is 4 nautical miles measured from straight baselines, while the Soviet Union claims 12 nautical miles. The Norwegian claim was measured from the line linking the terminus of the land boundary with Cape Kibergnes; the Russian claim was measured from an unnamed cape east of the terminus of the land boundary. The intersection of

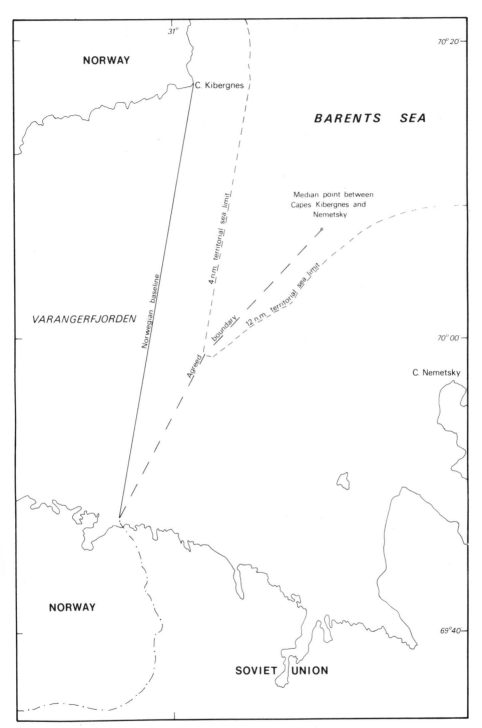

Figure 10.4 Varangerfjorden

these two claims was calculated to be at 69° 58' 50.22" north and 31° 6' 23.11" east by a joint commission, which published its report on 29 November 1957. The treaty also provided that neither country would extend its territorial sea beyond a straight line joining the point where the territorial seas intersected and the median point of the line joining Capes Kibergnes and Nemetsky. Although this agreement refers only to territorial waters, The Geographer (1970) has reasonably assumed the boundary also separates continental shelf claims. Despite negotiations between the two countries over many years it has not been possible to extend this short boundary of 24 nautical miles northwards into the Barents Sea. This particular problem is considered in the next section dealing with actual and potential disputes.

On 17 December 1973 Canada and Denmark signed a continental shelf agreement dealing with Baffin Bay and Davis and Nares Straits; the treaty was ratified on 13 March 1974. This boundary stretches for 1450 nautical miles; it commences in latitude 61° north and terminates at 82° 13' north in the Lincoln Sea. The line is defined by 127 turning points, and for most of its length it is a line of equidistance. There is a small gap in the boundary in the Kennedy Channel, because the two countries contest the ownership of Hans Island. This is not considered to be a major problem and it is clear that ownership of this island would only move the boundary a short distance in either direction.

While it is understood that the two countries wish to extend the maritime boundary northwards into the Lincoln Sea along a line of equidistance, it has not been possible to secure agreement on the use by Denmark of Beaumont Island as a basepoint. Beaumont Island, which is located near the mouth of Victoria Fjord on the north coast of Greenland, has the effect of pushing the median line 70 nautical miles westward at one point. The Canadian authorities appear to believe that this is a disproportionate effect for such a small island.

Denmark and Norway agreed on a continental shelf boundary between the Norwegian mainland and the Faeroes on 15 June 1979; the treaty was ratified in 1980. This short boundary of 32 nautical miles extends northwards from the trijunction agreed by Britain, Norway and Denmark. That trijunction was first set out in the Anglo-Norwegian Supplementary Protocol of 22 December 1978; the two countries had secured Danish approval of the position of this point on 15 June 1978. The northern terminus of this boundary is 200 nautical miles from the nearest land belonging to each country, and it was agreed that this continental shelf boundary would also act as the limit between the fishing zone around the Faeroes and the exclusive economic zone claimed by Norway.

The two agreements between Norway and Iceland dealing with the maritime boundaries south of Jan Mayen have some novel features. The first agreement signed on 28 May 1980 did not define a fisheries boundary and deferred the question of the continental shelf boundary for consideration by a conciliation commission. Provisions were set out for a joint fisheries commission and for regulating the catches of capelin. Stocks of this fish migrate between the waters of the two countries and it is an important resource for Icelandic fleets.

On 22 October 1981 the two countries agreed on a continental shelf boundary recommended by the conciliation commission. The shelf boundary is stated to coincide with the line of demarcation between the parties' economic zones. Now it was noted earlier that the fisheries boundary had not been defined, and the mystery is explained by reading the preambles to the two treaties. The 1981 treaty notes that the two countries had agreed in the earlier treaty that Iceland's economic zone is to be extended 200 nautical miles in the areas between Iceland and Jan Mayen, where the distance between the two sets of baselines is less than 400 nautical miles. There is no specific mention of this agreement in the 1980 treaty. However, in the preamble there are statements about Iceland's strong economic dependence on fisheries and the fact that Iceland has established an economic zone 200 nautical miles wide. So it appears that Norway has totally discounted Jan Mayen in drawing a fisheries and shelf boundary with Iceland.

Curiously there is no specification of the basepoints from which the Icelandic zone will be measured. For example will Iceland be able to claim from the small islet of Kolbeinsey? Denmark has strong reservations about that island being used by Iceland in delimiting a boundary with Greenland. Surely if Jan Mayen was discounted because of Iceland's view that it could not be considered an inhabited island, even though there were Norwegian scientists on it, then Kolbeinsey must also be ruled out as a basepoint. It is a puzzle why Norway was so unselfish in this matter. Jan Mayen is clearly an island, it cannot be considered to be a rock, and there is no requirement that islands should be inhabited or have an economic life of their own. The preamble makes reference to Article 71 of the Convention, but it is hard to see how that article applies in this case. This article states that the rights of landlocked and geographically disadvantaged states do not apply in respect of states whose economy is overwhelmingly dependent on the exploitation of the living resources of its exclusive economic zone. But Norway is neither landlocked nor geographically disadvantaged.

The second treaty also defined a rectangle of seabed which will be subject to some measure of joint operation, and again Norway's unselfishness is evident. The area occupies 45,470 square kilometres according to the treaty. The dividing line apparently cuts this rectangle in such a way that 32,750 square kilometres lie on the Norwegian side and 12,720 square kilometres lie on Iceland's side. Since each country is entitled to a quarter share in any petroleum operations which are undertaken in the joint zone lying beyond the boundary, it follows that Norway is yielding a quarter share in respect of an area two and a half times larger than the area within which its quarter share might be secured. There can be no surprise that Mr Johannesson, Iceland's Foreign Minister, described the treaty as sensible, fair and positive, and a potential example to other nations!

Actual and potential maritime boundary problems

Three potential disputes have already been mentioned, and they all deal with the effect to be given to small islands. If the United States and the Soviet Union decided to negotiate some other boundary than the 1867 meridian through Bering Strait, the question would arise of what effect should be given to Ostrov Gerald, a small islet east of Ostrov Vrangelya in the Chuckchi Sea. Settlement of the extension northwards of the boundary between Canada and Greenland has been delayed because of the Canadian view that Beaumont Island should not be given full effect as a basepoint. The Danish authorities take the same view as the Canadians when faced with the problem of drawing a maritime boundary between Greenland and Iceland. Iceland relies on Kolbeinsey as a basepoint, and it has always been specifically named in proclamations about Iceland's baselines. This islet measures about 70 metres long and 30 to 60 metres wide, with a maximum elevation of 8 metres. It is the view of the Danish authorities that this islet should be discounted, in the same fashion that Norway's Jan Mayen was discounted when the boundary with Iceland was drawn.

There is only one other maritime boundary problem in the Arctic Ocean and it concerns Canada and the United States in the Beaufort Sea. This problem follows the pattern of several other disputes, including those between China and Vietnam in the Gulf of Tongking, between the Soviet Union and the United States in the Bering Sea, and between Vietnam and Cambodia in the Gulf of Thailand. In each case the central fact is that an old treaty made reference to a straight line, which one of the modern contestants insists was meant to be a maritime boundary. In this case Canada is relying on the Anglo-Russian treaty of 1825 and the Russo-American treaty of 1867 to justify the use of meridian 141° west as the maritime boundary with the United States in the Beaufort Sea (Lawson 1981). Both treaties use the same words in respect of this meridian, for the first treaty defined the boundary between British and Russian North America, and the second treaty transferred sovereignty over the Russian zone to the United States.

the line of demarcation shall follow the summit of the mountains situated parallel to the Coast, as far as the point of intersection of the 141st degree of West longitude (of the same [Greenwich] meridian) and finally from the said point of intersection, the said meridian line of the 141st degree, in its prolongation as far as the Frozen ocean.   (Lawson 1981, 227–8)

Figure 10.5 shows the relationship of the meridian and the median line out to a distance of 200 nautical miles from the coast. The area in dispute measures 6600 square nautical miles, and there seems little doubt that the United States has the best title to this area. The words 'as far as the Frozen ocean' cannot be construed to mean that the meridian should continue to act as a boundary north of the coast. If it was argued that the line must continue until the ocean becomes frozen, then this view is rebuffed by the fact that the boundary would terminate at different points depending on the season. No one would suggest that negotiators would have produced such an uncertain and silly boundary. The unsatisfactory nature of Canada's assertion is further demonstrated by the reference in the same treaties to the meridian which passes through Bering Strait. This meridian, which never

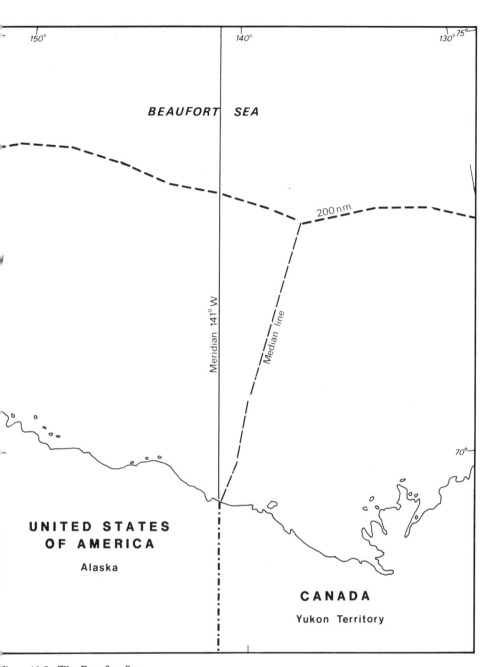

Figure 10.5 The Beaufort Sea

touches land, proceeds due north without limitation into the same Frozen Ocean. The treaty editors could not have intended the same sense to be applied to the phrases 'as far as the Frozen Ocean' and 'without limitation into the same Frozen Ocean'. There are no unusual circumstances along this coast and a median line would be an appropriate boundary.

The difficulty which Norway faced in negotiating a boundary with Iceland also exists in respect of Greenland. On 22 December 1976 Denmark declared fishing zones about the coasts of Greenland; they extended 200 nautical miles from specified baselines, but on the east coast the zone terminated at parallel 67° north, which is about the latitude of northern Iceland. On 29 May 1980 Norway declared a fishing zone 200 nautical miles wide around Jan Mayen, and three days later the Danish proclamation extending Greenland's fishing zone north of 67° north became effective. This proclamation also observed that Greenland's fishing zone would not be enforced beyond the median line. When the proclamation had to be renewed in September 1981, Denmark baldly asserted that 'where the island Jan Mayen lies opposite Greenland, the extent of the fisheries zone is 200 nautical miles'. This is the language which Iceland used so effectively and which was eventually accepted by Norway in May 1980.

Having yielded to Iceland's arguments Norway is now faced with identical views expressed by the Danish authorities. The remoteness of Jan Mayen from Norway; the transient nature of its small scientific population; and the fundamental importance of fishing in Greenland's economy form the core of the Danish case. Norway can counter by pointing out that the interest of Greenland's fleets in this area has been minimal until recently, in contrast with Iceland's major activities over a long period in the waters south of Jan Mayen. In any case fishermen from the Faeroes and Denmark have been more active than those from Greenland, and none of them has been as active as Norwegian fishermen in waters off eastern Greenland (Archer and Scrivener 1983, 65).

Under the terms of the Convention Jan Mayen is plainly an island not a rock. It has a length of about 30 miles and a width just less than 2 miles; its maximum elevation is 2276 metres on the peak of Haaken VII Toppen. While the vegetation is sparse there are alpine willows. Polar bears, arctic foxes and several kinds of sea birds live on the island at various times. Norway has operated a radio and meteorological station since 1921, and the island was annexed by Norway on 8 May 1929. While the special circumstances outlined in the Danish case might justify some discounting of claims from Jan Mayen it would be excessive to suggest that the island should be entirely disregarded in drawing the fishing zone of Greenland.

The main elements of the dispute between Canada and the United States in the Beaufort Sea have been reproduced in the Barents Sea where Norway and the Soviet Union are contesting some rich fishing grounds and underlying areas of wide continental shelf. Norway, playing the part of the United States, is in favour of a median line, while the Soviet Union follows Canada in extolling the merits of a meridian. There is an added complication in the Barents Sea. Both countries have major offshore archipelagos and Svalbard, which belongs to Norway, is subject to the terms of an international treaty agreed in 1920.

It has already been described how Norwegian and Russian territory meet in Varangerfjorden, and how that fjord has been divided by a maritime boundary which terminates at the mid-point of a line joining the Norwegian and Russian capes which mark its mouth. Four hundred nautical miles north of the Norwegian mainland lies Svalbard, an archipelago of a few large and many small islands. Norway acquired undisputed sovereignty over these islands on 9 February 1920. The treaty which established this situation was signed at the time by thirteen countries; since then a further thirty-six states have joined the treaty and the Soviet Union is one of them. The treaty confers absolute and full Norwegian sovereignty over all the islands 'great or small and rocks appertaining thereto', within an area bounded by meridians 10° and 35° east and parallels 74° and 81° north. Having done that the treaty then proceeds to qualify Norway's sovereignty. All the contracting parties enjoy equally hunting and fishing rights on the islands and in their territorial waters. In addition they must be admitted under the same conditions of equality to the exercise and practice of all maritime, industrial, mining or commercial enterprises on land and in the territorial waters.

The Russian archipelago Zemlya Frantsa Josifa lies 600 nautical miles north of the Soviet Union's mainland but only 200 nautical miles from Novaya Zemlya. This archipelago was one of a number which were confirmed as part of the Soviet Union in the 1926 proclamation, which set the meridian passing through Bering Strait according to the 1867 treaty with the United States as the eastern boundary of its Arctic sector, and meridian 32° 4' 35" east as the western boundary of the sector. At that time Finland still possessed an Arctic coast.

Norway disputed Russia's ownership of Zemlya Frantsa Josifa as recently as 1930, on the ground that Norwegian scientists and explorers had made more visits to the region than their Russian counterparts. However, since that period Russian sovereignty has not been challenged.

The area under dispute is shown in figure 10.6. The eastern limit is marked by the line of equidistance, giving full effect to all islands; the western boundary consists of meridian 32° 4' 35" east, except where it intersects the rectangle drawn by the Svalbard treaty of 1920. The total area is about 34,450 square nautical miles out to the edge of the 200 nautical mile zones. There is an additional area of seabed in the western half of the wedge of high seas which is located between Svalbard and Novaya Zemlya.

It is the Russian position that there are special circumstances which make it proper to draw the boundary westwards of the median line. The much larger population in the Kolskiy Poluostrov than in northern Norway and the much higher level of economic development on the Russian side of the boundary are facts which are advanced to justify the Russian claim. There is also the very important strategic aspect. The peninsula is the main base for the Soviet Union's northern fleet, and Russia regards unfettered access for that fleet as a prime consideration. Norway takes the view that special circumstances are found in the

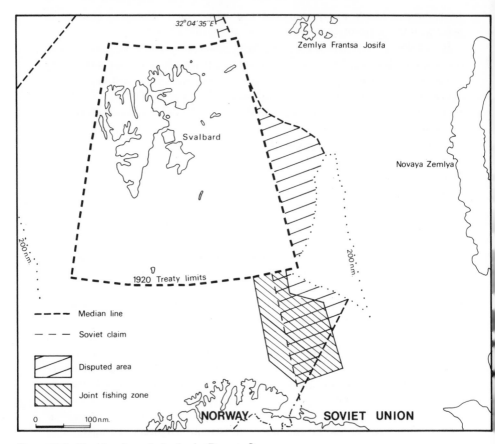

Figure 10.6   Maritime boundaries in the Barents Sea

realm of physical geography rather than the levels of population and the stage of economic development. Detecting no curious coastal configurations or inconveniently placed islands Norway regards the median line as the proper boundary.

During the mid-1970s Norway sent signals to the Soviet Union indicating that it would be prepared to consider an intermediate boundary between the median line and the Russian meridian, but these overtures did not lead to a final boundary. What did result was an interim arrangement for a shared fishing zone, the boundaries of which are shown in figure 10.6. The total area of this shared zone is about 19,000 square nautical miles: 11,600 square nautical miles lies between the boundaries claimed by Norway and the Soviet Union; 6750 square nautical miles lies west of the Russian claim, and 650 square nautical miles lies east of the Norwegian claim. The correspondence between the two countries regarding this interim arrangement made it clear that it did not prejudice the views of either party on the outer limits or common boundaries of claimed zones.

One of the strands of the discussions between the two countries concerns the legal status of waters and shelf around Svalbard. The Soviet Union insists that these areas are governed by the 1920 treaty. Norway takes the view that the treaty is quite specific, and that the only areas subject to the treaty are the land and the surrounding waters to the edge of the territorial sea, which is 4 nautical miles distant from the baselines. The second string to the Norwegian legal bow is that the shelf claims in the area of Svalbard, outside the territorial waters, are generated from the Norwegian mainland according to the principle of natural prolongation.

Since the Soviet Union appears to take an unyielding attitude to these negotiations; since there are now satisfactory arrangements for fisheries; and since both countries have large areas of shelf outside the disputed zone to explore, it seems unlikely that there will be an early solution to this quiescent problem.

Finally, it is necessary to consider a potential problem concerned with transit through Canada's Arctic archipelago. The famous Northwest Passage, which was first sought in 1576 and eventually forced in 1906 by Amundsen, periodically becomes the focus of attention by Canadian newspapers. One such occasion was in 1969, when the oil tanker *Manhattan* made an experimental voyage through the archipelago. The voyage was approved by Canada and a Canadian representative was on board. There have been very few completed voyages from the Atlantic Ocean to the Pacific Ocean via this route, and none has been a commercial undertaking.

However, it is possible that in the future new ship designs and a greater dependence on oil from the Arctic coast will encourage the movement of that oil by tanker to the east coast of North America. At that time Canada will have to consider what steps are necessary to ensure that such traffic is conducted in a safe fashion. Some legislation has already been enacted. Ships wishing to traverse the passage must meet certain construction specifications and minimum standards of manning and safety equipment. Canada's right to enact such legislation was endorsed retrospectively by Article 234 of the Convention. This article gives states the right to enforce non-discriminatory legislation to prevent, reduce and control pollution from ships in ice-covered areas, where severe climatic conditions create exceptional hazards to navigation. This legislation might have to be reviewed if the passage was used for commercial purposes on an increasing scale.

There has also been a long, unfinished and inconclusive debate in Canada about the propriety of drawing straight baselines around the Arctic archipelago. Canada has not done so, although there has been no statement to the effect that it will never do so. All the technical work for proclaiming baselines has been completed, so they could be announced at very short notice. Pharand (1973, 65–98) has made a detailed study of possible baselines for these offshore islands, and he comes to the sensible conclusion that they would conform with the rules that existed at that time and which have not been changed in any material way. That conclusion can only be confirmed by inspecting some of the baselines which have been proclaimed by countries in recent years. In comparison with such lines a set of

Canadian baselines around its Arctic archipelago would appear to be a very reasonable, if not modest, claim.

Conclusions

The Arctic Ocean is the smallest in the world, is the only one which has a large part of its surface covered with ice for most of the year, and is the ocean which has the highest proportion of its bed in surrounding continental margins. It is also the ocean which has the smallest amount of commercial traffic, although that traffic is locally important.

While no straight baselines have been drawn in the Arctic Ocean, a number have been drawn around the fretted coasts of Norway, Iceland, Greenland, Faeroes and Svalbard. With the exception of the baselines around Svalbard and southwest Iceland the baselines appear to conform to the spirit and letter of the rules for drawing straight baselines.

Only a few boundary agreements have been concluded, and while that between Greenland and Canada constitutes the longest marine boundary in the world, the segments drawn by Norway and the Soviet Union and by Norway and Denmark are very short. There are also two agreements for shared zones. Iceland and Norway have created a joint zone for exploration on the continental shelf, and Norway and the Soviet Union have created a shared fishing zone in the disputed area of the Barents Sea. The problems which remain fall into two general groups. First, there are disputes about the effect to be given to small or uninhabited islands belonging to one of the parties. Canada disapproves of a full claim from Greenland's Victoria Island; Greenland disapproves of a full claim from either Iceland's Kolbeinsey Island or Norway's Jan Mayen. Second, there are disputes over the question of whether a median line or a meridian is the appropriate boundary. The United States and Canada disagree on this question in the Beaufort Sea while Norway and the Soviet Union have a similar disagreement in the Barents Sea.

Fortunately it can be recorded that none of these problems is creating a high level of friction, nor is it evident that the existence of these problems seriously affects state relations in respect of other matters.

Once the bilateral boundaries have been agreed, countries will still face the problem of determining the outer edge of their continental margins. There is no evidence that any country is yet capable of fixing that limit with certainty. When that particular question is faced there will be considerable interest in the extent to which some of the transverse ridges, such as the Alpha and Lomonosov Ridges, form part of the continental margins of Canada, Greenland and the Soviet Union.

References

Archer, C. and Scrivener, D. (1983) 'Frozen frontiers and resource wrangles: conflict and cooperation in Northern Waters', *International Affairs*, 59, 59–76.

Lawson, K. L. (1981) 'Delimiting continental shelf boundaries in the Arctic: the United States–Canada Beaufort Sea boundary', *Virginia Journal of International Law*, 22 (1), 221–46.

Peary, R. E. (1910) *The North Pole*, London.

Pharand, D. (1973) *The Law of the Sea of the Arctic with Special Reference to Canada*, Ottawa.

Rintoul, B. (1975) 'Gulf of Alaska may offer best prospects for oil and gas', *Offshore*, 35, 82–90.

Tchernia, P. (1980) *Descriptive Regional Oceanography*, London.

The Geographer (1970) *Continental Shelf Boundary: Norway–Soviet Union*, 'Limits in the Seas' series, no. 17, Washington, DC.

The Geographer (1971) *Straight Baselines: Iceland*, 'Limits in the Seas' series, no. 34, Washington, DC.

11

The Baltic,
North and Irish Seas

Brest is so placed as though God had made it expressly for the purpose of destroying the commerce of these two Nations [England and Holland].   (Vauban 1693)

We have had to conclude, to our regret, that the general development of the law of the sea during the last decades, the culmination of which was the adoption of the Convention, has not been beneficial to Sweden. As a result of its geographical location, Sweden has only to a very limited extent been able to avail itself of the right to an enlarged coast State jurisdiction which is one of the main characteristics of the new law of the sea. On the contrary, Sweden has suffered serious drawbacks in particular as a result of the extension of the fishery zones of other States. I may recall here that during the Conference on the Law of the Sea Sweden joined the group of landlocked and geographically disadvantaged States, the members of which are the losers in the hard competition for the riches of the sea.

(United Nations 1982, 91–2)

Seldom in the history of Scotland can three words have had such an effective political impact as those in the statement 'It's Scotland's oil.'   (Brown 1978, 3)

Vauban's pithy analysis of the strategic importance of the location of Brest will remind readers that the seas off the north and west coast of Europe have been the scene of many battles in the ages of galleys, galleons and dreadnoughts. The statement by the Swedish delegate at the signing session of the Conference on the Law of the Sea indicates quite clearly that if countries were able to choose their location on one of the world's oceans, the Baltic Sea would be vying with the Caspian and Red Seas, for the title of 'Least Popular Sea'. Yet only a comparatively short distance to the west lies the North Sea, where the traditional resources of rich fishing grounds have been augmented by discoveries of oil, on a scale which revived the calls for Scottish independence.

The chief common characteristics shared by these seas is that they are semi-enclosed and shallow. The Baltic Sea is more enclosed than the others with only a single narrow entrance divided into three very narrow mouths; proceeding westwards the channels in the Kattegat are called Lille Baelt, Store Baelt and Oresund. The North Sea with outlets through the narrow English Channel and broad waters between the Shetland Islands and Norway is less enclosed than the Irish Sea. In all three seas the largest part of the seabed lies under waters less than 100 metres deep.

In the Baltic Sea there is a marked contrast between the coasts of the north and west, and those of the south and east. The shores of the Gulfs of Bothnia and Finland, and the east coast of Sweden north of Oland, have been cut into resistant material, and they resemble the *skjaergaard* of Norway, with many small islands fringing deep, narrow indentations. The south and east coasts have generally been formed in softer morainic material. On the coasts of east Denmark and West Germany there are drowned valleys which penetrate quite deeply into the land. The coasts of East Germany, Poland and the Soviet Union have been created by several spits and dunes formed by the westerly winds and the currents flowing eastwards. These depositional forms have tended to create smooth coastlines in this sector.

In the North Sea the rugged, indented coasts of Norway and eastern Scotland correspond to the northern coasts of the Baltic Sea, although the fringing islands are largely absent off Scotland. The smoother coasts of eastern England and Denmark, West Germany and the Netherlands can be related to the coasts of the south and east Baltic Sea. The drowned valleys are represented by the Humber and the Thames estuaries, and the coasts fringed with spits and dunes are found in the Netherlands, West Germany and western Denmark. This dichotomy is not evident in the Irish Sea where coasts are mainly characterized by deep embayments typical of submerged coasts.

In terms of economic activity and political relations there are also differences amongst the three seas. The North Sea is the scene of active fishing and oil industries, and across it passes a huge volume of commerce. The good political and economic relationships amongst the various states bordering the North Sea is apparent in the formation of the European Economic Community, even if certain decisions about particular policies are accompanied by long, sometimes strident debate. The Irish Sea has not yet yielded a crop of oil fields to match the harvest from fisheries, nor is there a large volume of trade between Britain and Eire. So long as there are serious differences over the future of Northern Ireland it is likely that relations between the two countries will be correct rather than cordial. Finally, in the Baltic Sea oil exploration activities have not produced large finds, and the fishing industry has suffered from rising levels of pollution and over-fishing (Fitzmaurice-Lachs 1982, 192–204). The surrounding countries belong to three major political and economic groupings. Denmark and West Germany are members of the European Economic Community and the North Atlantic Treaty Organization; East Germany, Poland and the Soviet Union are members of the Council of Mutual Economic Assistance and the Warsaw Pact. Finland and Sweden are members of the European Free Trade Association and are neutral and non-aligned. These divisions have not prevented co-operation and commerce, nor have they made such activities easier.

Straight baselines in the Baltic, North and Irish Seas

Of the thirteen countries which border these three seas only Belgium, the Netherlands and the Soviet Union have not proclaimed straight baselines along any part of their coasts. Because Norway's baseline south of parallel 68° 28.8′ north has already been considered (see pp. 259–60), attention in this chapter will be focused on the other countries. By Decree No. 9 of 1956 Poland closed its part of the Gulf of Gdansk with a single straight line. It measures 29.5 nautical miles and joins Hel, at the tip of the spit which masks the western part of the gulf, to the coastal terminus of the boundary between Russia and Poland. The proclamation, which was made before the 1958 Convention was concluded, makes no mention of the gulf being regarded as an historic bay. In any case, as Sebek (1979, 174–5) has observed, it is more difficult to justify historic claims to a bay which is shared by two countries. There can be no question that the natural entrance points of the gulf are found on Polish and Russian territory. It would be possible for Poland to shift the eastern terminus westwards for 10.5 nautical miles so that the new closing line measured exactly 24 nautical miles. That would still enclose most of the present internal waters, including the area called Zatoka Pucka which lies immediately south of the pronounced spit. Since the Soviet Union and Poland have concluded a lateral maritime boundary which disregards the present closing line, it is possible that Poland will maintain it on the grounds that it has not faced objections from the Soviet Union, the country with the most obvious right to protest.

Finland's straight baseline was decreed on 18 August 1956, and it could serve with the Norwegian baseline as a model which other straight baselines should strive to emulate. There are 180 turning points and no segment is more than 8 nautical miles long, because the decree provided that the longest segment should not measure more than twice the width of the territorial sea. This restriction means that the baseline faithfully follows the direction of the coast. It is also required by the decree that the basepoints should be revised at intervals of thirty years so that the most accurate definitions are available. The northern origin of the baseline is located on a line joining two islets, one belonging to Sweden and the other to Finland; this technique has also been used by Norway and Sweden and Denmark and West Germany.

The straight baselines proclaimed by Eire and the United Kingdom in 1959 and 1964 respectively lie entirely on the Atlantic coasts of those countries, and they will be considered in the chapter dealing with the Atlantic Ocean. The Swedish straight baseline was announced on 3 June 1966. It encloses most of the coastline with the exception of two short, smooth sections of coast in the south of the country, and similar sections on Oland and Gotland. There are thirteen sections in the system and 124 turning points. The first system of straight baselines had been published in 1934 (The Geographer 1972, 5); the new baselines conformed to the earlier pattern, although the number of turning points had been considerably reduced. The baselines could be criticized in some local areas because the coast is neither deeply indented nor fringed with islands, but in those areas the straight baselines have very little effect in advancing the outer edge of the territorial sea.

France's straight baselines were described in a decree dated 19 October 1967; only those parts drawn in the English Channel are considered here. There are five sectors of baseline in this region. The mouth of the Seine River is closed by a straight line measuring 8.5 nautical miles, and three roadsteads are closed on the Cherbourg peninsula. These three closing lines measure 14, 10 and 9 nautical miles in length, and their use represents a novel interpretation of Article 12 which permits roadsteads to be included within the territorial seas. These French road-steads would be included within territorial seas measured from the low-water mark, therefore it is not clear why these areas have been converted to internal waters by the use of closing lines. While all of these waters are in embayed areas none could be closed as a legal bay. The fifth sector begins near Granville on the east side of Baie du Mont St Michel, and after closing that legal bay continues around the coast of Bretagne and on to the mouth of the River Gironde. The fretted coast of this major peninsula, with deep indentations and some fringing islands, is an appropriate location for straight baselines.

East Germany made a general description of its internal waters in an ordinance dated 19 March 1964, and precise definitions were provided in a notice to mariners in January 1969 (The Geographer 1973, 1–2). Apart from one segment measuring 14 nautical miles which closes the legal bay of Wismar Bucht, the other seven segments serve to tie Rügen and its associated islands to the mainland. While exception may be taken to the fact that two bays called Tromper Wiek and Prorer Wiek have been closed although they fail the semicircular test, Rügen and its associated islands do fringe the coast and make straight baselines appropriate, as figure 11.1 shows.

Since 1970 West Germany has shown its straight baselines on charts of its coast. The main system extends from the eastern end of Juist eastwards through the remaining Ostfriesische Inseln and on to the boundary with Denmark. The coast in this region is masked by islands which are joined to the mainland by mud flats at extremely low tides. The northern terminus of the straight baseline is located in the sea, on a line joining a Danish and a German island. It is not known why West Germany failed to extend the system westwards to Memmert, but there may have been a desire to avoid any complications with the Netherlands over entry to the estuary of the Ems River. West Germany also drew straight baselines around Heligoland, although it is far from clear why this was considered necessary.

Denmark's straight baselines were first proclaimed on 21 December 1966; they were then modified slightly by a new decree on 19 April 1978. The new system deleted four basepoints and replaced an equal number. There are now seventy segments in the system and they are arranged in thirteen sectors. Some simply close river mouths and legal bays, while others either tie fringing islands to the mainland or surround offshore archipelagos. These archipelagos include Laeso, Sjaelland and Christianso. This last feature is a tiny collection of rocks and islets

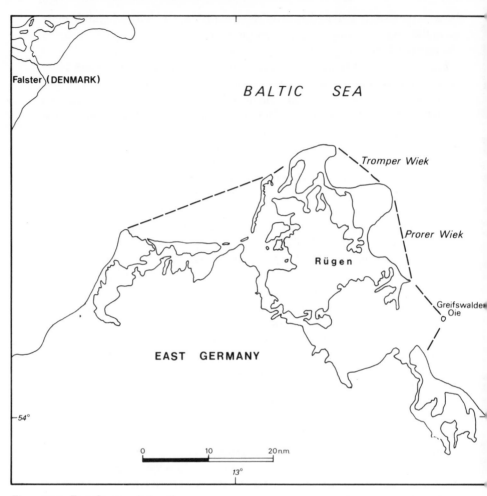

Figure 11.1   East Germany's baselines

situated east of Bornholm. While Lille Baelt has been closed Store Baelt has been left with a corridor of territorial waters, and Oresund is shared with Sweden, and special arrangements have been made for this strait. Although it is hard to find justification for some of the segments along the smooth coast of northeast Jylland, the baselines do not generally augment Denmark's claim to territorial seas.

Unilateral claims and agreed maritime boundaries

This is one of the few maritime regions of the world where the majority of coastal states claim territorial seas less than 12 nautical miles wide. Belgium, Denmark, Eire, East Germany, the Netherlands, the United Kingdom and West Germany all claim territorial seas 3 nautical miles wide. Finland and Norway still claim the traditional Scandinavian league of 4 nautical miles, and France, Poland, the Soviet Union and Sweden claim territorial seas 12 nautical miles wide. However, Sweden agreed with Denmark, in June 1979, to limit its claim to territorial waters to 3 nautical miles in those sections of coast opposite the Danish areas of Skagen, Laeso and Anholt in the Kattegat, and opposite Bornholm in the Baltic Sea. This act of self-denial on the part of Sweden was designed to ensure that there were no changes in the right of passage through these narrow waters.

Claims to fishing and exclusive economic zones show greater uniformity than claims to territorial waters. Finland and Poland claim only 12 nautical miles, and East Germany and Belgium claim to the median line with neighbouring claims; all the other states claim economic zones 200 nautical miles wide.

The semi-enclosed nature of these three seas requires many maritime boundaries to be settled between opposite and adjacent states. Several agreements have been made in the Baltic and North Seas and it is proposed to consider these two areas separately; no maritime boundaries have been agreed in the Irish Sea.

The maritime boundary agreed between Finland and the Soviet Union was settled in three stages. The territorial sea boundary was fixed in 1940, and extended 9 nautical miles in a southwest direction from the terminus of the land boundary. The co-ordinates of the maritime boundary's seaward terminus are 60° 15' 35" north and 27° 30' 43" east. This section of boundary was confirmed in the terms of the peace treaty between Finland and the United Nations on 10 February 1947. The boundary was continued in a general westerly direction by a treaty signed on 20 May 1965 and ratified on 25 May 1966. For the first 7.4 nautical miles the boundary continued to separate territorial seas, and the terminus of the territorial sea boundary was established at 60° 12' 19" north and 27° 18' 01" east. From this point a maritime boundary was then defined for a further 140 nautical miles by eighteen turning points. This boundary separated fishing and other areas and the continental shelves of both countries.

The equidistant line was extended for a further 44.5 nautical miles on 15 March 1968, when a treaty signed on 5 May 1967 came into force. The additional section was defined by another three turning points, and the terminus was left about 40 nautical miles short of the trijunction which is equidistant from the baselines of Sweden, Finland and the Soviet Union, as figure 11.2 shows.

Finland and Sweden defined their continental shelf boundary through the Gulf of Bothnia on 29 September 1972, and the agreement was ratified on 15 January 1973. The boundary extends for 420 nautical miles and is defined by seventeen turning points. The section of the boundary west of the Aland Islands is very old. On 19 January 1811, following the Hamina Peace Treaty, Sweden and Russia agreed on the topographical description of the frontier between their territories. Three of the points defined in that description, which had been corrected to conform with the revision of the agreement in 1888, were used as points to define the western boundary of the Aland Islands, which were the subject of a treaty on 20 October 1921 (League of Nations 1922, 217). This convention dealt with an

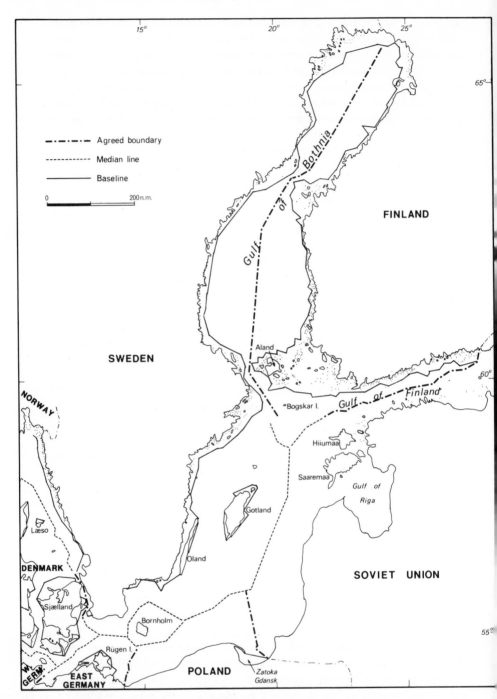

Figure 11.2 Maritime boundaries in the Baltic Sea

undertaking by Finland that the islands would not be fortified. Two of the points defined first in 1811 were then incorporated into the 1972 agreement. Further, the western boundary of the Aland Islands, defined in 1921, was effectively reproduced by the most southerly 85 nautical miles of the modern continental shelf boundary. The boundary lies close to the median line, but its course has been modified to produce a practical limit which is fair to both sides. The southern terminus of this boundary lies about 19 nautical miles northwest of the trijunction which is equidistant from the baselines of Sweden, Finland and the Soviet Union.

On 30 January 1932 Denmark and Sweden agreed on a territorial sea boundary which traversed the Oresund. The boundary stretches for 63 nautical miles and the two terminal sections are modified lines of equidistance. In the central section, where the Swedish island called Ven and the Danish island called Saltholm would cause sharp deviations in the course of the median line, a smooth agreed line has been substituted. There are nine turning points to identify the location of this boundary.

On 29 June 1974 East and West Germany agreed on a maritime boundary which continued their land boundary into Lubecker Bucht; the treaty was ratified on 1 October 1974. This boundary measures 8 nautical miles and apart from the first short segment, which is a median line, the boundary lies about 2 nautical miles closer to the coast of East Germany. It appears that the line lies close to the southeastern edge of the main shipping channel which leads to Travemunde and which was first established by the British occupation authorities in 1945 (The Geographer 1976, 2).

East Germany had settled its eastern lateral boundary with Poland on 29 October 1968. This boundary extends for 38 nautical miles and is defined by eight turning points. The line is based on the principle of equidistance, although some of the points have been adjusted very slightly to produce a more convenient line. The small German island called Griefswalder Oie has been given full effect in delimiting this line. Provision is made for the boundary to be extended beyond the present terminus to the trijunction with Danish claims. Providing Denmark's Bornholm Island is given full effect the trijunction lies about 6 nautical miles distant from the present terminus of the German–Polish boundary.

On 22 June 1978 East Germany agreed on a short maritime boundary separating its continental shelf and fishing zone from those of Sweden. The line measures 29 nautical miles and is defined by three turning points. It is located in the waters lying between Rügen, belonging to East Germany, and the Swedish coast between Trelleborg and Ystad. The agreement provides for the line to be extended in both directions to the trijunction with neighbouring states. In each case the neighbouring state will be Denmark, because it owns the islands of Bornholm to the east and Sjaelland to the west. The present termini appear to be within 1 nautical mile of the equidistant trijunctions with Denmark. The construction of this boundary was entirely a technical matter, because there was no dispute between the two countries. Once the basepoints on each coast had been agreed the equidistant line was calculated, and then that line was reduced to two straight segments to simplify administration and surveillance. Sensibly the two countries have specified the co-ordinates of the three turning points as they appear on both Swedish and German charts.

The Soviet Union and Poland delimited their territorial sea boundary by an agreement dated 18 March 1958; it came into force on 29 July 1958. The boundary was drawn perpendicular to the shoreline from the terminus of the land boundary. This boundary reaches the sand bar which encloses the lagoon called Vislinskiy Zaliv, at a point where that barrier is very gently curved; in such circumstances it is a comparatively simple matter to construct a perpendicular course for the boundary. It extends 3 nautical miles to the edge of Poland's territorial sea and then continues a further 9 nautical miles to the outer limit of Russia's territorial sea. In drawing this line it has evidently been agreed to ignore the Polish baseline which closes its half of the Gulf of Gdansk.

This boundary was extended as a continental shelf limit on 29 August 1969; the line became effective on 13 May 1970. The perpendicular line is extended for a further 4.8 nautical miles and then passes through an additional three turning points. The combined maritime boundaries measure 89 nautical miles, and the seaward terminus lies 3 nautical miles south of the trijunction with Sweden. Provision is made in the later agreement for the boundary to be extended to this trijunction.

The territorial sea boundary between Norway and Sweden has a long history. It was finally delimited in an arbitral award on 23 October 1909 after earlier agreements in 1661, 1897 and 1904 (The Geographer 1970, 2). On 24 July 1968 the two countries decided to extend that boundary seawards to divide the continental shelf. The boundary was continued southwestwards for 48 nautical miles and passed through four turning points. While the principle of equidistance guided the negotiations, the final line is a practical boundary; it terminated at the trijunction with Denmark, and that terminus became the point of origin for a boundary between Denmark and Norway in 1965.

The construction of continental shelf boundaries is more complete in the North Sea than in any other sea. The fact that these boundaries, with a single exception, were agreed in the period 1965 to 1972, in the face of two important obstacles, is a testimony to the spirit of co-operation between the coastal states. The two obstacles were physical and legal. The Norwegian Trench which sweeps around the coast of southern Norway, provided the physical problem. This depression has a depth of 370 fathoms in the south, where the width is about 20 nautical miles, and a depth of 260 fathoms in the north, where it has broadened to 75 nautical miles. If it had been judged that the trench constituted the proper boundary separating the natural prolongation of the British and Danish shelves on one side from the natural prolongation of the Norwegian shelf on the other side, the area of seabed available to Norway would have been sharply curtailed. The trench was ignored in drawing the boundary between these pairs of countries and lines of equidistance between the opposite coasts were used.

The legal problem stemmed from West Germany's zone-locked condition;

equidistant claims from the Netherlands and Denmark, which were mutually agreed on 31 March 1966, shut in claims from the concave coast of West Germany. West Germany objected to the use of median lines in this situation and successfully applied to the International Court of Justice for access to a larger area. A judgement in its favour was handed down on 20 February 1969, when the concept of natural prolongation was legally born. By the end of 1972 West Germany had been able to secure satisfactory seabed boundaries with the Netherlands and Norway, and had ratified an agreement with the United Kingdom by which West Germany inherited 8 nautical miles of boundary which had previously constituted the terminal sections of Britain's boundary with Denmark and the Netherlands. The British boundaries with those two countries were adjusted to provide new terminal points.

It is not proposed to describe each of these boundaries, which are completely described in the study by The Geographer (1974). Instead the boundaries are shown in figure 11.3 and their characteristics are summarized in table 11.1. All the agreements provide for consultation between the parties if a single field of petroleum or natural gas is found to straddle the boundary.

Although it is now usual for boundary agreements to include an article dealing with co-operation if a single field is found to straddle the line, actual cases of this event are rare. Gault (1979) has described the arrangements which were made for the Frigg gas field which was intersected by the Anglo-Norwegian boundary. This field was declared to be commercial in April 1972, and the companies which had rights in the area then had to agree on how the field should be exploited. It is

Table 11.1   Seabed boundaries in the North Sea

Countries	Date	Number of segments	Length (nautical miles)	Basis
Norway–United Kingdom	29.6.1965	8	359	Median line
	22.12.1978	2	140	Median line
Norway–Denmark	22.6.1966	8	255	Median line
Denmark–United Kingdom	6.2.1967	2	16	Median line
	7.12.1972[1]	2	11	Median line
Denmark–West Germany	27.5.1966	2	26	Median line
	7.12.1972	6	169	Agreed line
West Germany–United Kingdom	9.12.1972	3	8	Agreed line[2]
West Germany–Netherlands	18.9.1965	4	26	Median line
	7.12.1972	5	151	Agreed line
Netherlands–United Kingdom	26.12.1966	18	255	Median line
	7.12.1972[1]	Adjustment of northern terminus		

Notes:
1 These termini of existing boundaries were renegotiated after the verdict of the International Court of Justice, on 20 February 1969, in favour of West Germany.
2 This line is equidistant between Britain to the west and Denmark and the Netherlands to the east.

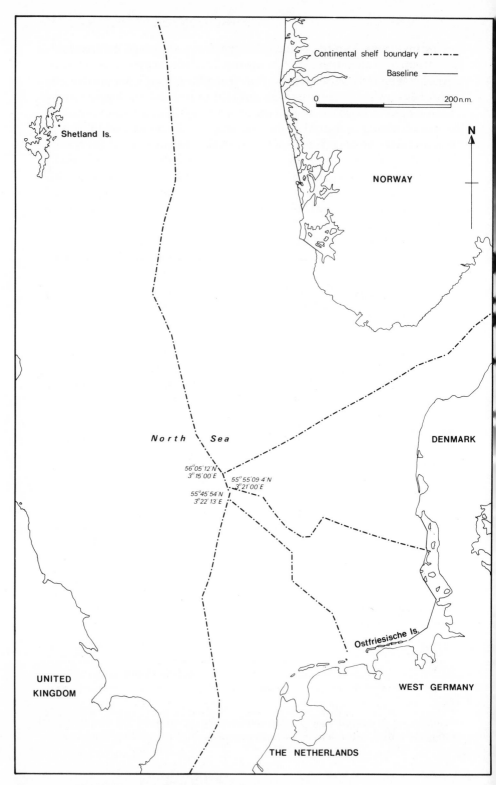

Figure 11.3 Maritime boundaries in the North Sea

recognized that unilateral action by two parties in respect of the same gas or petroleum field can prevent the maximum yield from being obtained. If wells are not sunk at the best location then pressure may fall and make subsequent recovery procedures costly. The answer in the Frigg field was to treat the deposit as a unit, so that it can be exploited in the most efficient way. That decision requires that agreement should be reached on the joint financing of the venture and the distribution of costs. Since the parties could not agree on the proportions of the field on each side of the boundary, they furnished all possible information regarding seismic and other data to a single expert who then made calculations which both parties accepted. There can be little doubt that problems of shared fields will become more common as more boundaries are drawn on the continental shelf and as the programme of exploration proceeds. Much detailed work remains to be done by lawyers so that as these problems arise they can be quickly solved. It seems that Gault has expounded the crucial principle on which such work should be based.

> The principle underlying the negotiations between all parties with an interest in the resolution of the Frigg problem was that unilateral exploitation was excluded because mutual respect for the rights of the other side must be observed. Apart from the violence unilateral action would do to the international legal order (especially if perpetrated by either the UK or Norway) the history of the petroleum industry points to the fruitlessness of non-cooperation in the exploitation of a joint deposit.   (Gault 1979, 311)

It is possible that the most intractable difficulties would be encountered in two different situations. First, if the two countries concerned had a record of poor or hostile relations, the idea of unilateral action to thwart the other country might be attractive. Second, if the two countries differed markedly, in the availability of other mineral resources, it is possible that the country with few alternative resources would find the more fortunate neighbour reluctant to enter into joint arrangements.

Belgium, which is a zone-locked country, has not concluded any maritime boundaries with its neighbours, and the remaining agreed boundary in this region is found in the English Channel and its Atlantic Ocean approaches. In 1975 Britain and France resolved to refer the question of their continental shelf boundary, west of 0° 30″ west, to a Court of Arbitration. The Court delivered its decision on 30 June 1977 (Court of Arbitration 1977). The central problem in this case concerned the presence of the British Channel Islands close to the French coast of Brittany and Normandy. If these islands are given full effect in delimiting a median line, then France is restricted to a small area of seabed in this region. Brown (1979) has provided his usual penetrating analysis of this judgement; and he concluded that the decision was important because it disposes of the fallacious notion that the concept of natural prolongation is of major relevance to the delimitation of continental shelves, and because it restricted the matters which might be introduced in applying equitable principles.

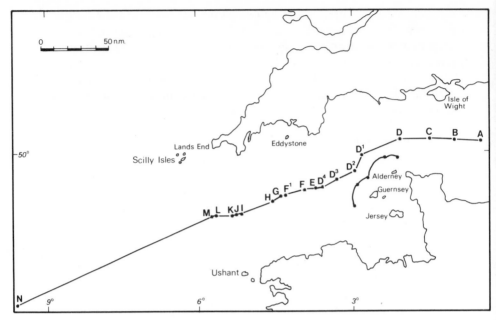

Figure 11.4   The Anglo-French maritime boundary in the English Channel

The boundaries determined by the Court are shown in figure 11.4. Between points A and D the line is equidistant from the British and French coasts. The line between points D^1 and D^4 was constructed as a median line ignoring the Channel Islands. Points E and F were also selected as median points giving full effect to the British and French coasts, and points G, H, I and J were selected on the same basis. The point F^1 was inserted because there had been a major disagreement between the two sides over the significance of Eddystone Rock. Britain urged that it be treated as a basepoint, while France argued that it should be discounted. The Court ruled that it should be treated as a basepoint; thus location F^1 is equidistant from Eddystone Rock and the French coast.

The boundary continued as a median line west of point J through points K and L. West of point L the Court considered that the Scilly Islands of Britain had a disproportionate influence on the course of the median line and so these islands were only given a half effect, and that is the principle which determined the boundary through points M and N. Point N is located on the 1000 metre isobath.

While the Court decided that it lacked competence to fix the boundary in the narrow waters between the Channel Islands and the French coast, it did delimit a boundary west and north of the islands. This boundary was fixed as a series of arcs of circles with a radius of 12 nautical miles.

This boundary definition did raise one very interesting point when it came to be applied by an expert appointed by the Court. Figure 11.5c shows how the half effect was applied to the location of the Scilly Islands. An area was defined by

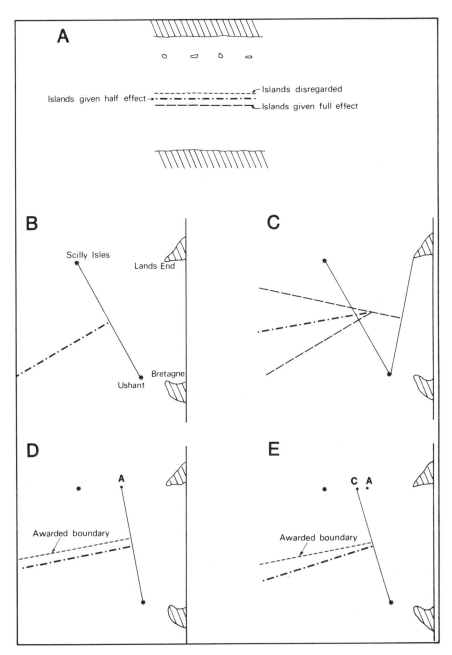

Figure 11.5 Methods of giving half effect to islands

constructing lines of equidistance between the Scilly Islands and Ushant and between Land's End and Ushant. The angle which these two lines created was bisected, and the bisector became the course of the boundary. Bowett (1979) has raised the question of how the concept of giving half effect should be applied in the case of adjacent coasts, for in the situation under examination the British and French basepoints were effectively adjacent rather than opposite.

In the case of opposite coasts the solution is very simple and unique. Figure 11.5a indicates a case where two countries are opposite each other and one country has a fringe of offshore islands. To calculate the boundary when the islands are given half effect, it is simply necessary to draw a line of equidistance using the islands, and another which totally ignores them, and then divide the area which lies between these two lines. The same effect would be achieved if the islands were notionally relocated half the distance from the coast.

Figure 11.5b shows the median line if the Scilly Islands are given full effect, and a comparison of figures 11.5b and 11.5c shows how the Court moderated the effect of the Scilly Islands to the benefit of France. However, there are other ways of moderating the full effect of the British islands, and they each produce unique lines. In figure 11.5d a median line has been drawn between Ushant and a point A which lies half-way between the Scilly Islands and Land's End. For comparison the boundary produced by the Court's method is also shown in this figure.

However, it is also possible to argue that the half effect should really be applied to the distance by which the Scilly Islands lie west of Ushant. The Court itself identified this as the main problem.

> The problem therefore is, without disregarding Ushant and the Scillies, to find a method of remedying in an appropriate measure the distorting effect on the course of the boundary of the more westerly position of the Scillies and the disproportion which it produces in the areas of the continental shelf accruing to the French Republic and the United Kingdom.
>
> (Court of Arbitration 1977, 217)

If the members of the Court had been asked to indicate the reference point for the phrase 'more westerly position', the answer must have been Ushant; it could not have been Land's End. It therefore seems sound to apply the principle of half effect to the distance by which the Scilly Islands lie west of Ushant. In figure 11.5e the median line has been drawn between Ushant and point C which is located at a distance from the Scilly Islands equal to half the distance which separates the meridians which pass through the Scilly Islands and Ushant. Once again the boundary produced by the Court's method has been shown to allow comparison.

Countries which agree to islands being given only a half effect would be wise to stipulate the means by which this calculation will be made. The British authorities learned to their cost that because the expert employed by the Court had worked on a chart based on a Mercator projection, the boundary had been deflected in France's favour. The straight line on the Mercator projection is a rhumb line which crosses the meridians at a constant angle. Maritime boundaries are usually defined as geodesics, which are the shortest distance on the surface of the sea between two turning points. Britain sought to have the location of the boundary calculated again as a geodesic, but the Court refused this application (Bowett 1979, 29).

Potential maritime boundary problems

It is noticeable that the construction of maritime boundaries has reached a more complete stage in the North Sea than in either the Baltic or Irish Seas. It appears likely that the negotiation of lateral territorial sea boundaries between Eire and Northern Ireland has been delayed because of difficult relations between Britain and Eire over the question of Northern Ireland. Agreements over maritime boundaries in the Irish Sea between the opposite coasts of Eire and the United Kingdom have probably made little progress because of the serious disagreement over the division of the continental shelf in the Atlantic Ocean in the vicinity of Rockall. This dispute is considered in the chapter dealing with that ocean.

In the Baltic Sea the completion of maritime boundaries has been made difficult by the existence of three groups of islands or islets. These features, which are owned by Finland, Sweden and Denmark give these countries an advantage in certain areas when median lines are drawn with neighbouring states.

Bogskar belongs to Finland. It is a collection of small islets and rocks located near the mouth of the Gulf of Bothnia. This territory was not apparently taken into account when the boundary was drawn with Sweden to divide the continental shelf. However, it was noted earlier that the boundary in this area reproduced the western limit of the Aland Islands as defined in the 1921 treaty dealing with that group. If Bogskar is used to compute a median line with Sweden and the Soviet Union, the trijunction of the various boundaries is pushed southwards by 16 nautical miles, to the benefit of Finland. The boundary between Russia and Finland terminated 20 nautical miles before Bogskar came into range as a possible basepoint. Finland would gain about 410 square nautical miles if it was allowed to use Bogskar as a basepoint instead of the straight baselines drawn around the coast of its mainland.

The largest island in the Baltic Sea is called Gotland, and this island, together with Faro and some small islets, belongs to Sweden; the group has been tied together by straight baselines. The position of Gotland 45 nautical miles off the Swedish coast pushes the median line with the Soviet Union eastwards, so that it lies 112 nautical miles from the Swedish mainland and only 39 nautical miles from the Latvian coast of the Soviet Union. Russia has sought to moderate the influence of Gotland and has tried to persuade Sweden that the median line should be drawn between the two mainlands. The area which Sweden gains by giving full effect to Gotland is about 4100 square nautical miles.

While Sweden has resisted this proposal it must be aware of the Russian sense of injustice, because 150 nautical miles to the southwest of Gotland Sweden finds its maritime claims constricted by the Danish island called Bornholm. This island, together with the associated group of islets called Christianso, lies in the mouth of the Baltic Sea just east of the Kattegat. Lying 72 nautical miles east of the Danish mainland, its maritime zones form an enclave surrounded by the zones of Sweden, East Germany and Poland. The area of seas and seabed which Bornholm permits Denmark to claim is about 2700 square nautical miles. It is the view of all three surrounding states that the claims from Bornholm should be discounted. While this seems to be a reasonable argument on the part of East Germany and Poland, which are only able to claim comparatively small areas of sea and seabed from their smooth coasts, it is not an argument which Sweden can use with conviction unless it is prepared to make concessions to Russia in the northern part of the Baltic Sea, where Gotland plays a critical role in fixing any median line.

Denmark also has to negotiate a territorial sea boundary with West Germany in the Baltic and North Seas. These negotiations are slightly complicated by the need to make some technical adjustments relating to agreements made shortly after the First World War, but the matter is not considered to be difficult or pressing by either country.

One of the reasons that there are so few problems in the North Sea and Irish Sea is that the members of the European Economic Community agreed on a common fisheries policy in January 1983. The agreement on 'a blue Europe', as the newspapers described it, followed nearly seven years of difficult, sometimes acrimonious debate. In geographical terms the important characteristic of the agreement is that it removes the need for negotiating common boundaries to separate fishing zones. Around each coastal state there is an exclusive zone 6 nautical miles wide, which is reserved for the fishermen of that country. A second band of waters, also 6 nautical miles wide lies outside this exclusive zone. In this second belt fishing is restricted to citizens of the coastal state and a specified number of foreign fishermen belonging to countries which have enjoyed historic rights to fish in these coastal waters. Outside the 12 nautical mile limit fishing is regulated by quotas rather than by special areas. For each type of fishery the total available catch has been determined by scientists. Each country is then granted a quote of the various stocks, and that country is responsible for supervising the activities of its fishermen and ensuring that statistics about volumes of fish caught are accurately recorded. The only exception to this rule is found in the vicinity of the Orkney and Shetland Islands, where frames have been drawn to indicate areas where only British fishermen and the fishermen of some other member countries may operate.

Conclusions

The Baltic, North and Irish Seas are shallow semi-enclosed seas, and in the case of the Baltic and North Seas there is a marked contrast between the rugged, indented coasts of the north and west regions, and the low, smooth coasts of the south and east areas.

The North Sea is more productive than the others in terms of fish and petroleum and natural gas; it is also the area where the highest density of traffic by merchant vessels is found. Further, the North Sea has been comprehensively divided by continental shelf boundaries whereas such boundaries are absent in the Irish Sea and rather incomplete in the Baltic Sea.

There are probably fewer serious maritime boundary problems in this region of the world's seas than in any comparable area. In the North Sea this is due to the similar political philosophies of the coastal states; to their determination to settle shelf boundaries to permit exploration and exploitation; and to the recent fisheries agreement. The difficulties which have been identified in the Baltic Sea are related to the effect which some island groups have upon the course of lines of equidistance. While these difficulties have prevented the conclusion of any boundary agreement between the countries concerned in the affected region, there is no evidence that the problems are a serious impediment to good relations.

References

Bowett, D. W. (1979) 'The arbitration between the United Kingdom and France concerning the continental shelf boundary in the English Channel and the south-western approaches', *The British Yearbook of International Law 1978*, Oxford, 1–29.

Brown, E. D. (1978) 'It's Scotland's oil. Hypothetical boundaries in the North Sea: a case study', *Marine Policy*, 2, 3–21.

Brown, E. D. (1979) 'The Anglo-French continental shelf case', *San Diego Law Review*, 16, 461–530.

Court of Arbitration (1977) *The United Kingdom of Great Britain and Northern Ireland and the French Republic. Delimitation of the Continental Shelf*, Geneva.

Fitzmaurice-Lachs, M. (1982) 'The legal regime of the Baltic Sea fisheries', *The Netherlands International Law Review*, 29, 174–251.

Gault, I. (1979) 'The Frigg gas field', *Marine Policy*, 3, 302–11.

League of Nations (1922) *Treaty Series*, 9, 211–21, Lausanne.

Sebek, V. (1979) *The Eastern European States and the Development of the Law of the Sea*, vol. I, New York.

The Geographer (1970) *Continental Shelf Boundary: Norway–Sweden*, 'Limits in the Seas' series, no. 2, Washington, DC.

The Geographer (1972) *Straight Baselines: Sweden*, 'Limits in the Seas' series, no. 47, Washington, DC.

The Geographer (1973) *Straight Baselines: East Germany*, 'Limits in the Seas' series, no. 52, Washington, DC.

The Geographer (1974) *Continental Shelf Boundary: North Sea*, 'Limits in the Seas' series, no. 10, revised, Washington, DC.

The Geographer (1976) *Maritime Boundary: Federal Republic of Germany–German Democratic Republic*, 'Limits in the Seas' series, no. 74, Washington, DC.

United Nations (1982) *Provisional Verbatim Record of the 187th Meeting, Third Conference on the Law of the Sea*, A/CONF.62/PV.187, New York.

Vauban, S. (1693) 'Memorandum regarding war expenditure on which the King might effect economies', cited in Roskill, S. W. (1956) *The War at Sea 1939–45*, vol. II, London.

12

The Mediterranean and Black Seas

The history of the Mediterranean world forms a natural whole. Separate histories
can be written of each of the lands and peoples that surround it, but so far as they are
separate they will be incomplete.   (Woodhouse 1977, 15)

The Mediterranean is of necessity the vital point of a naval war, and you can no more
change this than you can change the position of Mount Vesuvius.
                                                      (Admiral Sir J. A. Fisher 1900)

Probably to a greater extent than in any other semi-enclosed sea, the tides of
history have flowed across the Mediterranean and along its shores, tying the
various littoral territories together as empires, as enemies and as allies. The
Greek, Roman, Ottoman, French and Italian empires overlapped at various
times, and it would be difficult to find a higher concentration of battle sites on
land and sea in a region comparable in area to the Mediterranean basin.

But Mediterranean history is not entirely inbred. Fisher's comment on the
international strategic importance of the Mediterranean Sea, made at the beginning of the century, still has some application in its last fifteen years.

The Mediterranean and Black Seas, which are enclosed to a greater extent than
any other seas except the Caspian and Aral Seas, are dissimilar in physical,
political and economic properties. The Mediterranean Sea is nearly six times
larger than the Black Sea, and at its deepest point the Mediterranean Sea is twice
as deep as the Black Sea. The Mediterranean Sea occupies a basin which was
formed in two distinct stages. The convergence of the continental blocks of
Europe and Africa in Tertiary times produced the fringing fold mountains which
stretch from Switzerland in the west, through Yugoslavia, Albania and Greece to
Turkey in the east, and which in north Africa are represented by the Atlas Mountains. This crumpling of the earth's crust also produced the pronounced submarine basins, which are defined by steep continental slopes. These basins are
separated by submarine ridges which link Tunis to Genova via Sardegna and
Corse, Tunis to Reggio via Sicilia, and Tubruq to Kriti.

Subsequently the Mediterranean basin was widened as the continental blocks pulled apart. The main consequences of this trend have been the creation of the Adriatic Sea as the Italian and Dalmatian coasts separated; the creation of the Aegean Sea as the ranges linking southern Greece to Asia were fractured; and the creation of a connection between the Mediterranean and Black Seas. The existence of active volcanoes and the frequency of land movements indicate that these continental forces are still active.

The task of drawing maritime boundaries in the Mediterranean Sea has been made difficult by the existence of a multitude of islands, which are generally closer to the European and Asian rather than the African shore. Indeed, apart from the Iles Kerkenna off Tunisia, the African coast lacks offshore islands.

There are eighteen independent coastal states in the Mediterranean Sea and Britain owns Gibraltar and a base on Cyprus. There are some bitter disputes over maritime and territorial issues involving Greece and Turkey, Cyprus and Turkey, Spain and the United Kingdom, and Israel and its neighbouring Arab states.

The Mediterranean Sea is regarded as an important strategic zone by the western and Soviet blocs, and naval forces from both sides often conduct exercises in the region. This sea also provides an important avenue for European commerce with the Middle and Far East and for trade between littoral states.

The Black Sea was a deep brackish lake until the connection was formed with the Mediterranean Sea. Rising sea-levels drowned the shores of this lake, until stopped by the highlands of northern Turkey, Gruziya and southern Krym. Both seas have only comparatively small areas of discontinuous coastal plains. In both cases the major plains are associated with the principal rivers draining into the seas: the Rhône, Po and Nile Rivers in the case of the Mediterranean Sea and the Dnepr, Prutul and Dunarea in the case of the Black Sea. Ostrov Zmeinyy is the only island to complicate maritime boundaries in the Black Sea and its ownership is disputed by Romania and the Soviet Union. The widest area of continental shelf is found between the terminus of the land boundary between Bulgaria and Romania and Novorossiysk; the Sea of Azov has a maximum depth of only 8 fathoms.

There are two disadvantages suffered by the Black Sea which are not experienced by the Mediterranean Sea. The shallowness of the northern waters and the low level of salinity allow ice to form along the coast for periods lasting three months. Further, the fresh surface layers in the Black Sea overlie stagnant waters which possess high concentrations of hydrogen sulphide, and the living resources of this sea are poor by comparison with most other seas and oceans.

The Black Sea is surrounded by four countries, and three of those countries are governed by communist administrations; this region lacks the bitter disputes which characterize sections of the Mediterranean Sea. Traffic within the Black Sea is on a much smaller scale than in the Mediterranean Sea, primarily because it is a cul-de-sac, because Russia is the only large trading country, and because commerce originating in or destined for Turkey uses Mediterranean ports.

Straight baselines

In the Mediterranean Sea eight countries have proclaimed straight baselines; two others have announced the rules by which they will draw such baselines; and Libya has claimed an historic bay.

Albania proclaimed its straight baseline along a gently embayed coast on 1 March 1960 and has confirmed the line in a number of later Acts. The baseline has seven sectors which measure a total of 87 nautical miles. The Albanian coast between Kep i Rodonit and Kep i Gjuhezes offers a sharp contrast with the Yugoslav coast to the north. The Albanian topography has a grain which is transverse to the coast, while along the Dalmatian coast the grain of the mountains and islands is parallel to the coast. In Albania low limestone spurs covered with garrigue occur as headlands, and they alternate with smooth bays filled with alluvium, brought down by rivers such as the Drin and Shkumbin. Apart from a short detour to the island called Sazan, the baseline passes from headland to headland, enclosing two legal bays and five bays which do not satisfy the semicircular test. However, because the bays do not penetrate far into the land the baselines have only a small effect on the outer edge of Albania's territorial waters.

Turkey announced its straight baselines on 15 May 1964 and they became effective three months later. The lines were portrayed on a chart at the scale of 1:1.1 millions (The Geographer 1971, 2). There are four segments and three of these consist of a solitary line closing Iskenderun Korfezi, the bay southwest of Silifke, and the mouth of the Karadeniz Bogazi on the Black Sea. The two bays both satisfy the semicircular test. The fourth segment consists of 116 legs and measures 590 nautical miles. It extends from Av Burun in the southeast, near Antalya, to the coastal terminus of the boundary between Greece and Turkey in the northwest. This coast could be considered throughout its length to be deeply indented or fringed with islands.

Yugoslavia's straight baselines became effective on 2 May 1965. It was noted earlier that the topographic grain of the Dalmatian coast is parallel to the coast. The linear offshore islands represent the tops of mountain ridges which have been inundated and submerged beneath the sea. There are three segments of baseline marked by twenty-seven turning points, and the total length of the system is 244 nautical miles. The northern section along the coast of Istra encloses a coast which is deeply indented. The longer section from Rt Kamenjak to Dubrovnik connects a series of fringing islands. Yugoslavia has been modest in its claims to internal waters and has left the islands called Vis, Andrija, Susac and Bisevo outside the baseline system. The baselines along this coast could well serve as a model against which other baselines connecting fringing islands could be tested.

France's baselines were set out in a decree dated 19 October 1967. There are seven segments along the Mediterranean coast of the French mainland. The two longest segments enclose the coast from the Golfe de Fos, west of Marseilles, to Golfe Juan, east of Cannes, although short sections of low-water line are used to connect the straight baselines. The indented coast, with a sprinkling of offshore islands, makes the use of straight baselines appropriate. To the west and east of these main segments there are respectively two and three segments closing bays. There is some doubt whether Golfe les Flots d'Aigues Mortes is a legal bay, but its closing line does not significantly augment France's claim to territorial waters. A straight baseline has also been drawn around the southeast and west coasts of Corse, where there are a series of deep indentations.

On 10 December 1971 Malta proclaimed an act dealing with its territorial sea, and Section 3(1) provided for the construction of straight baselines. These lines were constructed in 1972. They join twenty-six basepoints and surround the entire territory of the country. The longest segment measures 11.9 nautical miles and joins Ras il-Wardija on Gozo to Ras il-Qaws on Malta. There are no basepoints on Comino, but the island called Fifla has been tied into the system by baselines which link Ras il-Qaws and Benghisa Point.

On 2 August 1973 Tunisia proclaimed straight baselines which extended from Ras Kaboudia in the north, via Iles Kerkenna to Ile de Jerba in the south. This line closes the Golfe de Gabes which is too large to be a legal bay but which might be considered to be an historic bay. Certainly it would not be reasonable to consider that the islands mentioned constitute a fringe in the immediate vicinity of the coast. This baseline was not taken into account when the International Court of Justice drew the boundary separating the continental shelves of Tunisia and Libya.

A Royal Decree dated 5 August 1977 defined Spain's straight baselines in the Mediterranean Sea and Atlantic Ocean; only the first set of lines are considered in this chapter. On the mainland coast there were three segments. The longest stretched from Punta Carbonera, east of Gibraltar, to Cabo de Salou, south of Tarragona. Two short segments link Barcelona to Arenys de Mar and Cabo Bagur to the terminus of the boundary with France. With a few exceptions, such as the promontory near Javea and the delta of the Ebro, the Spanish coast is too smooth and lacking in islands to justify the use of straight baselines. Fortunately, because the coast is so regular, the baselines do not push Spain's maritime claims seawards. Straight baselines have also been drawn around sections of the coasts of the Islas Baleares called Menorca, Mallorca, Ibiza and Formentera. The last two islands have been joined by straight lines, but it is hard to understand how such baselines can be justified around these islands. Apart from some small legal bays their coasts are neither deeply indented nor fringed with islands.

On 26 April 1977 Italy defined its baselines around the mainland, Sicilia and Sardegna. There are twenty-one segments of straight baselines around the mainland, and several consist of a single line. The longest segments link Capo Scalea to Capo d'Anzio, and Civitavecchia-Fanale to Punta di Portofino. There are several sections of these straight baselines which are open to criticism. For example, there is nothing in the Convention which could justify the baseline which passes from Punta Penna, north of Vasto, to a headland near Termoli, then to the Isole di Tremiti, and finally back to the mainland on the promontory called Gargano near Peschici. The coast throughout is lacking in indentations and the tiny group of islands is quite isolated, 13 nautical miles from the coast. It is also straining credulity in the vicinity of Isola d'Elba to consider Scoglio d'Africa and Isola di Gorgona as fringing islands. The Golfo di Taranto, which is closed by a single line, is claimed as an historic bay.

A total of ten segments have been drawn around Sicilia, and while there are parts of the southeast and west coast where straight baselines are appropriate, the north coast is too regular to justify those which have been drawn from Capo S. Vito to Capo Rasocolmo. The seven segments of straight baseline drawn about Sardegna appear to accord with the spirit and letter of the rules except in the east coast south of Capo di Monte Santo.

A decree dated 15 January 1951 defined the way in which straight baselines would be drawn about the Egyptian coast. On 28 December 1968 Syria followed suit with a similar declaration. In fact the Syrian coast and the Mediterranean coast of Egypt afford few opportunities for drawing straight baselines even according to their own rules. The main departures from the Convention permit shoals to be used as turning points, allow bays to be closed without any reference to width or depth, and authorize the inclusion of any islands within the system, either as an offshore archipelago or as fringing islands. Neither country appears to have produced charts showing straight baselines.

On 9 October 1973 Libya made its claim to Khalij Surt, a wide gulf west of Benghazi. The closing line was defined as parallel 32° 30′ north and it measures 296 nautical miles. This claim was justified on the grounds that Libya had exercised sovereignty over the waters throughout history and without any dispute, and that the area was crucial to the country's security. At one point on the closing line the nearest coast is 96 nautical miles distant; thus the straight baseline has a major effect in shifting the outer edge of Libya's territorial sea seawards.

As soon as the Libyan claim was made, objections began to be recorded by Britain, France, Italy, Greece, Russia, Turkey and the United States. The United States conducted ten naval exercises in the vicinity of the gulf in the period 1977–80. On a similar exercise in August 1981 two Libyan planes were shot down by American fighters. In short there is no evidence that Libya has exercised exclusive sovereignty over the claimed waters, even during the country's brief history, and plenty of evidence to show that Libyan claims to that effect have been challenged by other countries. It therefore appears that any claim to the gulf as an historic bay would fail. Further, there is no claim based simply on the perception of the coastal state that its security requires waters to be closed by straight lines. If such claims were accepted as part of international law there would be no need for any other rules about drawing straight baselines!

In the Black Sea, Bulgaria has claimed as internal waters the bays called Varna and Burgas. This claim was reiterated in the 1951 Decree dealing with territorial waters. Sebek (1979, 173) noted that the claim was originally made on 25 August 1935, in an earlier decree on the same subject.

Maritime claims and agreed maritime boundaries

In 1956 Israel declared the width of its territorial sea to be 6 nautical miles; that distance was selected because at that time 6 nautical miles was the most common width of territorial seas in the Mediterranean Sea. That regional characteristic has now disappeared and only Israel, Greece and Turkey still claim territorial seas 6 nautical miles wide. Turkey only claims that width in the Aegean Sea; in the Black and Mediterranean Seas it claims territorial seas 12 nautical miles wide. Greece apparently claims 6 nautical miles because any increase would provoke serious friction with Turkey over their rival claims in the Aegean Sea.

The remaining countries can be divided into three groups on the basis of their maritime claims. First, there are those countries which have coasts on wide oceans as well as on the Mediterranean or Black Seas. France, Morocco, the Soviet Union, Spain and the United Kingdom all claim fishing or exclusive economic zones 200 nautical miles wide. Apart from Britain which claims a territorial sea 3 nautical miles wide the other countries claim territorial waters 12 nautical miles in width.

Second, there is a majority of states which claim territorial waters 12 nautical miles wide, and in some cases claim a fishing zone which corresponds with the territorial seas. These states are Algeria, Tunisia, Libya, Egypt, Syria, Yugoslavia, Italy, Monaco, Cyprus, Bulgaria and Romania.

Finally, there are three countries which make unique claims. Albania, since 23 February 1976, has claimed territorial seas 15 nautical miles wide. There have been objections from several states to this claim in excess of 12 nautical miles. Malta, since 21 July 1978, has claimed an exclusive fishing zone 25 nautical miles wide, as well as a territorial sea 12 nautical miles in width.

Lebanon does not appear to have claimed any territorial sea, although there is a claim, dated 14 November 1921, by the French authorities to a fishing zone 6 nautical miles wide, and a claim to a security zone of the same width dated 16 May 1948.

Only one maritime boundary has been agreed in the Black Sea. Russia and Turkey signed a protocol defining their territorial sea boundary on 17 April 1973. The single straight line was drawn from the terminus of the land boundary at a bearing of 290°. When that line is drawn it is evident that the outer limits of the Turkish and Russian territorial seas intersect it at different points. The configuration of the coast causes the Turkish limit to cut the line 13.5 nautical miles from the shore, while the Soviet Union's limit intersects it 12 nautical miles from the land terminus (The Geographer 1974, 2).

Six maritime boundaries have been settled in the Mediterranean Sea and Italy has been involved in four of them. The exceptions involve Britain and Cyprus and Tunisia and Libya. When the Republic of Cyprus became independent Britain retained two bases on the island and the limits between the territorial waters of Cyprus and the British bases were specified. The four boundaries are not lines of equidistance, instead they appear to have been drawn perpendicular to the coast. As they proceed away from the coast the direction of the line changes, presumably because a greater length of coast is considered in determining its general direction (The Geographer 1972, 2). The boundaries do not have any seaward terminus and therefore they can accommodate the British claim of 3 nautical miles and the Cypriot claim of 12 nautical miles, as well as any extension of either claim.

On 24 February 1982 the International Court of Justice delivered its judgement in the case brought by Tunisia and Libya over their continental shelf boundary. This judgement was awaited with keen anticipation by many international lawyers, because it was considered that in view of the mass of technical evidence offered by both sides, the Court would make pronouncements which would clarify the importance of natural prolongation as a basis for claims to the continental shelf. Brown (1983) in an article sub-titled 'A missed opportunity' severely criticized the judgement, which had already been effectively attacked by the dissenting judgements of Oda and Evensen (International Court of Justice 1982). Brown's chief complaint was that the Court had failed to clarify the meaning of equitable principles, and he agrees with Oda that the line eventually drawn by the Court 'does not exemplify any principle or rule of international law' (Brown 1983, 159).

The boundary drawn by the Court consisted of two segments which are shown in figure 12.1. First a line was drawn from the terminus of the land boundary on a bearing of approximately 26° as far as parallel 34° 10′ 30″ north. This parallel was selected because it is the latitude which passes through the most westerly point of the Gulf of Gabes, which is judged to be the point where the Tunisian coastline makes a major change in direction. The bearing 26° was selected because a line along this bearing had been informally observed by both sides, for a few years, as the limits of concessions granted to oil companies. From the intersection of these lines the boundary was continued on a bearing of 52°. This bearing was determined by drawing lines from the most westerly point of the Gulf of Gabes to Ras Kaboudia and to the eastern edge of the Iles Kerkenna, and then bisecting the angle which they form. This bisector has an azimuth of 52°. The terminus of this second segment could not be specified because of the interests of third countries.

As figure 12.1 shows it is not clear where the terminus of the boundary between Libya and Tunisia will be located. After the boundary has extended 26 nautical miles it will reach point A which is on the line of equidistance between Tunisia and Italy, giving full effect to the Isole Pelagie. When it is discussed later it will be shown that the agreement between Italy and Tunisia, in August 1971, discounted those islands. But they were discounted in Tunisia's favour, for which Italy may well have secured certain benefits in other parts of the package of agreements. If the boundary awarded by the Court was continued beyond point A, it would mean that Libya was also benefiting because Italy was not making its full claim from the Isole Pelagie. The total area which could be involved is shaded on figure 12.1 and it measures 2000 square nautical miles. There seems to be no reason why

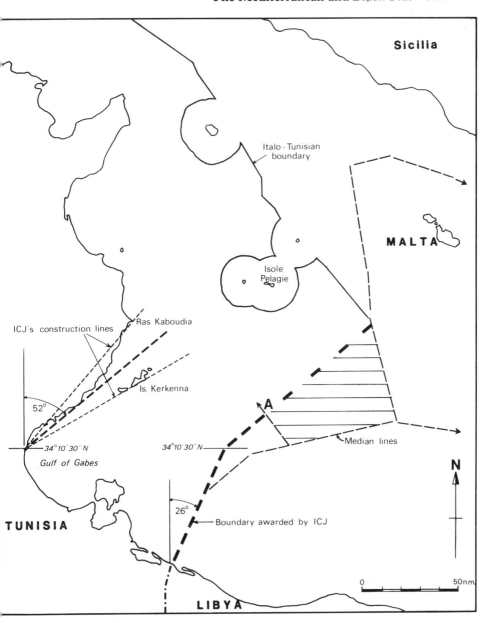

Figure 12.1   The maritime boundary between Libya and Tunisia

Italy should not claim the shaded area; the fact that the Isole Pelagie were
discounted as an act of favour for Tunisia does not mean that the islands also have
to be discounted for Libya or Malta.

On 21 January 1970 the continental shelf boundary between Italy and Yugo-slavia came into force; it had been signed on 8 January 1968. The negotiations were complicated by the presence of three Yugoslav islands and one Italian island which were distant from the coast of each country. The Yugoslav islands are called Jabuka, Pelagruz and Kajola; the Italian island is called Pianosa. If all these islands had been used as basepoints the line of equidistance would have favoured Yugoslavia. Instead of following this course it was agreed that Jabuka and Pianosa would be discounted and that the Yugoslav claim from the other two islands would be restricted to arcs with a radius of 12 nautical miles. As a result of these adjustments Yugoslavia conceded 900 square nautical miles which lay east of the median line, while it gained 120 nautical square miles which lay west of that line. The agreed line is shown in figure 12.2.

In the Sicilian Channel Italy has the advantage of offshore islands which Yugoslavia possessed in the Adriatic Sea. Happily Italy has shown itself as generous towards Tunisia as Yugoslavia was towards Italy. On 20 August 1971 Italy and Tunisia agreed on a continental shelf boundary and the treaty was ratified on 6 December 1978. The boundary extends from a point in the west, which is equidistant between the coasts of Tunisia and Sardegna, to an easterly terminus east of Isole Pelagie. The total length of the boundary is 443 nautical miles and it generally follows a median course except in the vicinity of Isola Pantelleria and Isole Pelagie. Around Isolotto Lampione in the Isole Pelagie the Italian claim is restricted to 12 nautical miles in the direction of Tunisia. Around the other islands in the group and around Isola Pantelleria the Italian claim is 13 nautical miles. If these restrictions had not been accepted by Italy a median boundary would have passed within 30 nautical miles of the Tunisian coast north of Iles Kerkenna.

Italy and Spain agreed on a continental shelf boundary between Menorca and Sardegna on 19 February 1974; it came into force on 16 November 1978. The boundary extends for 137 nautical miles and is defined by ten points. It is an equidistant line and has stopped short of the trijunctions with France to the north and Algeria to the south; in both cases these trijunctions lie about 7 nautical miles from the termini of the agreed boundary.

On 24 May 1977 Greece and Italy delimited their continental shelf boundary through the Ionian Sea; the agreement became effective on 12 November 1980. The boundary is defined by sixteen points and has a length of 268 nautical miles. The boundary is a median line except where some mutual minor adjustments were made. There appear to be two minor adjustments (The Geographer 1982, 4). The central point appears to lie 3 nautical miles on the Italian side of the median line, while the southern terminus lies 2.5 nautical miles on the Greek side of the median line. The agreement makes provision for the extension of the line to the trijunctions with neighbouring countries. The Libyan trijunction lies about 48 nautical miles to the south and the Albanian trijunction lies about 8 nautical miles to the north.

Italy and Yugoslavia signed a treaty dealing with the questions of Trieste and

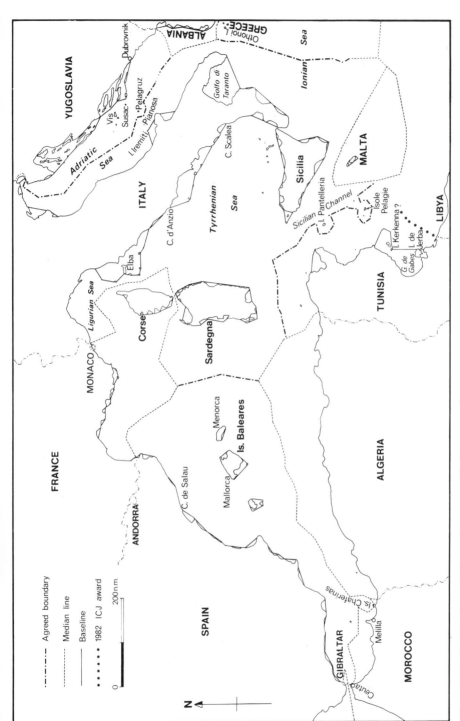

Figure 12.2 Maritime boundaries in the western Mediterranean Sea

Istria at Osimo on 10 November 1975; it was ratified on 3 April 1977. The main part of that treaty dealt with the land boundary between the two countries near the Adriatic coast. With minor modifications the Morgan Line, named after the Allied Commander in Trieste, was confirmed as the land boundary. Thus a provisional line became permanent after thirty years! The treaty also defined the boundary between the territorial waters of both countries in the Golfo di Trieste. It follows an unexceptionable course; after continuing the direction of the final segment of the land boundary towards the centre of the gulf, it swings west and then southwest until it reaches the outer limit of territorial waters west of Piran in Yugoslavia. Italy continues to have adequate channels to permit large vessels to reach Trieste.

Three other treaties which must be briefly mentioned deal with the narrow outlets from the Mediterranean Sea. After the Suez Canal had been opened on 17 November 1869 negotiations were held amongst various countries to secure its use by all nations. These efforts resulted in the Treaty of Constantinople on 29 October 1888. It was signed by Britain, Austria-Hungary, France, Germany, the Netherlands, Italy, Spain, Russia and Turkey (Colombos 1968, 202). Following the nationalization of the canal in 1956 by Egypt, that country affirmed its policy to respect the terms and spirit of the Constantinople Convention (Colombos 1968, 209). The canal was closed from 1967, following a war with Israel, until 1975, and it was May 1979 before ships from Israel were allowed to use the canal.

According to Colombos (1968, 220) the freedom of navigation through the Strait of Gibraltar is secured by the Anglo-French Declaration of 8 April 1904. Bruel (1947, 152) and Truver (1980, 178–9) take a different view. They believe that the Declaration affirmed a right to a free passage which was already considered to exist.

Passage through the Canakkale Bogazi and Karadeniz Bogazi, commonly known as the Dardanelles and the Bosporus, is governed by the Montreux Convention of 20 July 1936. It was signed by the British Empire, Turkey, France, Greece, Bulgaria, Japan, Romania, the Soviet Union and Yugoslavia. The Italian government, which had signed the Lausanne Treaty of 1923, adhered to the Montreux Convention subsequently.

The treaty stipulates that merchant vessels shall have the right of transit during peace or war, with the exception that transit can be denied to the vessels of countries at war with Turkey. There are different rules for the passage of small and large warships, depending on whether they belong to a state with a Black Sea coast or some other state, and whether Turkey is a belligerent or not. There are also restrictions on the tonnage of warships which countries beyond the Black Sea may have in those waters (Bruel 1947, 393–402).

Colombos (1968, 219) has noted that the Montreux Convention is in need of revision, but he holds out little prospect of that being achieved. He cites as a chief obstacle Russia's insistence that the Black Sea should be regarded as a closed sea, and that the Black Sea states alone have the right to draw up a new regime for these straits.

Potential problems over maritime boundaries

The potential problems fall into three classes. First there are the problems which arise because territory controlled by one country is claimed by another. In such cases it is generally impossible to make any progress in defining maritime boundaries. On opposite shores of the Strait of Gibraltar, Spain claims British territory and defends its own territory against Moroccan claims. Truver (1980, 160–75) has provided a useful account of the steps by which Gibraltar became a British possession. It was captured on 4 August 1704 by an Anglo-Dutch fleet for Archduke Charles of Austria. By the Treaty of Utrecht on 13 July 1713 Britain acquired Gibraltar.

> The Catholic King does hereby, for himself, his heirs and successors, yield to the crown of Great Britain the full and intire propriety of the town and castle of Gibraltar, together with the port, fortifications, and forts thereunto belonging; and he gives up the said propriety to be held and enjoyed absolutely with all manner of right for ever, without any exception or impediment whatsoever.
>
> But that abuses and frauds may be avoided by importing any kinds of goods, the Catholic king wills, and takes it to be understood, that the above-named propriety be yielded to Great Britain without any territorial jurisdiction, and without any open communication by land with the country round about.
>
> (Truver 1980, 247)

The arguments between Britain and Spain since 1713 have centred on the meaning of the words 'without any territorial jurisdiction'. Spain was clearly concerned to prevent Gibraltar being used as a base for smugglers, a development which occurred after the defeat of Napoleon in 1814. Britain was concerned to secure land and sea around Gibraltar which would facilitate its defence. There is no evidence to suggest that Britain will give Gibraltar back to Spain, or that Spain will agree to negotiate firm maritime boundaries between Spanish and British waters.

Across the strait from Gibraltar lies the Spanish town of Ceuta. It was secured by Spain in 1580 after it had passed through the hands of Phoenicians, Romans, Vandals, Goths and Portuguese. Nearly a century before, in 1497, Spain had captured Melilla, which had also been controlled by a series of former sovereigns. These two Spanish territories on the coast of Morocco are claimed by that country. In terms of making maritime claims Ceuta is more important than Melilla for two reasons. First, Ceuta is located on a promontory which terminates in Punta Almina, and therefore restricts claims from the adjoining coast of Morocco to a much greater extent than Melilla does, since the latter is situated on a smooth, concave coast south of Cap Tres Forcas. Second, Ceuta permits claims into the Strait of Gibraltar, whereas the waters off Melilla possess no important strategic qualities.

The third case in this category concerns Cyprus, which has been divided into two parts controlled by Greek and Turkish Cypriots respectively. Until the island is reunited it seems most improbable that the Cypriot authorities will agree to draw any maritime boundaries with Turkey.

The second class of potential problems is the largest and it concerns the presence of islands which deflect lines of equidistance to the disadvantage of neighbouring countries. These problems enjoy the same basic characteristic which provoked the case between Tunisia and Libya at the International Court of Justice. The Iles Kerkenna belonging to Tunisia have five counterparts.

Situated just west of the terminus of the land boundary between Morocco and Algeria lie the Islas Chaferinas, which belong to Spain. These three islands are called Isla del Congreso, Isla de Isabella II and Isla del Rey, and they lie about 4 nautical miles from Cap de Agua on the Moroccan coast. The islands were seized by Spain in 1848 in an attempt to forestall French occupation. The presence of this group of islands so close to the Moroccan coast, and the fact that it is located off a promontory with no other islands in the vicinity, result in the median line between Morocco and Spain being marked by a deep protuberance in favour of Spain. It would not be surprising if Morocco argued for a solution similar to that obtained by France in the case of the Channel Islands, if Spain insists on retaining these islands.

The next problem concerns Italy's Isole Pelagie in the channel between Malta and Tunisia. The agreement between Italy and Tunisia has been described, and it was explained that these islands had been heavily discounted in drawing the maritime boundary between the two countries. The eastern terminus of this boundary is 100 nautical miles from the nearest point on the Tunisian baseline, 50 nautical miles from Isola Lampedusa and 50.4 nautical miles from the nearest point of Malta. It is the view of the Maltese authorities that the Italian islands should also be discounted in drawing a boundary with Malta, so that Malta's claim can be extended westwards. Italy does not appear to be disposed to make the same concessions to Malta that were granted to Tunisia. This is probably due to the fact that the agreement with Tunisia involved a complete package involving joint fishing ventures which are not appropriate in the case of Malta. The Italian authorities may also take the view that since they have been generous towards Tunisia, it is for Libya to be generous with Malta.

Albania has not negotiated any maritime boundaries with its neighbours, but it is likely to seek relief from the constricting effect of the Greek islands called Kerkira, Erikousa and Othonoi. They overlap the Albanian coast and force the median line to follow a northerly course, severely restricting the claims which that country can make.

The most serious dispute over the effect to be given to islands occurs in the Aegean Sea. This dispute is particularly serious, first because Greece and Turkey have a history of conflict and hostility which is not conducive to concessions by either side, and second because a very large area is concerned. As figure 12.3 shows, a median line drawn between the Greek islands and the Turkish mainland would permit the latter country to claim only a small fringe of waters and continental shelf. There can be no question that the islands belong to Greece, and it is

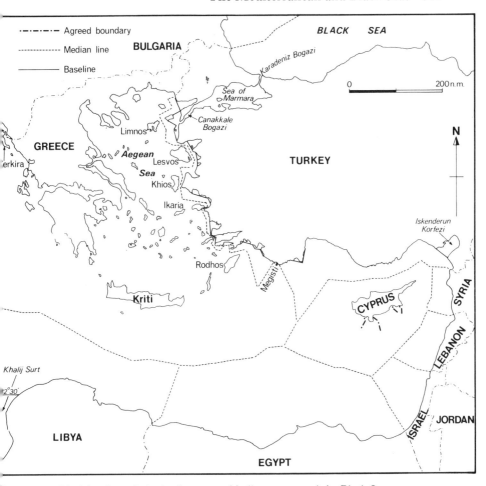

Figure 12.3 Maritime boundaries in the eastern Mediterranean and the Black Seas

equally clear that Turkey believes that they should not be given full effect. The two prime questions concern Turkey's claim to the continental shelf and the claims of both countries to territorial seas.

Turkey takes the view that equity is the overriding principle in this disagreement. Turkey is convinced that because the Aegean islands have an area of less than 5000 square kilometres and a population of less than half a million, they cannot be entitled to a larger share of the continental shelf than accrues to the Turkish Aegean coast, with a much larger area and a population of eight millions. Further, the Turkish authorities assert that the Greek islands are standing on the Turkish continental shelf and cannot supersede the claim from the mainland. They quote with approval the judgement in the Channel Islands case and draw attention to the concessions which Australia made to Papua New Guinea in Torres Strait, where Australian islands lie close to the coast of Papua.

It was noted earlier that Turkey and Greece each claim territorial waters 6 nautical miles wide in the Aegean Sea. While Greece would welcome an extension of this zone to 12 nautical miles it is known that in Turkey such a unilateral action is spoken of as a *casus belli*. There are three reasons why Turkey is so strongly opposed to territorial seas 12 nautical miles in the Aegean Sea. First, if both countries doubled the width of their territorial seas in the Aegean Seas, Greece's share of the waters would rise from 35 per cent to 64 per cent while Turkey's share would only grow from 9 per cent to 10 per cent. There would be a fall in the area of waters outside territorial seas from 56 per cent to 26 per cent. Second, except for short sections between Limnos and Lesvos, and between Khios and Ikaria, Turkish vessels would have to pass through Greek territorial waters to reach waters which were outside the regime of territorial seas. Even in these two cases the vessels would have reached waters which were totally surrounded by Greek territorial waters, so the problem of passing through Greece's territorial seas would have only been delayed if the ship was bound for the Suez Canal or the western Mediterranean Sea. Of course it would be possible for the vessels to hug the Turkish coast until they were east of Rodhos, but that is regarded as an unreasonable imposition.

Turkey's third objection to increased widths for territorial seas rests on the fact that such extensions would pre-empt the question of sovereignty over some parts of the continental shelf lying 6–12 nautical miles from land. This combination of objections led Turkey to vote against the adoption of the Convention in 1982.

Greece refutes Turkey's objections by drawing attention to the fact that islands can be used as basepoints from which continental shelf claims are made. Further, the view is expressed that the number of people living on the Aegean Islands, and their fairly uniform density from the Greek to the Turkish mainland, makes comparison with Britain's Channel Islands inappropriate (Gounaris 1980, 113). Presumably Greece also believes that Turkey should have enough confidence to rely on the right of innocent passage through the territorial seas of neighbours.

The International Court of Justice declined to become involved in this case and it therefore appears that the solution will be found in bilateral negotiations. Whatever solution is found to the problem of the Aegean Islands, it does seem that the most easterly Greek islands, called Megisti, are a special case. This small group of islands used to be called Kastellorizon, and they have an area of 4 square nautical miles. The location of these islands 60 nautical miles east of Rodhos, the closest Greek island, and only 1 nautical mile off the coast of Turkey, causes a major deviation of the median line between the two countries in Greece's favour. The area of sea and seabed which Greece gains directly from owning Megisti is 5240 square nautical miles.

It does appear that the characteristics of this small group of islands justify Turkey's enthusiasm for the judgement in the Channel Islands case, even if that enthusiasm is misguided in respect of the other Aegean Islands. Megisti is remote from the rest of Greece; it has only a small population; it is very close to the Turkish coast; and it would create an inequitable result if it was given full effect in drawing maritime boundaries. It could also be argued that this group of islands has only belonged to Greece for a comparatively short period of its history. Since 1306 the islands have belonged to the Knights of the Hospital, Egypt (1400), Naples (1450), Rodhos (1471), Turkey (1471), Rodhos (1472), Turkey (1512), Venice (1570), Turkey (1659), Greece (1832), Turkey (1832), Italy (1912), France (1915), Italy (1920), and Greece (1947). In any negotiations between the two countries, it appears that modifying the effect of Megisti is one concession which Greece could sensibly offer in exchange for Turkish concessions in the Aegean Sea.

There is only one island in the Black Sea which is distant from the shore and it is called Ostrov Zmeinyy. It lies 19 nautical miles due east of the terminus of the land boundary between the Soviet Union and Romania. It is occupied by the Soviet Union and claimed by Romania. While this is not an active dispute, it is understandable that Romania should feel a sense of injustice that this island serves to reduce significantly the area of sea and seabed it can claim according to median lines. The area which Romania can claim within median lines is 6430 square nautical miles; the area which Russia gains from owning Ostrov Zmeinyy is 2030 square nautical miles.

The last class of potential problems includes only one case. On 26 July 1982 Libya and Malta advised the International Court of Justice that an agreement between them referring the question of their continental shelves to the Court had now come into force. The agreement was signed on 23 May 1976 and came into force on 20 March 1982. The Court is asked to decide what principles and rules of international law apply to the delimitation of the continental shelves of the two countries, and how they should be applied to delimit a maritime boundary. The agreement stipulates that the two countries will enter into negotiations to determine their respective continental shelves in accordance with the decision of the Court.

There is a broad submarine valley between the Libyan coast and Malta, and it slopes gently eastwards towards the Ionian Basin where the deepest waters in the Mediterranean Sea are found. The Medina Bank stands as an isolated mound in this submarine valley; it is 67 nautical miles from Malta and 139 nautical miles from Libya. The Maltese authorities take the view that the boundary should be a line of equidistance, while the Libyan authorities believe that the boundary should lie north of the median line because Libya has a much longer coastline than Malta, and because the structural division of the continental shelf lies closer to Malta. There was a dispute in August 1980 when Malta began to drill the Medina Bank and was interrupted by a Libyan submarine.

Conclusions

While there are many important physical differences between the Mediterranean and Black Seas, they share the common attribute that neither contains rich fishing grounds and neither has been proved to overlie large fields of natural gas or crude petroleum. In terms of political characteristics there are also major differences. The small number of states which ring the Black Sea and the common political ideology of three of them partly explains the lack of maritime disputes. The fact that it is a cul-de-sac also means that extra-regional states are less concerned with the Black Sea than they are with the Mediterranean, which is both a vital avenue for commerce and a strategic theatre where rival navies manoeuvre.

The physical nature of the north coast of the Mediterranean Sea has encouraged Spain, Italy and Albania to draw straight baselines either where none is needed or where none can be justified. On the south coast both Libya and Tunisia have exploited normal geographical characteristics to draw straight baselines which can be easily criticized.

The most serious problems in the Mediterranean Sea are caused by the presence of islands close to the coast of neighbouring states. While Italy and Yugoslavia have both made concessions to discount their islands in the Sicilian Channel and the Adriatic Sea respectively, other difficult problems remain. It seems probable that the dispute between Greece and Turkey over the effect to be given to the Aegean Islands will prove the hardest to settle.

There are also problems at the western end of the Mediterranean because of the British and Spanish fragments of empire on the Spanish and Moroccan coasts respectively.

References

Brown, E. D. (1983) 'The Tunisia–Libya continental shelf case', *Marine Policy*, 7 (3), 142–62.
Bruel, E. (1947) *International Straits*, vol. II, London.
Colombos, C. J. (1968) *International Law of the Sea*, London.
Fisher, Admiral Sir J. A. (1900) Letter to Lord Selborne on 7 December. Quoted in Roskill, S. W. (1954) *The War at Sea 1939–45*, vol. I, London, 515.
Gounaris, E. (1980) 'The delimitation of the continental shelf of islands: some observations', *Revue hellénique de droit international*, 32 (1–4), 111–19.
International Court of Justice (1982) 'Continental Shelf (Tunisia–Libyan Arab Samahiriya): Judgement', *I.C.J. Reports*, The Hague.
Sebek, V. (1979) *The East European States and the Development of the Law of the Sea*, vol. I, New York.
The Geographer (1971) *Straight Baselines: Turkey*, 'Limits in the Seas' series, no. 32, Washington, DC.
The Geographer (1972) *Territorial Sea Boundary: Cyprus – Sovereign Base Area (UK)*, 'Limits in the Seas' series, no. 49, Washington, DC.
The Geographer (1974) *Territorial Sea Boundary: Soviet Union–Turkey*, 'Limits in the Seas' series, no. 59, Washington, DC.
The Geographer (1982) *Continental Shelf Boundary: Greece–Italy*, 'Limits in the Seas' series, no. 96, Washington, DC.
Truver, S. C. (1980) *The Strait of Gibraltar and the Mediterranean*, Germantown, Md.
Woodhouse, C. M. (1977) *Modern Greece*, London.

13

The Atlantic Ocean

The Atlantic Ocean, above all in its northern part, is the most travelled and best known of all the oceans.   (Tchernia 1980, 87)

The Atlantic is the vital area, as it is in that ocean and that alone that we can lose the war at sea.   (Churchill 1950, 771)

The posture of affairs thus being favourable to British designs, two warships, the Clio and the Tyne, were dispatched to the Falklands. The Clio first put in at Port Egmont, arriving on 20 December 1832.   (Goebel 1927, 455)

The Falkland Islands dispute, which has poisoned relations between Britain and Argentina for a very long time and which flared into destructive war in 1982, is not typical of maritime boundary disputes in the Atlantic Ocean. There are fewer problems of this nature in the Atlantic Ocean than in either the Indian or Pacific Oceans.

Three prime geographical facts contribute to this situation. First, along the coasts of South America, North America and Western Europe there are only thirteen countries or territories. This reduction in the potential for disagreement is strengthened by the fact that within the continental groupings political relations are good. Second, those islands found in the Atlantic Ocean are either isolated, so that boundaries are unnecessary, or in clearly defined groups owned by one country. Further, with a few notable exceptions the ownership of islands is not in dispute between countries. The third fact is that while there are twenty-one countries which share the west coast of the continent of Africa, this coast is remarkably smooth and uncomplicated and thus offers few circumstances which promote discord over maritime affairs.

The Atlantic Ocean has the shape of a letter S because the opposite coasts of North and South America and Western Europe and West Africa provide a good fit with each other. The ocean extends 6200 nautical miles from Iceland in the north to the line linking the southern tips of Africa and South America. Apart from the narrowing to about 1500 nautical miles between Brazil and Sierra Leone, the Atlantic Ocean has a width of about 3000 nautical miles.

Although not as large as the Pacific Ocean, the Atlantic Ocean drains a much larger area of the earth's surface. The mountain ranges of the continents which surround the Atlantic Ocean lie considerable distances from the coast and provide the source for rivers which are generally longer than those which flow into the Pacific Ocean. One effect of this circumstance is shown in the extensive continental rises found around the Atlantic littoral. Such features are only rarely found around the rim of the Pacific Ocean. The continental margin which borders the Atlantic Ocean occupies a larger proportion of the seabed than the margins in either the Pacific or Indian Oceans. However, it is noticeable that there are important variations within the Atlantic Basin in the extent of various components of the margin. The existence of wide continental rises has already been noted. It must also be recorded that the west coast of Africa tends to have narrower continental shelves and slopes than are found around the other three continents fringing the Atlantic Ocean.

The tendency for fishing grounds to be associated with continental margins means that the comparatively wide margins around the Atlantic Ocean provide many rich fishing grounds. The most notable lie between Iceland and the British Isles, on the Grand Banks south of Newfoundland, and off the coasts of Morocco and Namibia.

A map produced by The Geographer (1973b) showing the world's major shipping lanes reveals that the continents flanking the Atlantic Ocean are stitched together with a close network of routes. However, there is a lower density of routes between South America and Africa than between any other pair of continents. The chief hazards to navigation are fierce tropical storms and icebergs. About 7500 icebergs are calved from glaciers which grow rapidly on the west coast of Greenland between parallels 69° and 73° north. Only about 400 reach south of Newfoundland, and an average of fifty each year reach the southern limit of the Grand Banks.

The Mid-Atlantic Ridge forms a prominent and continuous feature on the seabed, near the middle of the ocean. A number of islands are associated with it, including the Azores, Ascencion, St Helena, Tristan da Cunha and Gough and Bouvet Islands. These are all volcanic in origin. There are also volcanic groups situated on the continental margins, including the Canary and Cape Verde Islands, and Fernando de Noronha. Major continental islands are also found in Newfoundland, the British Isles and the Falkland Islands. While there are a number of island states, such as Eire, the United Kingdom, Iceland and The Bahamas, which fringe the Atlantic Ocean, only Cape Verde and São Tomé and Príncipe are island states within the Atlantic Ocean.

The small number of countries which border the American and European margins of the Atlantic Ocean; the comparatively uncomplicated nature of the coastline of West Africa; and the relatively few serious actual and potential disputes, make it possible to consider this ocean in a single chapter. In the following sections dealing with straight baselines, maritime claims and agreed boundaries, and actual and potential problems, the ocean is treated in four continental sectors: South America, North America, Western Europe and West Africa. The Lesser Antilles and The Bahamas are treated as part of the Caribbean Sea.

Straight baselines

Argentina and Uruguay are the only countries in the South American sector of the Atlantic Ocean to have drawn straight baselines. On 30 January 1961 the two countries agreed that the estuary of the Rio de la Plata would be closed by a straight line joining Punta Rosa of Cabo San Antonio in the south and Punta del Este in the north. This line, which measures 120 nautical miles, is justified by reference to Article 13 of the 1958 Convention on the Territorial Sea and Contiguous Zone. This article permits the mouths of rivers flowing directly into the sea to be closed. It is certainly stretching the meaning of this article, and its equivalent Article 9 in the 1982 Convention, to consider the Rio de la Plata to be a river which flows directly into the sea.

On 29 December 1966 Argentina also defined three closing lines along its coast. Golfo Nuevo is a legal bay with a mouth of about 10 nautical miles. The same cannot be said of Golfo San Matias and Golfo de San Jorge. These are gulfs with wide mouths measuring 65 and 122 nautical miles respectively. There is no suggestion in the proclamation that they are considered to be historic bays, but that appears to be the only way in which these gulfs could be closed without breaching the provision on bays in the Convention.

While none of the other countries in this sector has drawn straight baselines, Guyana is in the remarkable position that its Caribbean neighbour, Venezuela, has drawn a straight baseline which terminates in Guyana's territory! By a decree dated 10 July 1968 Venezuela defined a straight baseline across the southern mouth of the Orinoco River. The baseline measures 99 nautical miles and it connects Punta Araguapiche, on the outer edge of the delta, with a location about 18 nautical miles east of Waini Point, on the smooth coast of Guyana. Two points should be made about this straight baseline. First, it cannot be justified by any article in the Convention. The line drawn cannot be considered to close the mouth of the Orinoco River, which lies at least 20 miles landward of the baseline. It does not close a legal bay, and there is no evidence that this section of coast is so unstable that the outer edge of the delta lay in the vicinity of the baseline in contemporary times. If the broad indentation is claimed as an historic bay then it would be necessary to provide evidence to justify the claim. In short, even if the claimed baseline was entirely within the territory of Venezuela, it is not clear how it would be justified in the terms of the Convention.

The second point is that there is no provision in any convention which permits a state to use the territory of another country for the terminus of its straight baseline. Presumably Venezuela would argue that it has a claim to western Guyana which has been maintained for a long time, and indeed there was an explanatory note which accompanied the decree (The Geographer 1970, 2). This note referred to the fact that Venezuela claimed territorial seas 12 nautical miles wide while Guyana only claimed 3 nautical miles. By this decree Venezuela was claiming the band of waters, 9 nautical miles wide, which lay outside Guyana's territorial waters, along that section of Guyana's coast claimed by Venezuela. It also reserved its claim to the territorial waters claimed by Guyana along the disputed coast, and to the internal waters created along the Guyanan coast by the Venezuelan straight baseline. On 4 October 1977 Guyana increased its claim to territorial waters 12 nautical miles wide; this means that since that date the band of waters 9 nautical miles wide specifically claimed by Venezuela is also claimed by Guyana.

On the coast of North America only Canada has proclaimed straight baselines. The United States has closed some legal bays but it has not drawn any straight baselines, to the disappointment of states such as Rhode Island. Canada announced its straight baselines along the south and east coasts of Newfoundland on 26 October 1967 and along the coast of Nova Scotia on 29 May 1969. In both cases the coasts are deeply indented and sometimes have fringes of islands. The seventy-five turning points on the coast of Newfoundland and the fifty-two turning points around the shore of Nova Scotia ensure that the baselines do not depart from the general direction of the coast. In meeting this requirement the Canadian baselines, like those of Finland, have been drawn in a meticulous fashion.

All the countries on the Atlantic coast of Western Europe have drawn straight baselines. On 25 September 1964 the United Kingdom announced baselines which tied the Western Isles to the mainland. The straight baselines consist of twenty-five sectors extending 283 nautical miles from Cape Wrath in the north to the Mull of Kintyre in the south. The islands on which the basepoints are located do fringe the coast, and sections of the islands are deeply indented.

Eire defined its straight baselines along the west and south coasts of its territory on 1 October 1959. There are six segments and all those in the west and southwest enclose coasts which are deeply indented and sometimes fringed with islands. The case for straight baselines is less obvious along the south coast east of Ram Head.

France's baselines, decreed on 19 October 1967, have already been described for the coasts of the English Channel and the Mediterranean Sea. In the Bay of Biscay, straight baselines defined by nineteen turning points have been defined from Pointe de Penmarch to Pointe de Grave, at the mouth of the River Gironde. While the northern part of this section of coast is indented, the baselines have been located offshore, joining islands which do not appear to form a fringe in the immediate vicinity of the coast. Isolated islands continue to provide basepoints along the southern sector where the coast is comparatively smooth.

Spain declared its straight baselines on 5 August 1977. Three segments occupy most of the Spanish coast of the Bay of Biscay and the Atlantic coast north of Portugal. These segments begin at Cabo Higuer in the east, near the French border, and terminate at Cabo Sillero, about 20 nautical miles north of the Portuguese boundary. While the Atlantic coastline is fretted and suitable for the construction of straight baselines, the coast of the Bay of Biscay appears to be too smooth and lacking a proper fringe of islands to justify the baselines which have been proclaimed. The fourth segment of baseline which has been drawn along the coast between the boundary with Portugual and Gibraltar encloses a smooth coast almost totally devoid of islands.

Spain also defined baselines around some of the Islas Canarias. Gran Canaria, Tenerife, Hierro and La Palma have individual baselines which surround all or most of their coastlines. The eastern group of the Islas Canarias, including Alegranza, Fuerteventura, Graciosa, Lanzarote, Lobos and Montana Clara have been tied together by a series of straight baselines. If it is eventually decided that the offshore archipelagos of continental states can be surrounded by archipelagos then this eastern group would certainly qualify. The construction of such baselines is becoming a fairly common occurrence, and this will be a trend difficult to reverse.

Portugal has drawn straight lines to enclose the bays at the mouths of the Rio Tejo and Rio Sado. The proclamation was made on 22 August 1966. The lines closing these bays measure 22 and 31 nautical miles respectively, and neither bay meets the semicircular test unless the waters within the estuaries of the rivers are included as part of the bays. Because the bay at the mouth of the Rio Sado is wider than 24 nautical miles, it could only be properly claimed as an historic bay.

Although the coast of West Africa is generally smooth and uncomplicated straight baselines have been drawn by Mauritania, Senegal, Guinea-Bissau, Guinea, Cameroon and Angola. Cape Verde and São Tomé and Príncipe have drawn archipelagic baselines around their territory. Mauritania enclosed the shallow waters over Banc d'Arguin by a baseline which linked Cap Blanc and Cap Timiris; it was announced on 21 January 1967. The single line measures 89 nautical miles along a section of coast which is neither deeply indented nor fringed with islands. Further, the line could only be considered to conform to the general direction of the coast if the entire coast of Mauritania was viewed in its entirety. The law defining the baseline makes no mention of any historic grounds on which the gently embayed area might be claimed. The Banc d'Arguin is a valuable fishing ground and the action may have been taken to strengthen measures against poaching by foreign fishing fleets.

On 5 July 1972 Senegal defined straight baselines along five sections of its coast. The first, short baseline closes the southernmost outlet of the Senegal River. The second segment measures 94 nautical miles and extends from near Cap Vert to the mouth of the Jumbas River. The third segment links Bird Island to the terminus of the northern boundary between Senegal and The Gambia. The remaining baselines lie south of The Gambia. The first extends for 33 nautical miles from the terminus of the southern boundary with The Gambia to the Casamance River, and the second measures 5 nautical miles and closes a minor indentation just north of Guinea-Bissau (The Geographer 1973a, 5). There can be no objection to the short segments which close the mouths of rivers, but the remaining parts of the baselines lie along a coast totally lacking in features which would justify the use of straight baselines. However, as in all such cases, these baselines along a smooth coast do not serve to push the outer limit of the territorial sea away from the land to any appreciable extent.

Three versions have appeared of Guinea-Bissau's straight baseline. On 22

August 1966 Portugal defined straight baselines for its mainland and its African colonies. The baseline for Guinea-Bissau was defined by twelve points and it extended for 154 nautical miles. This baseline surrounded the Arquipelago dos Bijagos, which consists of dozens of low alluvial islands and islets. These islands unquestionably fringe the coast in its immediate vicinity, and it is possible that the outer edges of the seaward islands are also unstable and subject to erosion, which would provide another ground under the Convention for drawing this straight baseline.

Guinea-Bissau became independent in September 1974 and little time was wasted in redefining the straight baseline. On 31 December 1974 new baselines were defined. In fact these baselines differed only slightly from those proclaimed eight years before by Portugal. Six basepoints were omitted and revised values were given for those retained. As figure 13.1 shows, the main changes occurred east of Ilha de Orango, and they had the result of reducing the area of internal waters claimed for Guinea-Bissau. It could be argued that by declining to use Poilau Ilha, the authorities had ensured that the baseline conformed more closely to the general direction of the coast.

On 19 May 1978 Guinea-Bissau published the third version of its baseline, and the conservative nature of earlier definitions was abandoned. Figure 13.1 shows that the new baseline is defined by four points. Cabo Roxo and the mouth of the Rio Cajet form the two termini on the mainland. The other two points are located in the sea so that 186 nautical miles of the baseline follows either the meridian which passes through Cabo Roxo or parallel 10° 40' north. The explanation for this baseline is found in the Luso-French boundary agreement of 12 May 1886. That agreement defined Portuguese Guinea, and the western boundary followed the course of the present baseline. There can be no doubt that the line defined in 1886 was simply intended to indicate which offshore islands fell to Portugal. This technique to avoid naming all the islands was common at that time. It was used by Russia and the United States in 1867, by China and France in 1887, by Britain and Queensland in 1893, and by Germany and Britain in 1899. It is unreasonable to describe the 1886 boundary as a baseline, and the current version is quite plainly against the letter and spirit of the Convention.

Guinea defined its territorial sea on 3 June 1964. The northern and southern limits were defined by the parallels which pass through the terminal points of Guinea's boundaries with Guinea-Bissau and Sierra Leone respectively. The problems which this claim creates for Guinea's neighbours will be discussed later. The territorial sea within these two limits is stated to be measured from a straight line defined in the following terms:

> a straight line passing by the southwest of Sene Island of the Tristao Group, and to the south, by the southwest foreland of Tamara Island, at low tide.
>
> (The Geographer 1972, 1)

This description does not make it clear that the line terminates at the two islands mentioned. It is possible that the line is drawn between the limiting parallels and

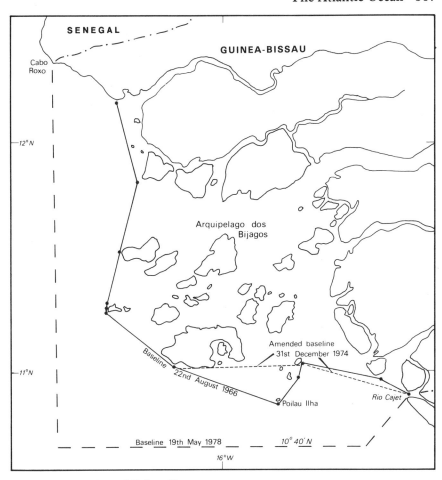

Figure 13.1 Baselines of Guinea-Bissau

does indeed pass by the two islands, presumably at no great distance from them. The coast of Guinea is neither deeply indented nor fringed with islands, so it is not known how the baseline can be justified.

Cameroon defined four straight lines along its coast on 5 December 1974. The lines closed four roadsteads in the Rio del Rey and the Akwafe, Bimbia and Wouri Rivers, and three small bays called Bibundi, Ambas and Navire de Guerre. Only the Baie du Navire de Guerre satisfies the semicircular test, but the baselines closing the other two embayments do not significantly augment the internal waters of Cameroon.

It was noted earlier that Portugal drew straight baselines for its African colonies on 22 August 1966. Those defined for Angola closed four legal bays. The Baia do

Bengo and an unnamed bay lie immediately north and south of Luanda, and the Baia do Mocamedes and Baia do Tigres lie near the boundary with Namibia.

Cape Verde defined a system of straight baselines encompassing all its islands on 1 October 1975. The decree defined the point of origin precisely and then gave general descriptions of the other eleven points, such as 'SW of Brava Island'. The waters within these baselines were identified as internal waters. Two years later on 31 December 1977 Cape Verde defined its baselines by fourteen points for which co-ordinates were provided. These new lines followed the same course as those set out in the earlier decree. This time, however, the waters within the baselines were defined as Cape Verde's archipelagic waters. It is therefore according to the rules for drawing archipelagic baselines that this system must be judged. The longest segment, linking Ponta Prainha and Ponta Preta, measures 137 nautical miles and the ratio of water to land is about 2:1. It would be possible for the baselines to be redrawn so that the longest line measures only 125 nautical miles and the water-to-land ratio does not exceed 9:1.

São Tomé and Príncipe defined its archipelagic waters on 16 June 1978. Twelve points define the various straight lines which satisfy the tests for drawing archipelagic baselines; the longest line measures 99 nautical miles and the ratio of water to land is 3:1.

Maritime claims and agreed maritime boundaries

Maritime claims in the southwest Atlantic Ocean fall into two distinct groups. The three large republics, Argentina, Brazil and Uruguay claim territorial seas 200 nautical miles wide and also claim identical exclusive economic or fishing zones. The three small countries between Brazil and Venezuela, that is Guyana, French Guiana and Surinam, claim territorial waters 12 nautical miles wide and exclusive economic or fishing zones 200 nautical miles in width.

The United States claims territorial waters 3 nautical miles wide compared with the 12 nautical miles claimed by Canada and by France from the islands of St Pierre and Miquelon. From each of these territories exclusive economic or fishing zones are claimed for a distance 200 nautical miles from the coast.

All the five countries occupying the Atlantic seaboard of Western Europe claim an exclusive economic zone 200 nautical miles wide, but while France, Portugal and Spain claim territorial seas 12 nautical miles wide the claims made by Eire and Britain are only 3 nautical miles.

Maritime claims by the countries of West Africa show a greater diversity than claims in any other area of comparable size in the world. The twenty-three countries and territories can be divided into ten groups. The prime division separates those countries which only claim territorial seas from those which claim an exclusive economic zone in addition. Equatorial Guinea and Zaire each claim only a territorial sea of 12 nautical miles. Although they claim only a territorial sea Cameroon and The Gambia each claim a width of 50 nautical miles. Congo,

Ghana and Liberia follow the South American pattern of claiming territorial seas 200 nautical miles wide.

The largest single group of countries claim territorial seas 12 nautical miles wide and an exclusive economic zone 200 nautical miles in width. The countries in this group are Cape Verde, Guinea, Guinea-Bissau, Ivory Coast, Morocco, Namibia, São Tomé and Príncipe, and South Africa. While the remaining countries, except Gabon, claim economic zones 200 nautical miles wide, they also claim territorial seas wider than 12 nautical miles. Angola's territorial seas are set at 20 nautical miles, while Nigeria and Togo have made claims to territorial waters 30 nautical miles from the shore. Mauritania has selected 70 nautical miles as the proper width for territorial waters, while Senegal has proclaimed territorial waters 150 nautical miles in width. Benin and Sierra Leone have announced identical bands of territorial seas and exclusive economic zones 200 nautical miles wide. Gabon has claimed territorial seas 100 nautical miles wide and an exclusive economic zone which extends for a further 50 nautical miles.

The claims described for Britain, Portugal and Spain are also made from the islands which lie in the Atlantic Ocean remote from their shores. The British possessions, all in the southern hemisphere, are Ascencion Island, St Helena, Tristan da Cunha and Gough Island, and the Falkland Islands and their dependencies. Also, Britain claims the rock called Rockall in the northern Atlantic Ocean; the problems associated with this insular feature are considered later. Portugal owns the Azores and the Madeira Islands, which include Ilhas Selvagens, lying midway between Madeira and Islas Canarias. Spain's sovereignty over the Islas Canarias permits maritime claims to be made to important fishing grounds in the northeast Atlantic Ocean. Norway owns the small, remote island of Bouvet and is entitled to claim territorial seas 4 nautical miles wide and an exclusive economic zone 200 nautical miles in width from it, as it does from its territories in the northern hemisphere.

As figures 13.2, 13.3 and 13.4 show there are fifty segments of international maritime boundaries to be settled in the Atlantic Ocean. Thirty-six separate adjacent states while the remainder divide waters and seabed between opposite states. There is a concentration of maritime boundaries along the littoral of West Africa, where thirty-five of the boundaries are located. Only eight maritime boundaries have been agreed in this area, however, it would be wrong to assume from this small number that there are many and serious complications about drawing maritime boundaries around the rim of the Atlantic Ocean. While there are problems, the majority of adjacent and some of the opposite boundaries which have to be drawn appear to be quite uncomplicated by geographical and historical circumstances.

Uruguay and Argentina agreed on 19 November 1973 on a maritime and continental shelf boundary (figure 13.2). The boundary was drawn in two sections. The first section lies entirely landward of the closing line of the Rio de la Plata. It originates near the point where the Rio Uruguay enters the extensive Playa Honda, which has Buenos Aires on its south coast. The boundary in the Rio

Figure 13.2 Maritime boundaries in the southwest Atlantic Ocean

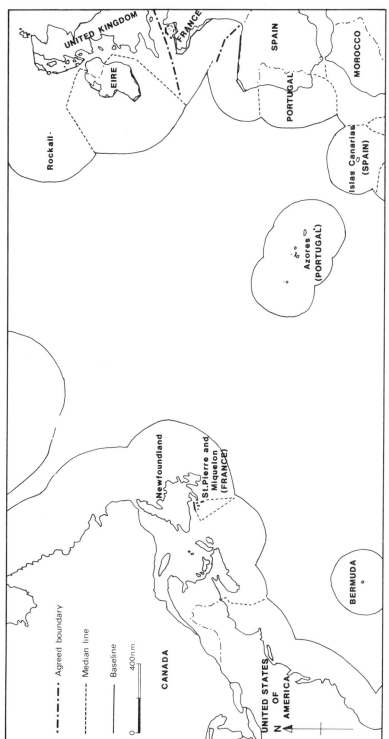

Figure 13.3 Maritime boundaries in the north Atlantic Ocean

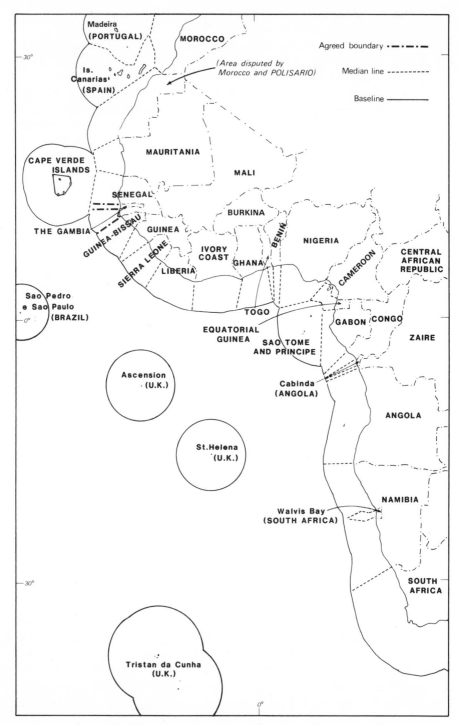

Figure 13.4 Maritime boundaries in the east Atlantic Ocean

Uruguay was settled by the treaty dated 7 April 1961, which came into force on 19 January 1966. The seaward terminus of the river boundary is located at the parallel 33° 56′ south which passes through Punta Gorda. The first point on the new maritime boundary is located at 34° 12′ south and 57° 57′ east. This maritime boundary then follows the navigable channel through the shallow Rio de la Plata to the centre point of the closing line of the estuary. The boundary measures 160 nautical miles and generally lies closer to the coast of Uruguay than to the coast of Argentina. Both countries also claim a zone of exclusive sovereignty over a coastal strip of waters from the closing line to a line joining Colonia in Uruguay and Punta Lara in Argentina; the zone is 7 nautical miles wide. Landward of the line linking Colonia and Punta Lara the zone shrinks to 2 nautical miles to the parallel of Punta Gorda.

The treaty which was ratified on 12 February 1974 proceeds to define the boundary seawards of the closing line of the Rio de la Plata as an equidistant line determined by the adjacent coasts method. The two countries also established a common fishing zone which is bounded by arcs of circles 200 nautical miles in radius, centred on Punta del Este and Cabo san Antonia. This common zone, which is shaped like a dome, does not include waters within 12 nautical miles of the coast.

The boundary between Brazil and Uruguay was agreed on 21 July 1972 and came into force on 12 June 1975. It consists of a single rhumb line drawn at a bearing of 128° from true north, and commences at the mouth of the Chuy Stream. This feature is not permanently fixed and accordingly the two countries have selected the point which they consider to be the mouth of the stream at the intersection of the coastline and a bearing of 128° from the Chuy Light. Provision is also made to construct works which will ensure that the Chuy Stream does have its mouth at the selected point.

Only one maritime boundary has been settled off the coast of North America and it concerns France and Canada. Those two countries signed an agreement on 27 March 1972 and it became effective immediately. The boundary separates Canada's territorial waters from the zones submitted to the fishery jurisdiction of France consequent upon its sovereignty over St Pierre and Miquelon (figure 13.3). The line measures 54 nautical miles and is defined by nine points, of which five are equidistant. Of the remaining four points two are located on Canadian islets, and two lie less than 1 nautical mile from the line of equidistance.

Two maritime boundaries have been agreed off the Atlantic coast of Western Europe (figure 13.3). The Anglo-French boundary, which was announced by the Court of Arbitration of 1977, was specifically designed to solve the problem presented by conflicting claims in the English Channel, but the boundary does continue on a fixed bearing to the 1000 metre isobath. France has also agreed on a boundary with Spain in the Bay of Biscay. On 29 January 1974 the two countries agreed on a boundary separating their territorial seas and contiguous zones. The boundary originated at the centre of the line linking Cabo Figuier in Spain and Pointe du Tombeau in France. It then continues through one defined point, which is equidistant, to the outer edge of the territorial sea, which is identified by a second equidistant point. This agreement was ratified on 5 April 1975.

A second agreement, also signed on 29 January 1974, extended a continental shelf boundary seawards from the terminal point of the territorial sea limit. The boundary continues on an equidistant course for 95 nautical miles before continuing for a further 150 nautical miles on a course which favours France. The terminus of the boundary, on a line joining Cabo de los Aguillones and Pointe du Raz, appears to be 30 nautical miles closer to Spanish territory than the equidistant point. The two countries also described a joint zone of nearly 900 square nautical miles, centred on a point with the co-ordinates of 45° 15′ north and 5° 20′ west.

Senegal is concerned in both the agreements which have defined maritime boundaries on the coast of West Africa (figure 13.4). The boundary with Guinea-Bissau was agreed between France and Portugal before either of the colonial territories became independent. That agreement on 26 April 1960 defined the boundary by a single line drawn from the light at Cabo Roxo on a bearing of 240°. Although it is not specified it seems likely that the bearing is from true north. This line appears to have been drawn perpendicular to the general direction of the coast, and it is therefore not a line of equidistance. Close to the coast the boundary favours Guinea-Bissau, while the more distant sections of the boundary favour Senegal. The point on the boundary which is 200 nautical miles from Senegal's coast is 192 nautical miles from Ilha Umbocomo in the Arquipelago dos Bijagos.

Senegal's boundaries with The Gambia were agreed on 4 June 1975 and they came into force on 27 August 1976. The northern boundary follows the parallel which passes through the coastal terminus of the land boundary; it is defined as 13° 35′ 36″ north. The southern boundary proceeds southwestwards for less than 1 nautical mile before swinging northwest for about 200 metres and then turning due west to follow the parallel 13° 3′ 27″ north. This parallel is 2′ 24″ south of the parallel which passes through the coastal terminus of the southern land boundary between the two countries. It is probable that the slight deviation near the coast was designed to prevent the boundary from passing too close to the Gambian shore which trends just north of west from the terminus of the land boundary.

Actual and potential maritime boundary disputes

Apart from the difficulty between Venezuela and Guyana over the straight baseline drawn by Venezuela, described earlier, there are no maritime boundary problems off the coast of South America. The dispute between Britain and Argentina over the Falkland Islands deals with territorial rather than maritime questions.

Off the coast of North America the United States faces difficulties in negotiating boundaries with both The Bahamas and Canada. Smith (1981, 405), in his survey of the United States' maritime boundaries, observes that the positions of

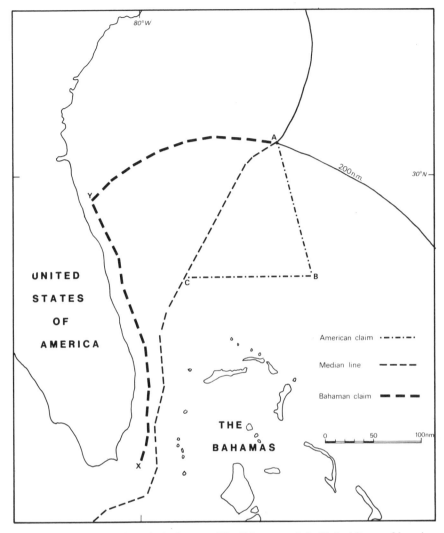

Figure 13.5 Maritime boundaries between The Bahamas and the United States of America

America and The Bahamas 'apparently differ significantly'. Unfortunately Smith, who must know a great deal about the potential dispute, did not feel able to describe the matters at issue. Fortunately the nature of the dispute is revealed in a study by Allen III (1981). On 1 March 1977 the United States published the limits of a fisheries conservation zone, within which it exercised exclusive fishery management authority. When the limits off Florida are plotted it is clear that they enclose areas which are closer to The Bahamas than to the United States. In figure 13.5 the American claim is shown where it deviates from the line of equidistance north of The Bahamas. The triangular area ABC, which is claimed by the United States but which is closer to The Bahamas, measures about 9500 square nautical miles. Allen III (1981, 227) records that American officials have asserted that special circumstances in this region require a departure from the median line, but that the special circumstances have not been made public.

Even though the American proclamation noted that the limits were without prejudice to any negotiations with neighbouring countries, The Bahamas evidently decided to make a counter claim. On 16 June 1977 an act declaring the claim by The Bahamas to fishery resources became effective. Except where the claim overlaps claims from neighbouring territories the outer limit of this fishing zone is 200 nautical miles from the baselines of The Bahamas. Where the claims overlap it is noted that negotiations will be held to fix a bilateral boundary. However, it is also remarkably provided that where no bilateral agreement exists, the outer edge of the zone pertaining to The Bahamas will be 12 nautical miles from the baseline of the neighbouring state. This claim is shown in figure 13.5 by the line XYA. The area thus apparently claimed by The Bahamas to the west of the median line measures about 16,000 square nautical miles. This extravagant claim only applies to fisheries in the water column; sedentary fisheries are only claimed as far as the median line. Allen III (1981, 227 and 231) asserts that the American limit refers both to the seas and the seabed. If that is correct, then it may be presumed that the special circumstances which officials believe justify deviations from the median line are related to questions of natural prolongation. In short, perhaps the United States holds the view that the Blake Plateau is a natural prolongation of the continent and quite unrelated to the coral banks built on submarine rises which provide the foundation for The Bahamas.

The dispute between Canada and the United States in the Gulf of Maine has proved a popular subject for academic analysis. Feulner (1976), McCrae (1981), and Rhee (1980 and 1981) are only a few of the authors who have tackled this problem, which has defied attempts to solve it through bilateral negotiations. Finally, the two countries referred the matter to a Chamber of the International Court of Justice. The Court has been asked to answer the following question.

What is the course of the single maritime boundary that divides the continental shelf and fisheries zones of the United States of America and Canada from a point in latitude 44° 11′ 12″ N, longitude 67° 16′ 46″ W to a point to be determined by the Court within an area bounded by straight lines connecting the following sets of geographic coordinates: latitude 40° N, longitude 67° W; latitude 40° N, longitude 65° W; longitude 42° N, 65° W?   (Rhee 1981, 602)

The limits which the Court must observe are shown in figure 13.6 which also shows the lines claimed by Canada and the United States.

The submarine topography of the Gulf of Maine consists of an amphitheatre which finds an outlet to the continental slope by the Northeast Channel, lying between Georges and Browns Banks. This depression was carved by ice during

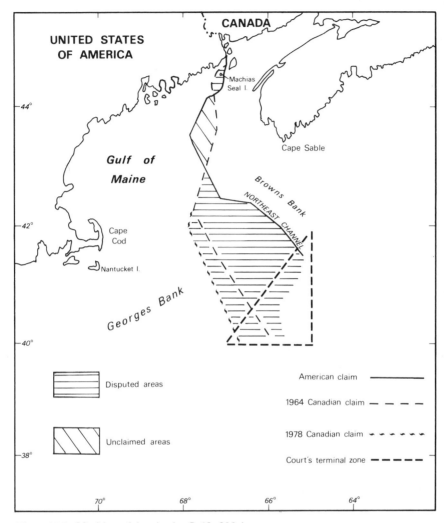

Figure 13.6 Maritime claims in the Gulf of Maine

the last glaciation, when much of the present continental shelf was above sea-level. The dispute has two main elements. First, both countries claim the small Machias Seal Island, which is composed of granite. Second, while Canada believes that the boundary should follow an equidistant course, the United States believes that it should follow the main axis of the depression and reach the continental slope via Northeast Channel.

The small northern disputed area is centred on Machias Seal Island, and that area is excluded from the consideration of the Court. The two countries will have to resolve this sovereignty matter, and if neither side is prepared to concede ownership to the other it is possible that they may agree on a joint zone around the island.

Immediately south of the point of origin given to the Court there is an area which is not claimed by either country! This area lies east of the American claim and west of the Canadian line. South of this unclaimed area lies the main prize in this dispute; this is the eastern end of Georges Bank. The waters over this bank contain valuable fish stocks and the mineral potential of the region is unknown. The United States argues that the Northeast Channel marks the proper divide between the continental shelves of the two countries, and also asserts that the channel marks a frontier between the Virginian faunal grouping to the south and the Boreal faunal grouping to the north.

When Canada ratified the 1958 Convention on the Continental Shelf on 6 February 1970, it entered the reservation that the presence of an accidental depression in the continental shelf should not be considered an interruption of the natural prolongation of national territory. Canada regards the Northeast Channel as such an accidental depression and therefore believes it should be disregarded in drawing a line of equidistance. Its position is the same as Norway's position *vis-à-vis* the United Kingdom and the Norwegian Trough, and Indonesia *vis-à-vis* Australia and the Timor Trough. Two Canadian boundaries are shown on the Georges Bank. The easterly line was proposed in 1964, when Canada issued exploration permits for areas at the eastern tip of Georges Bank. This line is simply a median line taking all the territory of both countries into account. On 15 September 1978 Canada substituted the western line. This median line ignores Cape Cod and Nantucket Island, which are now believed by Canada to distort the boundary unduly in favour of the United States.

It appears to be probable that until the dispute is resolved over the Gulf of Maine, there will be no solution to the other maritime problems which concern Canada and the United States in the Arctic and Pacific Oceans. If the Court brings down a judgement which favours one side in the Gulf of Maine, the other side may seek redress in one or more of the other disputed zones.

Rockall lies 200 nautical miles west of the Hebrides. It is a granite mass which has a height of 19 metres above high-water level, and it is surrounded on all sides by steep slopes. Landing on Rockall from a boat is only possible after a prolonged period of calm seas. Rockall was claimed for the United Kingdom on 18 September 1955 and incorporated into the County of Inverness in 1972. A navigation light has been established on the summit and has been maintained on a regular basis by crews transported by helicopters.

Rockall is the only part of the microcontinent of the same name which stands above high water. This massive submarine plateau measures about 600 nautical miles along its southwest-northeast axis and has a maximum width of about 240 nautical miles. This plateau is clearly defined by continental slopes on the west, south and east, but its northern limit is less obvious, and Bott (1975) has expressed the view that the microcontinent extends northwards to include the Faeroe Block.

Since portions of the microcontinent lie within 200 nautical miles of the

Faeroes, the United Kingdom and Eire, there is the problem of deciding which maritime boundaries should be drawn in this region.

Brown (1978) wrote a thorough analysis of the question before the final form of the Convention was agreed and before the judgement was delivered in the case between Libya and Tunisia. Even if some of his legal arguments are no longer relevant, he has provided a very useful survey of the geological evidence.

There seem to be two issues to be decided. The first is whether Rockall is an island or a rock. If it is an island then the United Kingdom is entitled to claim from it the entire suite of maritime zones. This would mean that if Rockall was not discounted in drawing boundaries with Eire, Britain would secure most of the microcontinent. Rockall is not very important in fixing median lines with the Faeroes; it would only serve as a basepoint for a short section of line.

If it was agreed that Rockall was a rock then it would be necessary to determine whether it could sustain human habitation or an economic life of its own. Brown (1978, 289) believes that Rockall is uninhabitable. If it was decided that the rock could sustain an economic life of its own then again Britain could use it as a basepoint for all permissible maritime claims. If it was agreed that Rockall had no economic life of its own and could not sustain habitation, then Britain could only use it to claim territorial seas, and it could not be used as a basepoint in any boundary determination with neighbours.

If Rockall is restricted to use as a basepoint for claiming territorial seas then the competing countries will have to argue on the basis of natural prolongation in their efforts to secure part of the seabed formed by the microcontinent. They will be able to claim the water column above the submarine plateau which lies within 200 nautical miles of their mainland baselines. Since it appears from maps produced by the United Nations (1978) and The Geographer (1973b) that the entire microcontinent lies within 350 nautical miles of the various mainlands, or within a line 100 nautical miles seaward of the 2500 metre isobath, there is no reason why the entire microcontinent should not be enclosed by continental shelf claims.

Ten years before Guinea-Bissau became an independent country Guinea claimed as territorial seas waters which lay much closer to Guinea-Bissau than to Guinea. Indeed the boundaries set by Guinea on 6 June 1964 included Poilau Ilha, which belongs to Guinea-Bissau. The boundary which Guinea unilaterally proclaimed between itself and what was then Portuguese Guinea followed parallel 10° 56' 42.55" north, which intersects the seaward terminus of the land boundary between the two countries. At that time Guinea claimed a territorial sea 130 nautical miles wide. Without changing the lateral limit, Guinea extended its territorial waters to 200 nautical miles on 31 December 1965.

On 10 September 1974 Guinea-Bissau became an independent country and on 19 May 1978 it announced its new straight baselines which followed the line drawn by France and Portugal, in the treaty of 12 May 1886, to enclose the islands which belonged to Portugal. This baseline, together with Guinea's unilateral claim, are shown in figure 13.7. Discussions between the representatives of both countries were held in 1977 and 1978 over the problem, and Guinea proposed that the southern boundary defined in the 1886 treaty should simply be

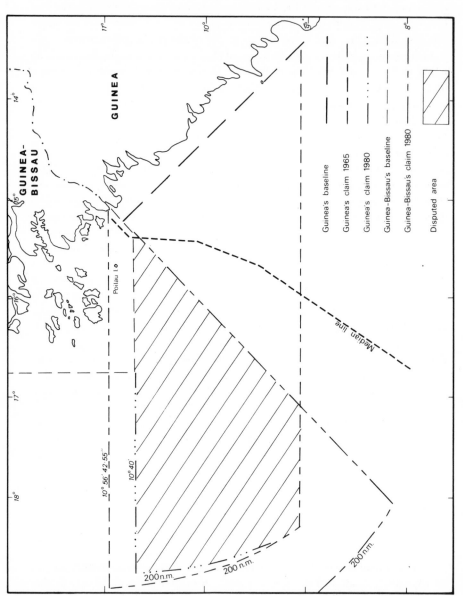

Figure 13.7 Maritime boundaries between Guinea and Guinea-Bissau

extended seawards. This southern boundary passes southwest, through the Pilot's Passage, from the mouth of the Rio Cajet, as far as parallel 10° 40' north. The line then follows that parallel westwards. This proposal meant that Guinea was prepared to move the lateral boundary southwards by 16' 42.55" of latitude. Not surprisingly Guinea-Bissau rejected this proposal.

Once again Guinea decided on unilateral action. On 25 January 1980 it awarded rights to a foreign oil company to explore a large area bounded on the north by parallel 10° 40' north. Six months later, on 30 July 1980, Guinea announced that it claimed an exclusive economic zone 200 nautical miles wide; the northern boundary was identical with the offer made to Guinea-Bissau in 1978 and refused by that country.

Figure 13.7 also shows two other lines. The first is the median line between the two countries. This line trends south of southwest and would converge with a median line drawn between Guinea and Sierra Leone. While they would not meet within 200 nautical miles of the coast, these lines would reduce the outer edge of Guinea's exclusive economic zone to about 30 nautical miles. The second line is drawn southwest from the mouth of the Rio Cajet; it is in effect an extension of the most easterly part of the boundary drawn in the sea in 1886. It is apparently a line which Guinea-Bissau is prepared to accept, according to a memorandum which Guinea-Bissau distributed to a number of African governments on 27 October 1980. This is a very modest claim by Guinea-Bissau; especially in view of Guinea's immodest, unilateral claims.

There is a potential problem concerning South Africa and Namibia because South Africa owns Walvis Bay and twelve islands along the Namibian coast. These territories are shown in figure 13.8. Ichaboe Island was annexed on 21 June 1861 by Britain, and the other islands were formally claimed on 5 May 1866. On 16 July 1866 the Governor of the Cape of Good Hope proclaimed British ownership over the twelve islands and their inclusion in his colony. Letters Patent were issued on 27 February 1867 appointing the Governor to be Governor of the islands, and authority was given to the Colony's Legislative Council and House of Assembly to request that the islands be transferred to the Colony. This process was completed on 6 July 1874. The islands provided supplies of guano, for which there had been much competition earlier in the century.

Walvis Bay was formally annexed by Britain on 12 March 1878. Letters Patent were issued on 14 December 1878, and on 7 August 1884 the Governor assented to the Act making Walvis Bay part of the Colony of the Cape of Good Hope. Walvis Bay is the best port on the coast of Namibia and during the colonial period Germany tried to secure its cession from Britain by offering large areas of territory along the border of Bechuanaland. This offer was refused, and Walvis Bay and the islands have remained as much part of South Africa as Cape Town or Durban.

The potential problem concerns the pattern of jurisdiction which would result if South Africa and Namibia each claimed areas of seas and seabed within 200 nautical miles of their territory according to the principle of equidistance. The area available to Namibia would be intersected by lateral corridors of South

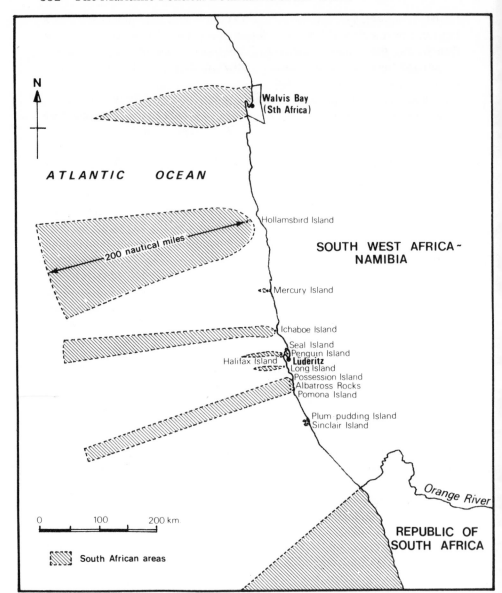

Figure 13.8 Maritime boundaries off the coast of Namibia

African zones in a manner which would make co-operation for fisheries super-vision essential.

While the internal political parties in Namibia hope that South Africa will agree to transfer sovereignty over Walvis Bay and the islands to Namibia after independence, South Africa insists that such questions can only be considered when

Namibia is independent, and in fact has only committed itself to discussing the availability of Walvis Bay to a democratically elected government of Namibia.

It is possible that Cameroon will make overtures to its neighbours in an effort to escape from its zone-locked condition. The island of Fernando Poo, which belongs to Equatorial Guinea, lies only 18 nautical miles off the coast of Cameroon, which is also placed at a disadvantage by the configuration of the delta of the River Niger to the west. The extent of the disadvantage is shown by the facts that Cameroon can only claim an economic zone measuring 4500 square nautical miles, while Nigeria and Equatorial Guinea can respectively claim 61,500 and 82,600 square nautical miles.

Conclusions

Although the south Atlantic Ocean provided the arena for pitched battles on land and sea in 1982, the Atlantic Ocean contains fewer maritime boundary problems than the Indian and Pacific Oceans. This fortunate circumstance owes much to the facts that there are few coastal states in South America, North America and Western Europe; that there are rarely islands which are located in a manner to give one country a decided advantage; and that the coasts of South America and West Africa are comparatively smooth, reducing the difficulties of drawing lateral equidistant boundaries.

The rim of the Atlantic Ocean is marked by fairly broad continental margins, in which the continental rise is usually an important part. This fact reflects the large volume of terrestrial sediments which are carried into the Atlantic by the many major rivers which drain the surrounding continents.

Not very many countries bordering the Atlantic Ocean have drawn straight baselines, a fact which owes much to the smooth nature of the coasts in the southern hemisphere and the decision of the United States to avoid the use of such baselines. However, some of those which have been drawn appear to breach the letter and spirit of the rules proposed in the Convention. The closure of the Rio de la Plata by Uruguay and Argentina, the straight baselines along Senegal's smooth coast, and the use of lines in excess of 125 nautical miles by Cape Verde provide three examples of unsatisfactory baselines.

In the southern hemisphere countries of the Third World in Africa and South America have established wide claims to territorial seas, with Africa providing the widest range of claims. While there have been only a few boundary agreements they have all been generally simple lateral lines, and it may be expected that more countries will be able to agree quickly on lateral boundaries similar to those of Guinea-Bissau and Senegal, and Uruguay and Brazil.

When existing boundary disputes are considered it is encouraging that Canada and the United States have agreed to arbitration in the matter of the Gulf of Maine, and that the dispute over the claims from Rockall appears to be of little present concern. The dispute between Guinea and Guinea-Bissau is potentially very serious, unless the good offices of the Organization of African Unity can be successfully applied. The potential problem over maritime zones claimed by South Africa and Walvis Bay will only be bitterly contested if the government of Namibia takes a hostile attitude towards South Africa. If relations between South Africa and the independent Namibia are good it seems likely that South Africa will not make unnecessary difficulties over the question of maritime boundaries. However, the outright cession of South African territory is not probable.

References

Allen III, P. A. (1981) 'Law of the sea: the delimitation of the maritime boundary between the United States and The Bahamas', *University of Florida Law Review*, 33, 207–39.

Bott, M. H. P. (1975) 'Structure and evolution of the North Scottish Shelf, the Faeroe Block, and the intervening region', in Woodland A. W. (ed.) *Petroleum and the Continental Shelf of North-west Europe*, vol. 1, Essex, 105–13.

Brown, E. D. (1978) 'Rockall and the limits of national jurisdiction of the United Kingdom', *Marine Policy*, 2, 181–211 and 275–302.

Churchill, W. S. (1950) *The Second World War*, vol. 2, London.

Feulner, G. R. (1976) 'Delimitation of continental shelf jurisdiction between States: the effect of physical irregularities in the natural continental shelf', *Virginia Journal of International Law*, 17 (1), 77–105.

Goebel, J. (1927) *The Struggle for the Falkland Islands*, London.

McCrae, D. M. (1981) 'Proportionality and the Gulf of Maine maritime boundary dispute', *Canadian Yearbook of International Law*, 19, 287–301.

Rhee, S.-M. (1980) 'The application of equitable principles to resolve the United States–Canada dispute over East Coast Fishery Resources', *Harvard International Law Journal*, 21 (3), 668–83.

Rhee, S.-M. (1981) 'Equitable solutions to the maritime boundary dispute between the United States and Canada in the Gulf of Maine', *American Journal of International Law*, 75 (3), 590–628.

Smith, R. W. (1981) 'The maritime boundaries of the United States', *Geographical Review*, 71, 395–410.

Tchernia, P. (1980) *Descriptive Regional Oceanography*, London.

The Geographer (1970) *Straight Baselines: Venezuela*, 'Limits in the Seas' series, no. 21, Washington, DC.

The Geographer (1972) *Straight Baselines: Guinea*, 'Limits in the Seas' series, no. 40, Washington, DC.

The Geographer (1973a) *Straight baselines: Senegal*, 'Limits in the Seas' series, no. 54, Washington, DC.

The Geographer (1973b) *Composite Theoretical Division of the Seabed* (map), Washington, DC.

The Geographer (1973c) *World Shipping Lanes*, a world map, scale 1 : 37 M, Washington, DC.

United Nations (1978) *Maps Illustrating Formulae for the Definition of the Continental Shelf*, Secretariat of the Conference on the Law of the Sea, New York.

14

The Caribbean Sea and the Gulf of Mexico

For many years I have felt that the old three-mile limit or twenty-mile limit should be superseded by a rule of common sense. For instance, the Gulf of Mexico is bounded on the south by Mexico and on the north by the United States. In many parts of the Gulf shallow water extends over very many miles off shore. It seems to me that the Mexican Government should be entitled to drill for oil in the southern half of the Gulf and we in the northern half of the Gulf. That would be far more sensible than allowing some European nation, for example, to come in there and drill.

(Roosevelt 1943)

Yesterday our Ambassador in Caracas advised me that the Government of Venezuela was proposing to us that we reactivate the Mixed Commission on Fisheries. To what end? Venezuela rejected the agreement reached by us with the former Government. . . . As far as I am concerned, I have had my fill of this fishy business, and as Prime Minister I wash my hands of it and turn it over to others.   (Williams 1975, 29)

The People's Revolutionary Government of Grenada has always taken the firm and clear position that our Caribbean Sea must be recognised and respected in practice as a zone of peace, independence and development.   (Whiteman 1982, 46)

President Roosevelt's thoughts in his memorandum to his Secretary of State under-lines an important difference between the Caribbean Sea and the Gulf of Mexico. The latter is regarded by the United States and Mexico as a lake which they share exclusively, apart from Cuba's small eastern portion. It is also interesting that the President's suggestion provided a preview of the debate over the American–Mexican treaty of 4 May 1978, and its rejection by the United States Senate.

Dr Eric Williams's outburst against Venezuela serves to focus attention on the facts that the Caribbean Sea, unlike the Gulf of Mexico, is bordered by a large number of small countries, and that while commentators often concentrate on the ideological divisions between the United States and Cuba in this region, there are also serious disagreements between other states within the Caribbean zone.

Mr Whiteman's remarks at the signing ceremony of the Law of the Sea Confer-ence, in December 1982, point to the volatility of events in the Caribbean. Within ten months of the Grenadan delegate making those comments, his country experi-enced a violent coup and an invasion by foreign armies.

Although they are sometimes jointly considered as the American Mediterreanean, the Caribbean Sea and the Gulf of Mexico differ from each other in important respects and have a more complex geological origin than the Mediterranean Sea. Emery and Uchupi (1973) have described how the narrow Caribbean crustal plate was trapped between the westward-moving plates of North and South America, and then sealed in position by underthrusting which raised the Lesser Antilles on a ridge which separates the Caribbean Sea from the Atlantic Ocean.

The Gulf of Mexico has a comparatively simple structure. The peninsulas of Yucatan and Florida, which stand as portals at the eastern outlet, are composed of broad limestone platforms of the Early Cretaceous period. The continental margin which fringes the American and Mexican coasts is narrowest off the delta of the Mississippi River and broadest off the northern edge of Yucatan and the west coast of Florida. The continental shelf is bounded by steep, clearly defined continental slopes which enclose the Sigsbee Abyssal Plain with depths in excess of 2000 fathoms. The basin received large volumes of sediment which provided a favourable environment for the creation of oil and gas fields (Emery and Uchupi 1973, 27), and the Gulf of Mexico contains a higher proportion of favourable petroleum areas than the Caribbean Sea. The Gulf of Mexico is surrounded by three countries, and the coastline of northern Cuba comprises only a small section of the surrounding coast compared with the long, equal sections occupied by the United States and Mexico.

The Caribbean Sea is slightly larger than the Gulf of Mexico and has a much more complex structure. A series of ridges enclose five submarine basins. In the northwest the ridge which separates the Gulf of Mexico and the Caribbean Sea lies almost east-west, between Yucatan and Cuba. The successive ridges, proceeding eastwards, gradually swing through an alignment northeast-southwest, between Honduras and Haiti, to a north-south alignment of the Aves Swell and the Lesser Antilles. Proceeding eastwards the basins are called the Yucatan Basin, the Cayman Trough, the Colombia and Venezuela Basins, separated by the Beata Ridge, and the Grenada Trough. With the exception of the Cayman Trough the basins have deeps in the order of 2500 fathoms. The favourable areas for hydrocarbon deposits are restricted to the continental margin of South America. Adjustments to the various crustal blocks is still proceeding around the periphery of the Caribbean Sea, where earthquakes and volcanic eruptions are experienced. In direct contrast to the Gulf of Mexico thirty-two political units share the coast of the Caribbean Sea; many of them are small countries and eleven territories still have a dependent relationship with a metropolitan country.

Straight baselines

Only three countries have proclaimed straight baselines and they are all located in the Greater Antilles. On 6 September 1967 the Dominican Republic defined certain closing lines for bays, which were described as straight baselines. Ten bays were closed and four satisfy the semicircular test; they are Manzanillo, Rincon, Samana and Neiba Bays. Escocesa and Santo Domingo Bays are claimed on historic grounds and are closed by lines measuring 45 and 32 nautical miles respectively. Bahia de Yuma, Andres Bay, Ocoa Bay and Ensenada de los Aguilas have also been closed although they fail the semicircular test and are not specifically mentioned in historic terms. In each case the closing line is less than 23 nautical miles long.

Haiti's straight baselines have been inferred from the declaration of 6 April 1972 (The Geographer 1973). The co-ordinates of the outer boundary of Haiti's territorial sea were not defined in the text but were shown on a map at a scale of 1:5 millions. When lines are drawn parallel to the boundaries shown, and 12 nautical miles landward, the baselines can be inferred. If the inference is correct Haiti has closed Golfe de la Gonave by a line measuring about 85 nautical miles. The declaration does not indicate whether this bay is claimed on historic grounds. It also appears that at least one of the turning points of the baseline is located in the sea, southwest of the southern land terminus of the boundary with the Dominican Republic.

On 24 February 1977 Cuba proclaimed straight baselines which surround the entire archipelago. They are not claimed to be archipelagic baselines and they do not satisfy the rules for drawing such lines; the ratio of water to land within the baselines is less than 1:1. However, there can be no objection, in principle, to a country which consists of an archipelago and which is unable to draw archipelagic baselines, drawing straight baselines along those parts of its coast which are indented or fringed with islands. Unfortunately Cuba has not observed these requirements closely. There are parts of the coast of the mainland which are fringed with islands for considerable distances and some other shorter parts which are deeply indented, but there are two aspects of these baselines which appear to contravene the spirit and letter of the rules for drawing straight baselines. First, baselines have been drawn along sections of the coast which are neither deeply indented nor fringed with islands. One section about 400 nautical miles long links Punta Maternillos on the north coast to Cabo Cruz, which is the eastern headland of the Golfo de Guacanayaro, on the south coast. Another long section with similar unexceptional characteristics stretches for 120 nautical miles between Punta Gobernadora and the Peninsula de Hicacos on the north, central coast.

The second objection centres on the fact that in using some offshore islands as basepoints, Cuba has failed to make the baselines conform to the general direction of the coast. This failing is particularly evident in the line from Cabo Cruz to Punta Cabeza del Este, which lies seaward of a line of small cays which would have provided more properly the sites of turning points preserving the general direction of the coast. The longest section measures 69 nautical miles and joins Cayo Puga and Cayo Trabuco. As it does so it traverses waters which are devoid of other islands, and makes an angle of 18° with the general direction of the coast.

It will be surprising if some archipelagic states in the Caribbean Sea do not proclaim archipelagic baselines in the future. It was noted that Cuba cannot satisfy the test for archipelagic baselines which requires that the ratio of water to land within the lines should be at least 1 : 1. Haiti and Trinidad and Tobago have the same disability. The territories which apparently could draw archipelagic baselines include Antigua, The Bahamas, Grenada, Jamaica and St Vincent and the Grenadines. The longest segment in any Antiguan system would measure 54 nautical miles and the baselines would enclose areas with a water-to-land ratio of 6.6 : 1. No ratio can be calculated for The Bahamas because it is not clear which areas are deemed to be steep-sided oceanic plateaus, enclosed or nearly enclosed by limestone islands and drying reefs. Waters over such features may be counted as land for the purposes of the calculation, and this variation in the rule was included for the express benefit of The Bahamas. The baseline system surrounding The Bahamas would meet all the other tests for archipelagic baselines. Jamaica, which possesses the Pedro and Morant Cays to the south of the main island, could employ a system of baselines which would have a longest segment of 102 nautical miles and a ratio of water to land of 1.2 : 1. A single set of baselines around the islands of Grenada would require a longest segment of 20 nautical miles and the system would provide a water-to-land ratio of 1.4 : 1. The tiny archipelago of Saint Vincent and the Grenadines could devise archipelagic baselines with a longest segment of 17 nautical miles and a ratio of 1.3 : 1.

Maritime claims and agreed maritime boundaries

The various maritime claims of countries in the region are listed in table 14.1. This table reveals three main points. First, twenty-four of the thirty-three territories claim an exclusive economic or fishery zone 200 nautical miles wide, and in addition Panama claims a single zone of territorial waters with the same width. Second, the single most common combination of claims is to territorial waters 12 nautical miles wide and an economic zone 200 nautical miles in width. The third main point is that the greatest diversity of claims is found amongst the independent island states in the region. It appears that some of these states which have only been independent for a short time have not yet altered the maritime claims which were inherited from the United Kingdom.

The first continental shelf boundary was drawn at the southern entrance to the Caribbean Sea. On 26 February 1942 Britain and Venezuela agreed on a boundary which separated areas of seabed in the Gulf of Paria and the Serpent's Mouth. Britain was then acting as the sovereign power in Trinidad and Tobago. That country became independent on 31 August 1962 and duly accepted the provisions of the earlier agreement. This boundary extends for 72 nautical miles and is defined by four points. The Geographer (1970) has drawn attention to problems of applying the defined co-ordinates to modern maps, but the two countries have not experienced any serious difficulties in this regard. After this early example of maritime boundaries, the next important phase of boundary construction began in 1977. Colombia and Venezuela have both been prominent in concluding arrangements with their neighbours. However, they have not managed to settle

Table 14.1 Maritime claims in the Caribbean Sea and the Gulf of
Mexico

Mainland independent states	Territorial sea (nautical miles)	Economic zone (nautical miles)
Belize	3	
Colombia	12	200
Costa Rica	12	200
Guatemala	12	200
Honduras	12	200
Mexico	12	200
Nicaragua	200	200
Panama	200	
United States of America	3	200
Venezuela	12	200
Island independent states		
Antigua and Barbuda	12	200
The Bahamas	3	200
Barbados	12	200
Cuba	12	200
Dominica	12	200
Dominican Republic	6	200
Grenada	12	200
Haiti	12	200
St Kitts and Nevis	3	
St Lucia	3	12
St Vincent and the Grenadines	3	12
Trinidad and Tobago	12	
Dependent territories		
Anguilla	3	
British Virgin Islands	3	200
Cayman Islands	3	200
Guadeloupe	12	200
Martinique	12	200
Montserrat	3	
Navassa Island	3	200
Netherlands Antilles	3	
Puerto Rico	3	200
Turks and Caicos	3	200
United States Virgin Islands	3	200

Source: Author's research.

the boundary which must eventually separate their respective waters and seabed,
and it is possible that their activity with other neighbours is designed to create
precedents which might be used in their negotiations with each other.

On 23 November 1970 Mexico and the United States agreed on boundaries to
separate their territorial seas in the Pacific Ocean and the Gulf of Mexico. The
agreement was ratified on 18 April 1972. The two countries have used a neat

solution to the problem posed by shifts in the mouth of the Rio Grande. Since the centre of this feature is the landward origin of the maritime boundary it would obviously be inconvenient if the alignment of the territorial sea boundary moved with the river. This problem was largely overcome by fixing a point which acts as a hinge in the boundary. This point is located 2000 feet east of the centre point of the river's mouth as it existed at the time the agreement was signed. Seawards of this fixed point the boundary is shown in a map attached to the agreement; it extends in a single straight line to a point 12 nautical miles from the coast. Since the United States only claims territorial waters 3 nautical miles wide, the boundary separates the Mexican territorial waters from the territorial sea and contiguous zone of the United States. Landward of the fixed hinge the boundary will consist of a straight line to the centre of the river's mouth, wherever it is located. This means that this short landward section of the maritime boundary will pivot about the hinge.

In 1978 Mexico and the United States agreed on a maritime boundary which extended the line agreed in 1970, but the United States Senate declined to ratify it and the treaty is in limbo. This question will be considered in the section dealing with actual and potential maritime problems.

It has not proved possible to obtain a copy of the agreement defining the maritime boundary between Cuba and Mexico, which came into effect on 26 July 1976. However, its location is shown on a map produced by the Mexican Department of External Relations in July 1978. The boundary is apparently defined by thirteen points and measures 352 nautical miles. Its northern terminus is the point where a line of equidistance is 200 nautical miles from each coast, and the southern terminus is the equidistant trijunction at which the claims of Cuba, Honduras and Mexico meet. The boundary is shown in figure 14.1 and appears to follow an equidistant course.

Colombia and Panama fixed their maritime boundaries in the Caribbean Sea and the Pacific Ocean on 20 November 1976; these boundaries entered into force on 30 November 1977. This boundary stretches for 538 nautical miles, and after commencing in the east as a boundary between adjacent countries, it becomes a boundary between the opposite territories of the Panamanian mainland and the various cays belonging to Colombia. The adjacent boundary is a slightly modified line of equidistance until it reaches about 210 nautical miles from the coast. As figure 14.1 shows, the section between the coast of Panama and the Colombian isles called Roncador Cay, Cayos del Este and Cayos de Alburquerque consists of a series of straight lines in a stepped formation. There are seven turning points along this section of line and only one of them is closer to Panamanian territory than to one of the Colombian isles. It appears that in locating the other six points the Colombian cays have been discounted. From the final point the agreement declares that the boundary continues on a bearing of 225° until it meets the claims of a third state, in this case Costa Rica.

The trijunction with Costa Rica was established in the agreement which that country signed with Colombia on 17 March 1977. It was fixed at the point where the final segment of the Colombia–Panama boundary, on a bearing of 225°, intersected parallel 10° 49′ north. The boundary proceeds westwards from this point along the parallel 10° 49′ north until it reaches meridian 82° 14′ west, where it turns north along the meridian and continues until it reaches the trijunction with Nicaragua. This boundary is not equidistant, and the western turning point lies 15 nautical miles closer to Costa Rican territory than to Cayos de Albuquerque. The exact co-ordinates of the trijunction of claims from Costa Rica, Panama and Colombia were set out in the agreement signed by Costa Rica and Panama on 2 February 1980; the agreement came into force on 11 February 1982. This treaty defined the maritime boundary as a single straight line between the terminus of the land boundary and a point at 10° 49′ north and 81° 26′ 08.2″ west. Although this boundary is described as a median line, it does not follow an equidistant course.

Cuba and the United States signed a treaty defining their common maritime boundary on 16 December 1977. This boundary extends for 313 nautical miles and connects twenty-seven points. Smith (1981) has described the interesting way in which this line was produced. The United States did not recognize the validity of some sections of Cuba's straight baselines along its northern coast, but instead of allowing this disagreement to stall the negotiations the United States created 'artificial construction lines' around the south coast of Florida. A line of equidistance was then constructed between the Cuban baseline and the American construction lines. A median line was also constructed between the low-water marks along the opposite coasts. An agreed line was then selected between these two median lines, so that the final boundary 'represented a negotiated settlement based on equitable principles' (Smith 1981, 402). While the western terminus is located 200 nautical miles from the coast of each country, the eastern terminus is close to the trijunction with The Bahamas.

Cuba and Haiti signed a boundary agreement on 10 October 1977. Starting from a point near the trijunction with The Bahamas, the line continued for 156 nautical miles along a course defined by fifty-one points. While both countries have drawn straight baselines along their sections of coast which flank the Windward Passage, where the boundary is located, there is an important difference between the characteristics of the two baselines. Although the Cuban baseline is not justified along this southern section of coast east of the Gran Bajo de Buena Esperanza, it lies very close to this comparatively smooth shore and would have practically no effect on the construction of a median line. The baseline drawn by Haiti, according to a reasonable inference from the declaration of 6 April 1972, closes the large Golfe de la Gonave, and its use would shift the median line about 13 nautical miles towards Cuba in some sections. It appears that the two countries have produced a median line related to the low-water marks of each coast, and modified slightly in some sections. The southern terminus of the boundary is located only 36 nautical miles from Navassa Island, which belongs to the United States of America, while the nearest points of Cuba and Haiti lie 65 nautical miles distant.

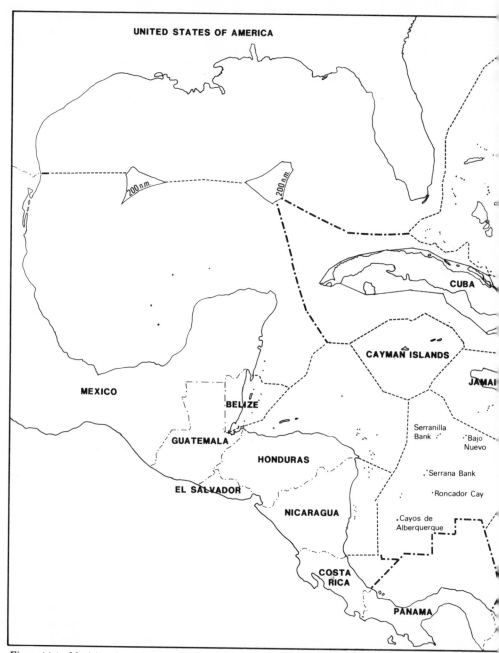

Figure 14.1 Maritime boundaries in the Gulf of Mexico and the Caribbean Sea

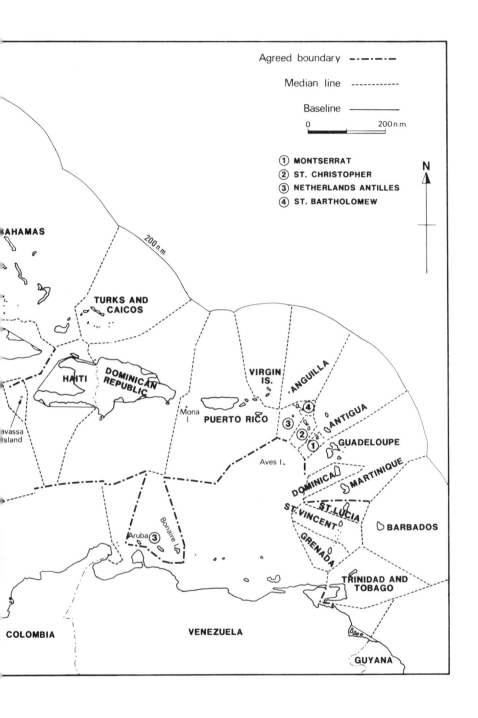

Agreed boundary ·–·–·–·–

Median line ----------

Baseline ——————

0   200 n.m.

① MONTSERRAT
② ST. CHRISTOPHER
③ NETHERLANDS ANTILLES
④ ST. BARTHOLOMEW

N

BAHAMAS

200 n.m.

TURKS AND
CAICOS

HAITI   DOMINICAN
         REPUBLIC

avassa
island

Mona
I.   PUERTO RICO

VIRGIN
IS.   ANGUILLA

③   ④
     ②   ANTIGUA
     ①   GUADELOUPE

Aves I.

DOMINICA   MARTINIQUE

ST. LUCIA

ST. VINCENT   ⚬BARBADOS

GRENADA

Bonaire
Aruba ③

TRINIDAD AND
TOBAGO

COLOMBIA   VENEZUELA

GUYANA

On 13 January 1978 Colombia and the Dominican Republic signed an agreement drawing a boundary separating their marine and submarine areas. The boundary, which measured 235 nautical miles, was defined by three points. The western terminus was close to the trijunction with Haiti, but the eastern terminus lay closer to the Netherlands Antilles than either Colombia or the Dominican Republic, and it also lay closer to Venezuela than to Colombia. Colombia and the Dominican Republic also defined a zone within which nationals from both countries could conduct scientific research and fish. The zone extended 20 nautical miles on each side of a section of boundary 77 nautical miles long.

One month later, on 17 February 1978, Colombia and Haiti agreed on a maritime boundary, which consisted of a single straight line 60 nautical miles in length. The eastern terminus coincided with the western terminus of the boundary which Colombia had agreed with the Dominican Republic. The western terminus was fixed 20 nautical miles closer to the Morant Cays of Jamaica than to the coasts of Haiti and Colombia. This western terminus is equidistant from Pointe de Gravois on Haiti, and Cabo la Ajuga and Cabo de la Vela on the Colombian coast. The remainder of this straight line is a median line between Pointe de Gravois and Cabo de la Vela.

Venezuela matched this Colombian activity by signing two agreements in a short time with the United States and the Netherlands. The boundary with the United States was signed on 28 March 1978 and it was ratified on 24 November 1980. This boundary extends for 299 nautical miles and it is defined by twenty-two points. While the eastern terminus is located at the trijunction with the Netherlands Antilles, the western terminus is equidistant only from Bonaire, which belongs to the Netherlands Antilles, and Mona, which is part of Puerto Rico. This unusual situation, which gives Venezuela waters and seabed which are closer to the Netherlands Antilles, was created by an agreement with the Netherlands which was ready, but unsigned, when the agreement with the United States was signed. The treaty with the Netherlands was signed on 31 March 1978 and it came into force on 15 December 1978. This agreement produced two boundaries. To the northeast of Aves Island, which is Venezuela's northern outpost, there was a short boundary measuring 27 nautical miles; it was defined by three points and the western terminus coincided with the eastern terminus of the boundary between Venezuela and the United States. The southern islands of the Netherlands Antilles, called Aruba, Curacao, and Bonaire, were separated from Venezuela by a boundary with three main segments. In the south the agreed boundary separated the mainland of Venezuela from the Netherlands' islands. The western segment trends north-south and separates the Venezuelan claim based on Los Monjes from the Netherlands claim based on Aruba. The eastern segment also trends north-south and separates the claims from the Netherlands' Bonaire from Islas de Aves which belongs to Venezuela, and which should not be confused with Aves Island. Quite remarkably, Venezuela was able to persuade the authorities in the Netherlands to concede 5200 square nautical miles of sea and seabed in the west and 7000 square nautical miles in the east which would have fallen to the Netherlands if median lines had been drawn. The north-south boundary segments mentioned earlier converged instead of diverging, as the median lines would have done. The northeastern terminus of the boundary between Venezuela and the Netherlands Antilles lay 12 nautical miles west of the terminus of Venezuela's boundary with the United States, although provision had been made in the agreement with the United States to extend that boundary west-wards along an azimuth of 274.23°, which would have reached the terminus of the boundary between the Netherlands Antilles and Venezuela. It is possible that the Netherlands agreed to discount the claim from its southern islands because they were so close to the Venezuelan coast and exercised such a restricting effect on claims from that mainland.

Venezuela did not in fact extend the boundary with the United States; instead it agreed with the Dominican Republic that a short section of its boundary with Venezuela should connect the termini agreed with the United States and the Netherlands. That agreement was signed on 3 March 1979. The agreement also defined the boundary between Venezuela and the Dominican Republic west of the Netherlands Antilles. This line commenced at the northwest terminus of the boundary between Venezuela and the Netherlands Antilles, and proceeded west-wards for 110 nautical miles through five points. Only the western third of this boundary is equidistant from Dominican and Venezuelan territory. The eastern two-thirds of the boundary appears to be a modified median line between the Dominican Republic and Aruba in the Netherlands Antilles! This boundary between Venezuela and the Dominican Republic overlaps the eastern section of the boundary which Colombia had agreed with the Dominican Republic a year earlier.

Venezuela also reached agreement with Trinidad and Tobago on common fishing zones on 12 December 1977. This agreement did not delineate a common fishing boundary, instead it defined two fishing zones. The first was situated to the north of Trinidad and west of Tobago, while the second occupied most of the area between the south coast of Trinidad and the mainland of Venezuela. Within these zones fishermen from both countries may operate providing they stay more than 2 nautical miles from the coast. Rules are laid down about the licensing of fishermen in these areas, the equipment to be used, and the proportion of the catch from the northern area which must be sold in Trinidad and Tobago. There are also three small areas lying in the western mouths of the Orinoco River where Venezuela will restrict fishing rights to vessels not exceeding 12 metres in length, with a storage capacity of not more than 1 ton (Nweihed 1980, 17). Half the catch from these three areas must be sold in Venezuela.

France has been active in negotiating maritime boundaries around Martinique and Guadeloupe. On 4 March 1981 an equidistant line was defined in an agreement signed with St Lucia to separate claims from that country and Martinique.

Potential and actual maritime boundary problems

It was noted earlier that Mexico and the United States signed an agreement defining their maritime boundaries in the Pacific Ocean and the Caribbean Sea on 4 May 1978. This agreement confirmed a provisional line which had been observed for one year (Smith 1981, 403–4). The Mexican Senate ratified the treaty on 20 December 1978, but ratification was refused by the American Senate, which decided in April 1981 to postpone action on the treaty until objections by geologists had been examined more carefully.

One of the leading critics of the boundary was Hedberg, who has written many useful articles on continental shelf boundaries. Hedberg raised three main points about the treaty in arguing that the United States had been awarded less than its fair share of the seabed of the Gulf of Mexico. First, he asserted that the international waters which lie more than 200 nautical miles from the coast should be eliminated. There are in fact two triangular areas of such waters. Second, Hedberg considered that it was unfair that Mexico should be allowed to make claims from the small islands which lie off the north coast of Yucatan. These features called Cayo Nuevo and Arrecife Alacran lie about 70 nautical miles off the coast of the peninsula. Finally, Hedberg argued that the proper boundary should be drawn midway between the locations of the foot of the continental slope which flank the Sigsbee Abyssal Plain. It is Hedberg's conclusion that if his advice is followed the United States will gain 25,000 square nautical miles of deep seabed which exploration has shown contains salt plugs which have trapped some oil formations (Hedberg 1980).

It is ironic that Hedberg contributed to the postponement of action by deploying arguments which do not bear his usual hallmark of soundness. The international waters lying more than 200 nautical miles from the coast cannot be eliminated without creating a precedent which would result in several other enclaves of international waters being annexed by countries. Nor is there any justification in existing or proposed rules for the claiming of waters more than 200 nautical miles from the coast. Hedberg appears to miss entirely the point that the seabed under the international waters has not been divided by the United States and Mexico. The treaty is silent on this matter, as Smith (1981, 403) has pointed out.

According to existing and proposed rules there is no reason why Mexico should not claim its maritime zones from the offshore islands north of Yucatan. Any suggestion that such actions were improper would create serious problems for the United States off Florida, southern California and Alaska, where the distribution of islands favours the United States.

Finally, there is no justification in the present rules to draw the limit between the continental margins of the two countries along a median line between the foot of the continental slopes. Even if it was decided to experiment with this concept in respect of the Sigsbee Abyssal Plain there is the difficulty of deciding which median line to select in this enclosed basin. The median line will depend on its point of origin. In one of his maps, Hedberg (1980) shows the line originating on the west side of the abyssal plain in the vicinity of meridian 95° west. However, it is possible that the median line drawn westwards from the mouth of the Rio Grande might intersect the foot of the continental slope to the north of the abyssal plain in the locality of meridian 91° west. If this latter point was the origin of the median line the United States would gain much less than the 25,000 square nautical miles which Hedberg predicted. Further, it is possible to imagine the long disputes which would be possible about defining the foot of the continental slope round the abyssal plain.

Colombia owns a series of islands in the western Caribbean Sea which are organized as the San Andres y Providencia Intendancy. The islands have a total area of 44 square kilometres and a population of about 25,000. Nicaragua disputes the ownership of some of these islands. It claims Roncador Cay, Bajo Nuevo, and the islands on the banks called Quita Sueno, Serrana and Serranilla. The other islands in the Intendancy are Cayos de Albuquerque, Courtown Cays, Isla de San Andres and Isla de Providencia. On 24 March 1928, while American marines were in Nicaragua at the request of its ruler, Nicaragua and Colombia signed a treaty regarding territory. In return for Colombian recognition of Nicaragua's control of the Mosquito Coast and the Great and Little Corn Islands, Nicaragua recognized Colombia's sovereignty over the islands in the San Andres Archipelago. The treaty noted that it was not concerned with the ownership of Roncador, Quita Sueno and Serrana, which were in dispute between the United States and Colombia. The United States claim rested on an act of 1856 dealing with unoccupied guano islands. The treaty did not mention Serranilla Bank or Bajo Nuevo.

In 1972 America and Colombia agreed on a treaty which included a provision withdrawing the claim by the United States to these guano islands. The treaty, which was ratified in 1982, did not recognize Colombian sovereignty over Roncador, Quita Sueno and Serrana. Nicaragua believes that neither the 1928 treaty nor the 1972 agreement are valid, and therefore it maintains its claim to these three islands, and it has added claims to Serranilla Bank and Bajo Nuevo. If it ever succeeded in this claim it would augment the area of its exclusive economic zone by about 70,000 square nautical miles.

In the Golfo de Honduras there is a problem which concerns Belize, Guatemala and Honduras. Guatemala claims the entire territory of Belize but would probably settle for the southern Toledo District, which is shown in figure 14.2 and which includes Ranguana and Sapodilla Cays. Honduras also claims Sapodilla Cay.

The origin of the dispute between Belize and Guatemala is found in the treaty signed between Britain and Guatemala on 30 April 1859. The treaty was ratified on 12 September 1859. This agreement defined the land boundary between the two territories, but according to Guatemala all the provisions of the treaty were not honoured and therefore the boundary does not exist and Belize belongs to Guatemala. As independence for Belize approached, the Guatemalan authorities modified their uncompromising stance and produced, with the British representatives, a statement of 'Heads of Agreement' on 11 March 1981. Seven of the sixteen headings deal with the question of Guatemala's access to the Caribbean Sea, and this quite clearly emerges as the major concern of Guatemala.

Figure 14.2 shows that if Belize and Honduras both claim territorial seas 12 nautical miles wide, Guatemala will only be able to reach the Caribbean Sea after passing through the territorial waters of its neighbours. Thus the various subjects in the 1981 agreement deal with Guatemala's permanent and unimpeded access to the high seas; Guatemala's use and enjoyment of Ranguana and Sapodilla Cays, together with their adjacent waters; Guatemala's right to free ports at Belize City and Punta Gorda; the improvement of communications between these ports and Guatemala; the need for agreements between Belize and Guatemala on fishing, pollution and navigation; and the joint development of seabed resources.

Belize has indicated that it is sympathetic to Guatemala's desire for unimpeded access beyond its territorial seas (Belize Government Information Service 1981, 2–3). The point is made that the boundaries will be drawn in such a way that Guatemala is not locked in by the territorial waters of its neighbours, and that Guatemala must have ownership of the access route to be sure the right of transit cannot be cancelled by another state. This appears to be a clear signal that Belize will give serious consideration to limiting its territorial sea claim in this region to 3 nautical miles. If it did restrict its claim in this way then Guatemala would have a corridor between the territorial waters of Belize and Honduras, even if the latter country claimed territorial waters 12 nautical miles wide.

Nor do the authorities in Belize see any serious difficulties with the other matters raised under the various headings, providing that none of them involves any diminution of Belize's sovereignty. For example, any joint development of seabed resources would be a commercial matter, there would be no question of joint ownership of the seabed which falls within the exclusive economic zone of Belize. Nor would any use and enjoyment by Guatemalans of Ranguana and Sapodilla Cays involve more than access and recreation, such as swimming. Commercial fishing is not one of the uses which would be considered.

While the 1859 treaty does not specifically mention these cays it does contain phrases which support the claim of Belize rather than Guatemala.

> Whereas the boundary between Her Britannic Majesty's settlement and possessions in the Gulf of Honduras, and the territories of the Republic of Guatemala, has not yet been ascertained and marked out. . . .
> ART I It is agreed between Her Britannic Majesty and the Republic of Guatemala that the boundary between the Republic and British settlements and possessions in the Bay of Honduras, as they existed to and on the 1st day of January 1850, and have continued to exist up to the present time, was and is as follows. . . . It is agreed and declared between the High Contracting Parties that all the territory to the north and east of the line of boundary above described, belongs to Her Britannic Majesty, and that all the territory to the south and west of the same belongs to the Republic of Guatemala.
>
> (Hertslet 1864, 345–6)

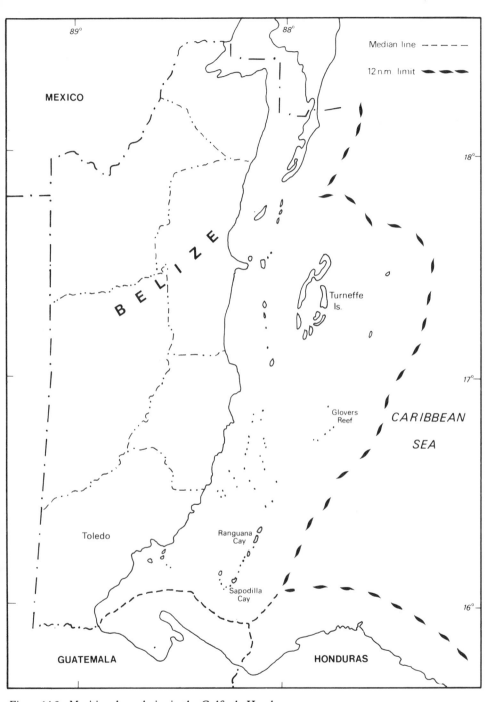

Figure 14.2 Maritime boundaries in the Golfo de Honduras

The cays which are claimed by Guatemala are certainly in the Golfo de Honduras, and they are indisputably north and east of the agreed boundary. Unless Guatemala is able to demonstrate that the cays were specifically excluded from the operations of the treaty in 1859 because they were not considered to be part of the British settlements and possessions, Belize seems to have a sound claim to these islands. It seems entirely possible that the cays were claimed by Guatemala as a means of securing a corridor of territorial seas to the Caribbean Sea.

The basis of Honduras's claim to Sapodilla Cay is not known, but if this claim was successful Guatemala would have to rely on Honduras to provide a corridor of territorial waters to the open sea.

It was noted earlier that despite their success in negotiating boundaries with neighbours, Colombia and Venezuela had not managed to resolve their dispute over the maritime boundary in the Golfo de Venezuela. This gulf, and its southern extension the Lago de Maracaibo, lie between the Sierra de Perija to the west and the Cordillera do Merida to the east. The boundary between Colombia and Venezuela skirts the western edge of this intermontane basin and reaches the coast on the western shore of the gulf at Castilletes, only 30 nautical miles from its mouth. Thus Venezuela secured all of the Lago de Maracaibo and most of the shore of the Golfo de Venezuela. This advantage in terms of constructing maritime boundaries is augmented to a considerable degree by Venezuela's possession on the small archipelago called Los Monjes in the mouth of the gulf.

As figure 14.3 shows, the problem relates to the proper course for the maritime boundary between the two countries from Castilletes to the trijunction with the Dominican Republic. It was the view of Colombia that a median line should be drawn from Castilletes to the trijunction, entirely disregarding Los Monjes. Once this had been done then the Venezuelan claim should be increased by a westward bulge in the vicinity of Los Monjes. The Venezuelan view was that the land boundary should be extended seawards in a straight line until a point was reached which was equidistant between Monje del Sur and the Peninsula de Guajira which belongs to Colombia. The maritime boundary should then continue as a median line giving full effect to Los Monjes.

Boggs (1950, 261) examined this problem and showed the lines of equidistance which ignored Los Monjes and which gave them full effect. In October 1980 discussions between the two countries produced a draft agreement on the delimitation of their maritime boundary. The proposed line started at Castilletes and proceeded due east along parallel 11° 51' 07.41" north until it reached the point equidistant between the two shores. It will be seen that this line, which is shown in figure 14.3, is not an equidistant line. The course of this first section of boundary corresponds with the closing line drawn by Venezuela in 1939 (Nweihed 1980, 9). This line, which connects Castilletes and Punta Salinas, was drawn after two incidents involving Italian ships, and it must be presumed that Venezuela was not prepared to consider a median line which would pass south of this parallel. The boundary then proceeded northwards to Point C which is equidistant from the mainlands of the two countries and Monje del Sur. From this point the

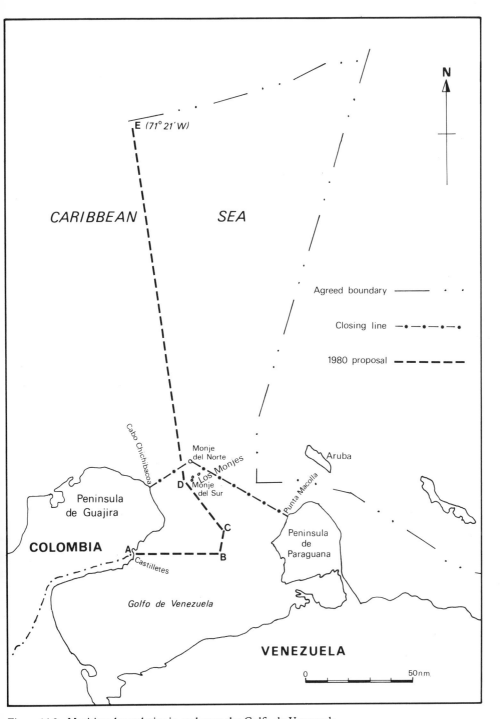

Figure 14.3 Maritime boundaries in and near the Golfo de Venezuela

boundary swings northwest to pass within 4 nautical miles of Los Monjes, before heading slightly west of north until meridian 71° 21' west is intersected. As figure 14.3 shows, Point E is located about 3 nautical miles southeast of the western terminus of the boundary which the Dominican Republic and Venezuela agreed in March 1979. In the draft agreement it was recorded that the boundary would proceed due northwards from Point E to the boundary with the Dominican Republic. It was also noted that the maritime zones of both countries would be measured seawards from a line which linked Punta Macolla on the Peninsula de Paraguana to Monje del Norte, and that island to Cabo Chichibacoa on the Peninsula de Guajira. This means that Venezuela had advanced its traditional baseline seawards and had permitted Colombia to use Monje del Norte as the eastern terminus of the Colombian baseline.

Quite remarkably, no political group in Venezuela was prepared to endorse this draft agreement and it lapsed. The draft agreement appeared to produce a boundary which was closer to the Venezuelan ideal described above than to the Colombian hope, but it was plainly not enough for the influential groups in Venezuela. Perhaps it is hoped that Colombia will be as amenable as the Netherlands, and those countries which have given full effect to Venezuela's claims from Aves Island. The intensity of feeling over this maritime boundary in the Golfo de Venezuela is revealed by the fact that Venezuela voted against the adoption of the Convention because it could not make reservations regarding Articles 15, 74 and 83, which deal with the delimitation of boundaries separating territorial seas, exclusive economic zones and continental shelves respectively, and Article 121 (3) which deals with claims which can be made from rocks. While Venezuela has oil deposits in the Lago de Maracaibo it can afford to delay a settlement which would permit exploration and exploitation of the seabed of the gulf.

Aves Island, which stands quite alone in the northeast Caribbean Sea, has given its name to the Aves Swell, on which it rests and which separates the Venezuela Basin from the Grenada Trough. This is a small sandy islet covered in purslane, inhabited by birds and breeding turtles. The Venezuelan authorities have built a platform and accommodation on the island and stationed a detachment of the National Guard there. The ownership of this islet was disputed by Venezuela, the Netherlands and the United States in the 1860s when guano islands were being exploited, but an arbitral award by Queen Isabel II of Spain confirmed Venezuela's sovereignty. That sovereignty has been recognized by the United States and the Netherlands, which have negotiated maritime boundaries with Venezuela. Further, these two countries have agreed that the islet should be given full effect in fixing those maritime boundaries.

There can be no question that Aves Island is an island and not a rock, and therefore it can be used as a basepoint in claiming the entire suite of maritime zones for Venezuela. The island enables Venezuela to claim 19,270 square nautical miles of sea and seabed which would not be available if Aves Island belonged to some other country. Territories which can only make small claims to maritime zones and which are severely restricted by the presence of Aves Island, are St Kitts and

Nevis, Dominica and St Vincent and the Grenadines. It will not be surprising if these territories seek to persuade Venezuela that maritime claims from Aves Island should be discounted, so that they can secure a more equitable share of the sea and seabed.

Another guano island owned this time by the United States is Navassa Island, located due west of the southern tip of Haiti. This small island is only occupied during the holiday season and there are a number of permanent houses which are used by visitors; in addition, United States' naval vessels visit the island. If equidistant lines were drawn about Navassa Island they would enclose an area of 4100 square nautical miles. However, it was noted earlier that Cuba and Haiti have agreed on a maritime boundary which cuts into this area about Navassa Island, and Haiti claims ownership of it.

Conclusions

There are important differences between the maritime characteristics of the Gulf of Mexico and the Caribbean Sea. The Gulf of Mexico has only three littoral states and Cuba's share of the gulf is small. The Caribbean Sea is surrounded by thirty-two territories, and it has a complex structure of basins separated by ridges and swells which contrasts with the simple submarine morphology of the Gulf of Mexico.

Only three countries have drawn straight baselines, and those drawn by Cuba and Haiti are open to criticism in terms of the rules of the Convention. It will be surprising if archipelagic baselines are not drawn around Antigua, The Bahamas, Grenada, Jamaica and St Vincent and the Grenadines. While the most common claim to maritime zones in this region sets the limit of territorial seas at 12 nautical miles and the limit of exclusive economic zones at 200 nautical miles, there is a wider diversity of claims amongst the island states in the Caribbean Sea than amongst the mainland states.

There has been good progress in drawing maritime boundaries between states in the Gulf of Mexico and the Caribbean Sea, with Cuba, Colombia, the United States and Venezuela taking leading roles. While there are a number of potential and actual maritime boundary problems in the Caribbean Sea, it appears that those involving Guatemala and Belize and Colombia and Venezuela will be the most difficult to solve.

There is a particular concern about the dangers of pollution from ships damaging the coastal environments of the Windward Islands. It is the view of some governments of these states that the waters of the mid-Atlantic Ocean act as a channel which convey rubbish and petroleum wastes to their eastern shores, and that this natural process endangers fishing grounds and tourist resorts. It seems certain that the island states in the Caribbean Sea will press hard for the full implementation of the provisions dealing with pollution which are contained in the Convention.

References

Belize Government Information Service (1981) *Government Explains Heads of Agreement*, Belmopan.

Boggs, S. W. (1950) 'Delimitation of seaward areas under national jurisdiction', *American Journal of International Law*, 45, 240–66.

Emery, K. O. and Uchupi, E. (1973) 'Petroleum production and pollution potential in the Caribbean Sea and the Gulf of Mexico', in *Caribbean Study Project Working Papers, Pacem in Maribus*, IV, Malta, 22–42.

Hedberg, N. D. (1980) 'Evaluation of the US–Mexico draft treaty on boundaries in the Gulf of Mexico', *Maritime Technology Society Journal*, 14 (1), 32–7.

Hertslet, L. (1864) *A Complete Collection of the Treaties and Conventions and Reciprocal Regulations at Present Subsisting between Great Britain and Foreign Powers*, vol. XI, London.

Nweihed, K. G. (1980) 'EZ (Uneasy) delimitation in the semi-enclosed Caribbean Sea: recent agreements between Venezuela and her neighbours', *Ocean Development and International Law*, 8 (1), 1–33.

Roosevelt, F. R. (1943) letter dated 9 June, in Department of State File No. 811, 0145/11-2844.

Smith, R. W. (1981) 'The maritime boundaries of the United States', *Geographical Review*, 71, 395–410.

The Geographer (1970) *Continental Shelf Boundary: Trinidad and Tobago–Venezuela*, 'Limits in the Seas' series, no. 11, Washington, DC.

The Geographer (1973) *Straight Baselines: Haiti*, 'Limits in the Seas' series, no. 51, Washington, DC.

Whiteman, U. (1982) *Speech Recorded in Provisional Verbatim Record of the 188th meeting, Third Conference on the Law of the Sea*, United Nations, A/CONF. 62/PV.188, New York.

Williams, E. (1975) *The Threat to the Caribbean Community*, Port of Spain, Trinidad.

Suggested reading list

Since 1974 there has been a large increase in the number of articles and books dealing with the law of the sea and maritime issues in general. Any scholar who tried to read all the studies published in the English language would have very little spare time for teaching or writing. The sources cited for each chapter are those which deal most directly with the subject under consideration. The following list, organized by chapters, provides additional titles which will lead the reader into the total literature.

1 Political geographers and the oceans

Alexander, L. M. (1980) 'The new geography of the world's oceans before and after the Law of the Sea', *Columbia Journal of World Business*, 15, 6–16.
Barnett, J. B. (1982) 'A guide to periodicals for the study of marine affairs', *Ocean Development and International Law*, 10, 357–77.
Wiktor, C. L. and Foster, L. A. (eds) (1980–) *Marine Affairs Bibliography*, Dalhousie Law School, Halifax, Nova Scotia.

2 The physical nature of oceans and coasts

Burk, C. A. and Drake, C. L. (1974) *The Geology of the Continental Margins*, New York.
Cotter, C. H. (1965) *The Physical Geography of the Oceans*, London.
Defant, A. (1961) *Physical Oceanography*, 2 vols, New York.
Fairbridge, R. W. (1966) *The Encyclopedia of Oceanography*, New York.
FAO Fisheries Department (1981) *Atlas of the Living Resources of the Sea*, Rome.
King, C. A. M. (1972) *Beaches and Coasts*, London.
Leonhard, A. T. (1982) 'The Peru Current and the search for a new legal regime for fisheries', *UCLA Pacific Basin Law Journal*, 1, 175–83.
Nairn, A. E. M. and Stehli, F. G. (1973, 1974, 1975) *The Ocean Basins and their Margins*, 3 vols, New York.
Shepard, F. P. and Wanless, H. R. (1971) *Our Changing Coastlines*, New York.
Warren, B. A. and Wunsch, C. (1981) *Evolution of Physical Oceanography*, New York.

3 National maritime claims

Brown, E. D. (1981) 'Delimitation of offshore areas: hard labour and bitter fruits at UNCLOS III', *Marine Policy*, 5, 172–84.
Clingan, T. A. (ed.) (1982) *Law of the Sea: State Practice in Zones of Special Jurisdiction*, Honolulu.
Conforti, B. (ed.) (1983) *La zona economica esclusiva* [The exclusive economic zone], Milan.
Hedberg, H. D. (1983) 'A critique of boundary provisions in the Law of the Sea', *Ocean Development and International Law*, 12, 337–48.
Hudson, C. (1980) 'Fishery and economic zones as customary international law', *San Diego Law Review*, 17, 661–89.

International Ocean Symposium (1982) *Exclusive Economic Zone*, Tokyo.

Jagota, S. P. (1981) 'Maritime boundary', *Académie de Droit International, Recueil des cours*, 171, 81–223.

Jayaraman, K. (1982) *Legal Regime of Islands*, New Delhi.

McDorman, T. L., Beauchamp, K. P. and Johnston, D. M. (1983) *Maritime Boundary Delimitation: An Annotated Bibliography*, Lexington, Mass.

Smith, R. W. (1983) 'A geographical primer to maritime boundary making', *Ocean Development and International Law*, 12, 1–12.

Van Dyke, J. and Brooks, R. A. (1983) 'Uninhabited islands: their impact on the ownership of the ocean's resources', *Ocean Development and International Law*, 12, 265–300.

4   International maritime boundaries

Adede, A. O. (1982) 'The basic structure of the disputes settlement part of the Law of the Sea Convention', *Ocean Development and International Law*, 11, 125–48.

Colson, D. A. (1978) 'The United Kingdom–France continental shelf arbitration', *American Journal of International Law*, 72, 95–112.

Feldman, M. B. (1982) 'The Tunisian–Libyan continental shelf case: geographic justice or judicial compromise', *American Journal of International Law*, 77, 219–38.

Fusillo, M. S. (1979) 'The legal regime of uninhabited rocks lacking an economic life of their own', *Italian Yearbook of International Law*, 4, 47–58.

Gaertner, M. P. (1982) 'The dispute settlement provisions of the Convention on the Law of the Sea: critique and alternatives to the International Tribunal for the Law of the Sea', *San Diego Law Review*, 19, 577–9.

Hirobe, K. (1980) 'Settlement of international maritime disputes', in *New Trends in Maritime Navigation*, 4th International Ocean Symposium, Tokyo, 84–6.

Pierce, G. A. (1981) 'Dispute settlement mechanisms in the Draft Convention on the Law of the Sea', *Denver Journal of International Law and Policy*, 10, 331–54.

Sebenius, J. K. (1981) 'The computer as mediator: the law of the sea and beyond', *Journal of Policy Analysis and Management*, 1, 77–95.

5   International maritime zones

Bentil, J. K. (1983) 'The foreshadowed global legal regime of deep seabed exploration and mining', *Lloyds' Maritime and Commercial Law Quarterly*, 260–82.

Brown, E. D. (1983) 'Freedom of the seas versus the common heritage of mankind: fundamental principles in conflict', *San Diego Law Review*, 20, 521–60.

Bush, W. M. (1981) 'An ocean-miner's view of the Draft Convention', *New York Law School Journal of International and Comparative Law*, 3, 27–37.

Joyner, C. C. (1981) 'The exclusive economic zone and Antarctica', *Virginia Journal of International Law*, 21, 691–726.

Larschan, B. and Brennan, B. C. (1983) 'The common heritage of mankind principle in international law', *Columbia Journal of Transnational Law*, 21, 305–37.

Post, A. M. (1983) *Deep Sea Mining and the Law of the Sea*, The Hague.

Teclaff, L. A. (1962) 'Shrinking the high seas by technical methods from the 1930 Hague Convention to the 1958 Geneva conference', *University of Detroit Law Journal*, 39, 660–84.

6   The Indian Ocean

Buzan, B. (1981) 'Naval power, the law of the sea, and the Indian Ocean as a zone of peace', *Marine Policy*, 5, 194–204.

Chandrasekhara, R. P. (1983) *The New Law of Maritime Zones: With Special Reference to India's Maritime Zones*, New Delhi.

Danseyar, A. E. (1982) 'Legal status of the Gulf of Aqaba and the Strait of Tiran: from customary international law to the Egyptian–Israeli peace treaty', *Boston College International and Comparative Law Review*, 5, 127–74.

Devaraj, M. (1982) 'A critique on Indian Ocean fisheries development', *Ocean Management*, 8, 97–123.

Lapidoth, R. (1983) 'The Strait of Tiran, the Gulf of Aqaba and the 1979 Treaty of Peace between Egypt and Israel', *American Journal of International Law*, 77, 84–108.

Lapidoth-Eschelbacher, R. (1982) *The Red Sea and the Gulf of Aden*, The Hague.

Lumb, R. D. (1981) 'The delimitation of maritime boundaries in the Timor Sea', *Australian Yearbook of International Law*, 7, 72–86.

Shyam, M. R. (1981) 'Extended maritime jurisdiction and its impact on South Asia', *Ocean Development and International Law*, 10, 93–112.

7   The south Pacific Ocean

Bath, C. R. (1974) 'Latin American claims on living resources of the sea', *Inter-American Economic Affairs*, 27, 59–85.

Broder, S. and Van Dyke, J. (1982) 'Ocean boundaries in the south Pacific', *University of Hawaii Law Review*, 4, 1–59.

Burmester, H. (1982) 'The Torres Strait Treaty: ocean boundary delimitation by agreement', *American Journal of International Law*, 76, 321–49.

Gallardo, V. A. (1976) *Chile's National Interest in the Oceans*, University of Chile, Santiago.

Grieg, D. W. (1981) 'The Beagle Channel arbitration', *Australian Yearbook of International Law*, 7, 332–85.

Lee, H. C. (1974) 'Archipelagic claim for Papua New Guinea', *Melanesian Law Journal*, 2, 91–107.

Phillips, J. C. (1982) 'The economic resources zone and the southwest Pacific', *International Lawyer*, 16, 265–78.

Prescott, J. R. V. (1982) 'An agenda of political maritime issues for Australia', in Bateman, S. and Ward, M. (eds) *Australia's Maritime Horizons*, Canberra, 51–65.

8   The South China Sea

Bethill, C. D. (1974) 'People's Republic of China and the law of the Sea', *International Lawyer*, 8, 724–51.

Johnston, D. M., Gold, E. and Tangsubkul, P. (eds) (1983) *International Symposium on the New Law of the Sea in Southeast Asia: Developmental Effects and Regional Approaches*, Halifax, Nova Scotia.

Kuribayashi, T. (1983) 'The new law of the sea and the Strait of Malacca' in Johnston, D. M., Gold, E. and Tangsubkul, P. (eds) *International Symposium on the New Law of the Sea in Southeast Asia: Developmental Effects and Regional Approaches*, Halifax, Nova Scotia, 146–51.

Lee, Y. C. (1978) *Southeast Asia and the Law of the Sea: Some Preliminary Observations on the Political Geography of Southeast Asian Seas*, Singapore.

O'Brien, R. (1977) *South China Sea Oil: Two Problems of Ownership and Development*, Singapore.

Park, C. (1981) 'Maritime claims in the China Seas: current state practices', *San Diego Law Review*, 18, 443–54.

Samuels, M. S. (1982) *Contest for the South China Sea*, London.

Sien, C. L. and MacAndrews, C. (eds) (1981) *Southeast Asian Seas: Frontiers for Development*, Singapore.

9   The north Pacific Ocean

Black III, W. L. (1983) 'Soviet fishing agreements with developing countries: benefit or burden', *Marine Policy*, 7, 163–74.

Copes, P. and Cook, B. A. (1982) 'Rationalisation of Canada's Pacific halibut fishery', *Ocean Management*, 8, 151–75.

Ely, N. and Pietrowski, R. F. (1975) 'Boundaries of seabed jurisdiction off the Pacific coast of Asia', *Natural Resources Lawyer*, 8, 611–29.

Feldman, M. B. and Aldrich, G. H. (1981) 'The maritime boundaries of the United States', *American Journal of International Law*, 75, 729–63.

Gregory, G. (1976) 'Japan and the law of the sea: uncertainties of the new order', *Australian Outlook*, 30, 44–64.

Hedberg, H. D. (1981) 'Ocean floor jurisdictional boundaries for the Bering Sea', *Marine Technology Society Journal*, 14, 47–53.

Okuhara, T. (1971) 'The territorial sovereignty over the Senkaku islands and problems in the surrounding continental shelf', *Japanese Annual of International Law*, 15, 97–106.

Ouchi, K. (1978) 'A perspective on Japan's struggle for its traditional rights on the oceans', *Ocean Development and International Law*, 5, 107–34.

Pak, C. Y. (1982) 'The continental shelf between Korea, Japan and China', *Marine Policy Reports*, 4/5.

10   The Arctic Ocean and associated seas

Auburn, F. M. (1973) 'International law and sea-ice jurisdiction in the Arctic Ocean', *International and Comparative Law Quarterly*, 22, 552–7.

Dehner, I. (1972) 'Creeping jurisdiction in the Arctic: has the Soviet Union joined Canada?', *Harvard International Law Journal*, 13, 271–88.

Dosman, E. J. (ed.) (1976) *The Arctic in Question*, Ottawa.

Evensen, J. (1981) 'La délimitàtion entre la Norvège et l'Islande du plateau continental dans le secteur de Jan Meyen' [The division of the continental shelf between Norway and Iceland, in the vicinity of Jan Mayen], *Annuaire français de droit international*, 27, 711–38.

Feder, B. J. (1978) 'A legal regime for the Arctic', *Ecology Law Quarterly*, 6, 785–829.

Johnston, D. M. (ed.) (1982) *Arctic Ocean Issues in the 1980s*, Halifax, Nova Scotia.

McRae, D. M. and Goundrey, D. J. (1982) 'Environmental jurisdiction in Arctic waters: the extent of Article 234', *University of British Columbia Law Review*, 16, 197–228.

Pharand, D. (1979) 'The legal status of the Arctic regions', *Académie de Droit International, Receuil des cours*, 163, 49–115.

Zaslow, M. (ed.) (1981) *A Century of Canada's Arctic Islands 1880–1980*, Ottawa.

11   The Baltic, North and Irish Seas

Alexanderssen, G. (1982) *The Baltic Straits*, The Hague.

Archer, C. (1977) 'Two North Sea policies: Danish and Norwegian attitudes compared', *Marine Policy*, 1, 289–300.

Grisel, E. (1970) 'The lateral boundaries of the continental shelf and the judgement of the International Court of Justice in the North Sea continental shelf cases', *American Journal of International Law*, 64, 562–93.

Johnson, B. (1976) 'The Baltic conventions', *International and Comparative Law Quarterly*, 25, 1–14.

Marston, G. (1981) *The Marginal Seabed: United Kingdom Legal Practice*, Oxford.

Reynolds, P. D. (1977) 'The EEC and the Law of the Sea', *Marine Policy*, 1, 118–31.

Rothpfeffer, T. (1972) 'Equity in the North Sea continental shelf cases: a case study in the legal reasoning of the International Court of Justice', *Nordisk tidsskrift for international ret*, 42, 81–137.

Watt, D. C. (ed.) (1980) *Greenwich Forum V: The North Sea: A New International Regime?*, Guildford, England.

Zaorski, R. (1975) 'The Gdansk Convention on fisheries and the conservation of living resources in the Baltic Sea and Belts', *Polish Yearbook of International Law*, 7, 7–19.

12   The Mediterranean and Black Seas

Bastianelli, F. (1983) 'Boundary delimitation in the Mediterranean Sea', *Marine Policy Reports*, 5/4.

Ben Achour, Y. (1983) 'L'Affaire de plateau continental tunisio–libyen (analyse empirique)' [An empirical analysis of the case of the continental shelf between Tunisia and Libya], *Journal de droit international*, 110, 247–92.

General Fisheries Council for the Mediterranean (1981) *Management of Living Resources in the Mediterranean Coastal Area*, Rome.

Gross, L. (1977) 'The dispute between Greece and Turkey concerning the continental shelf in the Aegean', *American Journal of International Law*, 71, 31–59.

Robal, R. T. (1977) 'The Aegean continental shelf case', *Harvard International Law Journal*, 18, 649–75.

Scovazzi, T. (1981) 'Implications of the new law of the sea for the Mediterranean', *Marine Policy*, 5, 302–12.

Spinnato, J. M. (1983) 'Historic and vital bays: an analysis of Libya's claim to the Gulf of Sidra', *Ocean Development and International Law*, 13, 65–85.

Timagenis, G. J. (1980) 'Protocol for the protection of the Mediterranean against pollution from land-based sources, Athens, 1980', *Hellenic Review of International Relations*, 1, 123–36.

13   The Atlantic Ocean

Akinsanya, A. (1976) 'The Nigerian territorial water decrees of 1967 and 1971', *Indian Journal of International Law*, 16, 276–86.

Chouraqui, G. (1977) 'L'Afrique et le droit de la mer' [Africa and the law of the sea], *Revue Juridique et Politique, Indépendance et Coopération*, 31, 1079–220.

Morris, M. A. (1977) 'The domestic context of Brazilian maritime policy', *Ocean Development and International Law*, 4, 143–70.

Nied, G. D. (1982) 'International adjudication: settlement of the United States–Canada maritime boundary dispute', *Harvard International Law Journal*, 23, 138–43.

Nwogugu, E. I. (1973) 'Problems of Nigeria's international offshore jurisdiction', *International and Comparative Law Quarterly*, 22, 349–62.

Rao, P. S. (1972) 'Offshore natural resources: an evaluation of African interests', *Indian Journal of International Law*, 12, 345–67.

VanderZwaag, D. L. (1983) *The fish feud: the United States and Canadian Boundary Dispute*, Lexington, Mass.

Zacklin, R. (1973) 'Latin America and the development of the law of the sea', *Annales d'études internationales*, 4, 31–54.

14   The Caribbean Sea and the Gulf of Mexico

Ayala Jiminez, C. A. (1978) *El Caribe, mar interior de los Américas* [The Caribbean, interior sea of the Americas], Bogota.

Brocard, G. (1979) *Le Statut juridique de la mer des Caraibes* [The legal status of the Caribbean], Paris.

Martz, M. J. R. (1977) 'Delimitation of marine and submarine areas: the Gulf of Venezuela', *Lawyer of the Americas*, 12, 301–17.

Mitchell, C. L. and Gold, E. (1982) *The Integration of Marine Space in National Development Strategies of Small Island States: The Case of the Caribbean States of Grenada and St Lucia*, Halifax, Canada.

Nweihed, K. G. (1981) *Delimitation Principles and Problems in the Caribbean*, Caracas.

Schmitt, K. M. (1982) 'The problem of maritime boundaries in United States–Mexican relations', *Natural Resources Journal*, 22, 139–53.

Suman, D. O. (1981) 'A comparison of the law of the sea claims of Mexico and Brazil', *Ocean Development and International Law*, 10, 131–73.

Glossary

ABYSSAL PLAIN. This refers to the deep seabed between depths of 2200 and 5500 metres. It is also used generally to refer to the seabed seaward of the continental rise.

ANADROMOUS FISH. This term refers to fish, such as the salmon, which return to freshwater rivers to spawn.

ARCHIPELAGIC BASELINES. Such baselines consist of a series of straight lines drawn by archipelagic states to connect the outermost points of their outermost islands. '

ARCHIPELAGIC STATE. Such states are composed entirely of groups of islands.

ARCHIPELAGIC WATERS. These waters lie inside the baselines which surround archipelagic states.

ARTIFICIAL ISLANDS. These are islands not formed by nature.

ATLANTIC TYPE OF COAST. See DISCORDANT COAST.

ATOLL. This is a coral island consisting of a circular reef enclosing a lagoon.

AZIMUTH. This is an angular bearing measured clockwise from true North; thus the azimuth of East is 90°.

BARRIER BEACH. Such features consist of sandy bars which are aligned on a similar azimuth to the coast, and which stand above high tide. They are separated from the coast by a lagoon.

BARRIER REEF. This feature consists of a coral reef aligned on a similar azimuth as the coastline, but separated from that coast by deeper lagoons or channels.

BASELINE. The baseline is the line on or near the coast of a state from which the territorial sea, contiguous zone and fishing or exclusive economic zones are measured.

BAY. This is a well-marked indentation in the coastline.

BEACH. This is a gently sloping accumulation of pebbles, shingle and sand along the coast between low tide and levels reached by storm waves.

BEARING. See AZIMUTH.

BIGHT. This regional feature refers to a wide, slightly curved indentation in a coastline. The Great Australian Bight is a good example.

CATADROMOUS SPECIES. Such fish, like eels, live in fresh water and spawn or mature in the sea.

CAY. This name is given to small islands built of coral and sand fragments on flat reefs which are sometimes uncovered by low tide.

CHART. This is a map specifically designed for air or sea navigation.

CLIFF. This name is given to rock faces, which are generally steep, along coasts.

COAST. This is a general term for the zone of contact between the land and sea.

COASTLINE. This term may be used as a synonym for COAST. It also refers specifically to the line on maps and charts which separates sea and land.

COASTAL STATE. Any state which possesses a coastline.

CONCORDANT COAST. Such a coast has a similar azimuth to the main relief lines of the hinterland. The coasts of Yugoslavia and western Canada provide good examples.

CONTIGUOUS ZONE. While the contiguous zone is measured from the same baseline as the territorial sea, the state has fewer rights in the contiguous zone, which may therefore be considered to lie seaward of the territorial sea.

CONTINENTAL DRIFT. See PLATE TECTONICS.

CONTINENTAL MARGIN. The submarine extension of the continents, which consists of the continental shelf, slope and rise.

CONTINENTAL RISE. This term refers to the accumulated debris from the continental shelf and slope, possibly augmented by material from the deep seabed, which accumulates at the foot of the continental slope, assuming a gentler gradient than the continental slope.

CONTINENTAL SHELF. In a geomorphological sense this term refers to the level projection of the land under the sea between the low water mark and the upper part of the continental slope. In the Law of the Sea documents the term refers to the continental margin, consisting of the continental shelf, slope and rise.

CONTINENTAL SLOPE. This term refers to the generally steep slope which links the continental shelf with the continental rise or deep seabed.

CORAL. This is the name given to rock formations produced by marine polyps capable of secreting lime.

CORAL REEF. Such features are rock masses composed of coral. They are normally found within 30° of the equator in warm waters.

COVE. This name is given to a small circular bay with a narrow mouth.

DALMATIAN COAST. This name is given to a CONCORDANT COAST which has been drowned by rising sea levels which have created chains of islands from the higher peaks of the former coastal ranges.

DELTA. This is a projection of land into the sea built by the deposition of alluvium by a river.

DIAPIR. This feature results from sediments being pierced and perhaps buckled upwards by intrusions of salt masses from beneath.

DISCORDANT COAST. This feature is formed when the coastline lies transverse to the grain of the relief of the hinterland. The west coast of Ireland provides a clear example.

EBB TIDE. This is the seaward flow of water after high tide.

ENCLOSED OR SEMI-ENCLOSED SEAS. This term refers to gulfs, basins or seas surrounded by two or more states and connected to the open seas by a narrow outlet, and to such features with wide mouths where most of the area is occupied by the territorial seas and exclusive economic zones of two or more states. The Black Sea and the Gulf of Thailand are examples of these features.

ENTREPOT. This is a regional centre through which regional and inter-regional trade is channelled.

EPEIRIC SEA. This term describes a shallow sea on the continental shelf, such as the North Sea.

ESTUARY. The term refers to the broad, tidal mouth of a river.

EUSTATISM. This name refers to long-term changes in sea-level through variations in the volume of water or the size of the ocean basins. They may be caused by tectonic changes, by increased sedimentation, and by the abstraction and release of water by the growth and decay respectively of ice sheets.

EXCLUSIVE ECONOMIC ZONE. This is an area of claimed ocean lying seawards of and adjacent to territorial waters, within which the claimant state has exclusive authority over the resources of the sea and the seabed.

FAST ICE. This term describes ice which covers an area of sea while remaining fastened to the land.

FIORD OR FJORD. This name is given to a long, narrow, deep glacial valley which has been drowned by a relative rise in sea-level.

FLAG STATE. This refers to any state which registers ships and permits those ships to fly its flag.

FLOE. This is a comparatively small, thin sheet of sea-ice which has broken off from a larger mass of sea-ice.

FLOOD TIDE. The landward movement of water after low tide.

FORE DEEP. This is a deep, linear trough in the seabed which lies close to island arcs such as the Philippines.

FRINGING REEF. Such a feature consists of a level platform of rock or coral attached to the coast of an island or continent. These features might be separated from the coast by a lagoon.

GEOGRAPHICAL CO-ORDINATES. Such co-ordinates are provided by the graticule of latitudes and longitudes which are drawn on globes, maps and charts.

GEOGRAPHICALLY DISADVANTAGED COUNTRIES. Such countries either have very short coastlines compared to their total area, such as Zaire, or possess a coastal configuration which restricts their claim to the continental shelf and exclusive economic zone to small areas; this latter situation is experienced by Iraq.

GROUND ICE. This describes ice which forms near the coast and which is attached to the seabed. It is common around the coast of Antarctica in winter.

GROYNE. This is a structure built at a right-angle to the coast, to arrest beach material moving along the shore and to build up the level of the beach.

GUYOT. This refers to a flat-topped mount rising from the seabed to within 1000 metres of the surface.

HIGHEST ASTRONOMIC TIDE. The highest level which can be predicted to occur under average meteorological conditions and under any combination of astronomical conditions. Higher levels may be reached during unusual meteorological conditions.

HIGHLY MIGRATORY SPECIES. Such species are those fish, including tuna, frigate mackerel, sailfish and swordfish, which travel across wide areas of ocean and might pass through the fishing or exclusive economic zone of several states.

HIGH SEAS. This is the area of the oceans which lies outside all national claims to internal waters, territorial seas, contiguous zones, and fishing and exclusive economic zones.

HISTORIC BAYS. Such bays are sometimes claimed as the exclusive property of states by virtue of that state's long and continuous control and use.

HOT PURSUIT. Patrol boats are permitted to pursue a vessel which appears to have breached the regulations of the coastal state into the high seas, providing that the offence was committed in either the internal waters, territorial waters, archipelagic waters, or contiguous zone, and the pursuit was commenced in one of those zones.

ICE AGE. A geological period when ice sheets covered extensive parts of the earth's surface.

ICE BARRIER. The term is associated with the edge of ice sheets in Antarctica.

ICEBERG. This is a large floating mass of ice which has broken off from an ice sheet or glacier.

INDIAN SPRING LOW WATER. This level for chart datum for Indian waters was proposed by Sir George Darwin. The sum of the semi-ranges of the principal lunar and solar semi-diurnal tides, and of the lunar and luni-solar diurnal tides is obtained and subtracted from mean sea-level to determine this value.

INNOCENT PASSAGE. This phrase refers to ships passing expeditiously through the territorial waters of a state in a manner which is not prejudicial to the peace, good order or security of that state.

INTER-GLACIAL PERIOD. This describes the interval between two ice ages.

INTERNAL WATERS. These waters lie on the landwards side of the baseline from which the state's territorial seas are measured.

ISLAND. An island is a naturally formed area of land, surrounded by water and above water at high tide.

ISTHMUS. This refers to a narrow neck of land between two areas of ocean, such as the Kra Isthmus between the Andaman Sea and the Gulf of Thailand.

LANDLOCKED STATE. Such states do not possess a coastline.

LATITUDE. This is the angular distance of a place north or south of the equator. The equator is 0° while the poles are each 90°.

LONGITUDE. This is the angular distance of a place east or west of the prime meridian which passes through Greenwich. The Greenwich meridian is 0°, and longitude is measured 180° east and west.

LOWEST ASTRONOMIC TIDE. The lowest level which can be predicted to occur under average meteorological conditions and under any combination of astronomical conditions. Lower levels may be reached during unusual meteorological conditions.

LOW-TIDE ELEVATION. Such features appear above the surface of the sea at low tide but are submerged at high tide.

LOW-WATER LINE. This is the general name given to a number of different levels reached by low tides throughout the year.

MANGANESE NODULES. These are spherical nodules, found mainly on the deep seabed, which consist of manganese, copper, cobalt, nickel and iron compounds and water.

MARGINAL DEEP. See FORE DEEP.

MARGINAL SEA. See EPEIRIC SEA.

MEAN HIGHER HIGH WATER. This height is the mean of the higher of two daily high waters over a long period.

MEAN HIGH-WATER SPRINGS. This level is the average of the heights of two successive high waters during those periods of 24 hours when the range of the tide is greatest.

MEAN LOWER LOW WATER. This height is the mean of the lower of two daily low waters over a long period.

MEAN LOW-WATER SPRINGS. This level is the average of the heights of two successive low waters during those periods of 24 hours when the range of the tide is greatest.

MEAN SEA-LEVEL. Mean sea-level is the average height of the sea's surface over a period of 18.6 years.

MEDIAN LINE. This is a line which at every point is equidistant from the shores between which it is being drawn.

MERIDIAN. This refers to any line of longitude, such as 90° west.

NAUTICAL MILE. A nautical mile is equal to one minute of latitude, which is 6076 feet.

NEAP TIDE. Such tides occur when the gravitational attraction of the moon and sun are operating at right angles to each other. The range of such tides is lower than average.

PACIFIC TYPE OF COAST. See CONCORDANT COAST.

PACK ICE. This refers to a mass of floating ice which has been formed by the congregation of floes.

PARALLEL. This refers to any line of latitude, such as 15° south.

PENINSULA. This describes an elongated projection of land into the sea, and can refer to local peninsulas such as Qatar, or regional peninsulas such as Malaya.

PLATE TECTONICS. This name is given to the process by which renewal of the seabed occurs and continents move.

REEF. Reefs consist of masses of rock or coral which either reach close to the surface or are exposed at low tide.

ROADSTEADS. These are areas of sea near ports where ships anchor, and where the transfer of cargo might occur.

SEA LANE. This is a corridor designated through an area of claimed waters, which should be followed by ships in passage.

SEAMOUNT. This is an isolated peak rising from the seabed to within 1000 metres of the surface. Seamounts are distinguished from GUYOTS by having pointed peaks.

SEDENTARY SPECIES. Such species are marine organisms which are either immobile on or under the seabed, or able to move only in contact with the seabed when they are in a harvestable stage.

SHELF ICE. This term refers to masses of floating ice formed by the conjunction of glaciers around the coast of Antarctica.

SHOAL. This is a shallow submarine bank formed of mud, sand or shingle.

SPIT. This is a ridge or embankment of sediment attached to land at one end and terminating in open water at the other end.

SPRING TIDE. This type of tide occurs twice each month when the gravitational attraction of the moon and sun are in the same direction. This conjunction results in higher high tides and lower low tides than normal.

STATES WITH SPECIAL GEOGRAPHICAL CHARACTERISTICS. This phrase refers to coastal states which either depend on the exploitation of the living resources in the exclusive economic zones of neighbouring states for adequate supplies of fish, or which, because of their coastal configuration, are unable to claim fishing or exclusive zones of their own.

STORM SURGE. This describes a rapid rise in sea-level above predicted tide levels due to strong onshore winds.

STRAIGHT BASELINES. Such baselines are substituted for low-water marks along coasts which are unstable, or which are deeply indented, or which have a near-by fringe of islands.

STRAITS USED FOR INTERNATIONAL NAVIGATION. This phrase refers to straits less than 24 nautical miles wide, which, before claims to territorial seas 12 nautical miles wide were introduced, possessed a central strip of high seas through which vessels could navigate without restriction.

SUBMARINE CANYON. This is a deep valley notched into the continental margin.

TERRITORIAL SEA. Proceeding seawards from the state's baseline the territorial sea is the first zone claimed. The state's rights within this zone are more comprehensive than in any other zone seaward of the baseline, and they extend to the underlying seabed and the overlying air.

THE AREA. This term comprehends the seabed and its subsoil beyond the limits of national jurisdiction.

THE ASSEMBLY. This is one of the organs of The Authority; each state which adheres to the Convention on the Law of the Sea will be a member of the Assembly.

THE AUTHORITY. This is the organization through which states that are party to the Convention on the Law of the Sea will administer activities in the deep seabed.

THE COUNCIL. This organ of The Authority will consist of thirty-six elected members.

THE ENTERPRISE. This organ of The Authority will be responsible for mining and associated activities on the deep seabed on behalf of The Authority.

TIDAL FLAT. This describes an area of mud or sand exposed at low tide.

TIDE. This name is given to the periodic rise and fall of coastal waters resulting from the gravitational attraction of the moon and sun.

TOMBOLO. This is a spit which ties an island to the mainland.

TRAFFIC SEPARATION SCHEME. This is a safety arrangement which ensures that in narrow straits ships travelling in opposite directions do so along different sea lanes.

TRANSIT PASSAGE. This is almost a euphemism for innocent passage through international straits but there are some differences. Transit passage includes overflight, it cannot be suspended and it does not apply to warships.

TRANSIT STATE. This term refers to a state through which the trade of a landlocked country passes, whether or not the transit state has a coastline.

TSUNAMI. This is a large wave produced by seismic activity on the seabed. Such waves might travel long distances before reaching the continental margin when their amplitude is increased before reaching the shore.

Name index

Subject index

Note: emboldened figures refer to maps and diagrams